A

POPULAR ACCOUNT

OF

THE ANCIENT EGYPTIANS.

REVISED AND ABRIDGED FROM HIS LARGER WORK,

BY SIR J. GARDNER WILKINSON, D.C.L., F.R.S., &c.

IN TWO VOLUMES.

VOL. II.

Illustrated with Five Hundred Woodcuts.

ISBN: 978-1-63182-823-2

All Rights reserved. No part of this book maybe reproduced without written permission from the publishers, except by a reviewer who may quote brief passages in a review to be printed in a newspaper or magazine.

Printed: March 2023

Published and Distributed By:
Lushena Books
607 Country Club Drive, Unit E
Bensenville, IL 60106
www.lushenabks.com

ISBN: 978-1-63182-823-2

CONTENTS OF VOL. II.

CHAPTER VI.

PAGE

The different classes of Egyptians—Third class:—The husbandmen—Agriculture—Productions of Egypt—Harvest—Festivals of the peasants—Gardeners, huntsmen, boatmen of the Nile .... A

CHAPTER VII.

Fourth class:—Artificers, tradesmen or shopkeepers, musicians, builders, carpenters, boat-builders, masons, potters, public weighers and notaries, pounders — Glass — False stones — Lamps — Fine linen — Looms—Flax—Leather—Papyrus—Potters—Carpenters—Boxes—Boats—Metals—Tin—Gold mines—Iron—Bronze—Casting—Stone knives—Pounding in mortars.................................. 56

CHAPTER VIII.

The fifth class:—Pastors, poulterers, shops, fowlers, fishermen, labourers, brickmakers, and common people—Jews—People giving an account of their mode of living—Laws—Judges—Crimes and Punishments—Thieves—Debtors—Sales and deeds—Marriages—Parents—Lawgivers—Provinces and governors—Revenues—Gold—Mensuration—Three seasons—Intercalation—Sothic year—Land measures—Cubit—Weights and measures................................ 168

CHAPTER IX.

Egyptian art — Remains of Nineveh — Human figure — Drawing and painting—Architecture—Orders of architecture—Some devices copied from nature—Too great symmetry avoided—Use of large stones—Antiquity of the arch—Bricks—Progress of architecture—Use of limestone—Colossi—Monoliths—Machinery—Masons—Early Egyptian inventions—Dresses—Wigs—Dresses of women—Ornaments—Ointments—Mirrors—Doctors—Magic............................. 262

CHAPTER X.

Funeral rites—Offerings to the dead—Tombs—Funeral processions—Trials of the dead—Sacred lake—Burial—Embalming—Sarcophagi—Papyri, &c. 356

LIST OF WOODCUTS

In Vol. II.

Those with ** prefixed are new woodcuts; with * new woodcuts copied from lithographs of the previous work.

** Frontispiece.
Mode of transporting a large colossus from the quarries. The statue is bound upon a sledge with ropes; on the knee stands a man beating time with his hands, and giving out a verse of a song; another stands on the base, and pours a green liquid, evidently grease, from a vase, before the sledge. In the upper line are companies of soldiers carrying green twigs; then four rows of men, forty-three in each, dragging the statue with ropes; and in the lowest line are others bearing implements, and vases of grease, or other liquids, followed by "superintendents," or task-masters; and behind the statue are other "superintendents," and perhaps reliefs of men.

CHAPTER VI.

Vignette — Page
H. *Khónfud*, or clod-crushing machine 1

Woodcut
356. *Shadóof* for watering the lands 4
357. Cattle rescued from the inundation....................... 6
358. Sowing.. 12
359. Ploughing and hoeing................................... 13
360. Yoke of an ancient plough found in a tomb............... 15
361. Wooden hoes... 16
362. Wooden hoes in the Berlin Museum 17
363. Hoeing and sowing the land and felling trees 18
364. Pigs; rarely seen in the sculptures 18
365. Plants from the sculptures.............................. 36
366. Ploughing, sowing, and reaping 40
367. Harvest scene 41

THE ANCIENT EGYPTIANS.

Woodcut	Page
368. The *Tritura*	42
369. Song of the threshers to the oxen	43
370. Harvest scene	44
371. *Tritura* or threshing, and winnowing	45
372. Wheat bound in sheaves	47
373. The oxen driven round the heap; contrary to the usual custom	48
374. Gathering the *Doora*, and wheat	50
375. Gathering the *Doora*, and stripping off the grain	51
376. Ostrich, with the feathers and eggs	54

Vignette
I. The *Nóreg*, a machine used by the modern Egyptians for threshing corn 55

CHAPTER VII.

Vignette
K. Modern boats of the Nile; on the opposite bank is a whirlwind of sand 56

Woodcut
377. Glass-blowers 58
378. Glass bottles, and a bead with the name of Amun-m-het 59
379. Bottles, and selvage of cloth 68
380. Chinese bottles found in the Egyptian tombs. The inquiry respecting these bottles, which has limited their date to a much later time than was formerly supposed, was instituted by Dr. Bowring, our Plenipotentiary in China; and Mr. Medhurst's paper is one of several on this curious question (*see Trans. China Branch of R. Asiatic Soc.*, Part 3, 1851–2, p. 34) 69
381. A guard apparently with a lantern 72
382. Women weaving and using the spindle 85
383. Men spinning and making a sort of network, horizontal loom, or perhaps mat-making 86
384. A piece of cloth on a frame, and an upright loom 87
385. Spindles 88
386. Preparing flax; beating it, and making it into twine and cloth 89
387. Wooden comb found with some tow 91
388. Netting-needle and wooden plane for smoothing cloth 91
**389. Goeffreying machine 92

LIST OF WOODCUTS IN VOL. II.

Woodcut	Page
390. Part 1, Cutting and twisting thongs of leather Part 2, Carpenters	94
391. Currier holding a strap of leather with his toes	104
392. Part 1, Shoemakers Part 2, Men polishing a column, probably of wood	105
393. Fullers	106
394. Potters' earthenware vases	108
395. Carpenters' tools, and the basket that held them	112
396. Veneering and the use of glue	114
397. Different boxes	116
398. Bandaging mummies and making the cases	118
**399. Making a papyrus boat	120
400. Boats for carrying cattle and goods	124
401. A boat with the mast and sail taken down, having a chariot and horses on board	124
402. Boat of the Nile, showing how the sail was fastened to the yards, and the nature of the rigging	128
403. Goldsmiths; fusing, weighing, and other processes	137
404. Goldsmiths	138
405. Blow-pipe and small fire-place	139
406. Golden baskets in the tomb of Remeses III.	140
407. Ḳabbáneh, or public weighers and notaries	148
408. Rings of gold and silver	149
409. Vases of the time of Thothmes III.	162
410. Flint knives	164
411. Pounding various substances in stone mortars with metal pestles	166

Vignette
*L. Boats with coloured and embroidered sails; from the tomb of Remeses III. at Thebes. 167

CHAPTER VIII.

Vignette
M. Cattle during the inundation in the Delta 168

Woodcut
412. Modern ovens for hatching eggs 170
413. Herdsmen and poulterers treating sick animals and geese...... 173
414. Geese brought and numbered 174
415. A deformed ox-herd 175

Woodcut	Page
416. Giving an account to two scribes of the stock on the estate	176
417. Herdsmen giving an account of the cattle	177
418. Cattle, goats, asses, and sheep, with their numbers over them	179
419. Bird-traps	180
420. Fishing and fowling scenes	181
421. Clap-nets, from the sculptures	183
422. A poulterer's shop	184
423. Fowlers catching geese, and poulterers	185
424. Fishing with ground bait	186
425. Fishing with a drag-net	187
426. Leads with part of a net	188
427. A sort of landing-net	189
428. Bringing in fish and preparing them for salting	190
429. Another mode of carrying large fish	190
430. The *oxyrhinchus* fish, in bronze	191
431. The *oxyrhinchus* at the Oasis	191
432. A bronze *Lepidotus*	192
433. Foreign captives employed in making bricks at Thebes	196
**434. Features of two of the brickmakers	198
435. Persons coming to be registered	200
436. Persons brought before the scribes	200
437. The Goddess of Truth and Justice	205
438. The Goddess of Truth " with her eyes closed"	205
439. The bastinado	211
440. Women bastinadoed	211
441. Workmen beaten	212
442. Bastinado for petty theft	215
443. The 12 Egyptian months	253

Vignette
**N. Pointed arch at Tusculum, in Italy (built while the Kings ruled at Rome?) 261

CHAPTER IX.

Vignette
O. View of the modern town of Manfalóot 262

Woodcut
**444. Egyptian mode of drawing the human figure in squares on a wall, showing the proportions during the 18th and 19th dynasties 267
445. A scribe writing on a tablet 276

LIST OF WOODCUTS IN VOL. II.

Woodcut	Page
446. Scribe with his inkstand on the table; one pen is put behind his ear	276
447. Artists painting on a board, and colouring a statue	277
448. Section of one of the *southern* grottoes of Beni Hassan	283
449. Columns of the *northern* grottoes of Beni Hassan	284
450. Five of the Egyptian orders of columns	285
450a The remaining three of the orders of columns	286
451. Heads of enemies, once supporting something now removed	287
452. True and false arches; mode of commencing a quarry	303
453. Removing a stone from the quarries of El Māsara	306
454. Levelling and squaring a stone	313
455. Polishing granite statue	314
456. Standing figure of a king painted to represent granite	314
457. Bellows	316
458. Siphons used as early as 1430 B.C.	318
459. Men's dresses	321
460. Dress of the king	323
461. Head-dresses	325
462, 463. Wigs	326
464. Women carrying children	330
465. Sandals	331
466. Sandals and shoes	332
467. Dresses of women	334
468. Head-dress of a lady	335
469. Hands of a wooden figure of a woman, with many rings	336
470. Rings, signets, bracelets, and earrings	338
471. Various necklaces	340
472. Combs found at Thebes	343
473. Boxes, or bottles, for holding the *kohl* for staining the eyelids	344
474. Needles, pins, and earrings	345
475. Metal mirrors. (Metal, and even glass, mirrors were also used at Rome, but *these differed from some of the Roman " specula"* used as ornaments for rooms; from which the Venetians borrowed their mirrors, with figures upon them)	346
476. Other metal mirrors	347
477. Walking sticks	347
478. Priests and other persons of rank walking with sticks	348
479. A lady in the bath with her attendants	349
480. Doctors and patients; or perhaps barbers	352
481. Exvotos	354
**482. A boat or *baris* of the dead	355

THE ANCIENT EGYPTIANS.

CHAPTER X.

Vignette — Page
P. Tomb of Sakkára, arched with stone, of the time of Psammitichus II. 356

Woodcut
483. Services performed to the dead 357
484. Members of the family present when the services were performed 358
485. A woman embracing, and weeping before, her husband's mummy 358
486. Conveying the mummies on sledges to the closets in which they were kept 359
487. Pouring oil over a mummy 360
488. An altar in the British Museum 361
489. A table with cakes and ducks 362
490. Seals found near the tombs 364
491. Closets containing figures of gods 366
492. The mummy's head seen at an open panel of the coffin 368
493. A peculiar attendant at a funeral 371
494. Certain personages present at funerals, and grease poured before the sledge 373
495. A stone scarabæus with silver wings 395
496. Different forms of mummy-cases 398

Vignette
Q. Interior of a mummy-pit, and a woman seeking for ornaments .. 400

MANNERS AND CUSTOMS

OF

THE ANCIENT EGYPTIANS.

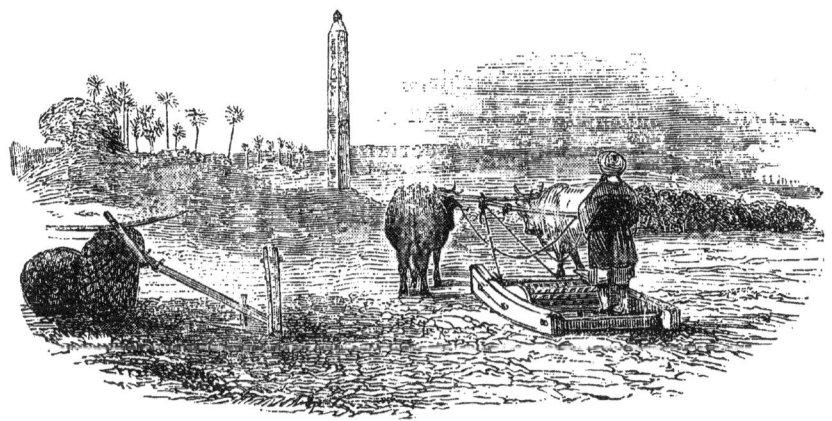

II. *Khonfud*, or clod-crushing machine used after the land is ploughed. *Heliopolis—Cairo in the distance.*

CHAPTER VI.

THE DIFFERENT CLASSES OF EGYPTIANS—THE THIRD CLASS—THE HUSBANDMEN—AGRICULTURE—PRODUCTIONS OF EGYPT—HARVEST—FESTIVALS OF THE PEASANTS—GARDENERS, HUNTSMEN, BOATMEN OF THE NILE.

THE high estimation in which the priestly and military professions were held in Egypt placed them far above the rest of the community; but the other classes had also their degrees of consequence, and individuals enjoyed a position and importance in proportion to their respectability, their talents, or their wealth.

According to Herodotus, the whole Egyptian community was divided into seven tribes, one of which was the sacerdotal, another of the soldiers, and the remaining five of the herdsmen, swineherds, shop-keepers, interpreters, and boatmen. Diodorus states that, like the Athenians, they were distributed into three classes—the priests; the peasants or husbandmen, from whom the soldiers were levied; and the artisans, who were employed in handicraft and other similar occupations, and in common offices among the people—but in another place he extends the number to five, and reckons the pastors, husbandmen, and artificers, independent of the soldiers and priests. Strabo limits them to three, the military, husbandmen, and priests; and Plato divides them into six bodies, the priests, artificers, shepherds, huntsmen, husbandmen, and soldiers; each peculiar art or occupation, he observes, being confined to a certain subdivision of the caste, and every one being engaged in his own branch without interfering with the occupation of another. Hence it appears that the first class consisted of the priests; the second of the soldiers; the third of the husbandmen, gardeners, huntsmen, boatmen of the Nile, and others; the fourth of artificers, tradesmen, and shop-keepers, carpenters, boat-builders, masons, and probably potters, public weighers, and notaries; and in the fifth may be reckoned pastors, poulterers, fowlers, fishermen, labourers, and, generally speaking, the common people. Many of these were again subdivided, as the artificers and tradesmen, according to their peculiar trade or occupation; and as the pastors, into ox-herds, shepherds, goatherds, and swineherds; which last were, according to Herodotus, the lowest grade, not only of the class, but of the whole community, since no one would either marry their daughters or establish any family connection with them. So degrading was the occupation of tending swine, that they were looked upon as impure, and were even forbidden to enter a temple without previously undergoing a purification; and the prejudices of the Indians against this class of persons almost justify our belief in the statement of the historian.

Without stopping to inquire into the relative rank of the different subdivisions of the third class, the importance of agriculture in a country like Egypt, where the richness and productiveness of the soil have always been proverbial, suffices to claim the first place for the husbandmen.

ABUNDANCE OF CORN.

The abundant supply of grain and other produce gave to Egypt advantages which no other country possessed. Not only was her dense population supplied with a profusion of the necessaries of life, but the sale of the surplus conferred considerable benefits on the peasant, in addition to the profits which thence accrued to the state; for Egypt was a granary where, from the earliest times, all people felt sure of finding a plenteous store of corn;* and some idea may be formed of the immense quantity produced there, from the circumstance of " seven plenteous years" affording, from the superabundance of the crops, a sufficiency of corn to supply the whole population during seven years of dearth, as well as "all countries" which sent to Egypt " to buy" it, when Pharaoh by the advice of Joseph† laid up the annual surplus for that purpose.

The right of exportation, and the sale of superfluous produce to foreigners, belonged exclusively to the government, as is distinctly shown by the sale of corn to the Israelites from the royal stores, and the collection having been made by Pharaoh only; and it is probable that even the rich landowners were in the habit of selling to government whatever quantity remained on hand at the approach of each successive harvest; while the agricultural labourers, from their frugal mode of living, required very little wheat and barley, and were generally contented, as at the present day, with bread made of the *Doora*‡ flour; children, and even grown persons, according to Diodorus, often living on roots and esculent herbs, as the papyrus, lotus, and others, either raw, toasted, or boiled.

The Government did not interfere directly with the peasants respecting the nature of the produce they intended to cultivate; and the vexations of later times were unknown under the Pharaohs. They were thought to have the best opportunities of obtaining, from actual observation, an accurate knowledge on all subjects connected with husbandry; and, as Diodorus observes, "being from their infancy brought up to agricultural

---

* Gen. xii. 2, and xlii. 2. † Gen. xli. 29.
‡ The Holcus Sorghum.

pursuits, they far excelled the husbandmen of other countries, and had become acquainted with the capabilities of the land, the mode of irrigation, the exact season for sowing and reaping, as well as all the most useful secrets connected with the harvest, which they had derived from their ancestors, and had improved by their own experience." "They rented," says the same historian, "the arable lands belonging to the kings, the priests, and the military class, for a small sum, and employed their whole time in the tillage of their farms;" and the labourers who cultivated land for the rich peasant, or other landed proprietors, were superintended by the steward or owner of the estate, who had authority over them, and the power of condemning delinquents to the bastinado. This is shown by the paintings of the tombs; which frequently represent a person of consequence inspecting the tillage of the field, either seated in a chariot, walking, or leaning on his staff, accompanied by a favourite dog.*

Their mode of irrigation was the same in the field of the peasant as in the garden of the villa;† and the principal differ-

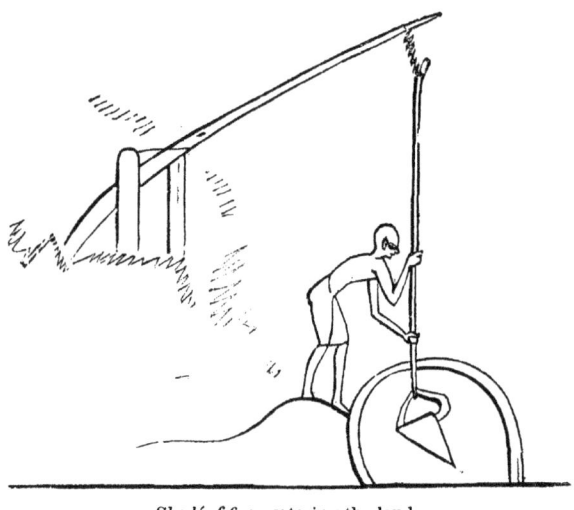

356.   *Shadóof* for watering the lands.   *Thebes.*

* *See* woodcut 368, *fig.* 1, and vol. i. p. 32.   † Vol. i. p. 33, 34, 35.

ence in the mode of tilling the former consisted in the use of the plough.

The usual contrivance for raising water from the Nile for watering the crops was the *shadóof*, or pole and bucket, so common still in Egypt; and even the water-wheel appears to have been employed in more recent times.

The sculptures of the tombs frequently represent canals conveying the water of the inundation into the fields; and the proprietor of the estate is seen, as described by Virgil, plying in a light painted skiff or papyrus punt, and superintending the maintenance of the dykes, or other important matters connected with the land. Boats carry the grain to the granary, or remove the flocks from the lowlands; as the water subsides, the husbandman ploughs the soft earth with a pair of oxen; and the same subjects introduce the offering of first-fruits to the gods, in acknowledgment of the benefits conferred by "a favourable Nile." The main canal was usually carried to the upper or southern side of the land, and small branches, leading from it at intervals, traversed the fields in straight or curving lines, according to the nature or elevation of the soil.

The inundation began about the end of May, sometimes rather later: but about the middle of June the gradual rise of the river was generally perceived; and the comparatively clear stream assumed a red and turbid appearance, caused by the floods of the rainy season in Abyssinia: the annual cause of the inundation. It next assumed a green appearance, and being unwholesome during that short period, care was taken to lay up in jars a sufficient supply of the previous turbid but wholesome water, which was used until it reassumed its red colour. This explains the remark of Aristides, "that the Egyptians are the only people who preserve water in jars, and calculate its age as others do that of wine;" and may also be the reason of water-jars being an emblem of the inundation, though the calculation of the "age" of the water is an exaggeration. Perhaps, too, the god Nilus being represented of a blue and a red colour, may allude to the two different appearances of the low and high Nile.

In the beginning of August, the canals were opened, and the waters overflowed the plain. That part nearest the desert, being

357. Cattle rescued from the inundation. Beni Hassan.

Part 1. Figs. 1 and 3. Men calling to others to drive the cattle towards the boat. 2. Rower. 4. Pulling a cow by a noose to the boat. Part 2. Fig. 5. Driving the cattle towards the boat. 6. Throwing a noose, in order to drag them after the boat (the end of it is effaced). 7. The rowers. 8. A man on the bank fishing. (See the Vignette at the head of Chap. VIII.)

the lowest level, was first inundated ; as the bank itself, being the highest, was the last part submerged, except in the Delta, where the levels were more uniform, and where, during the high inundations, the whole land, with the exception of its isolated villages, was under water. As the Nile rose, the peasants were careful to remove the flocks and herds from the lowlands; and when a sudden irruption of the water, owing to the bursting of a dyke, or an unexpected and unusual increase of the river, overflowed the fields and pastures, they were seen hurrying to the spot, on foot, or in boats, to rescue the animals, and to remove them to the high grounds above the reach of the inundation. Some, tying their clothes upon their heads, dragged the sheep and goats from the water, and put them into boats; others swam the oxen to the nearest high ground ; and if any corn or other produce could be cut or torn up by the roots, in time to save it from the flood, it was conveyed on rafts or boats to the next village. And though some suppose the inundation does not now attain the same height as of old, those who have lived in the country have frequently seen the villages of the Delta standing, as Herodotus describes them, like islands in the Ægean Sea, with the same scenes of rescuing the cattle from the water.

Guards were placed to watch the dykes, which protected the lowlands, and the utmost care was taken to prevent any sudden influx of water, which might endanger the produce still growing there, the cattle, or the villages. And of such importance was the preservation of the dykes, that a strong guard of cavalry and infantry was always in attendance for their protection ; certain officers of responsibility were appointed to superintend them, being furnished with large sums of money for their maintenance and repairs ; and in the time of the Romans, any person found destroying a dyke was condemned to hard labour in the public works or in the mines, or was branded and transported to the Oasis. According to Strabo, the system was so admirably managed, "that art contrived sometimes to supply what nature denied, and, by means of canals and embankments, there was little difference in the quantity of land irrigated, whether the inundation was deficient or abundant." "If," continues the geographer, "it rose only to the height of eight cubits, the usual idea was that a famine would ensue; fourteen being required for a plentiful harvest: but when Petronius was præfect of Egypt, twelve cubits gave the same abundance, nor did they suffer from want even at eight:" and it may be supposed that long experience had taught the ancient Egyptians to obtain similar results from the same means, which, neglected at a subsequent period, were revived, rather than, as Strabo thinks, first introduced, by the Romans.

In some parts of Egypt, the villages were liable to be overflowed when the Nile rose to a more than ordinary height, by which the lives and property of the inhabitants were endangered; and when their crude brick houses had been long exposed to the damp, the foundations gave way, and the fallen walls, saturated with water, were once more mixed with the mud from which they had been extracted. On these occasions, the blessings of the Nile entailed heavy losses on the inhabitants; for, according to Pliny, "if the rise of the water exceeded sixteen cubits, a famine was the result, as when it only reached the height of twelve." In another place he says, "a proper inundation is of sixteen cubits . . . . in twelve cubits, the country suffers from famine, and feels a deficiency even in thirteen; fourteen cause joy, fifteen security, sixteen delight; the greatest rise of the river to this period being of eighteen cubits, in the reign of Claudius; the least during the Pharsalic war."

From all that can be learnt respecting the rise of the Nile, it is evident that the actual height of the inundation is the same now as in former times, and maintains the same proportion with the land it irrigates; and that, in order to arrive at great accuracy in its measurement, the scales of the Nilometers ought, after certain periods, to be raised in an equal ratio, as may be seen by any one who visits those of Cairo and Elephantine. For the bed of the river gradually rises from time to time; and the level of the land, which always keeps pace with that of the river, increases in a ratio of six inches in a hundred years in some places (as about Elephantine), and in others less—varying according to the distance down the stream. The consequence, and indeed the proof, of which is, that the highest scale in the Nilometer at the island of Elephantine, which served to measure the inundation in the reigns of the early Roman emperors, is now far below the level of the ordinary high Nile; and the obelisk of Matareeh or Heliopolis, the Colossi of the Theban plain, and other similarly situated monuments, are flooded to a certain height by the waters of the inundation, and imbedded in a stratum of alluvial soil deposited around their base.

The continual increase in the elevation of the bed of the river naturally produced those effects mentioned by Herodotus and other writers, who state that the Egyptians were obliged from time to time to raise their towns and villages, in order to secure them from the effects of the inundation; and that the same change in the levels of the Nile and the land took place in former ages as at the present day, is shown by the fact of Sabaco having found it necessary to elevate the towns throughout the country, which had been previously protected by similar means in the reign of Sesostris. This was done by the inhabitants of each place, who had been condemned for great crimes to the public works. Bubastis was raised more than any other city; and the lofty mounds of Tel Basta, which mark its site, fully confirm the observation of Herodotus, and show, from the height of those mounds above the present plain, after a lapse of 770 years, that "the Ethiopian monarch elevated the sites of the towns much more than his predecessor Sesostris had done," when that conqueror employed his captives in making the canals of Egypt. And if its height was in proportion to the number of its criminals, Bubastis could not boast of the morality of its inhabitants.

On a rough calculation, it may be said that the land about Elephantine has been raised about nine feet in 1700 years; at Thebes, about seven; and in a less degree towards the Delta and the sea, where the extensive surface of the land (compared to the narrow valley above Memphis) alters the proportions in its elevation, until at the mouths of the Nile there is no perceptible rise of the soil from alluvial deposit.

There is another singular fact connected with the inundation in different places: that throughout the valley lying to the S. of the Delta, the actual banks of the Nile are much more elevated than the land of the interior at a distance from the river, and are seldom quite covered with water even during the highest inundations; though the bank then projects very little above the level of the stream; and, in some places, the peasant is obliged to keep out the water by temporary embankments. This difference of level may be accounted for partly by the continued cultivation of the soil by the river side, which, being more conveniently situated for artificial irrigation, has a constant succession of crops; for it is known that tillage has the effect of raising land, from the accumulation of decayed vegetable substances, the addition of dressing, and other causes; and the greater depression of the plain in the interior is owing, in some degree, to the numerous channels in that direction, and to the effect of the currents which pass over it as the water covers the land: though they are not sufficient to account for the great difference between the height of the bank and the land near the edge of the desert, which is often 12 or 15 feet, as may be seen from the comparative height of the same horizontal dyke at those two points.

These elevated roads, the sole mode of communication by land from one village to another during the inundation, commence on a level with the bank of the river, and, as they extend to the interior, are there so much higher than the fields, that room is afforded for the construction of arches to enable the water to pass through them; though the larger bridges are only built on those parts, where ancient or modern canals have caused a still greater depression of the land.

The canals, like the dykes, were the constant care of the magistrates in old times; and they were furnished with sluices and other appliances to regulate the supply of water, and to turn the fisheries to good account.

The water of the inundation was differently managed in

various districts. This depended either on the relative levels of the adjacent lands, or on the crops they happened to be cultivating at the time. When a field lay fallow, or the last crop had been gathered, the water was permitted to overflow it as soon as its turn came to receive it from the nearest sluices; or, in those parts where the levels were low and open to the ingress of the rising stream, as soon as the Nile had arrived at a sufficient height; but when the last autumn crop was in the ground, every precaution was taken to keep the field from being inundated, and "as the water rose gradually, they kept it out by small dams, which could be opened if required, and closed again without much trouble."*

As the Nile subsided, the water was retained in the fields by proper embankments; and the mouths of the canals being again closed, it was prevented from returning into the falling stream. By this means the irrigation of the land was prolonged considerably, and the fertilizing effects of the inundation continued until the water was absorbed. And so rapidly does the hot sun of Egypt, even at this late period of the season—in the months of November and December—dry the mud when once deprived of its covering of water, that no fevers are generated, and no illness visits those villages which have been entirely surrounded by the inundation.

The land being cleared of the water, and presenting in some places a surface of liquid mud, in others nearly dried by the sun and the strong N.W. winds (that continue at intervals to the end of autumn and the commencement of winter), the husbandman prepared the ground to receive the seed, which was either done by the plough and hoe, or by more simple means, according to the nature of the soil, the quality of the produce they intended to cultivate, or the time the land had remained under water.

When the levels were low, and the water had continued long upon the land, they often dispensed with the plough, and, like their successors, broke up the ground with hoes, or simply dragged the moist mud with bushes after the seed had been thrown upon the surface, and then merely drove a number of

* Diodor. i. 36.

Fig. 4. Goats treading in the grain, when sown in the field, after the water has subsided. 6 is sprinkling the seed from the basket he holds in his left hand; the others are driving the goats over the ground. The hieroglyphic word above, Sk, or Skai, signifies "tillage," and is followed by the demonstrative sign, a plough. *Tombs near the Pyramids.*

CHAP. VI.

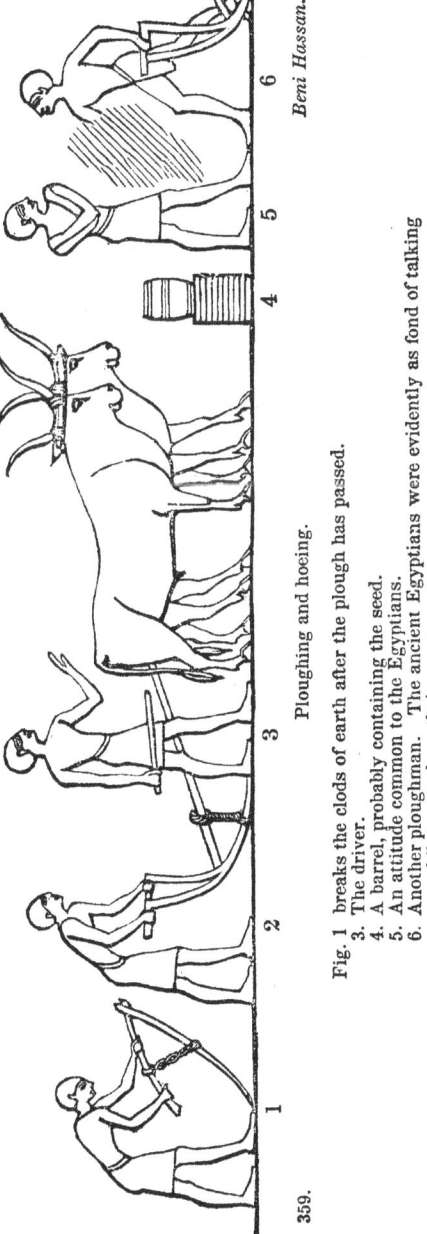

Ploughing and hoeing.   Beni Hassan.

Fig. 1 breaks the clods of earth after the plough has passed.
3. The driver.
4. A barrel, probably containing the seed.
5. An attitude common to the Egyptians.
6. Another ploughman. The ancient Egyptians were evidently as fond of talking while at work as their successors.

cattle, asses, pigs, sheep, or goats into the field to tread in the grain. " In no country," says Herodotus, " do they gather their seed with so little labour. They are not obliged to trace deep furrows with the plough, and break the clods, nor to partition out their fields into numerous forms, as other people do; but when the river of itself overflows the land, and the water retires again, they sow their fields, driving the pigs over them to tread in the seed; and this being done, every one patiently awaits the harvest." On other occasions they used the plough, but were contented, as we are told by Diodorus and Columella, with " tracing slight furrows with light ploughs on the surface of the land;" and others followed with wooden hoes* to break the clods of the rich and tenacious soil.

The modern Egyptians sometimes substitute for the hoe a machine,† called *khonfud*, " hedgehog," which consists of a cylinder studded with projecting iron pins, to break the clods after the land has been ploughed; but this is only used when great care is required in the tillage of the land; and they frequently dispense with the hoe, contenting themselves also with the same slight furrows as their predecessors, which do not exceed the depth of a few inches, measuring from the lowest part to the summit of the ridge. It is difficult to say if the modern Egyptians derived the hint of the "*hedgehog*" from their predecessors; but it is a curious fact that a clod-crushing machine, not very unlike that of Egypt, has only lately been invented in England, which was shown at the Great Exhibition of 1851.

The ancient plough was entirely of wood, and of as simple a form as that of modern Egypt. It consisted of a share, two *handles*, and the pole or beam; which last was inserted into the lower end of the stilt, or the base of the handles, and was strengthened by a rope connecting it with the heel. It had no coulter, nor were wheels applied to any Egyptian plough; but it is probable that the point was shod with a metal sock, either of bronze or iron. It was drawn by two oxen; and the plough-

* Woodcuts 359, *fig.* 1, 361 and 362.
† See the Vignette at the beginning of this chapter.

CHAP. VI.   THE PLOUGH.   15

man guided and drove them with a long goad, without the assistance of reins, which are used by the modern Egyptians. He was sometimes accompanied by another man, who drove the animals,* while he managed the two handles of the plough; and sometimes the whip was substituted for the more usual goad.

Cows were occasionally put to the plough; and it may not have been unknown to them that the cow ploughs quicker than the ox.

The mode of yoking the beasts was exceedingly simple. Across the extremity of the pole, a wooden yoke or cross-bar, about fifty-five inches or five feet in length, was fastened by a strap lashed backwards and forwards over a prominence projecting from the centre of the yoke, which corresponded to a similar peg, or knob, at the end of the pole; and occasionally,

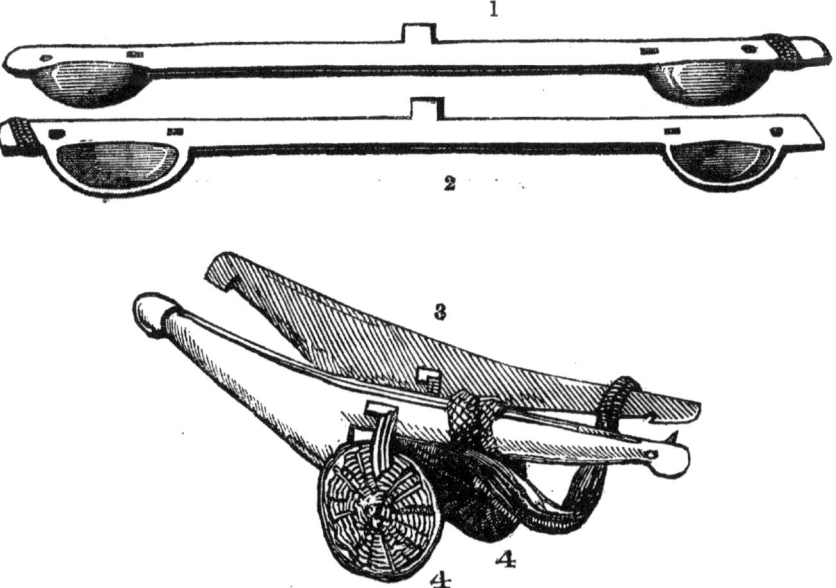

360.   Yoke of an ancient plough found in a tomb.   *Collection of S. d'Athanasi.*
   Figs. 1, 2. The back and front of the yoke.
      3. Collar or shoulder pieces attached to the yoke.
      4, 4. The pieces of matting for protecting the two shoulders from friction.

* *See* instances of both in woodcut 34, vol. i. p. 32.

in addition to these, was a ring passing over them as in some Greek chariots. At either end of the yoke was a flat or slightly concave projection, of semicircular form, which rested on a pad placed upon the withers of the animal; and through a hole on either side of it passed a thong for suspending the shoulder-pieces which formed the collar. These were two wooden bars, forked at about half their length, padded so as to protect the shoulder from friction, and connected at the lower end by a strong broad band passing under the throat.

Sometimes the draught, instead of being from the withers, was from the head, the yoke being tied to the base of the horns;* and in religious ceremonies oxen frequently drew the bier, or the sacred shrine, by a rope fastened to the upper part of the horns, without either yoke or pole.

From a passage in Deuteronomy, "Thou shalt not plow with an ox and an ass together," it might be inferred that the custom of yoking two different animals to the plough was common in Egypt; but it was evidently not so; and the Hebrew lawgiver had probably in view a practice adopted by some of the people of Syria, whose country the Israelites were about to occupy.

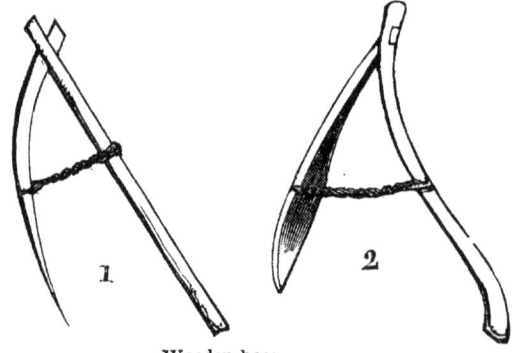

361.
Wooden hoes.
Fig. 1. From the sculptures.   Fig. 2. Found in a tomb.

The hoe was of wood, like the fork, and many other implements of husbandry, and in form was not unlike our letter A,

* As in woodcut 359, p. 13.

CHAP. VI.   HOES.   17

with one limb shorter than the other, and curving inwards. The longer limb, or handle, was of uniform thickness, round and smooth, sometimes with a knob at the end; and the lower extremity of the blade was of increased breadth, and either terminated in a sharp point, or was rounded at the end. The blade was frequently inserted into the handle,* and they were bound together, about the centre, with a twisted rope. Being the most common tool, answering for hoe, spade, and pick, it is frequently represented in the sculptures; and several, which have been found in the tombs of Thebes, are preserved in the museums of Europe.

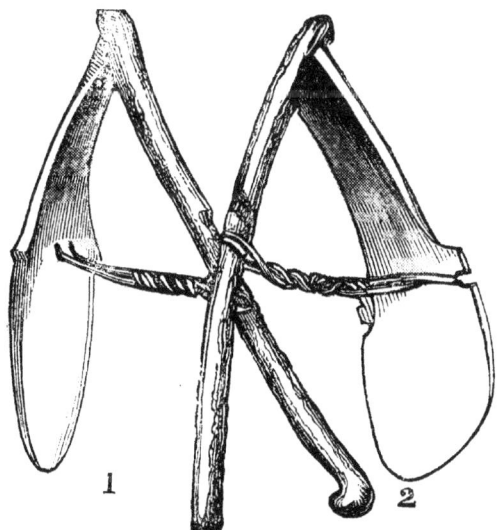

362.   Wooden hoes.   *Berlin Museum.*

The hoe in hieroglyphics stands for the letter M, though the name of this instrument was in Egyptian, as in Arabic, *Tôré*. It forms the commencement of the word *Mai*, " *beloved,*" and enters into numerous other combinations.

There are no instances of hoes with metal blades, except of very late time, nor is there any proof of the ploughshare having been sheathed with metal.

* Woodcut 361, *fig.* 2.

363. Hoeing and sowing the land, and felling trees. *Thebes.*

The axe had a metal blade, either bronze or iron; and the peasants are sometimes represented felling trees with this implement, while others are employed in hoeing the field preparatory to its being sown—confirming what I before observed, that the ancient, as well as the modern Egyptians frequently dispensed with the use of the plough.

The admission of swine into the fields, mentioned by Herodotus, should rather have been before than after they had sowed the land, since their habits would do little good to the farmer,

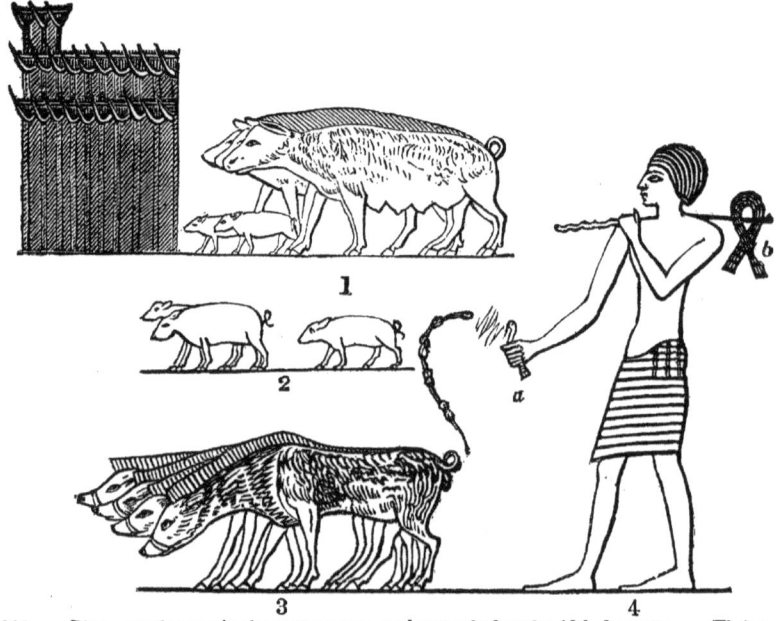

364. Pigs; rarely seen in the sculptures; and never before the 18th dynasty. *Thebes.*
1. Sows with young pigs. 2. Young pigs. 3. Boars.
a is a whip, knotted like some of our own. *b* a *gayd*, or noose, often used as the emblem of a shepherd.

and other animals would answer as well for "treading in the grain;" but they may have been used before for clearing the fields of the roots and weeds encouraged by the inundation; and this seems to be confirmed by the herd of pigs with water plants represented in the tombs.

They sometimes used a top dressing of nitrous soil, which was spread over the surface; a custom continued to the present day: but this was confined to certain crops, and principally to those reared late in the year; the fertilizing properties of the alluvial deposit answering all the purposes of the richest manure. Its peculiar quality is not merely indicated by its effects, but by the appearance it presents; and when left upon rock, and dried by the sun, it resembles pottery, from its brightness and consistence. Its component parts, according to the analysis given by Regnault in the "Mémoires sur l'Egypte," are—

11 water.
9 carbon.
6 oxide of iron.
4 silica.
4 carbonate of magnesia.
18 carbonate of lime.
48 alumen.
———
100

the quantity of silica and alumen varying according to the places whence the mud is taken, which frequently contains a great admixture of sand near the banks, and a larger proportion of argillaceous matter at a distance from the river.

The same quality of soil and alluvial deposit seems to accompany the Nile in its course from Abyssinia to the Mediterranean; and though the *White* River is the principal stream, being much broader, bringing a larger supply of water, and coming from a greater distance than the Blue (*Black*) River, or Abyssinian branch, which rises a little beyond the lake Dembea, still this last claims the merit of possessing the real peculiarities of the Nile, and of yielding those fertilizing properties which mark its course to the sea. The White River, or western branch, likewise overflows its banks, but no rich mud accompanies its inundation; and though, from the force of its stream (which brings down numbers of large fish and shells at the commencement of its rise, probably from passing through some large lakes), there is evidence of its being supplied by an abundance of heavy rain, we may conclude that the nature of the soil, along the whole of its course, differs considerably from that of the Abyssinian branch.

And here I may mention that the name Bahr el Azrek, opposed to Bahr el Abiad, or "*White* River," should be translated *Black* (not *Blue*) River; azrek, though signifying "blue," being also used in the sense of our "jet black;" and hossán *azrek* is a "*black* (not a blue) horse."

Besides the admixture of nitrous earth, the Egyptians made use of other kinds of dressing, and sought, for different productions, the soils best suited to them. They even took advantage of the edge of the desert for growing the vine and some other plants, which, being composed of clay and sand, was peculiarly adapted to such as required a light soil; and the cultivation of this additional tract, which only stood in need of proper irrigation to become highly productive, had the advantage of increasing considerably the extent of the arable land of Egypt. In many places we still find evidence of its having been tilled by the ancient inhabitants, even to the late time of the Roman empire; and in some parts of the Fyoom, the vestiges of beds and channels for irrigation, as well as the roots of vines, are found in sites lying far above the level of the rest of the country.

The occupation of the husbandman depended much on the produce he had determined on rearing. Those who solely cultivated corn had little more to do than to await the time of harvest; but many crops required constant attention, and some stood in need of frequent artificial irrigation.

In order to give a general notion of the quality of the crops, and other peculiarities relating to their agriculture, I shall introduce the principal productions of Egypt in the two following tables, of which the first presents those raised after the retirement of the inundation:

CHAP. VI.   PRODUCTIONS AFTER THE INUNDATION.   21

English Name.	Botanical Name.	Remarks.
Wheat	Triticum sativum. (Arab. *Kumh.*)	Sown in ____; reaped in beginning of April, a month later than barley. *Comp.* Exod. ix. 32.
Barley	Hordeum vulgare. (Arab. *Shayéer.*)	Sown at the same time; reaped, some in 90 days, some in the 4th month.*
Beans	Vicia faba. (Arab. *Fool.*)	Sown in October or November; cut in about 4 months.
Peas?	Pisum arvense. (Arab. *Bisilleh.*)	Sown in the middle of November; ripen in 90 or 100 days.
Lentils	Ervum lens. (Arab. *Ads.*)	} Sown in the middle or end of November; ripen in 100 or 110 days.
Vetches	(Hommos) Cicer arietinum. (Arab. *Hommos.*)	
Lupins	Lupinus Termis. (Arab. *Termus.*)	*Id.* Called θαρμος in Coptic, which is still retained in the modern Arabic name Termus.
Clover	Trifolium Alexandrinum. (Arab. *Bersim.*)	Sown in beginning of October; first crop after 60 days, second after 50 more days, third left for seed; if a fourth crop is raised by irrigation, it produces no seed.
	Trigonella fœnum-græcum. (Arab. *Helbeh.*)	The Helbeh, or Trigonella fœnum-græcum, sown in November; cut in about 2 months.
	Lathyrus sativus. (Arab. *Gilbán.*)	Lathyrus sativus, a substitute for clover, gathered in 60 days; seed ripens in 110.
A sort of French Bean	Dolichos lubia. (Arab. *Loobieh.*)	Sown at same time as wheat in November; ripens in 4 months. A crop raised by the Silóof in August, gathered in about 3 months; its beans for cooking in 60 days.

* Pliny says in the sixth, and wheat in the seventh, month after sowing, xviii. 7.

English Name.	Botanical Name.	Remarks.
Safflower	Carthamus tinctorius. (Arab. *Kortum*.)	The flowers used for dyeing: the seeds giving an oil. Sown middle of November; seeds ripen in 5 months.
Lettuce	Lactuca sativa. (Arab. *Khus*.)	Cultivated for oil. Sown in middle of November; seeds ripen in 5 months.
Flax	Linum usitatissimum. (Arab. *Kettán*.)	Sown middle of November; plucked in 110 days.
Coleseed	Brassica oleifera. (Arab. *Selgam*.)	
Hemp?	Cannabis sxa. (Arab. *Hasheésh*.)	Yields an oil. Sown middle of November; cut in 110 days.
Cummin	Cuminum Cyminum. (Arab. *Kammoon*.)	
Coriander	Coriandrum sativum. (Arab. *Koosbera*.)	Sown middle of December; cut in 4 months.
Poppy	Papaver somniferum. (Arab. *Afm*.)	Sown end of November; seeds ripen in April. The Arabic name signifies father (of) sleep.
Water Melon, and several other Cucurbitæ	Cucurbita citrullus. (Arab. *Batéekh*.)	Sown middle of December; cut in 90 days.
Cucumber, and other Cucumis	Cucumis sativus. (*Kheár*) &c.	Cut in 60 days.
Doora	Holcus Sorghum. (Arab. *Doora Sayfee*.)	Independent of the crop raised by the *Shadóof*, and that *during* the inundation; sown middle of November; ripens in 5½ months.

All these, the ordinary productions of modern Egypt, appear to have been known and cultivated in old times; and according to Dioscorides, from the *Helbeh*, or Trigonella, was made the ointment, called by Athenæus "Telinon." The Carthamus tinctorius and the pea are now proved, by the discovery of their seeds in a tomb at Thebes, to have been ancient Egyptian plants; the coleseed appears also to have been an indigenous production; and hemp is supposed to have been used of old for its intoxicating qualities.

The Carthamus was not only cultivated for the dye its flower produced, but for the oil extracted from its seeds. The ancient, as well as the modern Egyptians, also obtained oil from other plants, as the olive, *simsim* or sesamum, the *cici* or castor-berry tree, lettuce, flax, and *selgam* or coleseed. This last, the Brassica oleifera of Linnæus, appears to be the Egyptian *raphanus* mentioned by Pliny, as "celebrated for the abundance of its oil," unless he alludes to the *seemga*, or Raphanus oleifer of Linnæus, which is now only grown in Nubia and the vicinity of the first cataract. The seeds of the *simsim* also afforded an excellent oil, and they were probably used, as at the present day, in making a peculiar kind of cake, called by the Arabs *Koosbeh*, which is the name it bears when the oil has been previously extracted. When only *bruised* in the mill, and still containing the oil, it is called *Taheéneh;* and the unbruised seeds are strewed upon cakes, or give their name and flavour to a coarse conserve called *Haloweh simsemeéh*. The oil of *simsim* (called *seerig*) is considered the best lamp oil of the country; it is also used for cooking, but is reckoned inferior in flavour to that of the lettuce.

The castor-berry tree is called by Herodotus Sillicyprion, and the oil kiki (*cici*), which he says is not inferior to that of the olive for lamps, though it has the disadvantage of a strong unpleasant smell. Pliny calls the tree *cici*, which, he adds, "grows abundantly in Egypt, and has also the names of croton, trixis, tree sesamum, and ricinus;" and he records his very natural dislike of castor oil. The mode he mentions of extracting the oil by putting the seeds into water over a fire, and skimming the surface, is the manner now adopted in Egypt; though he says the ancient Egyptians merely pressed them after sprinkling them with salt. The press, indeed, is employed for this purpose at the present day, when the oil is only wanted for lamps; but by the other method it is more pure, and the coarser qualities not being extracted, it is better suited for medicinal purposes. Strabo says, "Almost all the natives of Egypt used its oil for lamps, and workmen, as well as the poorer classes, both men and women, anointed themselves with it," giving it the same name, *kiki*, as Pliny, which he does not confine, like Herodotus, to the oil; and of all those by which it was formerly known in Egypt or Greece, no one is retained by the modern Egyptians. It grows in every part of Upper and Lower Egypt, but the oil is now little used, in consequence of the extensive culture of the lettuce, the coleseed, the olive, the carthamus, and the *simsim*, which afford a better quality for burning; it is, therefore, seldom employed except for the purpose of adulterating the lettuce and other oils; and the Ricinus, though a common plant, is rarely cultivated in any part of the country.

"The *cnicon*, a plant unknown in Italy, according to Pliny, was sown in Egypt for the sake of the oil its seeds afforded;" the chorticon, urtica, and amaracus were cultivated for the same purpose, and the cypros, "a tree resembling the ziziphus in its foliage, with seeds like the coriander, was noted in Egypt, particularly on the Canopic branch of the Nile, for the excellence of its oil." Egypt was also famed for its "oil of bitter almonds;" and many other vegetable productions were encouraged for the sake of their oil, for making ointments, or for medicinal purposes.

In the length of time each crop took to come to maturity, and the exact period when the seed was put into the ground, much depended upon the duration of the inundation, the state of the soil, and other circumstances; and in the two accompanying tables I have been guided by observations made on the crops of modern Egypt, which, as may be supposed, differ in few or no particulars from those of former days, the causes that influence them being permanent and unvarying.

PRODUCTIONS OF THE SUMMER.

English Name.	Botanical Name.	Remarks.
Rice	Oryza sativa. (Arab. *Rooz* or *Aroos*.)	Cut in 7 months: in October. Grown in the Delta.
Doora	Holcus Sorghum. (Arab. *Doora Kaydee*.)	Sown in beginning or end of April; cut at rise of Nile in 100 days. Its seed sown as Byoód.
Byoód or autumn *Doora*	Holcus Sorghum. (Arab. *D. Byood*, or *Dimeeree*.)	Sown middle of August; cut in 4 months; but its seed, no longer prolific, is all used for bread.
Yellow Doora	Id. (Arab. *D. Saffra*.)	Sown when the Nile is at its height, in middle of August, and banked up from the inundation: ripens in 120 days. Only in Nubia and the Oases: sown at same time as the Doora.
Millet	Holcus saccharatus. (Arab. *Dokhn*.)	Planted in March and summer. In good soil some is gathered the 5th month.
Cotton	Gossypium herbaceum. (Arab. *Koton*.)	Gives an oil. Ripens in about 100 days. Sown 10 days after the Doora Byoód. *See above*, p. 23.
Simsim, Sesame	Sesamum orientale. (Arab. *Simsim*.)	Sown in April: the first crop in 70 days; second in 40; third in 30; fourth in 25, in the first year: it is then left and again in March. Then the first crop is cut after 40 days; second in 30; third in 30; and the same in the third year. After three years it is renewed from seed. The first year's crop is the best.
Indigo	Indigofera argentea. (Arab. *Neeleh*.)	
Henneh	Lawsonia spinosa et inermis.	Used for the dye of its leaves.
Water Melon	and other Cucurbitæ. (Arab. *Bateekh*, &c.)	During the rise of the Nile, and in March, on the sand taks of the river.
Onion (Leek, and Garlic)	Allium Cepa, &c. (Arab. *Bussul*.)	Sown in August.
Bámia	Hibiscus esculentus. (Arab. *Bámia*.)	Mostly in gardens. Gathered in 50 or 60 days, in September and October. Many other vegetables raised at different seasons, by artificial irrigation.

In the foregoing table are enumerated the chief productions sown the half year before, or during the inundation. They may be called the plants of the summer season; which succeeding the other crops, either immediately or after a short interval, are produced solely by artificial irrigation. But the use of the *shadóof* is not confined to the productions of summer; it is required for some in spring, and frequently throughout the winter, as well as in autumn, if the inundation be deficient; and the same system was, of course, adopted by the ancient Egyptians.

Having, in the preceding tables, shown the seasons when the principal productions of Egypt were raised, I proceed to mention those which appear, from good authority, to have been grown by the ancient Egyptians. Wheat, barley, *doora*, peas, beans, lentils, *hommos*, *gilbán*? (Lathyrus sativus), carthamus, lupins, *bamia* (Hibiscus esculentus), *figl* (Raphanus sativus, *var.* edulis), *simsim*, indigo, sinapis or mustard, origanum, succory, flax, cotton, cassia, senna, colocinth, cummin, coriander, several Cucurbitæ, " cucumbers, melons, leeks, onions, garlic," lotus, nelumbium, cyperus esculentus, papyrus, and other Cyperi, are proved to have been cultivated by them; and the learned Kircher mentions many productions of the country, principally on the authority of Apuleius, and early Arab writers. But the greater part of these last are wild plants; and, indeed, if all the indigenous productions of Egypt (which unquestionably grew there in ancient as well as modern times) were enumerated, a large catalogue might be collected, those of the desert alone amounting to nearly 250 species. For though the Egyptian Herbarium is limited to about 1300, the indigenous plants constitute a large proportion of that number, and few countries have a smaller quantity introduced from abroad than Egypt, which, except in a few instances, has remained contented with the herbs and trees of its own soil; and the plants of the desert may be considered altogether indigenous, without, I believe, one single exception.

The following is a brief enumeration of those mentioned by Pliny, together with the most striking characteristics or properties he ascribes to them. I have arranged them in the order in which they are given by the naturalist, not according to their botanical classification, some being unknown.

EGYPTIAN PLANTS FROM PLINY.

Name from Pliny.	lib.	c.	Botanical Name.	Remarks.
A plant producing ladanum	12	17	Cistus ladaniferus.	"The plant which produces ladanum, introduced into Egypt by the Ptolemies." *Plin.*
Tree producing Myrobalanum, Myrobalanus	12	21	Moringa aptera? (Arab. *Yessur*; fruit, *Hab-ghâlee.*)	"Producing a fruit from which an oil or ointment was extracted. Growing in the Thebaïd." *Plin.*
Palma called Adipsos.	12	22	?	"Gathered before ripe: that which is left is called Phœnicobalanus, and is intoxicating." *Plin.*
Sphagnos, Bryon, or Sphacos	12	23 28	Parmelia parietina? (Arab. *Shegeret e'neddeh.*)	"Said to grow in Egypt." *Plin.* A sort of lichen growing on trees. Oil and oil from it. *Plin.* 13. 1.
Cypros	12	24	Lawsonia spinosa et inermis. (Arab. *Henneh.*)	"Bearing leaves like the Zizyphus. Used in oil to make the ointment called Cyprus. The best grown about Canopus. Leaves dye the hair." *Plin.*
Maron	12	24	Teucrium Iva? (Arab. *Miskeh?*)	There are four or five other species of Teucrium in Egypt.
(——)	12	25	Amyris Opobalsamum. (Arab. *Belisân.*)	Balsam in Egypt, according to Dioscorides and Strabo, till lately cultivated at Heliopolis.
Elate (Abies?) Palma, or Spathe	12	28	?	"Of use for ointments." *Plin.* It is supposed to be the sheath of the palm flowers. *Ide Dioscor.* 1. 150. (Arab. *'a'.át*, comp. *Spat he*)
Amygdalus, Almond	13	1	Amygdalus communis. (Arab. *Lóz.*)	"Oil of bitter almonds made in Egypt." *Plin.*
Palma, Palm	13	4	Phœnix dactylifera. (Arab. *Nakhl.*)	See vol. i. p. 55. "Thebaïc palms." *Plin.* 23. 4.
Myxa	13	5	Cordia Myxa, Sebestena domestica, *Alpin.* (Arab. *Mokhayt.*)	"Wine made from the fruit in Egypt." *Plin.* They now make birdlime from it.
Ficus Ægyptia	13	7	Ficus Sycamorus. (Arab. *Gimmayz.*)	"Fruit growing on the stem itself." *Plin.* and *Athen. Deipn.* ii. p. 51.
(Ceraunia siliqua)	13	8	Ceratonia Siliqua. (Arab. *Kharoób.*)	(Locust tree, or *Kharoób*, said by Pliny *not* to grow in Egypt. It is now an Egyptian tree.)

	lib.	c.	Botanical Name.	Remarks.
Persica or Peach	13 15	9 12	Amygdalus Persica. (Arab. *Khokh.*)	"Pliny rejects the idle tale of the peach being a poisonous fruit introduced by the Persians into Egypt." *See* lib. xv. 13.
Cuci	13	9	Cucifera Thebaïca. (Arab. *Dôm.*)	"Like to a palm, but with spreading branches. Fruit fills a man's hand; of a brown yellow olour. That within large and hard; turned and made into pulleys or sail rings. The nucleus within it eaten when young; exceedingly hard when dry (and ripe)." *See* above, vol. i. p. 56.
Spina Ægyptia, the Acanthus of Herodotus and Strabo.	13 24	9 11 11 12	Mimosa Nilotica. (Arab. *Sont.*)	"Seed pods used for tanning." "Produces gum." *Plin. See Athen.* xv. p. 680. Groves of it at Tûs, Memphis, and Abydus: the two last still remain. My ther Mimosas in Egypt. Pliny (xiii. 10) mentions a sensitive acacia about Memphis. One is now common on the nkes of the Nile above Dongola (the *Acacia Asperata*?). The mimosa Lebbek also grew of old in Egypt, and the Copt Christians have a silly legend of its worshipping the Saviour.
Quercus, Oak	13	9	Quercus ———	"About Thebes, where the Persica, olive (and spina) grow." *Plin.* The oak is uknown in Egypt. Grows in the Eastern desert of the Thebaid. *See Descr. de l'Egypte. Bot.*, pl. 28. fig. 1.
(Perséa)	13	9	Balanites Ægyptiaca. (Arab. *Egleeg*; fruit, *Lalôb.*)	
Oliva, Olive	13 15	9 3	Olea Europæa. (Arab. *Zaytôon.*)	"The olives of Egypt very fleshy, but with little oil." *Plin.* xv. 13. This is very true. Strabo says, "the Arsinoïte nome alone (excepting the gardens of Alexandria) produces the olive. The oil is very good if carefully extracted; if not, the quantity is great, but with a strong odour." xvii. p. 556.

CHAP. VI.   EGYPTIAN PLANTS FROM PLINY.   29

Prunus Ægyptia	13	10	Rhamnus Spina Christi or R. Nabeca, Forsk. (Arab. *Nebk*.)	"Near Thebes."
Papyrus or Biblus	13 24	11 12 11	Cyperus papyrus. (Arab. *Berdi?*)	*See* below in chap. vii. Strabo, xvii. p. 550.
Lotus	13 24	17 2	Nymphæa Lotus. (Arab. *Beshnín*.)	*See* vol. i. p. 57, 79, 256, 257.
Punicum malum or Granatum, Pomegranate	13	19	Punica Granatum. (Arab. *Roománn*.)	"The flower called Bal ustin." *Plin.* It is the ancient rub or rose, which was used for its dye, and gave its name to the island of Rhodes. It is therefore on the reverse of the coins of that island.
Tamarix, Myrice, Tamarisk	13 24	21 9	Tamarix Gallica. (Arab. *Tarfa*.)	"Called also Myrice, or wild brya, very abundant in Egypt and Syria." " ng, or bryonia, commonly called Arbor infelix." *Plin.*
Ferula	13 20	22 23	Ferula communis? or Bubon tortuosum? (The Crythmum Pyrenaicum of Forskal.) (Arab. *Shebet e' Gebel*.)	"Knotted and hollow stem, very light, good for ahs. Some called the sed *Thapsia*." *Plin.* Two kinds, like the anethum. A large umbelliss plant, supposed to be a sort of wild fennel.
Capparis	13	23	Capparis spinosa. (Arab. *Lussuf*.)	The Caper. The fruit of the Egyptian pr, or *Lusseuf*, is very large, like a small cucumber, about 2½ inches long, which is eaten by the Arabs.
Sari	13	23	Cyperus dives? or C. fastigiatus? (Arab. *Dees*.)	*See Theophr.* iv. 9. "It grows on the banks of the Nile, with a hd (*coma*) like the papyrus, and is eaten in the same manner." *Pln.*
Vitis, Vine	14 16	3 7 18	Vitis vinifera. (Arab. *Enéb*.)	*See* above, vol. i. p. 39 to 45. Pliny says that no trees, not even vines, lose their leaves about Memphis and Elephantine. Lib. xvi. 21.
Cici, Croton, Trixis, or wild Sesamum	15	3	Ricinus communis. (Arab. *Kharwah*.)	Castor-berry tee, or Palma Christi. "Oil extracted from it abounds in Egypt." *Plin.*

Name from Pliny.	lib.	c.		Remarks.
Raphanus	15 19	7 5	Raphanus oleïfer, or the Brassica oleïfer. (*Seemga* of Nubia; or the *Selgam* of Egypt?)	"Oil made from its seeds in Egypt." *Plin.* It is probably the *Seemga* or Raphanus oleifer, and not the sativus, that he alludes to. He may perhaps have had in view the *Selgam* (Brassica oleifer), or coleseed, so common throughout Egypt. The seemga is now confined to Nubia and the extremity of the Thebaid.
Chorticon, a Grass	15	7		"Oil ... made from it." *Plin.*
Sesama	15	7	Sesanum orientale. (Arab. *Simsim*.)	"... used for its oil." See above, p. 23.
Urtica, called Cnecimum, or Cnidium	15 22	7 13	Urtica pilulifera. (Arab. *Fiss el Keláb*.)	"Giving an oil." "The Alexandrian the best quality." "Used also medicinally." *Plin.* Supposed to be a nettle. Perhaps of Greek introduction.
Pyrus Alexandria, Pear of Alexandria	15	15	Pyrus communis? (Arab. *Koomittree*.)	It is a singular fact, that the small fruit of the wild fig of the Egyptian desert, and of Syria, is called by the Arabs *Kottayn*, since Pliny says, "the small Syrian figs are called *Cottana*." Lib. xiii. c. 5. The tree is called *Hamát*.
Ficus, Fig.	15	18	Ficus Carica. (Arab. *Tin*.)	
Myrtus, Myrtle	15 21	29 11	Myrtus communis. (Arab. *As*, or *Mersia*.)	"The myrtle of Egypt is the most odoriferous." *Plin.* and *Athen.* 15. It is only now grown in gardens. Pliny in another place says, "the flowers of Egypt have very little odor," xxi. 7, probably on the authority of Theophrastus. *Hist. Plant.* vi. 6; *De Cas. Plant.* vi. 27.
Calamus, Reed	16	36	Arundo Donax, and Arundo Isiaca. (Arab. *Kussub* and *Boos*.)	"Used by many nations for arrows, so that half the world has been conquered by reeds," *Plin.* (See vol. i. p. 352, 353.)
Hordeum, Barley	18		Hordeum vulgare. Arab. *Sha'*	

CHAP. VI. EGYPTIAN PLANTS FROM PLINY. 31

Triticum, Wheat......	18	8	Triticum sativum. (Arab. *Kumh*.)	
Zea	18	8	Triticum Zea? (Arab. *Kumh*.)	"The Egyptians make a medicinal decoction of olyra for children, which they call Athara." *Plin.* xxii. 25.
Dra		10	Holcus Sorghum? (Arab. *Dóora*.)	
The		11	Triticum Spelta?	
Faba, Beans	18	12	Vicia Faba. (Arab. *Fool*.)	"With a prickly stalk." *Plin.*
Lens, Lentils	18	12	Ervums Lens. [*duz*] (Arab. *Atz, Adz,* or *Ad-*)	"Two kinds of lentils in Egypt." *Plin.*
Linum, Flax	19	1	Linum usitatissimum. (Arab. *Kettán*.)	"Four kinds, the Tanitic, Pelusiac, Butic, and Tentyritic." *Plin.*
Gossipion, Cotton...	19	1	Gossypium herbaceum. (Arab. *Kóton*.)	"Called Gossipion, or Xylon: the cloths made from it are named Xylina." *Plin.*
Aron	19	5	Arum Col casia. (Arab. *Kolkás*.)	"about the size of a squill;" "with a bulbous root." *Plin.*
Aris	24	16	Arum Arisarum?	"Like the aron, but smaller; the root being the size of an olive." *Plin.*
Allium, Garlic......	19	6	Allium sativum. (Arab. *Tóm*.)	"Both ranked by the Egyptians among gods, in taking an oath." *Plin.*
Cepa, Onion	19	6	Allium Cepa. (Arab. *Bussal*.)	
Porrum, Leek......	19	6	Allium Porrum) (Arab. *Korrát*.)	"The best kind is in Egypt." *Plin.*
Cuminum, Cummin {	19	8	Cuminum Cyminum, and Nigella sativa. (Arab. *Kammoon-abiad* and *Kammoon-asved*.)	Pliny speaks of two, one whiter than the other, used for the same purpose, and put upon cakes so of bread at Alexandria. The white and black film are called by the Arabs *Kammoon abiad* and *Kammoon asved*: the latter is the Nigella tiwa. See above, vol. i, p. 177, 266.
	20	15		
Origanum	19	8	Origanum Ægyptiacum. (Arab. *Bardakoosh*.)	
	20	17		
	25	4		

Name from Pliny.	lib.	c.		Remarks.
Sinapis, Mustard	19	8	Sinapis juncea. (Arab. *Khardel*, or *Kubbr*.)	"The best seed is the Egyptian. Called also Napy, Thaspi, and Saurion." *Plin.*
Cichorium, or Intubus erraticus	20	8	Cichorium Intybus. (Arab. *Shakorieh*.)	"In Egypt, the wild endive is called Cichorium; the garden endive, Seris." *Plin.*
Seris	21	15	Cichorium Endivia?	
	20	8	(Arab. *Hendebeh*.)	
Anisum, Aniseed	20	17	Pimpinella Anisum. (Arab. *Yensoon*.)	"The Egyptian is the best quality after the Cretan." *Plin.*
Coriandrum	20	20	Coriandrum sativum. (Arab. *Kosbar* or *Koozbareh*.)	"The best is from Egypt." *Plin.*
Buceros, or Fœnum Græcum	21	7	Trigonella Fœnum Græum. (Arab. *Helbeh*.)	"Without any scent." *Plin.*
	24	19		
(*Helenium*)	21	10	Teucrium Creticum?	(Helenium (according to Dioscorides), a native of Egypt. This and four other species of Teucrium now grow there.)
	21	21		
Amaracus	21	11	Origanum Majorana.	"What is called by Dioscorides, is known in Egypt and Syria as the Sampsuchum." "An oil made from it." *Plin.* Athenæus (xv. p. 676) says, "the Amaracus is in Egypt;" and in lib. v. he mentions "Amaracine ointment."
	21	22		
Melilotus	21	11	Trifolium Melilotus Indica. (Arab. *Rekrak* or *Nafal?*)	"Grows every where." *Plin.*
Rosa, Rose	21	11	Rosa centifolia. (Arab. *Werd*.)	If by "In Ægypto sine odore hæc omnia," Pliny means that *all* the flowers mentioned in this chapter are Egyptian, many others might be here introduced.
Viola, Violet	21	11	Viola odorata. (Arab. *Benefsig*.)	

EGYPTIAN PLANTS FROM PLINY.

Name	Bk.	Ch.	Description
Colocasia or Cyamus, or Faba Ægyptia	21	15	Nymphæa Nelumbo, or Nelumbium.	"Growing in the Nile." "one of the wild plants," and so plentifully in Egypt." *Plin.* Æn. iii. p. 72. Æ, xvii. p. 550.
Anthalium	21 21	15 29	Supposed to be the Cyperus esculentus? ? (which is in Arab. *Hab el âzeez*.)	"Grows some distance from the Nile." "Fruit like a medlar, without husk or nut. Leaf of the Cyperus. No other use but for food." *Plin.* Some suppose it the Cyperus seul atus, with is very full.
Œtum	21	15	Supposed to be the Arachis hypogæa ?	"Also eaten in Egypt. Few l ass ; large root." *Plin.* this says, it has a long root, gathered at the time of the inundation, and used for crowning the ads. Lib. i. c. l. 11.
Arachidna	21	15	?	"These two are spreading and numerous roots ; but no leaf, nor anything above the ground." *Plin.*
Aracos	21	15	?	
Condrylla	21	15	Lactuca ; ms? (Arab. *Khuss*.)	Lettuce ?
Hypocheris	21	15	Hyoseris kta.	All esculent plants.
Caucalis	21	15	this daucoïdes ? this ms.	
Anthriscum	21	15	(Arab. *Özer e'shaytán*.)	
Scandix, or Tragopogon	21	15	Tragopogon picroides ?	"Leaves like a crocus." *Plin.* The *Edıhbáh* is of the *order Syngenesia*, and the flower is of a purplish colour. Dioscorides describes its flower with a white circuit and yellow within.
Parthenium	21 22 25	15 17 5	30 Matricaria Parthenium, or M. Chamitta.	
Strychnum, or Strychnus, or Trychos, or Solanum	21 21 27	15 31 13	Solanum Dulcamara, or Solanum nigrum. (rab. *Eneb e' teeb*.)	"Used in Egypt for chaplets : the leaves like ivy : of two kinds ; one has red berries (in a sort of bladder) full of grains, and is called Halicacabus, or Callion, and, in Italy, *Vesicaria* : the third kind is very poisonous." Nightshade.

Name from Pliny.	lib.	c.	Botanical Name.	Remarks.
Corchorus	21	15	Corchorus olitorius. (Arab. *Melokhéïh*.)	"Eaten at Alexandria." *Plin.*
Aphace	21	32	Leontodon Taraxacum.	"Flowers all the winter and spring, till the summer." *Plin.* Dandelion.
Acinos	21	15	Thymus Acinos, or Ocymum Zátarhendi. (Arab. *Zátar*.)	"The E grows the Acinos for making chaplets and for food. It appears the same as the Ocimum, but its leaves and stalks are more hirsute." *Plin.*
	21	27		
Epipetron	21	15	Sedum confertum. (Arab. *Heialem*.)	"Never flowers." *Plin.* Some editions of Pliny make this and the Acinos the same; but they are generally said to be different.
Cnicus, or Atractylis	21	15	Carthamus tinctorius? (Arab. *Koortum*.) The other is perhaps the Carthamus Creticus?	S ... to be the Carthamus. "Unknown in Italy. Oil ... from the seeds, and of great value. Two kinds; the wild and the cult ... ed; and two ... s of the former. Remedy against the ... on of scorpions and other reptiles." *Plin.* It is ... that the Cnicus and Atractylis are ... t the same plant.
	21	32		
Tribulus	21	16	Trapa natans?	"... s about the Nile in marshes, and is eaten. Leaf like the elm." *Plin.*
	22	10		
Pirdicium	21	17	?	"E ... n by other people, as by the Egyptians." *Plin.*
	22	17		" ... s on walls and tiles of houses."
Ornithogale	21	17	Ornithogalum Arabicum?	
Juncus	21	18	Juncus acutus? (Arab. *Sumár*.)	"Sieves made of it in Egypt." *Plin.*
Cypirus	21	18	Gladiolus communis.	"With a bulbous root." *Plin.*
Cyperus	21	18	Cyperus Niloticus, and many other species.	"A triangular rush." *Plin.*

CHAP. VI.   EGYPTIAN PLANTS FROM PLINY.   35

Heliochrysum, or Chrysanthemum.	21 25 21 33	Gnaphalium Stœchas. ———?	"Gods crowned with it; a custom particularly observed by Ptolemy, King of Egypt." *Plin.* "Grown in gardens in Egypt, for making chaplets." *Plin.*
Persoluta			
Lotometra	22 21	A large kind of cultivated lotus, or Nymphæa Lotus.	"Coming from the garden lotus, from whose seed, like millet, the Egyptian bakers make bread." *Plin.*
(*Rhus*)	24 11	Rhus oxyacanthoïdes. (Arab. *Errīn.*)	("Rhus: leaves like myrtle, used for dressing skins." Though Pliny does not mention it as an Egyptian plant, it is indigenous in the desert, and the leaves and wood are used by the Arabs for tanning.)
Egyptian Clematis, or Daphnoides, or Polygonoides	24 15	Vinca major et minor?	"Mostly produced in Egypt." *Plin.*
Ophiusa	24 17	———?	"About Elephantina." *Plin.*
Stratiotis	24 18	Pistia Stratiotes. (Arab. *Heialem el ma.*)	"Only in Egypt during the inundation of the Nile." *Plin.*
Nepenthes	25 2 21 21	Perhaps the *Bust* or *Hasheesh*, a preparation of the Cannabis sativa.	" r attributes the glory of s to Egypt. He mentions ny given to Helen by the wife of the Egyptian King, ly the Nepent , w d oblivion of sorrow." *Plin.*
Absinthium marinum, or Seriphium	27 7 21 21	Artemisia Judaica? (Arab. *Bytherán.*)	"The b st at Taposiris in Egypt: a bunch of it carr d at the fête of s." *Plin.*
Myosotis	27 12	Myosotis arvensis.	"T e Egyptians e that if, on the 27th day of s (Thoth), w h n s arly to our August, any one an nts lf w h its juice before he s in the morning, he will be free from ess of the eyes all that year." *Plin.*

The trees of ancient Egypt represented on the monuments are the date, *dôm*, sycamore, pomegranate, persea, tamarisk, and Periploca Secamone; and the fruit, seeds, or leaves of the *nebk*, vine, fig, olive, *Mokkayt* (Cordia Myxa), *Kharoob* or locust-tree, palma Christi or *cici*, *Sont* or acanthus, bay, and *Egleeg* or balanites, have been found in the tombs of Thebes; as well as of the Areca, Tamarind, Myrobalanus, and others, which are the produce either of India, or the interior of Africa. And though these last are not the actual productions of Egypt, they are interesting, as they show the constant intercourse maintained with those distant countries. One instance has been met with of the pine-apple, in glazed pottery. The sculptures also represent various flowers, some of which may be recognized, while others are less clearly defined, and might puzzle the most expert botanist.

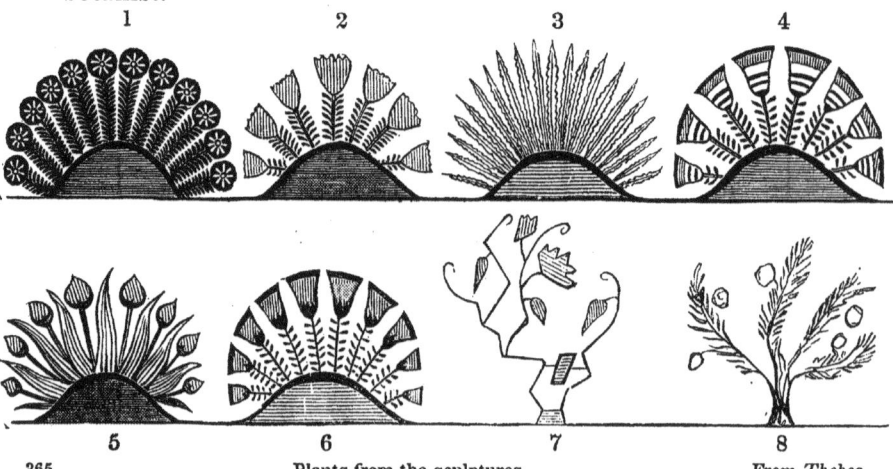

365. Plants from the sculptures. *From Thebes.*
Figs. 1 to 6, inclusive, from the tomb of Remeses III.
Figs. 1 and 5 perhaps the same as the two flowers in *fig.* 10, woodcut 260.

Little attention is paid by the inhabitants of modern Egypt to the cultivation of plants, beyond those used for the purpose of food, or to the growth of trees, excepting the palm, large groves of which are met with in every part of the country; and if the statement of Strabo be true, that "in all (Lower) Egypt the palm was sterile, or bore an uneatable fruit, though of excellent quality in the Thebaïd," this tree is now cultivated with more success in Lower Egypt than in former times, some of the best quality of dates being produced there, particularly at Korayn, to the east of the Delta, where the kind called A'maree is superior to any produced to the north of Nubia.

Few timber trees are reared in these days either in Upper or Lower Egypt. Some sycamores, whose wood is required for water wheels and other purposes; a few groups of *Athuls*, or Oriental tamarisks, used for tools and other implements requiring a compact wood; and two or three groves of *Sont*, or Mimosa Nilotica, valuable for its hard wood, and for its pods used in tanning, are nearly all that the modern inhabitants retain of the many trees grown by their predecessors. But their thriving condition, as that of the mulberry-trees (planted for the silkworms), which form, with the Mimosa Lebbek, some shady avenues in the vicinity of Cairo, and of the Cassia fistula (bearing its dense mass of blossoms in the gardens of the metropolis), shows that it is not the soil, but the industry of the people, which is wanting to encourage the growth of trees.

The *Egleeg*, or balanites (the supposed Persea), no longer thrives in the valley of the Nile; many other trees are rare, or altogether unknown; and the extensive groves of Acanthus, or *Sont*, are rather tolerated than encouraged, as the descendants of the trees planted in olden times near the edge of the cultivated land.

The thickets of Acanthus, alluded to by Strabo, still grow above Memphis, at the base of the low Libyan hills: in going from the Nile to Abydus, you ride through the grove of Acacia, once sacred to Apollo, and see the rising Nile traversing it by a canal, as when the geographer visited that city, even then reduced to the condition of a small village: and groves of the same tree may here and there be traced in other parts of the Thebaïd, from which it obtained the name of the Thebaïc thorn.

Above the cataracts, the *Sont* grew in profusion a few years ago upon the banks of the Nile, enabling the poor Nubians to send abundance of charcoal for sale to Cairo; and its place is supplied in the desert by the *Séáleh* and other of the Mimosa tribe, which are indigenous to the soil.

The principal woods used by the Egyptians were the date, *Dôm*, sycamore, several acacias, the two tamarisks, the *Egleeg* or balanites, ebony, fir, and cedar. The various purposes to which every part of the palm or date-tree was applied have been already noticed, as well as of the *Dôm*, or Theban palm. Sycamore wood was employed for coffins, boxes, small idols, doors, window shutters, stools, chairs, and cramps for building; for handles of tools, wooden pegs or nails, cramps, idols, small boxes, and those parts of cabinet work requiring hard compact wood, the *Sont* (Acacia Nilotica) was usually preferred; and spears were frequently made of other acacias, which grew in the interior, or on the confines of the desert.

For cramps in walls, and tools of various kinds, the wood of the Tamarix orientalis was much used, and even occasionally for pieces of furniture, for which purpose the Egleeg was also employed; but the principal woods adopted by the cabinet-maker for fine work were ebony, fir, and cedar. Of these three the first came from Africa, and formed, with ivory, gold, ostrich feathers, dried fruits, and skins, the principal object of the annual tribute brought to Egypt by the conquered tribes of Ethiopia and the Soodán; but fir and cedar were imported from Syria, the two last being in great demand for common furniture, small boxes, coffins, and various objects connected with the dead.

Other woods of a rare and valuable kind were brought to Egypt by the people of Asia tributary to the Pharaohs; and the importance attached to them may be estimated by their being frequently imitated, for the satisfaction of those who could not afford to purchase furniture or trinkets of so expensive a material.

Egypt also produced some fungi useful for dyeing; the pods of the Acacia Nilotica, the bark of the *séáleh* acacia, and the wood and bark of the *Errin*, or Rhus oxyacanthoïdes, for tanning; and the Periploca Secamone for curing skins.

White crops were, of course, the principal cultivated productions in the valley of the Nile, and the wheat and barley were grown in every part of Egypt.

Like the Romans, they usually brought the seed in a basket, which the sower held in his left hand, or suspended on his arm (sometimes with a strap round his neck), while he scattered the seed with his right ; and he sometimes followed the plough, in those fields which required no further preparation with the hoe, or were free from the roots of noxious weeds. The mode of sowing was what we term broadcast ; the seed was scattered loosely over the surface, whether ploughed or allowed to remain in its unbroken, muddy state ; and in no agricultural scene is there any evidence of drilling or dibbling.

Corn, and those productions which did not require constant irrigation, were sown in the open field, as in other countries ; but for indigo, esculent vegetables, and herbs, the fields were portioned out into the usual square beds,* surrounded by a raised border of earth to keep in the water, which was conducted into them by channels from the *shadóof*, or poured in with buckets.†

Wheat was cut in about five, barley in four months ; the best quality, according to Pliny, being grown in the Thebaïd. The wheat, as at the present day, was all bearded, and the same varieties, doubtless, existed in ancient as in modern times; among which may be mentioned the seven-eared quality described in Pharaoh's dream.‡ This is the kind which has been lately grown in England, and which is *said* to have been raised from grains found in the tombs of Thebes. It is no longer cultivated in Upper Egypt, being only grown in small quantities in the Delta; and this is the more remarkable, as it renders the substitution of modern for ancient wheat at Thebes very improbable.

The wheat was cropped a little below the ear§ with a toothed sickle, and carried to the threshing-floor in wicker panniers upon asses,∥ or in rope¶ nets, the gleaners following to collect the

---

* *See* these square beds in woodcut 39, *fig.* c, vol. i. p. 35.
† *See* p. 4, and vol. i. p. 33.   ‡ Gen. xli. 22.
§ *Comp.* Job, xxiv. 24, " Cut off as the tops of the ears of corn."
∥ Woodcut 368, *figs.* 4 and 5.   ¶ Woodcut 367, *figs.* 5 and 7.

Part 1.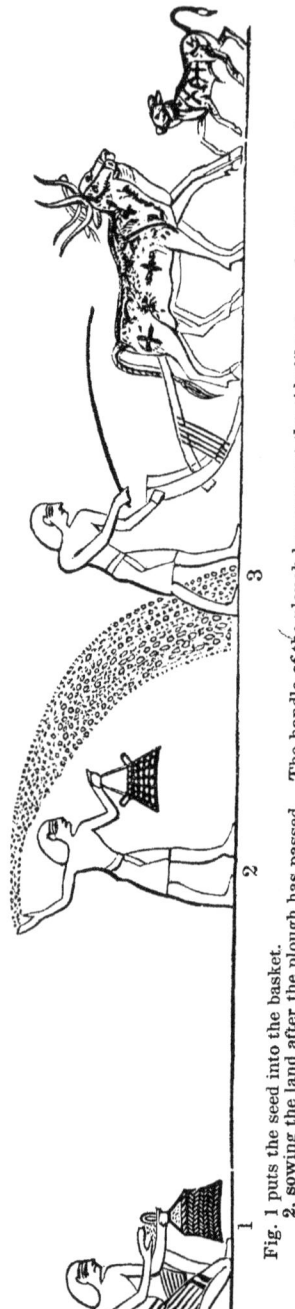

Fig. 1 puts the seed into the basket.
2, sowing the land after the plough has passed. The handle of the plough has a peg at the side like the modern Egyptian plough, which may be seen in the Vignette.

Part 2.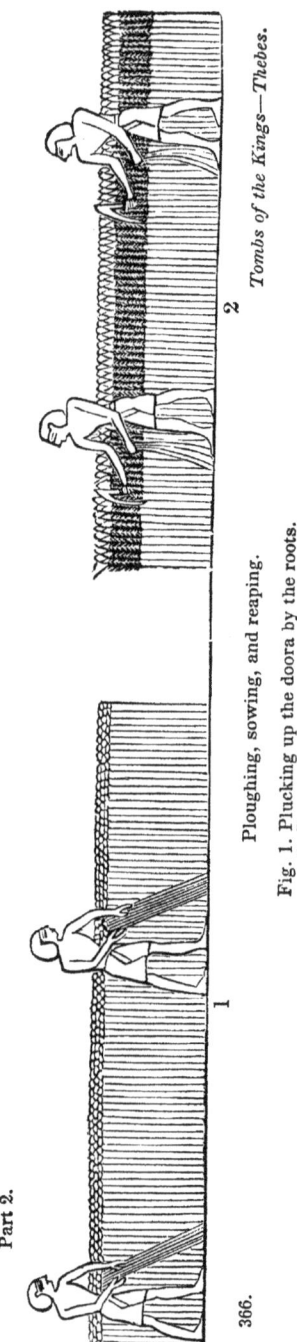

Ploughing, sowing, and reaping.
Fig. 1. Plucking up the doora by the roots.
2. Reaping wheat.

Tombs of the Kings—Thebes.

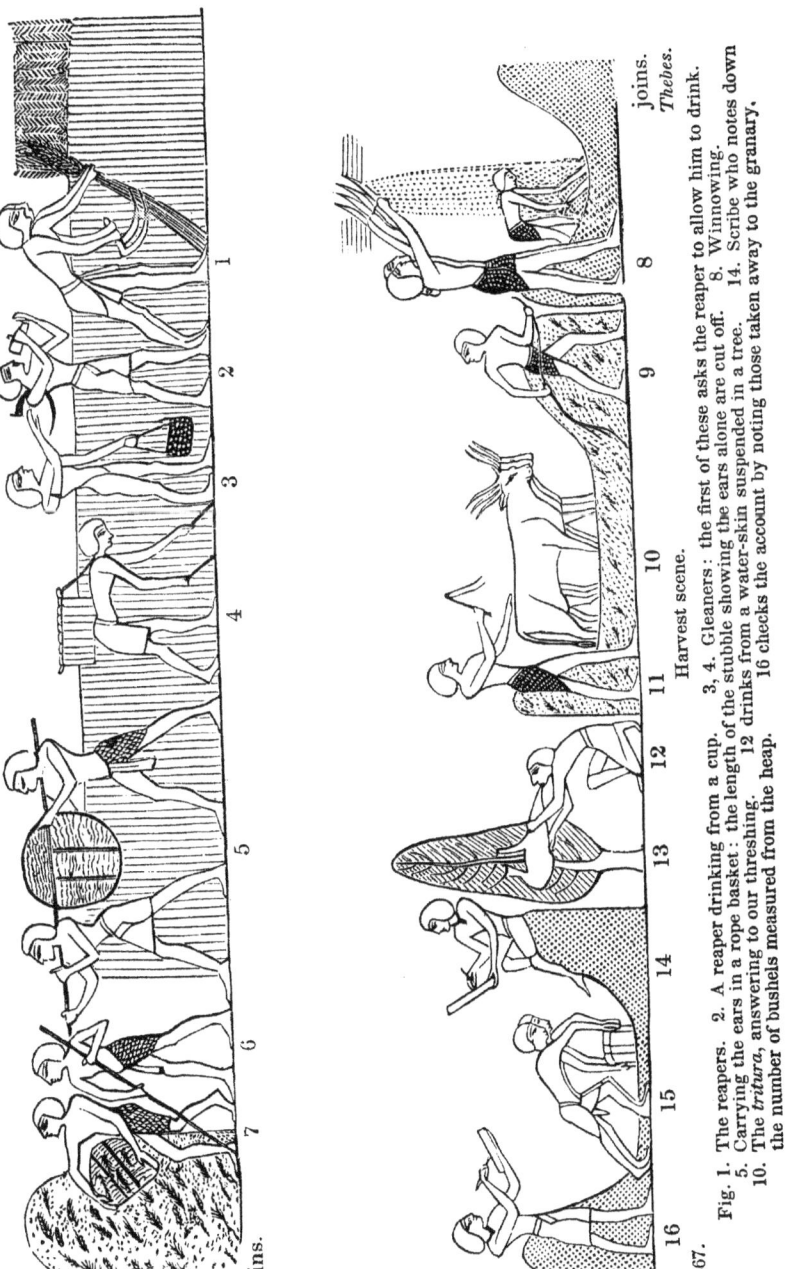

Fig. 1. The reapers. 2. A reaper drinking from a cup. 3, 4. Gleaners: the first of these asks the reaper to allow him to drink. 5. Carrying the ears in a rope basket: the length of the stubble showing the ears alone are cut off. 8. Winnowing. 10. The *tritura*, answering to our threshing. 12 drinks from a water-skin suspended in a tree. 14. Scribe who notes down the number of bushels measured from the heap. 16 checks the account by noting those taken away to the granary.

Harvest scene. *Thebes.*

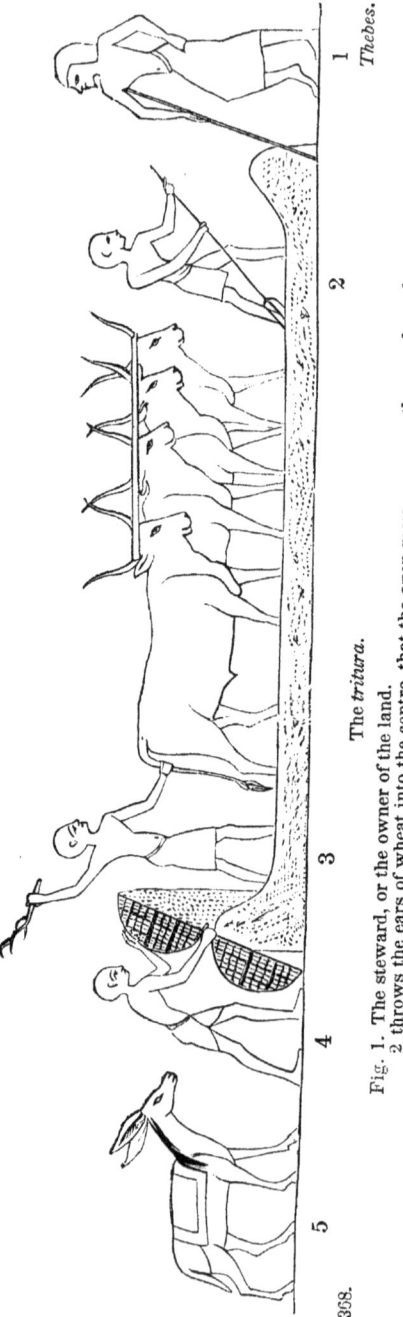

The *tritura*. Thebes.

Fig. 1. The steward, or the owner of the land.
2. throws the ears of wheat into the centre, that the oxen may pass over them and tread out the grain.
3. The driver.
4. brings the wheat to the threshing-floor in baskets carried on asses.
The oxen are yoked together, that they may walk round regularly.

368.

fallen ears in hand baskets. The rope net, answering to the *Shenfeh* of modern Egypt, was borne on a pole by two men; and the threshing-floor was a level circular area near the field, or in the vicinity of the granary, where, when it had been well swept, the ears were deposited, and cattle were driven over it to tread out the grain. While superintending the animals so employed, the Egyptian peasants, like their modern successors, relieved their labours by singing; and in a tomb at Eileithyias this song of the threshers is written in hieroglyphics over oxen

369.   Song of the threshers to the oxen.   *Eileithyias.*

treading out the grain: "(1) Thresh for yourselves (*twice, a*), (2) O oxen, (3) thresh for yourselves (*twice, b*), (4) measures for yourselves, (5) measures for your masters." The discovery and translation of this are due to Champollion, to whom all who study hieroglyphics are under such infinite obligations, and whose talents were beyond all praise.

A certain quantity was first strewed in the centre of the area, and when this had been well triturated by the animals' feet, more was added by means of large wooden forks, from the main

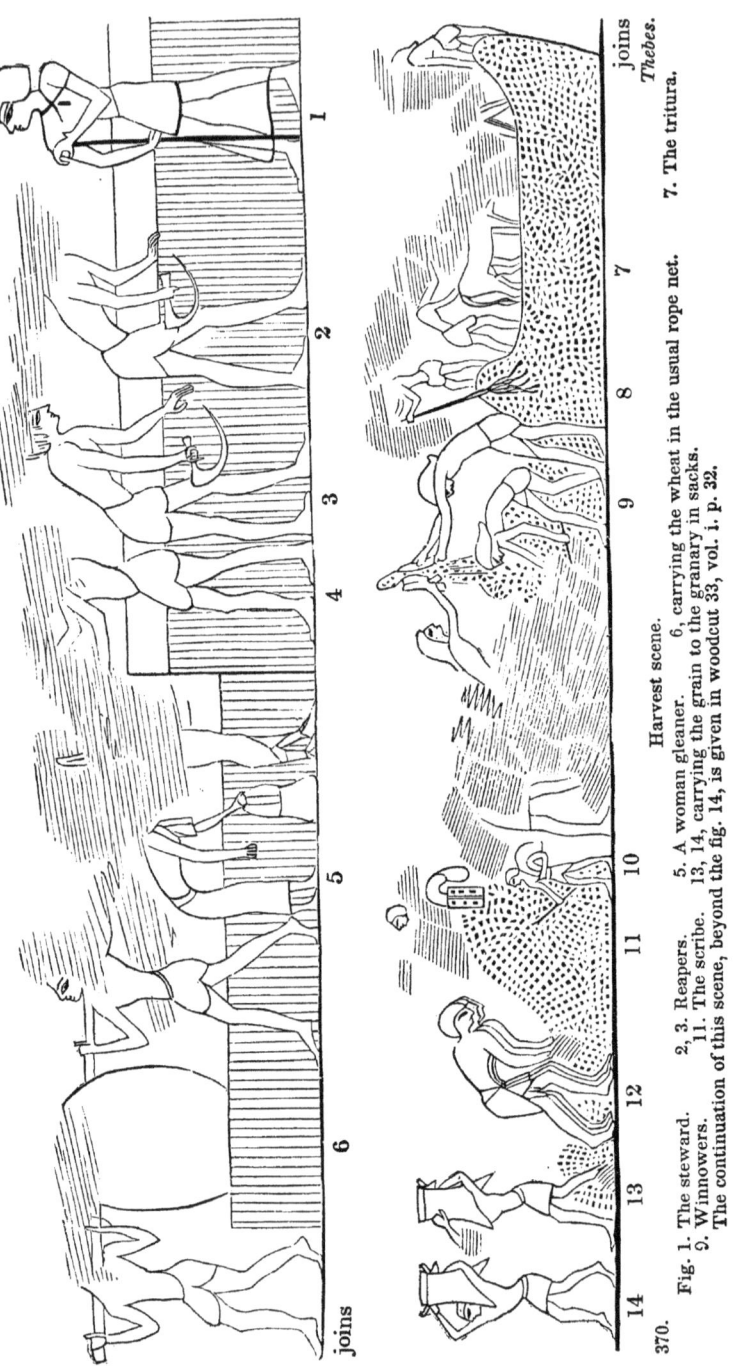

370. Harvest scene.

Fig. 1. The steward. 2, 3. Reapers. 5. A woman gleaner. 6, carrying the wheat in the usual rope net. 9. Winnowers. 11. The scribe. 13, 14, carrying the grain to the granary in sacks. 7. The tritura. The continuation of this scene, beyond the fig. 14, is given in woodcut 33, vol. i. p. 32.

Thebes.

TREADING OUT THE GRAIN.

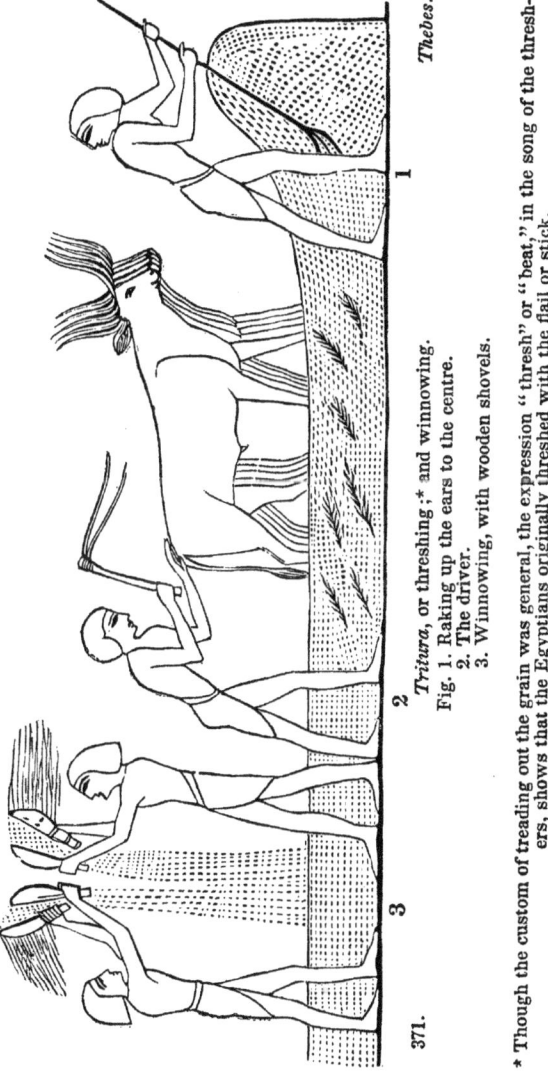

371. *Tritura*, or threshing;* and winnowing.
Fig. 1. Raking up the ears to the centre.
2. The driver.
3. Winnowing, with wooden shovels.

Thebes.

* Though the custom of treading out the grain was general, the expression "thresh" or "beat," in the song of the threshers, shows that the Egyptians originally threshed with the flail or stick.

heap, raised around, and forming the edge of, the threshing-floor; and so on till all the grain was trodden out. This process, called *trituration*, was generally adopted by ancient, as by some modern people. Sometimes the cattle were bound together by a piece of wood or a rope fastened to their horns or necks, in order to force them to go round the heap and tread it regularly, the driver following behind them with a stick.*

After the grain had been trodden out, they winnowed it with wooden shovels; it was then carried to the granary in sacks, each containing a fixed quantity, which was determined by wooden measures; a scribe noting down the number, as called by the teller who superintended its removal. Sweepers with small hand-brooms were employed to collect the scattered grain that fell from the measure; and the " immense heaps of corn" mentioned by Diodorus, collected from " the field which was round every city,"† accord well with the representation of the paintings in the tombs,‡ and with those seen at the present day in the villages of the Nile. Sometimes two scribes§ were present; one to write down the number of measures taken from the heap of corn, and the other to check them by entering the quantity removed to the granary,‖ as well as the number of sacks actually housed—a precaution quite in character with the circumspect habits of the Egyptians.

Oxen, as Herodotus says, were generally used for treading out the grain; and sometimes, though rarely, asses were employed for that purpose.

The Jews had the same custom, and, like the Egyptians, they suffered the ox to tread out the corn unmuzzled, according to the express order of their lawgiver.¶ In later times, however, it appears that the Jews used "threshing instruments;" though, from the offer made to David by Ornan, of "the oxen also," and the use of the word *dus*, "treading," in the sentence, "Ornan was *threshing* wheat,"** it is possible that the *trituration* is here alluded to, and that the threshing instruments only refer to the winnowing-shovels, or other implements used on those occasions; though the "new sharp threshing instrument having teeth,"

---

* Woodcuts 368, 373.   † Gen. xli. 48. Diodor. i. 36.
‡ Woodcuts 367, 370.   § Woodcut 367.
‖ Of the granary, see vol. i., woodcuts 11, 32, 33.
¶ Deut. xxv. 4.   ** 1 Chron. xxi. 20, and 23.

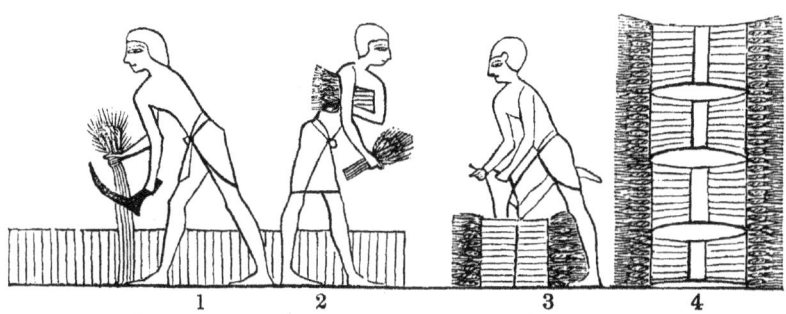

372.   Wheat bound in sheaves.   *Thebes.*
Fig. 1. Reaping. 2. Carrying the ears. 3. Binding them in sheaves put up at fig. 4.

mentioned in Isaiah,* seems to be the *nóreg*, or corn-drag, still employed in Egypt, which the Hebrew name " *moreg*" so closely resembles; and this same word is applied to the "threshing instruments" of Ornan. The Jews, like the Greeks, bound up the wheat, when cut, into sheaves;† which was sometimes done by the Egyptians, though their usual custom was to put it into baskets or rope nets, and to carry it loose to the threshing-floor.

The modern Egyptians cut the wheat close to the ground—barley and doora being plucked up by the roots—and having bound it in sheaves, carry it to a level and cleanly-swept area near the field, in the centre of which they collect it in a heap, and then taking a sufficient quantity, spread it upon the open area, and pass over it the *nóreg* drawn by two oxen: the difference in the modern and ancient method being that in the former the *nóreg* is used, and the oxen go round the heap, which is in the centre, and not at the circumference, of the threshing floor. Some instances, however, occur of the heap being in the centre, as at the present day.

The *nóreg* is a machine consisting of a wooden frame, with three cross-bars or axles, on which are fixed circular iron plates, for the purpose of bruising the ears of corn and extracting the grain, at the same time that the straw is chopped up: the first and last axles having each four plates, and the central one three:

* Isaiah, xli. 15.   † Gen. xxxvii. 7.   Levit. xxiii. 10.   Deut. xxiv. 19, &c.

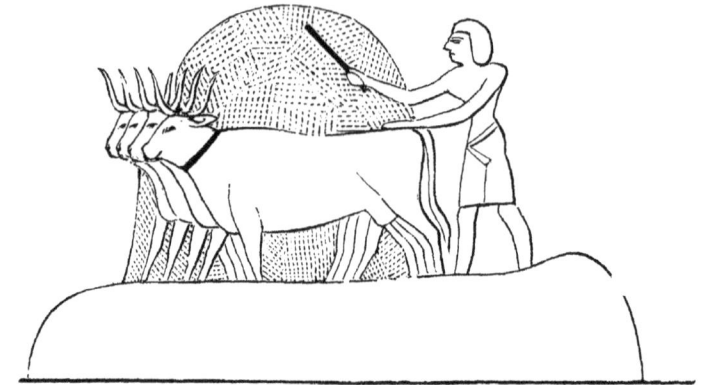

373. The oxen driven round the heap; contrary to the usual custom. *Thebes.*

and at the upper part is a seat on which the driver sits, his weight giving additional effect to the machine.* Indeed, the Roman *tribulum*, described by Varro, appears not to have been very unlike the *nóreg*. It was " a frame made rough by stones or pieces of iron, on which the driver, or a great weight, was placed; and this being drawn by beasts yoked to it, pressed out the grain from the ear."

While some were employed in collecting the grain and depositing it in the granary, others gathered the long stubble from the field, and prepared it as provender to feed the horses and cattle; for which purpose it was used by them, as by the Romans, and the modern Egyptians. They probably preferred reaping the corn close to the ear, in order to facilitate the trituration; and afterwards cutting the straw close to the ground, or plucking it by the roots, they chopped it up for the cattle; and this, with dried clover (the *drees* of modern Egypt), was laid by for autumn, when the pastures being overflowed by the Nile, the flocks and herds were kept in sheds or pens on the higher grounds, or in the precincts of the villages.

This custom of feeding some of their herds in sheds accords with the Scriptural account of the preservation of the cattle,

* See Vignette at the end of this chapter.

which had been "brought home" from the field; and explains the apparent contradiction of the destruction of "*all* the cattle of Egypt" by the murrain, and the *subsequent* destruction of the cattle by the hail;* those which "were in the field" alone having suffered from the previous plague, and those in the stalls or "houses" having been preserved.

An instance of stall-fed oxen from the sculptures has been given in the account of the farmyard† and villas of the Egyptians.

The first crop of wheat having been gathered, they prepared the land for whatever produce they next intended to rear; the field was ploughed and sowed, and, if necessary, the whole was inundated by artificial means, as often as the quality of the crop or other circumstances required. The same was repeated after the second and third harvest, for which the peasant was indebted to his own labours in raising water from the Nile—an arduous task, and one from which no showers relieved him throughout the whole season. For in Upper Egypt rain may be said to be unknown: five or six slight showers, that annually fall there, scarcely deserving that name; and in no country is artificial irrigation so indispensable as in the valley of the Nile.

In many instances, instead of corn they reared clover, or leguminous herbs, which were sown as soon as the water began to subside, generally about the commencement of October; and at the same time that corn, or other produce, was raised on the land just left by the water, another crop was procured by artificial irrigation. This, of course, depended on the choice of each individual, who consulted the advantages obtained from certain kinds of produce, the time required for their succession, or the benefit of the land; for though no soil recovers more readily from the bad effects arising from a repetition of similar crops, through the equalizing influence of the alluvial deposit, it is at length found to impoverish the land, and the Egyptian peasant is careful not to neglect the universal principle in husbandry of varying the produce on the same ground.

---

* Exod. ix. 6 and 19, &c. † Woodcut 31, vol. i. p. 27.

Besides wheat, other crops are represented in the paintings of the tombs; one of which, a tall grain, is introduced as a production both of Upper and Lower Egypt. From the colour, the height to which it grows, compared with the wheat, and the appearance of a round yellow head it bears on the top of its bright green stalk, it is evidently intended to represent the *doora*, or Holcus Sorghum. It was not reaped by a sickle, like the wheat and barley, but men, and sometimes women, were employed to pluck it up;* which being done, they struck off the earth that adhered to the roots with their hands, and having bound it in sheaves, they carried it to what may be termed the threshing-floor, where, being forcibly drawn through an instrument armed

374.   Gathering the doora and wheat.   *Thebes.*
Fig. 1. Plucking up the plant by the roots.
2. Striking off the earth from the roots.
3. Reaping wheat.

at the summit with metal spikes, the grain was stripped off, and fell upon the well-swept area below. This ancient contrivance is the more remarkable, as something of the kind has lately been proposed in England for a similar purpose.†

Much flax was cultivated in Egypt, and the various processes of watering it, beating the stalks when gathered, making it into twine, and lastly into a piece of cloth, are represented in the

---

* Woodcuts 374 and 375.   † Woodcut 375, *fig.* 3.

GATHERING THE HARVEST.

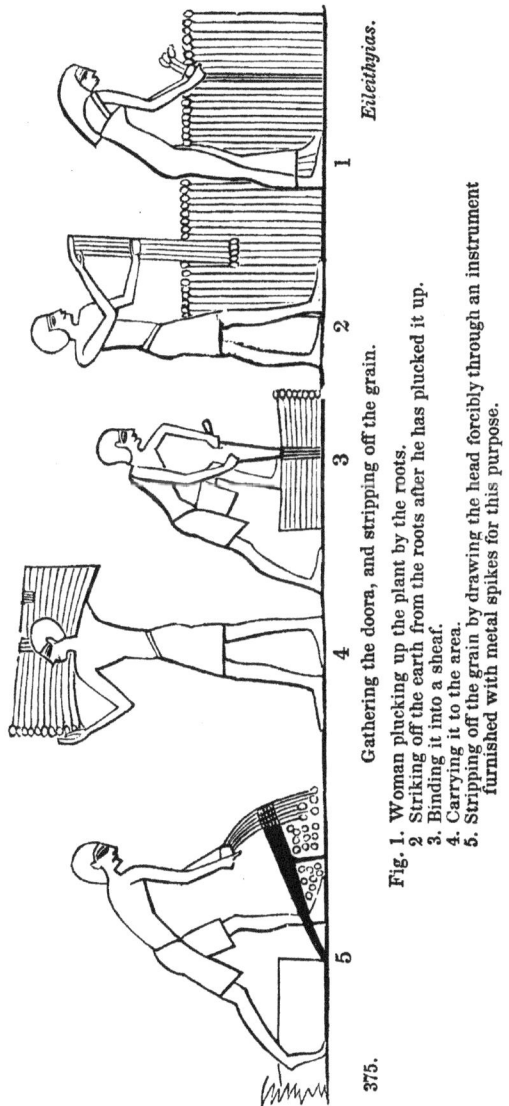

Fig. 1. Woman plucking up the plant by the roots.
2. Striking off the earth from the roots after he has plucked it up.
3. Binding it into a sheaf.
4. Carrying it to the area.
5. Stripping off the grain by drawing the head forcibly through an instrument furnished with metal spikes for this purpose.

Eileithyias.

paintings. These will be mentioned in the account of the arts and manufactures of Ancient Egypt.

At the end of summer, the peasant looked anxiously for the

return of the inundation, upon which all his hopes for the ensuing year depended. He watched with scrupulous attention the first rise of the river; the state of its daily increase was noted down and proclaimed by the curators of the Nilometers at Memphis and other places; and the same anxiety for the approaching inundation was felt on each succeeding year. But during this interval he was not idle, and the quantity of water required for artificial irrigation entailed on the peasant incessant labour, except when the Nile was at its highest; and even while watching his water-melons, and various cucurbitaceous plants (like the modern *felláh*, under the shade of a rude " lodge in a garden of cucumbers"), he occupied himself in preparing something that might be serviceable on a future occasion.

During the inundation, when the Nile had been admitted by the canals into the interior, and the fields were covered with water, the peasantry indulged in various amusements which this leisure period gave them time to enjoy. Their cattle were housed, and supplied with dry food, which had been previously prepared for the purpose; the tillage of the land and all agricultural occupations were suspended; and this season was celebrated as a harvest home, with recreations of every kind. They indulged in feasting, and in all the luxuries of the table that they could afford; they attended the public games held in some of the principal towns, where the competitors contended for prizes of cattle, skins, and other things well suited to the taste or wants of the peasant; and they amused themselves with wrestling-matches, bull-fights, and various sports. Many a leisure hour was passed in singing and dancing; and among the songs of the Egyptian peasant, Julius Pollux mentions that of Maneros; who was even celebrated as the inventor of husbandry—an honour generally given to the still more mysterious Osiris. But some songs and games were exclusively appropriated to certain festivals, and this adaptation of peculiar ceremonies to particular occasions is quite consistent with the character of the Egyptians.

They had many festivals connected with agriculture and the produce of the soil, which happened at different periods of the year. In the month Mesoré, they offered the first-fruits of their lentils to the god Harpocrates, " calling out at the same time, The tongue is Fortune, the tongue is God;" and the allegorical festival of "the delivery of Isis was celebrated immediately after the Vernal Equinox," to commemorate the beginning of harvest. " Some," says Plutarch, " assimilate the history of these gods to the various changes which happen in the air, during the several seasons of the year, or to those accidents which are observed in the production of corn, in its sowing and ripening; ' for,' they observe, ' what can the burial of Osiris more aptly signify than the first covering the seed in the ground after it is sown? or his reviving and reappearing, than its first beginning to shoot up? and why is Isis said, upon perceiving herself to be with child, to have hung an amulet about her neck on the 6th of the month Phaophi, soon after sowing time, but in allusion to this allegory? and who is that Harpocrates, whom they tell us she brought forth about the time of the winter *tropic*, but those weak and slender shootings of the corn, which are yet feeble and imperfect?'—for which reason it is that the first-fruits of their lentils are dedicated to this god, and they celebrate the feast of his mother's delivery just after the vernal equinox." From this it may be inferred that the festival of the lentils was instituted when the month Mesoré coincided with the end of March; for since they were sown at the end of November, and ripened in about 100 or 110 days, the first-fruits might be gathered in three months and a half, or " just after the vernal equinox," or the last week in March; which would carry back the original institution of the festival to about 2650 years before our era, or some time after the reign of Menes.

" On the 19th day of the first month (Thoth), which was the feast of Hermes, they eat honey and figs, saying to each other, ' how sweet a thing is truth!' "—a satisfactory proof that the month itself, and not the first day alone, was called after and dedicated to Thoth, the Egyptian Hermes; and another festival, answering to the " Thesmophoria of the Athenians," was established to commemorate the period when " the husbandmen began to sow their corn, in the Egyptian month Athyr."

Many of the sacred festivals of the Egyptians were connected with agriculture; but these I have already introduced among their religious ceremonies. The gardeners have also been noticed in mentioning the villas of the Egyptians.*

The huntsmen formed another subdivision of this class.

They were employed in great numbers to attend and assist the amateur sportsmen, during their excursions in pursuit of the wild animals of the country, the scenes of which were chiefly in the deserts of Upper Egypt.† They conducted the dogs to the field; they had the management of them in loosing them for the chase, and they secured and brought home the game, after having contributed by their own skill to increase the sport of the chasseur. They also followed the occupation on their own account, making a considerable profit by catching the animals most prized for the table; by the reward they received for destroying the hyæna, and other animals hostile to the husbandman or the shepherd; and by the lucrative chase of the ostrich, which was highly valued for its plumes and eggs, and was sold to the wealthier Egyptians.

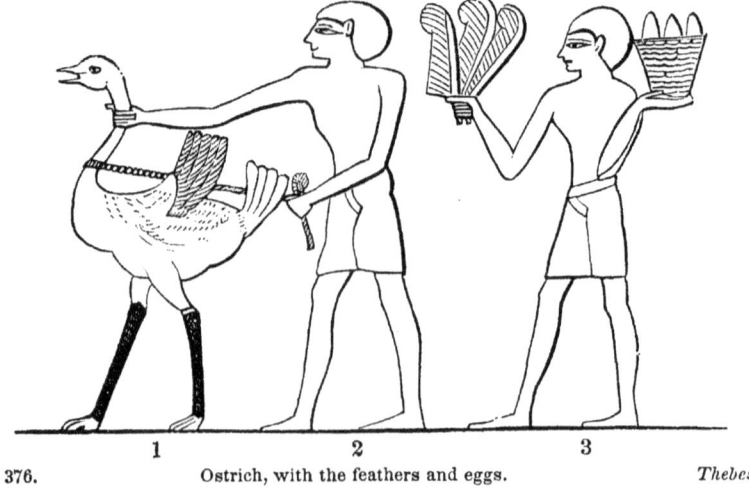

376.   Ostrich, with the feathers and eggs.   *Thebes.*

* Vol. i. p. 296 to 301, and 33 to 45, and 55, 56, 57.
† *See* beginning of chap. iv.

CHAP. VI. BOATMEN OF THE NILE. 55

The boatmen of the Nile belonged to the same third class.

They were of different grades; some belonging to the private sailing or pleasure boats of the grandees, others to those of burden. They also differed from the sailors of the "long ships" employed at sea, and even from those of the war galleys on the Nile, which acted as guard-boats, and were also used in the expeditions undertaken by the Pharaohs into Ethiopia.* These government boatmen were sometimes employed by the kings in transporting large blocks of stone to ornament the temples; and the immense monolith of granite, brought by Amasis from the first cataract to Saïs, was dragged overland by 2000 boatmen; but those who carried stones in lighters from the quarries were an inferior order, and ranked among the common boatmen of the Nile. Even among them the office of steersman seems always to have been very important; and as the pilots of the ships of war had a high rank above the "able seamen" of the fleet, so the helmsman in the ordinary boats of the Nile was looked upon as little inferior to the captain, standing in the same relative position as the *Mestámel* to the *Ryïs* of the modern *Cangia*.

* See above, vol. i. p. 411, on their sailors and ships of war.

I.   The *Nóreg*, a machine used by the modern Egyptians for threshing corn.

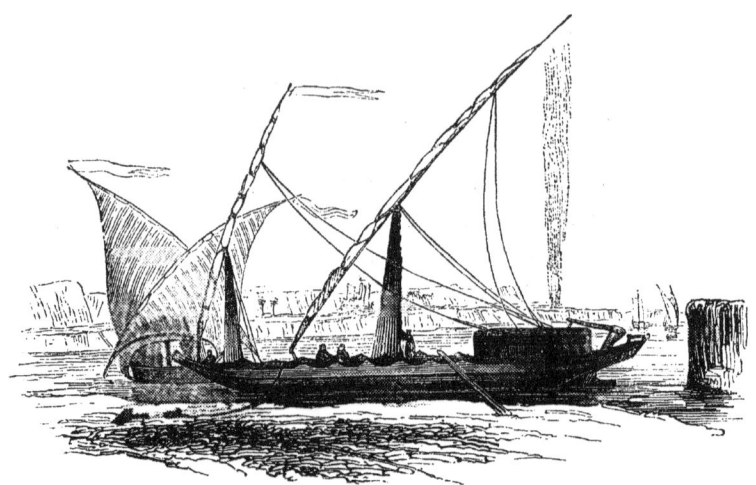

K. Modern boats of the Nile. On the opposite bank is a whirlwind of sand.

CHAPTER VII.

FOURTH CLASS:—ARTIFICERS, TRADESMEN OR SHOPKEEPERS, MUSICIANS, BUILDERS, CARPENTERS, BOAT-BUILDERS, MASONS, POTTERS, PUBLIC WEIGHERS AND NOTARIES, POUNDERS — GLASS — FALSE STONES—LAMPS—FINE LINEN—LOOMS—FLAX—LEATHER—PAPYRUS—POTTERS—CARPENTERS—BOXES—BOATS—METALS—TIN—GOLD MINES—IRON—BRONZE—CASTING—STONE KNIVES—POUNDING IN MORTARS.

In the fourth class were included the workers in glass, metals, wood, and leather; the manufacturers of linen and various stuffs; dyers, tanners, carpenters, cabinet-makers, masons; and all who followed handicraft employments, or any kind of trade. The musicians, who gained their livelihood by singing and playing, the leather-cutters and the carvers in stone, and ordinary painters (distinct of course from sculptors and artists) were included in the same class, which was mostly composed of people living in towns. Each craft (as is generally the case in modern Egypt also) had its own quarter of the town, called after it; as the quarter of the goldsmiths, of the leather-cutters, and others; and no one presumed to interfere with the occupation of a different trade from his own. It is even said that every one was obliged by law to follow the very same trade as his father; at all events, whether allowed in the beginning of his career to choose for himself or no, he was forced to continue in the one he first belonged to, and each vied with his neighbour in improving his own branch.

According to Diodorus, "no tradesman was permitted to meddle in political affairs, or to hold any civil office in the state, lest his thoughts should be distracted by the inconsistency of his pursuits, or by the jealousy and displeasure of the master in whose business he was employed. They feared that, without such a law, constant interruptions would take place, in consequence of the necessity, or the desire, of becoming conspicuous in a public station; that their proper occupations would be neglected, and that many would be led, by vanity and self-sufficiency, to interfere in matters out of their sphere. They also considered that to follow more than one occupation would be detrimental to their own interests and to those of the community; and that when men, from a motive of avarice, are induced to engage in numerous branches of art, the result generally is, that they are unable to excel in any. Such," he adds, "is the case in some countries, where artisans engage in agricultural pursuits, or in commercial speculations, and frequently in two or three different arts at once. Many, again, in those communities which are governed on democratic principles, are in the habit of frequenting popular assemblies, and, dreaming only of their own interests, receive bribes from the leaders of parties, and do incredible mischief to the state. But with the Egyptians, if any artisan meddled with political affairs, or engaged in any other employment than the one to which he had been brought up, a severe punishment was instantly inflicted upon him; and it was with this view that the regulations respecting their public and private occupations were instituted by the early legislators of Egypt."

Many arts and inventions were in common use in Egypt for centuries before they are generally supposed to have been known; and we are now and then as much surprised to find that certain things were old 3000 years ago, as the Egyptians would be if they could hear us talk of them as late discoveries. One of them is the use of glass, with which they were acquainted, at least, as early as the reign of the first Osirtasen, more than 3800 years ago; and the process of glass-blowing is represented, during his reign, in the paintings of Beni Hassan, in the same manner as it is on later monuments, in different parts of Egypt, to the time of the Persian conquest.

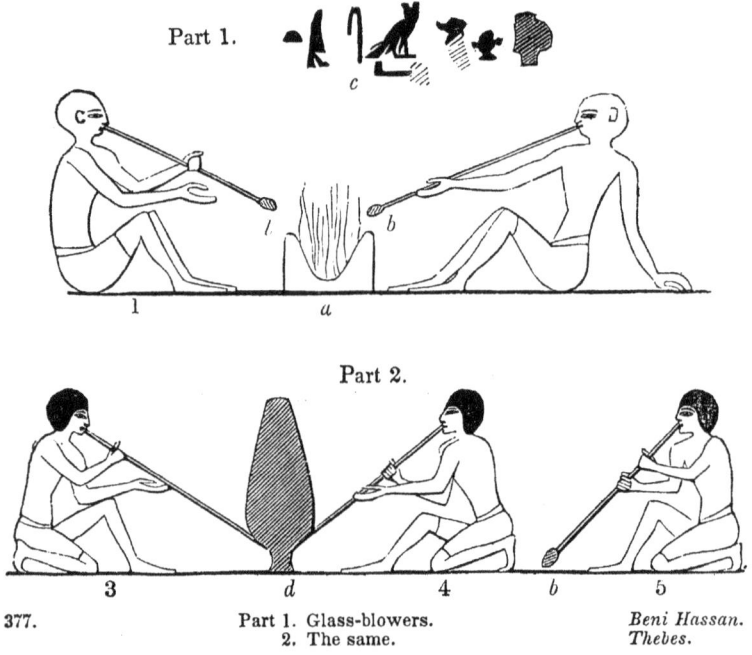

377. Part 1. Glass-blowers.   *Beni Hassan.*
      2. The same.   *Thebes.*

The glass at the end of the blowpipe *b b* is coloured green.
a is the fire.   *d* a glass bottle.

The form of the bottle and the use of the blow-pipe are unequivocally indicated in those subjects; and the green hue of the fused material, taken from the fire at the point of the pipe, sufficiently proves the intention of the artist. But, even if we had not this evidence of the use of glass, it would be shown by those well-known images of glazed pottery, which were common at the same period; the vitrified substance that covers them being of the same quality as glass, and containing the same in-

EARLY USE OF GLASS.

gredients fused in the same manner. And besides the many glass ornaments known to be of an earlier period is a bead, found at Thebes, bearing the name of a Pharaoh who lived about 1450 B.C., the specific gravity of which, 25° 23′, is precisely the same as of crown glass, now manufactured in England.

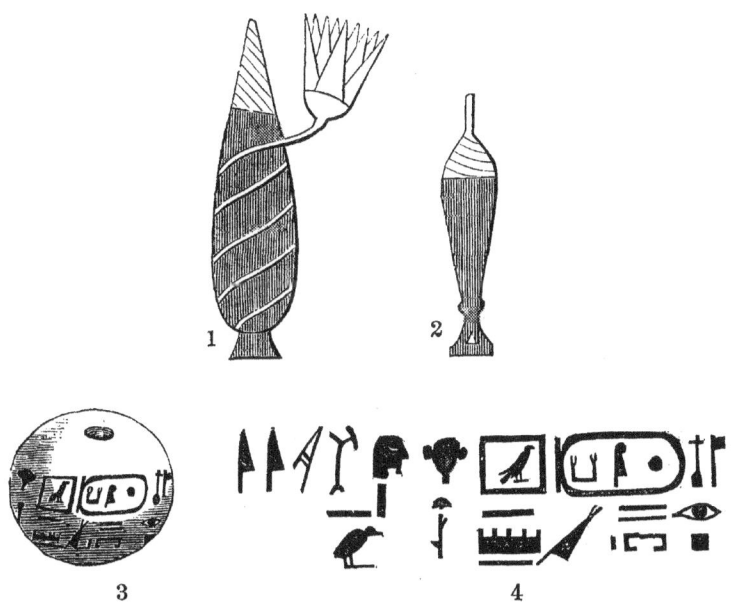

378. Figs. 1, 2. Glass bottles represented in the sculptures of Thebes.
3. Captain Henvey's glass bead. About the real size.
4. The hieroglyphics on the bead, containing the name of Amun-m-het, who lived about B.C. 1450.

Glass bottles, similar to those in the above woodcut (*figs.* 1, 2), are even met with on monuments of the fourth dynasty, dating long before the Osirtasens, or more than 4000 years ago; the transparent substance shows the red wine they contained; and this kind of bottle is represented in the same manner among the offerings to the gods, and at the fêtes of individuals, wherever wine was introduced, from the earliest to the latest times. Bottles, and other objects of glass, are commonly found in the tombs; and though they have no kings' names or dates inscribed upon them (glass being seldom used for such a purpose), no doubt exists of their great antiquity; and we may consider it a fortunate chance that has preserved *one* bead with the name of a sovereign of the 18th dynasty. Nor is it necessary to point out how illogical is the inference that, because other kinds of glass have not been found bearing a king's name, they were not made in Egypt, at, or even before, the same early period.

Pliny ascribes the discovery of glass to some Phœnician sailors accidentally lighting a fire on the sea-shore; but if an effect of chance, the secret is more likely to have been arrived at in Egypt, where natron (or subcarbonate of soda) abounded, than by the sea side; and if the Phœnicians really were the first to discover it on the *Syrian* coast, this would prove their migration from the Persian Gulf to have happened at a very remote period. Glass was certainly one of the great exports of the Phœnicians; who traded in beads, bottles, and other objects of that material, as well as various manufactures, made either in their own or in other countries; but Egypt was always famed for its manufacture; a peculiar kind of earth was found near Alexandria, without which, Strabo says, " it was impossible to make certain kinds of glass of many colours, and of a brilliant quality;" and some vases, presented by an Egyptian priest to the Emperor Hadrian, were considered so curious and valuable that they were only used on grand occasions.

Glass bottles, of various colours, were eagerly bought from Egypt, and exported into other countries; and the manufacture, as well as the patterns of many of those found in Greece, Etruria, and Rome, show that they were of Egyptian work; and though imitated in Italy and Greece, the original art was borrowed from the workmen of the Nile.

Such, too, was their skill in making glass, and in the mode of staining it of various hues, that they counterfeited with success the emerald, the amethyst, and other precious stones; and even arrived at an excellence in the art of introducing numerous colours into the same vase, to which our European workmen, in spite of their improvements in many branches of this manufacture, are still unable to attain. A few years ago the glass-makers of Venice made several attempts to imitate the variety of colours found in antique cups; but as the component parts were of different densities, they did not all cool, or set, at the same rapidity, and the vase was unsound. And it is only by making an inner foundation of one colour, to which those of the outer surface are afterwards added, that they have been able to produce their many-coloured vases, some of which were sent to the Great Exhibition of 1851.

Not so the Egyptians, who combined all the colours they required in the same cup, without the interior lining: those which had it being of inferior and cheaper quality. They had even the secret of introducing gold between two surfaces of glass; and in their bottles, a gold band alternates within a set of blue, green, and other colours. Another curious process was also common in Egypt in early times, more than 3000 years ago, which has only just been attempted at Venice, whereby the pattern on the surface was made to pass in right lines directly through the substance; so that if any number of horizontal sections were made through it, each one would have the same device on its upper and under surface. It is, in fact, a Mosaic in glass, made by fusing together as many delicate rods of an opaque glass, of the colour required for the picture, in the same manner as the woods in Tunbridge-ware are glued together, to form a larger and coarser pattern. The skill required in this exquisite work is not only shown by the art itself, but the fineness of the design; for some of the feathers of birds, and other details, are only to be made out with a lens; which means of magnifying was evidently used in Egypt, when this Mosaic glass was manufactured. Indeed, the discovery of a lens of crystal by Mr. Layard, at Nimroud, satisfactorily proves its use at an early period in Assyria; and we may conclude that it was neither a recent discovery there, nor confined to that country.

Winckelmann is of opinion that "the ancients carried the art of glassmaking to a higher degree of perfection than ourselves, though it may appear a paradox to those who have not seen their works in this material ;" and we may even add that they used it for more purposes, excepting of course windows, the inconvenience of which, in the hot sun of Egypt, would have been unbearable ; or even in Italy ; and only one pane of glass has been found at Pompeii, in a place not exposed to the outer light.

Winckelmann also mentions two pieces of glass mosaic, " one of which, though not quite an inch in length, and a third of an inch in breadth, exhibits, on a dark and variegated ground, a bird resembling a duck, in very bright and varied colours, rather in the manner of a Chinese painting than a copy of nature. The outlines are bold and decided, the colours beautiful and pure, and the effect very pleasing, in consequence of the artist having alternately introduced an opaque and a transparent glass. The most delicate pencil of a miniature painter could not have traced with greater sharpness the circle of the eyeball, or the plumage of the neck and wings; at which part this specimen has been broken. But the most surprising thing is, that the reverse exhibits the same bird, in which it is impossible to discover any difference in the smallest details ; whence it may be concluded that the figure of the bird continues through its entire thickness. The picture has a granular appearance on both sides, and seems to have been formed of single pieces, like mosaic work, united with so much skill, that the most powerful magnifying glass is unable to discover their junction. From the condition of this fragment, it was at first difficult to form any idea of the process employed in its manufacture ; and we should have remained entirely ignorant of it, had not the fracture shown that filaments of the same colours, as on the surface of the glass, and throughout its whole diameter, passed from one side to the other ; whence it has been concluded that the picture was composed of different cylinders of coloured glass, which, being subjected to a proper degree of heat, united by (partial) fusion. I cannot suppose they would have taken so much trouble, and have been contented to make a picture only the sixth of an inch thick, while, by employing longer filaments,

CHAP. VII. GLASS MOSAICS. EMERALDS. 63

they might have produced one many inches in thickness, without occupying any additional time in the process; it is therefore probable this was cut from a larger or thicker piece, and the number of the pictures taken from the same depended on the length of the filaments, and the consequent thickness of the original mass. The other specimen, also broken, and about the size of the preceding one, is made in the same manner. It exhibits ornaments of a green, yellow, and white colour, on a blue ground, which consist in volutes, strings of beads, and flowers, ending in pyramidical points. All the details are perfectly distinct and unconfused, and yet so very minute, that the keenest eye is unable to follow the delicate lines in which the volutes terminate; the ornaments, however, are all continued, without interruption, through the entire thickness of the piece."

Winckelmann is quite right respecting the mode of forming these glass mosaics, which was made more intelligible by a specimen found in Egypt. It consisted of separate squares, whose original division was readily discovered in a bright light, as well as the manner of adjusting the different parts, and of uniting them in one mass; and here and there the heat applied to cement the squares had caused the colours to run between them, in consequence of partial fusion from too strong a fire.

Not only were these various parts made at different times, and afterwards united by heat, rendered effective on their surfaces by means of a flux applied to them, but each coloured line was at first separate, and, when adjusted in its proper place, was connected with those around it by the same process.

The immense emeralds mentioned by ancient authors were doubtless glass imitations of those precious stones. Such were the colossal statue of Serapis, in the Egyptian labyrinth, nine cubits, or thirteen feet and a half, in height; an emerald presented by the King of Babylon to an Egyptian Pharaoh, which was four cubits, or six feet, long, and three cubits broad; and an obelisk in the temple of Jupiter, which was forty cubits, or sixty feet, in height, and four cubits broad, composed of four emeralds; and to have formed statues of glass of such dimensions, even allowing them to have been of different pieces, was a greater triumph of skill than imitating the stones.

That the Egyptians, more than 3000 years ago, were well acquainted not only with the manufacture of common glass, for beads and bottles of ordinary quality, but with the art of staining it of divers colours, is sufficiently proved by the fragments found in the tombs of Thebes; and so skilful were they in this complicated process, that they imitated the most fanciful devices, and succeeded in counterfeiting the rich hues, and brilliancy, of precious stones. The green emerald, the purple amethyst, and other expensive gems, were successfully imitated; a necklace of false stones could be purchased at an Egyptian jeweller's, to please the wearer, or deceive a stranger, by the appearance of reality; and some mock pearls (found by me at Thebes) have been so well counterfeited, that even now it is difficult with a strong lens to detect the imposition.

Pliny says the emerald was more easily counterfeited than any other gem, and considers the art of imitating precious stones a far more lucrative piece of deceit than any devised by the ingenuity of man; Egypt was, as usual, the country most noted for this manufacture; and we can readily believe that in Pliny's time they succeeded so completely in the imitation as to render it "difficult to distinguish false from real stones."*

Many, in the form of beads, have been met with in different parts of Egypt, particularly at Thebes; and so far did the Egyptians carry this spirit of imitation, that even small figures, scarabæi, and objects made of ordinary porcelain, were counterfeited, being composed of still cheaper materials. A figure, which was entirely of earthenware, with a glazed exterior, underwent a somewhat more complicated process than when cut out of stone, and simply covered with a vitrified coating; this last could therefore be sold at a low price: it offered all the brilliancy of the former, and its weight alone betrayed its inferiority; by which means, whatever was novel, or pleasing from its external

* Plin. xxxvii. 12.

appearance, was placed within reach of all classes, or at least the possessor had the satisfaction of seeming to partake in each fashionable novelty.

Such inventions, and successful endeavours to imitate costly ornaments by humbler materials, not only show the progress of art among the Egyptians, but strongly argue the great advancement they had made in the customs of civilized life; since it is certain, that until society has arrived at a high degree of luxury and refinement, artificial wants of this nature are not created, and the poorer classes do not yet feel the desire of imitating the rich, in the adoption of objects dependent on taste or accidental caprice.

Glass bugles and beads were much used by the Egyptians for necklaces, and for a sort of network, with which they covered the wrappers and cartonage of mummies. They were arranged so as to form, by their varied hues, numerous devices or figures, in the manner of our bead purses, and women sometimes amused themselves by stringing them for ornamental purposes, as at the present day.

The principal use to which glass was applied by the Egyptians (besides the beads and fancy work already noticed), was for the manufacture of bottles, vases, and other utensils; wine was frequently brought to table in a bottle, or handed to a guest in a cup of this material; and a body was sometimes buried in a glass coffin. Occasionally a granite sarcophagus was covered with a coating of vitrified matter, usually of a deep green colour, which displayed, by its transparency, the sculptures or hieroglyphic legends engraved upon the stone; a process well understood by the Egyptians, and the same they employed in many of the blue figures of pottery and stone, commonly found in their tombs.

In their glass mosaics, the colours have a wonderful brilliancy; the blues which are given by copper are vivid and beautifully clear; and one of the reds has all the intenseness of rosso antico, with the brightness of the glassy material in which it is found, thus combining the qualities of a rich enamel.

Many of the porcelain cups discovered at Thebes present a tasteful arrangement of varied hues, and show the skill of the

Egyptians, and the great experience they possessed in this branch of art. The manner in which the colours are blended and arranged; the minuteness of the lines, frequently tapering off to an almost imperceptible fineness; and the varied directions of twisted curves, traversing the substance, but strictly conforming to the pattern designed by the artist, display no ordinary skill, and show that they were perfect masters of the means they employed.

The Egyptian porcelain should perhaps be denominated glass-porcelain, as partaking of the quality of the two, and not being altogether unlike the porcelain glass invented by the celebrated Réaumur, who discovered, during his curious experiments on different qualities of porcelain, the method of converting glass into a substance very similar to chinaware.

The ground of Egyptian porcelain is generally of one homogeneous quality and hue, either blue or green, traversed in every direction by lines or devices of other colours—red, white, yellow, black, light, or dark blue, and green, or whatever the artist chose to introduce; and these are not always confined to the surface, but frequently penetrate into the ground, sometimes having passed half, or entirely, through the fused substance; in which respect they differ from the porcelain of China, where the flowers or patterns are applied to the surface, and justify the use of the term glass-porcelain. In some instances, the yellows were put on after the other colours, upon the surface of the vase, which was then again subjected to a proper degree of heat, and after this, the handles, the rim, and the base were added, and fixed by a repetition of the same process. It was not without considerable risk that these additions were made to their porcelain and glass vases, and many were broken during the operation; to which Martial alludes, in an epigram on these fragile cups of the Egyptians.

That the Egyptians possessed considerable knowledge of chemistry and the use of metallic oxides, is evident from the nature of the colours applied to their glass and porcelain; and they were even acquainted with the influence of acids upon colour, being able, in the process of dyeing or staining cloth, to bring about certain changes in the hues, by the same means adopted in our own cotton works, as I shall show in describing the manufactures of the Egyptians.

The art of cutting glass was known to them at the most remote periods, hieroglyphics and various devices being frequently engraved upon vases and beads; they also ground glass; and some, particularly that which bears figures or ornaments in relief, was cast in a mould. Some have supposed that the method of cutting glass was unknown to the ancients, and have limited the period of its invention to the commencement of the 17th century of our era, when Gaspar Lehmann, at Prague, first succeeded in it, and obtained a patent from the Emperor Rodolph II.; but the specimens of ancient glass, cut, engraved, and ground, discovered in Egypt, suffice to prove the art was practised there of old.

We find that in Rome the diamond was used for cutting hard stones; for Pliny tells us that diamonds were eagerly sought by lapidaries, who set them in iron handles, having been found to penetrate anything, however hard. He also states that emeralds and other hard stones were engraved, though in early times it was "considered wrong to violate gems with any figures or devices;" and "all gems could be engraved by the diamond." And though we do not know the precise method adopted by the Egyptians for cutting glass and hard stones, we may reasonably conclude they were acquainted with the diamond, and adopted it for engraving them. Emery powder and the lapidary's wheel were also used in Egypt; and there is little doubt that the Israelites learnt the art of cutting and engraving stones in that country.*

Some glass bottles were enclosed in wicker-work very nearly resembling what is now called by the Egyptians a *damagán*; which holds from one to two gallons of fluid; and some of a smaller size, from six to nine inches in height, were protected by a covering made of the stalks of the papyrus or *cyperus* rush, like the modern bottles containing Florence oil; others, again, appear

* The stones engraved by the Israelites were the "sardius, topaz, and carbuncle; the emerald, sapphire, and *diamond*; the ligure, agate, and amethyst; the beryl, onyx, and jasper." Exod. xxviii. 17, 18, 19, 20, 21, and xxxix. 6.

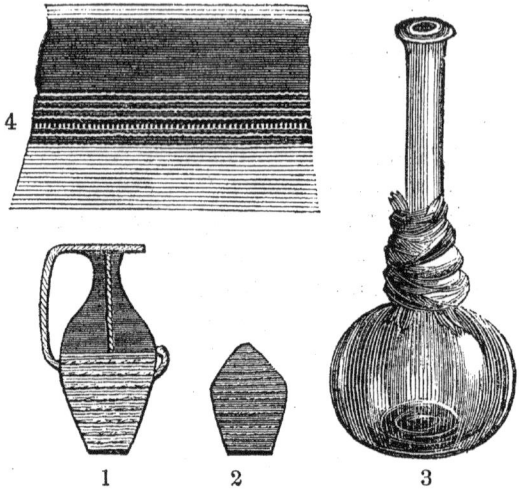

379. Fig. 1 has apparently leather sewed over the glass.
2 glass *damagán* enclosed in wicker work.
3 small glass bottle covered with papyrus rush, like the Florence oil flasks.
4 a piece of cloth with a border of a blue colour.

to have been partly cased in leather, sewed over them, much in the same manner as some now made for carrying liquids on a journey. (*Figs.* 1, 3, *and* 2.)

Among the many bottles found in the tombs of Thebes, and other places, none have excited greater curiosity and surprise than those of Chinese manufacture, presenting inscriptions in that language. Their number is considerable, and I have seen more than twenty from Thebes and other places. But though found in ancient tombs, there is no evidence of their having really been deposited there in early Pharaonic or even Ptolemaic times; and so many of the tombs have been occupied till a recent period by the Moslem population, that they may have been left there by these their more recent inmates. Professor Rosellini, however, mentions one he met with " in a previously unopened tomb, of uncertain date, which" he refers, " from the style of the sculptures, to a Pharaonic period, not much later than the 18th dynasty ;" and, were it not for this, we might suppose them brought from India by Arab traders. They are about two

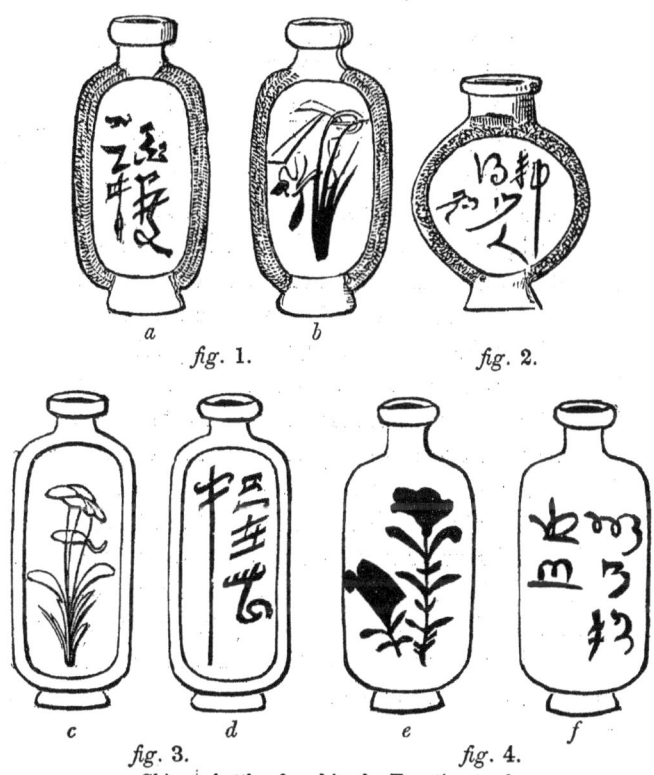

380. Chinese bottles found in the Egyptian tombs.
Fig. 1, in the Museum of Alnwick Castle.
2, one of two presented by me to the British Museum.
3, belonging to Mr. W. Hamilton.
4, in my possession. From Thebes.

inches in height; one side presents a flower, and the other an inscription, containing, according to Sir J. Davis (in three out of eight he examined), the following legend: "The flower opens, and lo! another year;" and another has been translated by Mr. Thoms: "During the shining of the moon the fir-tree sends forth its sap" (which in a thousand years becomes amber).

The quality of these bottles is very inferior, and of a time, as Sir J. Davis thought, "when the Chinese had not yet arrived at the same perfection in making porcelain as at present." They appear to have been only prized for their contents; and after they were exhausted, the valueless bottle was applied to the ordinary purpose of holding the *Kohl*, or Collyrium, used by women for staining their eyelids.*

It has been questioned if the Egyptians understood the art of enamelling upon gold or silver, but we might infer it from an expression of Pliny, who says: "The Egyptians paint their silver vases, representing Anubis upon them, the silver being painted and not engraved;" and M. Dubois had in his possession a specimen of Egyptian enamel. The reason of the doubt is our finding so many small gold figures with ornamented wings and bodies, whose feathers, faces, or other coloured parts are composed of a vitrified composition *let into* the metal. But they may have adopted both processes; and it is probable that many early specimens of *encaustum* were made by tooling the devices to a certain depth on bronze, and pouring a vitrified composition into the hollow space, the metal being properly heated at the same time; and, when fixed, the surface was smoothed down and polished.

Both the encaustic painting in wax, and that which consisted in burning in the colours, were evidently known to the ancients, being mentioned by Pliny, Ovid, Martial, and others; and the latter is supposed to have been on the same principle as our enamelling on gold.

Bottles of various kinds, glass, porcelain, alabaster, and other materials, were frequently exported from Egypt to other countries. The Greeks, the Etruscans, and the Romans received them as articles of luxury, which, being remarkable for their beauty, were prized as ornaments of the table; and when Egypt became a Roman province, part of the tribute annually paid to the conquerors consisted of glass vases, from the manufactories of Memphis and Alexandria.

The intercourse between Egypt and Greece had been constantly kept up after the accession of Psammitichus and Amasis;

---

* Since the above was written, a paper has been presented by Mr. Medhurst to the Royal Asiatic Society, which would establish the fact of their having been brought by the Arab traders, if, as here stated, the style of the characters did not come into use till the 3rd century of our era; and the poems, from which the sentences were taken, were not written till the 8th and 11th centuries. The earliest mention of porcelain in China is also limited to the 2nd century B.C. A similar bottle was found by Mr. Layard at Arban, on the Khaboor.

and the former country, the parent of the arts at that period, supplied the Greeks and some of the Syrian tribes with numerous manufactures. The Etruscans, too, a commercial people, appear to have had an extensive trade with Egypt, and we repeatedly find small alabaster, as well as coloured glass, bottles in their tombs, which have all the character of the Egyptian; and not only does the stone of the former proclaim by its quality the quarries from which it was taken, but the form and style of the workmanship leave no doubt of the bottles themselves being the productions of Egyptian artists. The same remark applies to many objects found at Nineveh.

It is uncertain of what stone the famous murrhine vases, mentioned by Pliny, Martial, and other writers, were made; it was of various colours, beautifully blended, and even iridescent, and was obtained in greater quantity in Carmania than in any country. It was also found in Parthia and other districts of Asia, but unknown in Egypt; a fact quite consistent with the notion of its being fluor-spar, which is not met with in the valley of the Nile; and explaining the reason why the Egyptians imitated it with the composition known under the name of false murrhine, said to have been made at Thebes and Memphis. The description given by Pliny certainly bears a stronger resemblance to the fluor-spar than to any other stone, and the only objection to this having been murrhine is our not finding any vases, or fragments, of it; and some may still doubt if the substance is known to which the naturalist alludes. But the fluor-spar appears to have the strongest claim; and the glass-porcelain of Egypt, whose various colours are disposed in waving lines, as if to imitate the natural waves of that crystallized substance, may be the false murrhine of the ancients. (*Woodcuts* 170, *fig.* 2; 171, *fig.* 5.)

It is difficult to say whether the Egyptians employed glass for the purpose of making lamps or lanterns: ancient authors give us no direct information on the subject; and the paintings offer few representations of lamps, torches, or any other kind of light.*

Herodotus mentions a " fête of burning lamps," which took

* In the funeral processions one person carries what seems to be a candle or torch.

place at Saïs, and indeed throughout the country, at a certain period of the year, and describes the lamps used on this occasion as "small vases filled with salt and olive oil, on which the wick floated, and burnt during the whole night;" but he does not say of what material those vases were made, and they may either have been of glass or of earthenware.

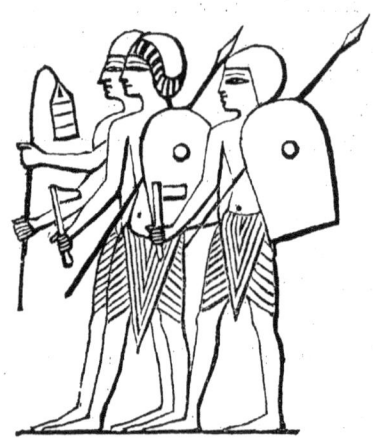

381. A guard apparently with a lantern. Tel-el-Amarna.

The sculptures of Tel-el-Amarna, again, represent a guard of soldiers, one of whom holds before him what appears to be a lamp, and resembles the cloth or paper lanterns so common in Egypt at the present day.

The Egyptians were always celebrated for their manufacture of linen and other cloths, and the produce of their looms was exported to, and eagerly purchased by, foreign nations. The fine linen and embroidered work, the yarn and woolen stuffs, of the upper and lower country, are frequently mentioned, and were highly esteemed. Solomon purchased many of those commodities, as well as chariots and horses, from Egypt; and Chemmis, the city of Pan, retained the credit it had acquired in making linen stuffs till about the period of the Roman conquest.

Woolen garments were chiefly used by the lower orders: sometimes also by the rich, and even by the priests, who were permitted to wear an upper robe in the form of a cloak of this material; but under garments of wool were strictly forbidden them, upon a principle of cleanliness; and as they took so much pains to cleanse and shave the body, they considered it inconsistent to adopt clothes made of animals' hair. No one was allowed to be buried in a woollen garment, in consequence of its engendering worms, which would injure the body; nor could any priest enter a temple without taking off this part of his dress.*

* See vol. i. p. 333.

The quantity of linen manufactured and used in Egypt was very great; and, independent of that made up into articles of dress, the numerous wrappers required for enveloping the mummies, both of men and animals, show how large a supply must have been kept ready for the constant demand at home, as well as for that of the foreign market.

That the bandages employed in wrapping the dead are of linen, and not, as some have imagined, of cotton, has been already ascertained by the most satisfactory tests; and though no one among the unscientific inhabitants of modern Egypt ever thought of questioning the fact, received opinion in Europe had, till lately, decided that they were cotton ; and it was forbidden to doubt that " the bands of *byssine* linen," said by Herodotus to have been used for enveloping the mummies, were cotton.

The actual experiments made, with the aid of powerful microscopes, by Mr. Bauer, Mr. Thomson, Dr. Ure, and others, on the nature of the fibres of linen and cotton threads, have shown that the former invariably present a cylindrical form, transparent, and articulated, or jointed like a cane, while the latter offer the appearance of a flat riband, with a hem or border at each edge ; so that there is no possibility of mistaking the fibres of either, except, perhaps, when the cotton is in an unripe state, and the flattened shape of the centre is less apparent. The results having been found similar in every instance, and the structure of the fibres thus unquestionably determined, the threads of mummy cloths were submitted to the same test, and no exception was found to their being linen ; nor were they even a mixture of linen and cotton thread.

The fact of the mummy cloths being linen is therefore decided. The name *byssus*, it is true, presents a difficulty ; owing to the Hebrew *shash* being translated "*byssus*" in the Septuagint version, and, in our own, " fine linen ;" and to shash being the name applied by the Arabs at this day to fine muslin, which is of cotton and not of linen ; but as the mummy cloths said by Herodotus to be " of *byssine sindon*," are known to be invariably linen, the byssus cannot be cotton. Herodotus, indeed, uses the expression " treẽ wuc to denote cotton; and Julius Pollux adopts the same name, distinguishing it also from byssus, which he calls a species of Indian flax. The use of the two words *byssus* and *linon* presents no difficulty, since they might be employed, like our flax and linen, to signify the plant, and the substance made from it.

Cotton cloth, however, was among the manufactures of Egypt, and dresses of this material were worn by all classes. Pliny states that the Egyptian priests, though they used linen, were particularly partial to cotton robes; and "cotton garments," supplied by the government for the use of the temples, are distinctly mentioned in the Rosetta Stone. Herodotus and Plutarch affirm that linen was preferred, owing as well to its freshness in a hot climate, as to its great tendency to keep the body clean, and that a religious prejudice forbade the priests to wear vestments of any other quality; this, however, refers to the inner portion of the dress; and the prohibition of entering a temple with cotton or woollen garments led to the notion that none but linen were worn by them at any time. The same custom was adopted by the votaries of Isis when her rites were introduced by the Greeks and Romans; and linen dresses were appropriated to those who had been initiated in the sacred mysteries.

Whatever restrictions may have been in force respecting the use of cotton among the priesthood, other individuals were permitted to consult their own choice on this point; and it was immaterial whether they preferred, during life, the coolness of flax, or the softness of cotton raiment, provided the body, after death, was enveloped in bandages of linen; and this regulation accounts for the mummy cloths of the poorest individuals being also found of that material.

It was not only for articles of dress that cotton was manufactured by the Egyptians: a great quantity was used for the furniture of their houses, the coverings of chairs and couches, and various other purposes; and a sort of cloth was made of the united filaments of flax and cotton. This is mentioned by Julius Pollux, who, after describing the cotton-plant as an Egyptian production, and stating that cloth was manufactured of the "wool of its nut," says they sometimes "make the woof of it, and the warp of linen;" a quality of cloth still manufactured by the modern Egyptians.

From the few representations which occur in the tombs of Thebes, it has been supposed that the Egyptian looms were of rude construction, and totally incapable of producing the fine linen so much admired by the ancients; and as the paintings in which they occur were executed at a very early period, it has been conjectured that, in after times, great improvements took place in their construction. But when we consider with what simple means oriental nations are in the habit of executing the most delicate and complicated work, we cease to feel surprised at the apparent imperfection of the mechanism, or instruments, used by the Egyptians; and it is probable that their far-famed "fine linen," mentioned in Scripture, and by ancient writers, was produced from looms of the same construction as those represented in the paintings of Thebes and Eileithyias. Nor was the praise bestowed upon that manufacture unmerited; and the quality of one piece of linen found near Memphis fully justifies it, and excites equal admiration at the present day, being to the touch comparable to silk, and not inferior in texture to our finest cambric.

The mummy cloths are generally of a very coarse quality; and little attention was bestowed on the disposition of the threads, in the cloths of ordinary manufacture. Mr. Thomson, who examined many specimens of them, is of opinion that the number of threads in the warp invariably exceeded those of the woof, occasionally even by four times the quantity; and as his observations are highly interesting, I shall introduce an extract from his pamphlet on the subject.

"Of the products of the Egyptian loom, we know scarcely more than the mummy pits have disclosed to us; and it would be as unreasonable to look through modern sepulchres for specimens and proofs of the state of manufacturing art amongst ourselves, as to deduce an opinion of the skill of the Egyptians from those fragments of cloth which envelope their dead, and have come down, almost unchanged, to our own time. The curious or costly fabrics which adorned the living, and were the pride of the industry and skill of Thebes, have perished ages ago. There are, however, amongst these remains, some of which are not worthy of notice, which carry us back into the workshops of former times, and exhibit to us the actual labours of weavers and dyers of Egypt, more than 2000 years ago.

"The great mass of the mummy cloth, employed in bandages and coverings, whether of birds, animals, or the human species, is of coarse texture, especially that more immediately in contact with the body, which is generally impregnated with resinous or bituminous matter. The upper bandages, nearer the surface, are finer. Sometimes the whole is enveloped in a covering coarse and thick, and very like the sacking of the present day: sometimes in cloth coarse and open, like that used in our cheese-presses, for which it might easily be mistaken. In the College of Surgeons are various specimens of these cloths, some of which are very curious.

"The beauty of the texture and peculiarity in the structure of a mummy cloth given to me by Mr. Belonzi were very striking. It was free from gum, or resin, or impregnation of any kind, and had evidently been originally white. It was close and firm, yet very elastic. The yarn of both warp and woof was remarkably even and well spun. The thread of the warp was *double*, consisting of two fine threads twisted together. The woof was single. The warp contained 90 threads in an inch; the woof, or weft, only 44. The fineness of these materials, estimated after the manner of cotton yarn, was about 30 hanks in the pound.

"The subsequent examination of a great variety of mummy cloths showed that the disparity between the warp and woof belonged to the system of manufacture, and that the warp generally had twice or thrice, and not seldom four times, the number of threads in an inch that the woof had: thus, a cloth containing 80 threads of warp in the inch, of a fineness of about 24 hanks in the pound, had 40 threads in the woof: another with 120 threads of warp, of 30 hanks, had 40; and a third specimen only 30 threads in the woof. These have each respectively double, treble, and quadruple the number of threads in the warp that they have in the woof. This structure, so different from modern cloth, which has the proportions nearly equal, originated, probably, in the difficulty and tediousness of getting in the woof, when the shuttle was thrown by hand, which is the practice in India at the present day, and which there are weavers still living old enough to remember the universal practice in this country."

Mr. Thomson then mentions some fragments of mummy cloths, sent to England by the late Mr. Salt, which he saw in the British Museum. They were " of different degrees of fineness; some fringed at the ends, and some striped at the edges." "My first impression," he continues, " on seeing these cloths, was, that the finest kinds were *muslin*, and of Indian manufacture, since we learn from the 'Periplus of the Erythrean Sea,' ascribed to Arrian, but more probably the work of some Greek merchant himself engaged in the trade, that muslins from the Ganges were an article of export from India to the Arabian Gulf: but this suspicion of their being cotton was soon removed by the microscope of Mr. Bauer, which showed that they were all, without exception, linen. Some were thin and transparent, and of very delicate texture. The finest appeared to be made of yarns of near 100 hanks in the pound, with 140 threads in the inch in the warp, and about 64 in the woof. A specimen of muslin in the museum of the East India House, the finest production of the Dacca loom, has only 100 threads in an inch in the warp, and 84 in the woof; but the surprising fineness of the yarns, which, though spun by hand, is not less than 250 hanks in the pound, gives to this fabric its unrivalled tenuity and lightness.

"Some of the cloths were fringed at the ends, and one, a sort of scarf, about four feet long, and twenty inches wide, was fringed at both ends. Three or four threads twisted together with the fingers to form a strong one, and two of these again twisted together, and knotted at the middle and at the end to prevent unravelling, formed the fringe, precisely like the silk shawls of the present day.

"The selvages of the Egyptian cloths are generally formed with the greatest care, and are well calculated by their strength to protect the cloth from accident. Fillets of strong cloth or tape also secure the ends of the pieces from injury, showing a knowledge of all the little resources of modern manufacture.

Several of the specimens, both of fine and coarse cloth, were bordered with blue stripes of various patterns, and in some alternating with narrow lines of another colour. The width of the patterns varied from half an inch to an inch and a quarter. In the latter were seven blue stripes, the broadest about half an inch wide nearest the selvage, followed by five very narrow ones, and terminated by one an eighth of an inch broad. Had this pattern, instead of being confined to the edge of the cloth, been repeated across its whole breadth, it would have formed a modern gingham, which we can scarcely doubt was one of the articles of Egyptian industry.

"A small pattern about half an inch broad formed the edging of one of the finest of these cloths, and was composed of a stripe of blue, alternating with three lines of a fawn colour, forming a simple and elegant border. These stripes were produced in the loom by coloured threads previously dyed in the yarn. The nature of the fawn colour I was unable to determine. It was too much degraded by age, and the quantity too small, to enable me to arrive at a satisfactory conclusion. Though I had no doubt the colouring matter of the blue stripes was indigo, I subjected the cloth to the following examination. Boiled in water for some time, the colour did not yield in the least; nor was it at all affected by soap, nor by strong alkalies: sulphuric acid, diluted only so far as not to destroy the cloth, had no action on the colour. Chloride of lime gradually reduced, and at last destroyed it. Strong nitric acid, dropped upon the blue, turned it orange, and in the same instant destroyed it. These tests prove the colouring matter of the stripes to be indigo.

"This dye was unknown to Herodotus, for he makes no mention of it. It was known to Pliny, who, though ignorant of its true nature, and the history of its production, has correctly described the most characteristic of its properties, the emission of a beautiful purple vapour when exposed to heat. Had his commentators been acquainted with the sublimation of indigo, it would have saved many learned doubts. We learn from the Periplus, that it was an article of export from Barbarike on the Indus, to Egypt, where its employment by the manufacturers of that country, probably from a remote period, is clearly established by the specimens here described."

In *woodcut* 379, *fig.* 4, is a piece of cloth, brought from Thebes, which offers a very good instance of the coloured border mentioned by Mr. Thomson. It is of ordinary quality; the number of threads in the inch is ninety-six in the warp, and thirty-four in the woof; and the border consists of one broad band and six narrow stripes, of a blue colour, evidently died with indigo; the band which is nearest the selvage is one inch and two tenths in breadth; the others consist each of two threads, in the direction of the warp, with the exception of the innermost one, which is of five threads, and the dividing line between the fourth and fifth is varied by the introduction of a blue thread down the centre. The rest of the cloth has the usual yellowish tinge, " supposed to arise from some astringent preparation employed for its preservation," which, according to Mr. Thomson, imparts to water a similar colour, but offers no trace of tannin. " In none of the specimens I have examined," he adds, " did either gelatine or albumen, or solution of iron, afford any precipitate; but the subacetate of lead produced a cloud, indicating the presence of extractive matter."

It is evident that the colour was imparted to the threads previous to the cloth being made,* as the blue remains unaltered; and the cloths with broad coloured borders are the more curious, as they illustrate the representations in the paintings, and show that they were similar to those made by the looms in the age of the Pharaohs of the 12th and 18th dynasties; and the Nubians wear shawls with the same blue borders, manufactured in the valley of the Nile at the present day. The Egyptians also dyed old dresses, as in these days.

Another piece of linen, from Thebes, has 152 threads in the warp, and 71 in the woof, to each inch; it is of a much darker hue than the cloth just mentioned, and was perhaps dyed with the *carthamus tinctorius*, or safflower. But the most remarkable piece of fine linen is that found near Memphis, before mentioned;

---

* As with the threads used by the Israelites, Exod. xxxv. 25. " And all the women that were wise-hearted did spin with their hands, and brought that which they had spun, both of blue, and of purple, and of scarlet, and of fine linen " and some idea may be given of its texture, from the number of threads in the inch, which is 540 (or 270 double threads) in the warp; and the limited proportion of 110 in the woof shows the justness of Mr. Thomson's observation, that this disparity belonged to their " system of manufacture," since it is observable even in the finest quality of cloth. It is also of a light brown colour. Another very remarkable circumstance in this specimen is, that it is covered with small figures and hieroglyphics, so finely drawn, that here and there the lines are with difficulty followed by the eye, and as there is no appearance of the ink having run in any part of the cloth, it is evident they had previously prepared it for this purpose. The perfection of its threads is equally surprising; the knots and breaks, seen in our best cambric, are not found in holding it to the light—an ancient mode of proving fine cloth, which led to that beautiful Greek expression $\varepsilon\iota\lambda\iota\kappa\rho\iota\nu\eta\varsigma$, " sincere," borrowed from this test of light, which is far superior to the Latin *sincerus*, derived from honey, *sine cerâ*.

Pliny cites four qualities of linen, particularly noted in Egypt; the Tanitic and Pelusiac, the Butine and the Tentyritic; and mentions in the same place the cotton-tree of Egypt, which he confines to the Upper country. He also states that the quantity of flax cultivated in Egypt was accounted for by their exporting linen to Arabia and India; and the quality of that produced by the Egyptian looms was far superior to any other.

The threads used for nets were remarkable for their fineness; and Pliny says " some of them were so delicate that they would pass through a man's ring, and a single person could carry a sufficient number of them to surround a whole wood. Julius Lepus, who died while governor of Egypt, had some of these nets, each string of which consisted of 150 threads; a fact perfectly surprising to those who are not aware that the Rhodians preserve to this day, in the Temple of Minerva, the remains of a linen corslet presented to them by Amasis, king of Egypt, whose threads are composed each of 365 fibres; and in proof of the truth of this, Mutianus, who was thrice consul, lately affirmed at Rome that he had examined it; and the reason of so few fragments remaining was attributable to the curiosity of those who had frequently subjected it to the same scrutiny."

CHAP. VII. EMBROIDERY. 81

Herodotus mentions this corslet, and another, presented by Amasis to the Lacedæmonians, which had been carried off by the Samians; "it was of linen, ornamented with numerous figures of animals, worked in gold and cotton. Each thread of the corslet was worthy of admiration. For, though very fine, every one was composed of 360 other threads, all distinct; the quality being similar to that dedicated to Minerva, at Lindus, by the same monarch."

Many of the Egyptian stuffs presented various patterns worked in colours by the loom, independent of those produced by the dyeing or printing process, and so richly composed, that Martial says they vied with the Babylonian cloths embroidered with the needle.

The art of embroidery* was commonly practiced in Egypt; and the Hebrews, on leaving the country, took advantage of the knowledge they had there acquired to make a rich "hanging for the door of the tent, of blue, and purple, and scarlet, and fine twined linen, wrought with needlework;"† a coat of fine linen was embroidered for Aaron; and his girdle was " of fine twined linen, and blue, and purple, and scarlet, of needlework."‡

The gold thread used for these purposes is supposed to have been beaten out with the hammer,§ and afterwards rounded; and even the delicate net made by Vulcan, which was so fine that the gods themselves were unable to see it, is represented to have been forged on his anvil with the hammer.‖ Pliny mentions cloth woven with gold threads, sometimes entirely of those materials, without any woollen or linen ground, as were the garment of Agrippina, the tunic of Heliogabalus, and that worn by Tarquinius Priscus, mentioned by Verrius.

Pliny says, "Coloured dresses were known in the time of Homer, from which the robes of triumph were borrowed: and from the Phrygians having been the first to devise the method

* Ezekiel, xxvii. 7, " Fine linen, with broidered work from Egypt."
† Exod. xxvi. 36, xxvii. 16, xxxvi. 37, and xxxviii. 18.
‡ Exod. xxviii. 39, and xxxix. 29.
§ Exod. xxxix. 3, "And they did beat the gold into thin plates, and cut it into wires, to work it in the blue, and in the purple, and in the scarlet, and in the fine linen."   ‖ Hom. Od. viii. 274.

of giving the same effect with the needle, they have been called *Phrygiones*. But to weave cloth with gold thread was the invention of the Asiatic king, Attalus, from whom the name Attalie was derived; and the Babylonians were most noted for their skill in weaving cloths of various colours."

The question still remains undecided respecting the time when silver thread came into use; and as no mention of silver stuffs occurs in the writings of ancient authors, it has been supposed that its introduction was of late date. Silver wire, however, was already known in Egypt about 3300 years ago, being found at Thebes of the third Thothmes: nor is there any reason to suppose it was then a novel invention; and it was probably known and used nearly as soon as gold wire, which we find attached to rings bearing the name of Osirtasen the First, who lived more than 600 years earlier.

This wire is supposed not to have been drawn, like our own, through holes in metal plates, but to have been beaten out, and rounded with the file; but the appearance of some found at Thebes justifies the conclusion that a mode of drawing it was not unknown to them; and the omission of every representation of the process in the paintings is no argument against it, since they have also failed to introduce the casting of metals, and various other arts, with which we see they were acquainted.

Wire-drawing was first attempted with the most ductile metals, gold and silver being used before brass and iron, because the wire was originally employed for ornamental purposes. Gold thread and wire were always made entirely of metal, even to the time of the latter Roman Emperors; and there is no instance of flattened wire wound round silk or linen threads, or of silver or other wire gilt, though gilding was so common on vases and other articles of bronze. That the Egyptians had arrived at great perfection in the art of making the thread is evident, from its being sufficiently fine for weaving into cloth, and for embroidery; and the exceeding delicacy of the linen corslet of Amasis, on which numerous figures of animals were worked in gold, required a proportionate degree of fineness in the gold thread used for the purpose.

The coloured dresses represented in the Egyptian paintings, worn by women of rank, and by the deities, much resemble our modern chintzes in the style of their patterns, though it is probable that they were generally of linen instead of calico: some appear to have been worked with the needle, and others woven with gold threads.

Another very remarkable discovery of the Egyptians was the use of mordants. They were acquainted with the effect of acids on colour, and submitted the cloth they dyed to one of the same processes adopted in our modern manufactories; and while, from his account, we perceive how little Pliny understood the process he was describing, he at the same time gives us the strongest evidence of its truth. " In Egypt," he says, "they stain cloths in a wonderful manner. They take them in their original state, quite white, and imbue them, not with a dye, but with certain drugs which have the power of absorbing and taking colour. When this is done, there is still no appearance of change in the cloths; but so soon as they are dipped into a bath of the pigment, which has been prepared for the purpose, they are taken out properly coloured. The singular thing is, that though the bath contains only one colour, several hues are imparted to the piece, these changes depending on the nature of the drug employed: nor can the colour be afterwards washed off; and surely if the bath had many colours in it, they must have presented a confused appearance on the cloth."

From this it is evident that the cloth was prepared before steeping; the *momentary* effect he mentions could only be produced by the powerful agency of mordants; and they not only used them to make the cloth take the colour equally, but also to change the hues.

Whether the Egyptians really understood the principle on which the salts and acids of the mordants acted, or calculated their effects solely from the experience they had acquired, it is difficult to decide. They had long been used in Europe, before their chemical agency was properly explained; and when the term mordant was first applied by the French dyers, they imagined "that the intention of passing the substances, which were to be dyed, through certain saline liquors, was to corrode something that opposed the entering of the colouring principle, and to enlarge the pores of the substances" (the effect of acids in changing the hues being a later discovery); we cannot therefore positively prove that the Egyptians had a knowledge of chemistry, though from their long experience, and from their skill in the employment of the metallic oxides, we may find strong reasons to infer it. For if at first ignorant of the reason of such changes, it is probable that, in process of time, they were led to investigate the causes by which they were effected.

Many discoveries, and even inventions, are more the effect of chance than of studious reflection, and the principle is often the last to be understood. In discoveries this is generally the case, in inventions frequently. But when men have observed, from long practice, a fixed and undeviating result, their curiosity naturally becomes excited, the thirst for knowledge, and, above all, the desire of benefiting by the discovery, prompt them to scrutinize the causes to which they have been so much indebted; and few people, who have made any advance in the arts of civilized life, long remain ignorant of the means of improving their knowledge.

We may therefore suppose some general notions of chemistry, or at least of chemical agency, were known to the Egyptians; and the beautiful colours they obtained from copper, the composition of various metals, and the knowledge of the effects produced on different substances by the salts of the earth, tend to confirm this opinion.

The Egyptian yarn seems all to have been spun with the hand, and the spindle is seen in all the pictures representing the manufacture of cloth. Spinning was principally the occupation of women; and our word "wife" is nearly related to "woof," "weaving," and "web." But men were also employed at the spindle and the loom; though not, as Herodotus would lead us to suppose, to the exclusion of women, who he pretends undertook the duties of men in other countries, "by going to market, and engaging in business, while the men, shut up in the house, worked at the loom." Men, to this day, are employed in making cloth in

CHAP. VII.   MAKING THREAD. THE LOOM.   85

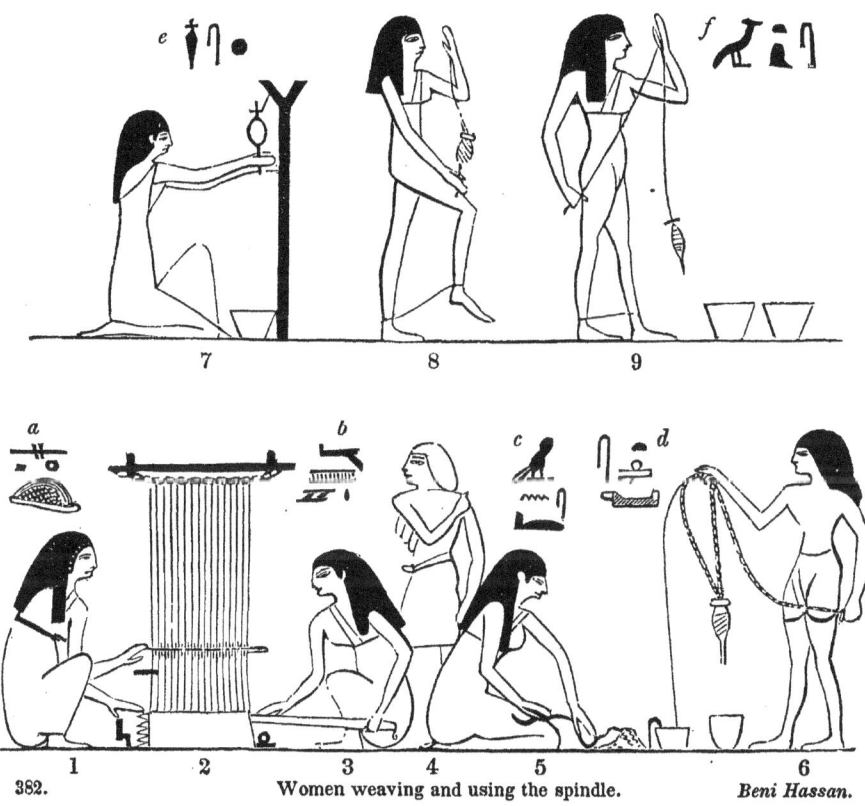

382.   Women weaving and using the spindle.   Beni Hassan.

Egypt and in other countries, but it cannot be said that they have relinquished their habits for those of women; and we find from the paintings executed by the Egyptians themselves, that both men and women were employed in manufacturing cloth.

"Other nations," continues the historian, "make cloth by pushing the woof upwards, the Egyptians, on the contrary, press it down;" and this is confirmed by the paintings* which represent the process of manufacturing cloth; but at Thebes,† a man who is engaged in making a piece of cloth, with a coloured

---

* In woodcut 382, *fig* 2.   † Woodcut 384, *fig.* 2.

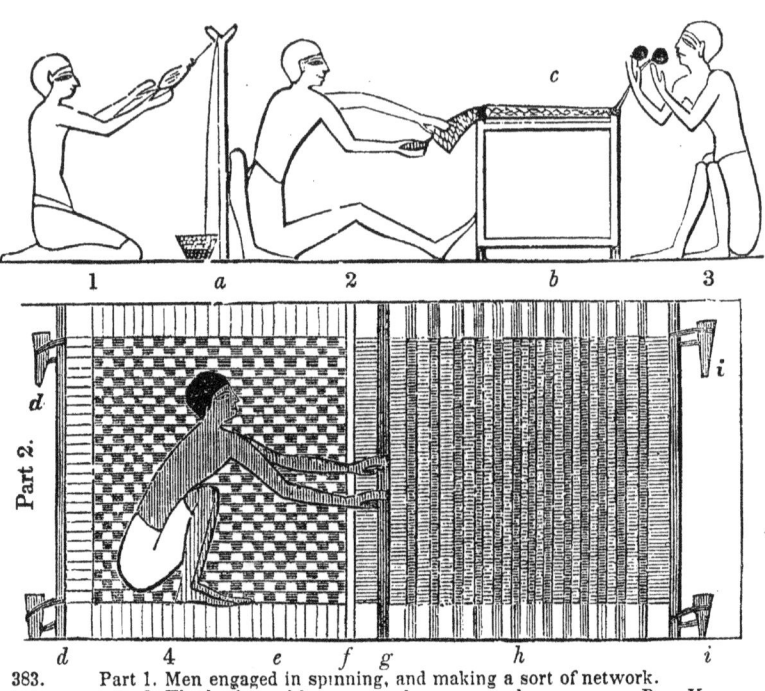

383. Part 1. Men engaged in spinning, and making a sort of network.
2. The horizontal loom, or perhaps mat-making.   *Beni Hassan.*

border or selvage, appears to push the woof upwards, the cloth being fixed above him to the upper part of the frame. They had also the horizontal loom, which occurs at Beni Hassan and other places; and at El Bersheh we see the mode of taking up the increasing length of the cloth by pegs in the ground (as still done in Ethiopia), and how the women wound off numerous threads from balls placed within a slight framework, the fineness of which is indicated by the number taken to form one twist.

In the hieroglyphics over persons employed with the spindle, it is remarkable that the word *saht*, which in Coptic signifies to "twist," constantly occurs. The spindles were generally small, being about one foot three inches in length, and several, found at Thebes, are now in the museums of Europe.* They were generally of wood, and in order to increase their impetus in turning,

* One of those in the British Museum, which I found at Thebes, had some of the linen thread with it. Woodcut 385, *fig.* 2.

CHAP. VII   LOOMS.   FLAX.   87

384.   Fig. 1. A piece of cloth on a frame.   *Eileithyias.*
       2. A loom.   *Thebes.*
k is a shuttle, not thrown, but put in with the hand. It had a hook at each end. See
woodcut 382, fig. 2.

the circular head was occasionally of gypsum, or composition; some, however, were of a light plaited work, made of rushes, or palm leaves, stained of various colours, and furnished with a loop of the same materials, for securing the twine after it was wound.*

Besides the use of the spindle, and form of the loom, we find the two principal purposes, to which flax was applied, represented in the paintings of the tombs; and at Beni Hassan the mode

* Woodcut 385, *fig.* 5.   Another of wood, *fig.* 6.

385.   5   4   3   2   1
         Spindles.   *British and Berlin Museums.*

Fig. 1 is a sort of cane split at the top to give it a globular shape.
2 has the head of gypsum.
3 entirely of wood.
4 of plaited or basket work.
5 the loop to put over the twine.
6 a ring of wood for securing the twine.

of cultivating the plant, in the same square beds now met with throughout Egypt (much resembling our salt pans), the process of beating the stalks, and making them into ropes, and the manufacture of a piece of cloth, are distinctly pointed out.

It is, however, possible that the part of the picture, where men are represented pouring water from earthen pots, may refer to the process of steeping the stalks of the plant, after they were cut; the square spaces would then indicate the different pits in which they were immersed, containing some less, some more,

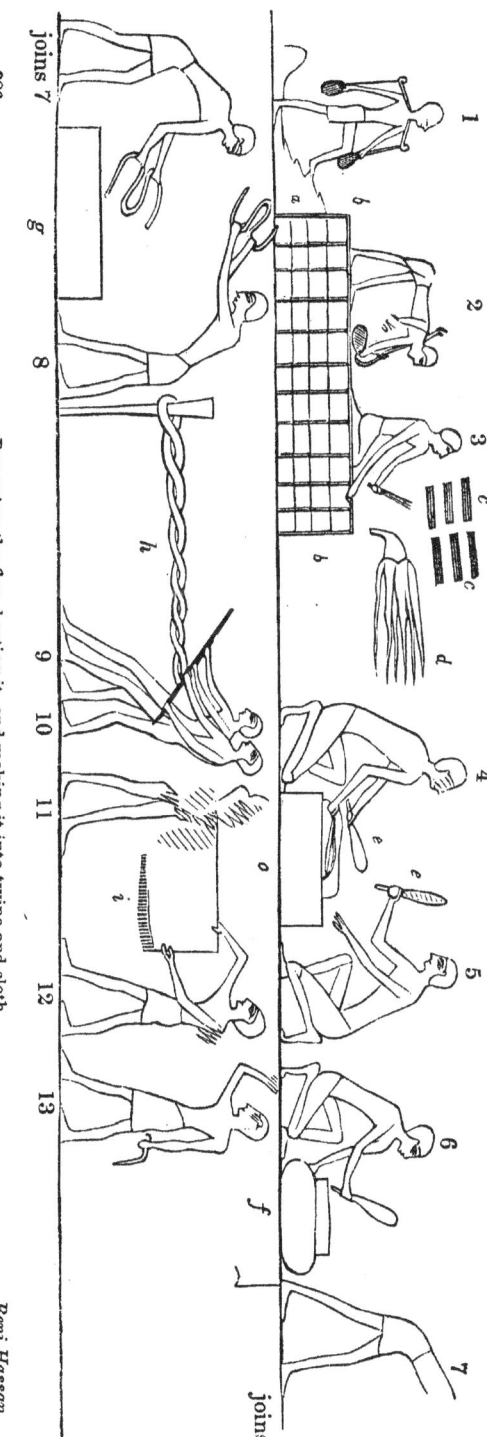

386.   Preparing the flax, beating it, and making it into twine and cloth.   *Beni Hassan.*

Fig. 1 brings water in earthen pots. *a*, steps leading up to the top of the pits. *b b*, where the flax was steeped. *c c*, the flax taken by fig. 3 to dry, previous to beating. *d*, the stalks fresh cut. 4 and 5 are engaged in beating it with mallets, *e e*. 7 and 8, striking it, after it is made into yarn, on a stone, *g*. 9 and 10, twisting the yarn into a rope. 11 and 12 show that a piece of cloth, *i*, has been made of the yarn. 13, a superintendent.

water, according to the state in which they were required; and this is rendered more probable by the flight of steps, for ascending to the top of the raised sides of the pits, which would not have been introduced if the level ground were intended.

The steeping, and the subsequent process of beating the stalks with mallets, illustrate the following passage of Pliny upon the same subject: "The stalks themselves are immersed in water, warmed by the heat of the sun, and are kept down by weights placed upon them; for nothing is lighter than flax. The membrane, or rind, becoming loose is a sign of their being sufficiently macerated. They are then taken out, and repeatedly turned over in the sun, until perfectly dried; and afterwards beaten by mallets on stone slabs. That which is nearest the rind is called *tow*, inferior to the inner fibres, and fit only for the wicks of lamps. It is combed out with iron hooks until all the rind is removed. The inner part is of a whiter and finer quality. Men are not ashamed to prepare it. . . . . After it is made into yarn, it is polished by striking it frequently on a hard stone, moistened with water; and when woven into cloth it is again beaten with clubs, being always improved in proportion as it is beaten."

They also parted and cleansed the fibres of the flax with a sort of comb, probably answering to the iron hooks mentioned by Pliny; two of which, found with some tow at Thebes, are preserved in the Berlin Museum; one having twenty-nine, the other forty-six, teeth. (*Woodcut* 387.)

The border of some of their cloths consists of long fringes, formed by the projecting threads of the warp, twisted together, and tied at the end in one or more knots, to prevent their unravelling, "precisely," as Mr. Thomson observes, "like the silk shawls of the present day;" and specimens of the same borders, in pieces of cloth found in the tombs, may be seen in the British Museum, and other collections.

The sculptures, as well as the cloths which have been discovered, perfectly bear out Herodotus in his statement that they had the custom of leaving a fringe to their pieces of linen, which, when the dresses were made up, formed a border round the legs; but they do not appear to have been universally worn. This

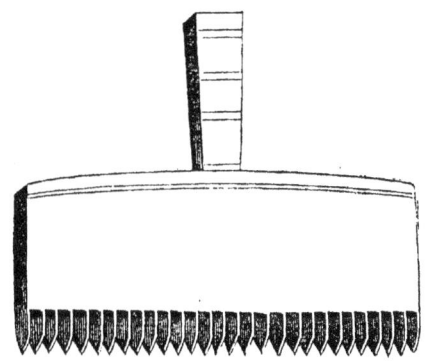

387.   Wooden comb found with some tow.   *Berlin Museum.*

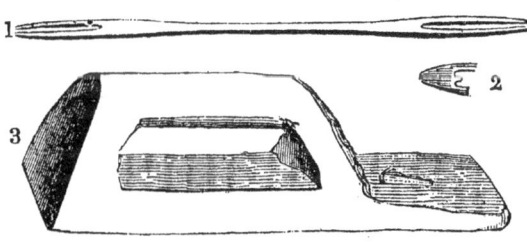

388.   Fig. 1. Netting needle of wood.
       2. Part of another of bronze, of later date, found by me at Berenice.
       3. Wooden plane for smoothing or pressing cloth.   *From Thebes.*

kind of dress he says was called *calasaris*. When the fringe was wanting, the border was hemmed, which had the same effect of preventing the unravelling of the cloth; and a fringe was sometimes sowed on, as in many of our imitation shawls. The Jews wore a similar kind of fringed dress, and Moses commanded the children of Israel to "make them fringes in the borders of their garments . . . and . . . put upon the fringe of the borders a riband of blue." (*Numbers* xv. 38.)

Besides the process of making cloth, that of smoothing, or calendering, is represented in the paintings, which seems to have been done by means of wooden rods, passed to and fro over the surface; but from the appearance of some of the fine linen found in the tombs, we may conjecture that much greater pressure was sometimes used for this purpose, such as could only be applied by a press, or cylinders of metal.

For smoothing linen, a wooden substitute for what we call an *iron* was also used; some of which have been found at Thebes, six inches in length, made of tamarisk wood;* but this belonged chiefly to the washerwomen, who had also a wooden instrument for geoffreying fine linen, by which the waving lines were made, so commonly seen in the dresses of the kings and priests.

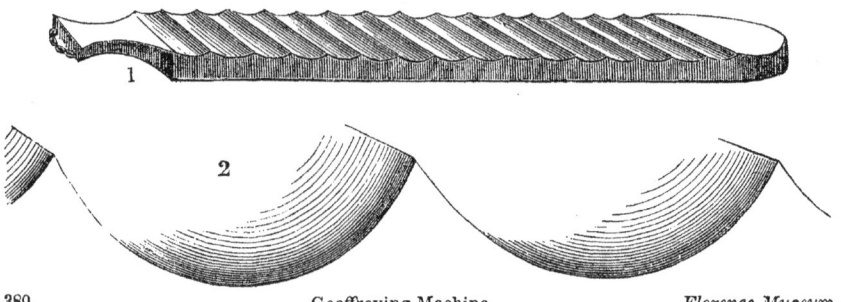

389.   Geoffreying Machine.   *Florence Museum.*

I have already stated that the Egyptians had carpets, which were a very early invention, being mentioned by Homer, who gives them the same name they are still known by, *Tapeta*, whence *tapis* and *tapestry*. They were used in houses, and were even spread for the sacred animals in Egypt. They were of wool, but of their quality we are unable to form any opinion, the fragments discovered in the tombs being very imperfectly preserved, though there is no doubt of their being portions of carpets. A small rug was also brought to England, and is now in the possession of Mr. Hay.

It is eleven inches long by nine broad, and is made like many carpets of the present day, with woollen threads on linen string. In the centre is the figure of a boy in white, with a goose above it, the hieroglyphic of " child," upon a green ground; around which is a border composed of red and blue lines; the remainder is a ground of yellow, with four white figures above and below, and one at each side, with blue outlines and red ornaments; and the outer border is made up of red, white, and blue lines, with a fancy

---

* Woodcut 388, *fig.* 3.

device projecting from it, with a triangular summit, which extends entirely round the edge of the carpet. Its date is uncertain; but from the child, the combination of the colours, and the ornament of the border, I am inclined to think it really Egyptian.

I have noticed the use of flax for making ropes, string, and various kinds of twine; for large ropes, however, of ordinary quality, and for common purposes, the *leef*, or fibres of the date tree, were employed, as at the present day; and many specimens of these durable materials have been found in the excavations of Upper and Lower Egypt.

In a tomb at Thebes, of the time of Thothmes III., is represented the process of twisting thongs of leather, which, as it is probably the same as that adopted in rope-making, may be properly introduced here.

The ends of four thongs were inserted and fastened into a hollow tube, from the side of which a bar projected, surmounted by a heavy metal ball; and the man, who twisted them, held the tube in his right hand, whirling it round, as he walked backwards, by means of the impetus given from the ball. A band, attached to a ring at the other end of the tube, went round his body, in order to support it and give it a free action, and the ring turned upon a nut, to prevent the band itself from twisting.

At the other extremity of the walk, his companion, seated on the ground, or on a low three-legged stool, let out the separate thongs, and kept them from becoming entangled. Behind him sat another, who, with the usual semicircular knife, cut the skin into strips, as he turned it round; showing that what we term "the circular cut" was known to the ancient Egyptians 3300 years ago, and that they had already adopted this mode of obtaining the longest thongs from a single piece of leather. Such, too, was Dido's method, when she persuaded the unsophisticated natives to give up a piece of land as large as she could cover with a bull's hide, upon which she built Byrsa, the citadel of Carthage.

But the name Byrsa, said to be derived from the "hide," seems rather to be related to the fortress itself; being found in the names of Birs-Nimroud, Borsippa, the mounds of Boursa, and other places in the East, where towers, or citadels, once stood.

Part. 1. Cutting and twisting thongs of leather.

a, a skin hanging up in the shop, indicating the trade of leather cutter. *b*, cutting thongs out of a circular piece of skin. *d* arranges the separate thongs, which are twisted by *i*, and when finished are bound together and hung up in the shop, *g h*. *k*, a weight, which gives a greater impetus to the tube, *l*, when thrown round. *m*, cobbler, perforating the sole of a sandal to receive the thong. *n n*, thongs ready for fixing to the sole. *o*, pieces of leather, ready for cutting into soles. *p*, an awl. *q*, a stand.

Part. 2. Carpenters.

r, drills a hole in the seat of a chair, *s*. *t t*, legs of chairs. *u u*, hatchets. *v*, a right angle. *w*, man planing or polishing the leg of a chair.

390.

When finished, the twisted thongs were wound round a hollow centre, through which the end was passed, and repeatedly bound over the concentric coils in the same manner as we tie up ropes.

Some, indeed, have supposed the present subject to represent rope-making; but the presence of the skin on the left, and the shoemakers on the right, forming a continuation of the picture, sufficiently prove that they are engaged in preparing leathern thongs for sandals, and other similar purposes.

Their nets were made of flax-string,* both for fishing and fowling, and portions of them have been discovered at Thebes. The netting needles† were of wood, very like our own, split at each end, and between ten and eleven inches in length, and others were of bronze, with the point closed.

Sieves were often made of string, but some of an inferior quality, and for coarse work, were constructed of small thin rushes or reeds (very similar to those used by the Egyptians for writing, and frequently found in the tablets of the scribes); a specimen of which kind of sieve is in the Paris Museum. The paintings also represent them made of the same materials; and the first they used were evidently of this humble quality, since the hieroglyphic indicating a sieve is borrowed from them. Horse-hair sieves are ascribed by Pliny to the Gauls; the Spaniards, he says, made them of string; and the Egyptians of papyrus-stalks and rushes.

The Egyptians were not less famed for their manufacture of paper, than for the delicate texture of their linen. The plant from which it was made, the *Cyperus papyrus* of modern botanists, mostly grew in Lower Egypt, in marshy land, or in shallow brooks and ponds formed by the inundation of the Nile, where they bestowed much pains on its cultivation.

The right of growing and selling it belonged to the government, who made a great profit by its monopoly; and though we frequently read of the *byblus* or *papyrus* being used for constructing canoes or rude punts, for making baskets, parts of

---

* *Comp.* Isaiah, xvii. 9, " They that work in fine flax, and they that weave networks." Plin. 19, 1, and above, p. 80. † Woodcut 388, *figs.* 1, 2.

sandals, sails, and for numerous other common purposes, it is evident that we are to understand, in these instances, some other species of the numerous family of Cyperus; which is also shown by Strabo's distinguishing the *common* from "the *hieratic* byblus."

The real *papyrus*, or hieratic *byblus*, was particularly cultivated in the Sebennytic nome; other parts of the Delta also produced it, and probably even some districts in Upper Egypt. The paper made from it differed in quality, being dependent upon the growth of the plant, and the part of the stalk whence it was taken; and we find many of the papyri which have been preserved vary greatly in their texture and appearance. They are generally fragile, and difficult to unroll, until rendered pliant by gradual exposure to steam, or the damp of our climates; and some are as brittle as if they had been purposely dried.

We are, however, less surprised at the effect of the parched climate of Upper Egypt, when we consider the length of time they have been kept beyond the reach of moisture; and our drawing paper, after a very few years, becomes so dry in that country, that it is too brittle to fold without breaking. Indeed, those papyri which have not been exposed to the same heat, being preserved in the less arid climate of Lower Egypt, still keep their pliability; and I have a fragment of one from Memphis, which may be bent, and even twisted in any way, without breaking, or without being more injured than a piece of common paper. The hieroglyphics from their style show it to be of an ancient Pharaonic age, and they contain the name of the city where the papyrus was found, " Menofr (or Memphis), the land of the Pyramid."

The mode of making papyri was this: The interior of the stalks of the plant, after the rind had been removed, was cut into thin slices in the direction of their length, and these being laid on a flat board in succession, similar slices were placed over them at right angles; and their surfaces being cemented together by a sort of glue, and subjected to a proper degree of pressure, and well dried, the papyrus was completed. The length of the slices depended, of course, on the breadth of the intended sheet, as that of the sheet on the number of slices placed in succession beside each other, so that though the breadth was limited, the papyrus might be extended to an indefinite length.

The papyrus is now no longer used, paper from linen rags and other materials having superseded it; but some few individuals continue to make it in Sicily as a curiosity; and sheets from the plant, which still grows in the Anapus, near Syracuse, are offered to travellers, as curious specimens of an obsolete manufacture. I have seen many of these small sheets of papyrus; the manner of placing the pieces is the same as that practised in former times; but the quality of the paper is very inferior to that of ancient Egypt, owing either to the preparation of the slices of the stalk, before they are glued together, or to the coarser texture of the plant itself, certain spots occurring here and there throughout the surface, which are never seen on those discovered in the Egyptian tombs. The plant is now unknown in Egypt; and the only streams that produce it are the Anapus in Sicily, and a small one two miles north of Jaffa, where it was found by the Rev. S. Malan.

Pliny thus describes the plant and the mode of making paper: "The papyrus grows in the marsh lands of Egypt, or in the stagnant pools left inland by the Nile, after it has returned to its bed, which have not more than two cubits in depth. The root of the plant is the thickness of a man's arm; it has a triangular stalk, growing no higher than ten cubits (15 feet), and decreasing in breadth towards the summit, which is crowned as with a thyrsus, containing no seeds, and of no use except to deck the statues of the gods. They employ the roots as fire-wood, and for making various utensils. They even construct small boats of the plant; and out of the rind, sails, mats, clothes, bedding, and ropes; they eat it either crude or cooked, swallowing only the juice; and when they manufacture paper from it, they divide the stem, by means of a kind of needle, into thin plates, or laminæ, each of which is as large as the plant will admit. . . . ."

"All the paper is woven upon a table, and is continually moistened with Nile water, which being thick and slimy, furnishes an effectual species of glue. In the first place, they form, upon a table perfectly horizontal, a layer the whole length of the papyrus; which is crossed by another placed transversely, and afterwards inclosed within a press. The different sheets are then hung in a situation exposed to the sun, in order to dry, and the process is finally completed by joining them together, beginning with the best. There are seldom more than twenty slips or stripes produced from one stem of the plant.

"Different kinds of broad paper vary in breadth. The largest, in old times, was the Hieratic, for holy purposes. . . . . The best is now thirteen digits broad; the hieratic two less. . . The Saitic is under nine, being only the breadth of the mallet; and the paper used for business is only six digits broad. Besides the breadth, the fineness, compactness, whiteness, and smoothness are particularly regarded; . . . . when it is coarse it is polished with a (boar's) tooth, or a shell; but then the writing is more readily effaced, as it does not take the ink so well." Some sheets of papyrus, of ancient date, were much broader than any he mentions, thirteen digits or fingers being only about nine inches and two thirds; and the Turin Papyrus of Kings was at least fourteen inches and a half in breadth.

Pliny makes a strange mistake when he supposes that the papyrus was not used for making paper before the time of Alexander the Great, as papyri are of the most remote Pharaonic periods; and the same mode of writing on them is shown from the sculptures to have been common in the age of Suphis, or Cheops, the builder of the Great Pyramid, 2000 years before Alexander's conquest of Egypt.

It is uncertain until what period paper made of the papyrus continued in general use: there are some deeds and other documents in the Vatican of the fifth and sixth centuries, and in the Munich Library of the seventh, in *minuscules;* and there is evidence of its having been occasionally employed, to the end of the seventh century, when it was superseded by parchment. All public documents, under Charlemagne and his dynasty, were written on this last, and the papyrus was then entirely given up.

Parchment, indeed, had been invented long before, and is supposed to have been first used for writing in the year 250 before our era, by Eumenes, king of Pergamus; who, being desirous of collecting a library which should vie with that of Alexandria, and being prevented by the jealousy of the Ptolemies from obtaining a sufficient quantity of papyrus, had recourse to this substitute; and this adoption of it at Pergamus obtained for it the lasting name of Pergamena (*parchment*). It was made of the skins of sheep and of calves; but to the former the name of parchment is more correctly applied, as to the latter that of vellum. The use of parchment, or of prepared skins, for writing upon, was not, however, first suggested at Pergamus; it had been known ages before in Egypt; and "records kept in the temple" are mentioned in the time of the eighteenth dynasty, 1200 years before Eumenes, written upon skins called *Thr*, or *Tahar*—a name which, as Mr. Birch thinks, resembles the Chaldee *Tzar*. Rolls of leather are also found in the tombs, buried with the deceased in lieu of papyri, which are of a very early period, and were adopted in consequence of the high price of the papyrus paper.

The monopoly of the papyrus in Egypt so increased the price of the commodity, that persons in humble life could not afford to purchase it for ordinary purposes; few documents, therefore, are met with written on papyrus, except funereal rituals, the sales of estates, and official papers, which were absolutely required; and so valuable was it, that they frequently obliterated the old writing, and inscribed another document on the same sheet. The same happened afterwards with those on parchment; Cicero mentions *palimpsests* in his time; and one of his own treatises (de Republicâ) was subjected to this treatment.

For common purposes, pieces of broken pottery, stone, board, and leather were used; an order to visit some monument, a soldier's leave of absence, accounts, and various memoranda, were often written on the fragments of an earthenware vase; an artist sketched a picture, which he was about to introduce in a temple or a sepulchre, on a large flat slab of limestone, or on a wooden panel prepared with a thin coating of stucco; and even parts of funereal rituals were inscribed on square pieces of stone, on stuccoed cloth, or on leather. But though a rigid monopoly secured the value of the paper, it did not ensure the employment of the plant in its manufacture; other and better materials were at length discovered for making paper; and the remarkable prophecy of Isaiah (xix. 7) has come to pass, which foretold the papyrus should " be no more" in Egypt; " The paper reeds by the brooks, by the mouth of the brooks, ... shall wither, be driven away, and be no more;" and this Egyptian plant no longer grows in Egypt. Yet its name is destined to survive: the "Bible," or book, is so called from the *byblus*, and its other name, *papyrus*, will be perpetuated in " paper."

It was perhaps the desire to increase its value that caused its disappearance from Egypt, having been rooted out from every spot except where its cultivation was permitted by the government; and Pliny either says "it *only* grew in the nome of Sebennytus;" or that "nothing was grown in that district but the papyrus."

In the infancy of society various materials were employed for writing, as stones, bricks, tiles, plates of bronze, lead, and other metals, wooden tablets, the inner bark (hence *liber*) and leaves of trees, and the shoulder bones of animals. Wooden tablets, covered with wax, were long in use among the Romans, as well as the papyrus; and the inner bark of trees and pieces of linen had been previously adopted by them about B.C. 440.

Many Eastern people still write on the leaves of trees, or on wooden tablets, and *wáraka* continues to signify, in Arabic, both "paper" and a "*leaf*."

The early Arabs committed their poetry and compositions to the shoulder-bones of sheep; they afterwards obtained the papyrus paper from Egypt, on which the poems called *Moallaquât* were written, in gold letters; and after their conquests in Asia and Africa, these people so speedily profited by the inventions of the nations they subdued, that parchment was manufactured in Syria, Arabia, and Egypt, which in colour and delicacy might vie with our modern paper. It speedily superseded the use of the papyrus, and continued to be employed until the discovery of the method of making paper from cotton and silk, called *Carta bombycina*, which is proved by Montfaucon to have been known at least as early as A.D. 1100; and is supposed to have been invented about the beginning of the ninth century. Being introduced into Spain from Syria, it was denominated *Carta Damascena;* and manuscripts on cotton paper are said to exist in the Escurial, written in the eleventh century. There are also some on cotton paper in the Munich library, of the eleventh century; and of linen at the beginning of the fourteenth.

It is a matter of doubt to what nation, and period, the invention of paper manufactured from linen ought to be ascribed. The Chinese were acquainted with the secret of making it from various vegetable substances long before it was known in Europe; the perfection to which they have carried this branch of art continues to excite our admiration; and "the librarian Casiri relates," according to Gibbon, "from credible testimony, that paper was first imported from China to Samarcand A.H. 30 (A.D. 652), and *invented,* or rather introduced, at Mecca A.H. 88 (A.D. 710)."

It may, however, be questioned whether it was made from linen at that early period, and we have no positive proof of linen paper being known even by the Saracens prior to the eleventh century. The Moors, as might be expected, soon introduced it into Spain, and the Escurial library is said to contain manuscripts written on this kind of paper as old as the twelfth century.

But paper of mixed cotton and linen, which was made at the same time, appears to have been in more general use; and linen paper continued to be rare in most European countries till the fifteenth century. That it was known in Germany as early as the year 1312 has been satisfactorily ascertained by existing documents, and a letter on linen paper, written from Germany to Hugh Despencer, about the year 1315, is preserved in the Chapter-house at Westminster; which, even to the water-mark, resembles that made at the present day.

It was not till the close of the sixteenth century that paper was manufactured in England. The first was merely of a coarse brown quality, very similar to that of the modern Arabs, whose skill in this, as in many arts and sciences, has been transferred to people once scarcely known to them, and then greatly their inferiors; and writing or printing paper was not made in London before 1690; France and Holland having, till that time, supplied us with an annual importation, to the amount of nearly 100,000 pounds.

The tanning and preparation of leather was also a branch of art, in which the Egyptians evinced considerable skill; the leather cutters constituted one of the principal subdivisions of the fourth class; and a district of the city was exclusively appropriated to them, in the Libyan part of Thebes, where they were known as "the leather-cutters of the Memnonia."

Leather is little capable of resisting the action of damp, and other causes of destruction, so that we cannot reasonably expect to find much of it in a good state of preservation; but the fine quality of the straps, placed across the bodies of mummies, discovered at Thebes, and the beauty of the figures stamped upon them, satisfactorily prove the skill of "the leather cutters," as well as the antiquity of embossing; and those bearing the names of Sheshonk (Shishak), the contemporary of Solomon, and the other kings of that dynasty, are perfectly preserved.

Many of the occupations of their trade are portrayed on the painted walls of the tombs at Thebes. They made shoes, sandals, the coverings and seats of chairs or sofas, bow-cases, and most of the ornamental furniture of the chariot; harps were also adorned with coloured leather, and shields and numerous other things were covered with skin prepared in various ways. They also made skins for carrying water, wine, and other liquids, coated within with a resinous substance, as is still the custom in Egypt.

Part of the process of curing the skins is introduced in the sculptures; and that of dyeing them is mentioned in the Bible,* being doubtless borrowed by the Jews from Egypt. In one instance, a man is represented dipping the hide into a vase, probably containing water, in which it was suffered to soak, preparatory to the lime being applied to remove the hair; a process very similar to that adopted at the present day in the East.

The Arabs prefer the acrid juice of a plant growing in the desert for the purpose, as its effect is still more rapid, and as it has the advantage of making the skin better and more durable.

* Exod. xxv. 5, "And rams' skins dyed red."

This plant is the Periploca Secamone; its stalks contain a white milky juice, which exudes from it when bruised, and which is so acrid as to be highly injurious to the eye, or to the wounded skin. It supports itself by winding around every neighbouring shrub, and its not ungraceful stalks appear to have been occasionally used by the ancient Egyptians, for the same ornamental purpose as the ivy, the nightshade, and the convolvulus, in forming festoons. But though there is no proof of its having been employed by them in curing skins, it is very probable, as they were so well acquainted with the properties of the plants of the desert and the valley of the Nile; and curriers are represented in the sculptures of Thebes, pounding something in a mortar, which is either the *periploca*, lime, or some other substance required for the purpose.

According to the Arabs, the method of preparing skins with the periploca (their *Ghulga*) is as follows: "The skins are first put into flour and salt for three days, and are cleansed of all the fat and impurities of the inside. The stalks of the plant, being pounded between large stones, are then put into water, which is applied to the inner side of the skin for one day, and the hair having fallen off, the skin is left to dry for two or three days, and the process is completed."

The mode of stretching or bending leather over a form is frequently represented at Thebes; and the semicircular knife, similar to that of our modern curriers, is commonly used by them. The curriers and shoemakers had also a sort of chisel, the common awl (specimens of which have been found at Thebes, similar to our own), a stone for polishing the leather, the cutting table, the bending form, the horn, and a few other utensils; and a prepared skin, the emblem of their trade, was suspended, together with ready-made shoes and other articles, to indicate their skill, and to invite a customer. (*Woodcuts* 333, 390, *and* 392, *part* 1.)

The shops of an Egyptian town were probably similar to those of Cairo and other Eastern cities, which consist of a square room, open in front, with falling or sliding shutters to close it at night; and the goods, ranged on shelves or suspended against the walls, are exposed to the view of those who pass. In front is generally a raised seat, where the owner of the shop and his customers sit during the long process of concluding a bargain previous to the sale and purchase of the smallest article; and here an idle lounger frequently passes whole hours, less intent on benefiting the shopkeeper than in amusing himself with the busy scene of the passing crowd.

Among the many curious customs introduced in the paintings, and still retained in the East, is that of holding a strap of leather, or other substance, with the toes, which, if always free

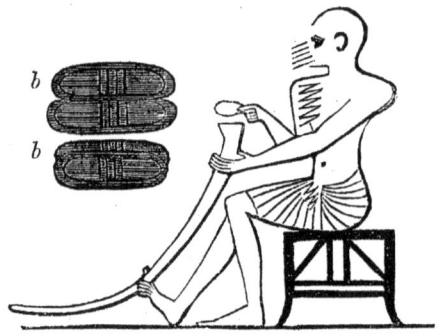

391.   Currier holding a strap of leather with his toes, while cutting it.   *Thebes.*
b b are straps tied up, and deposited in the shop.

and unencumbered with tight shoes, retain their full power and pliability; and the singular, I may say primitive, mode of tightening a thong with the teeth, while sewing a shoe, is also portrayed in the paintings of the same time.

It is probable that, as at the present day, they ate in the open front of their shops, exposed to the view of every one who passed; and to this custom Herodotus may allude, when he says, "the Egyptians eat in the street."

There is no direct evidence that the ancient Egyptians affixed the name and trade of the owner of the shop, though the presence of hieroglyphics, denoting this last, together with the emblem which indicated it, may seem to argue in favour of the custom; and the absence of many individuals' names in the sculptures is readily accounted for by the fact, that these scenes refer to the occupation of the whole trade, and not to any particular person.

Of all people, we may suppose Egyptian shop-keepers most likely to display the patronage received from royalty, the name

SHOPS. LEATHER.

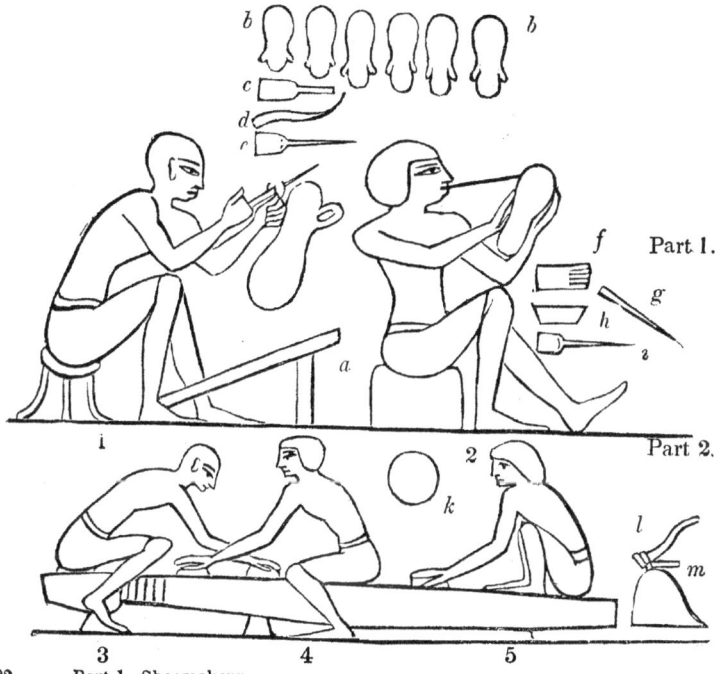

392. Part 1. Shoemakers.
      Part 2. Men employed in polishing a column, probably of wood. *Thebes.*
    Fig. 1. Making a hole with an awl.   2. Tightening a thong with his teeth.
    b b. Sandals hanging up in the shop.   *c* to *i*. Various tools, *l* an adze.

of a monarch being so often introduced in the most conspicuous manner on the coffins of private individuals, and in the paintings of the tombs; many of the scarabæi they wore presenting the name of a king, and the most ordinary devices being formed to resemble a royal oval. But whether or not they had this custom, or that of affixing the name and occupation of the tradesman, it is difficult to determine; and indeed in those cities where certain districts were set apart for particular trades, the latter distinction was evidently uncalled for and superfluous.

The great consumption of leather in Egypt, and the various purposes to which skins, both in the tanned and raw state, were applied, created a demand far greater than could be satisfied by the produce of the country; they, therefore, imported skins from foreign countries, and part of the tribute levied on the conquered tribes of Asia and Africa consisted of hides, and the skins of wild animals, as the leopard, fox, and others; which are frequently represented in the paintings of Thebes, laid before the throne of a Pharaoh, together with gold, silver, ivory, rare woods, and the various productions of each vanquished country.

For tanning they used the pods of the *Sont*, or Acacia (Acacia, or Mimosa, Nilotica), the *acanthus* of Strabo and other writers, which was cultivated in many parts of Egypt, being also prized for its timber, charcoal, and gum; and it is probable that the bark and wood of the Rhus oxyacanthoïdes, and the bark of the Acacia *Seál*, both natives of the desert, were employed for the same purpose.

Many persons, both men and women, were engaged in cleaning cloths and stuffs of various kinds; and the occupations of the fuller form some of the numerous subjects of the sculptures. It is probable that they were only a subdivision of the dyers. In

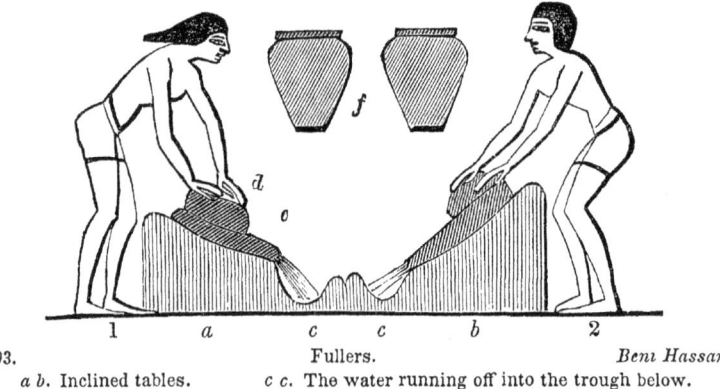

393.   Fullers.   *Beni Hassan.*
a b. Inclined tables.   *c c.* The water running off into the trough below.

early times, before, and even after, the invention of soap, potash, nitre, and several earths, were employed for cleansing cloths, as well as various herbs, many of which are still in use among the Arabs, one of which was doubtless the alkaline plant *boréeth*, mentioned by Jeremiah (ii., 22) and Malachi (iii., 2). Many of the Suædas and Salsolas, and other alkaline plants, are found in the Egyptian deserts, as well as the *gilloo*, also called "the soap plant;" and the people of Cairo and the Barbary coast use certain woods for cleansing manufactured stuffs.

A far more numerous class were the potters; and all the processes of mixing the clay, and of turning, baking, and polishing the vases, are represented in the tombs of Thebes and Beni Hassan.

They frequently kneaded the clay with their feet, and after it had been properly worked up, they formed it into a mass of convenient size with the hand, and placed it on the wheel, which was of very simple construction, and generally turned with the hand. The various forms of the vases were made out by the finger during their revolution; the handles, if they had any, were afterwards affixed to them; and the devices and other ornamental parts were traced with a wooden or metal instrument, previous to their being baked. They were then suffered to dry, and for this purpose were placed on planks of wood; they were afterwards arranged with great care in trays, and carried, by means of the usual yoke, borne on men's shoulders, to the oven.

Many of the vases, bottles, and pans of ordinary quality were very similar to those made in Egypt at the present day, as we see from the representations in the paintings, and from those found in the tombs, or in the ruins of old towns; and judging from the number of Coptic words applied to the different kinds, their names were as varied as their forms. Coptos and its vicinity were always noted for this manufacture; the clays found there were peculiarly suited for porous vases to cool water; and their qualities are fully manifested, at the present day, in the *goolleh* or *bardak* bottles, of the neighbourhood, made at the modern towns of Kéneh and Ballás.

That the forms of the modern *goollehs* are borrowed from those of an ancient time is evident, from the fragments found amidst the mounds of ancient towns and villages, as well as from the many preserved entire; and a local tradition asserts that the modern manufacture is borrowed from, and has succeeded without interruption to, that of former days.

It is impossible to fix the period of the invention of the potter's wheel, and the assertion of Pliny, who attributes it to Corœbus the Athenian, is disproved by the evidence of the Egyptian

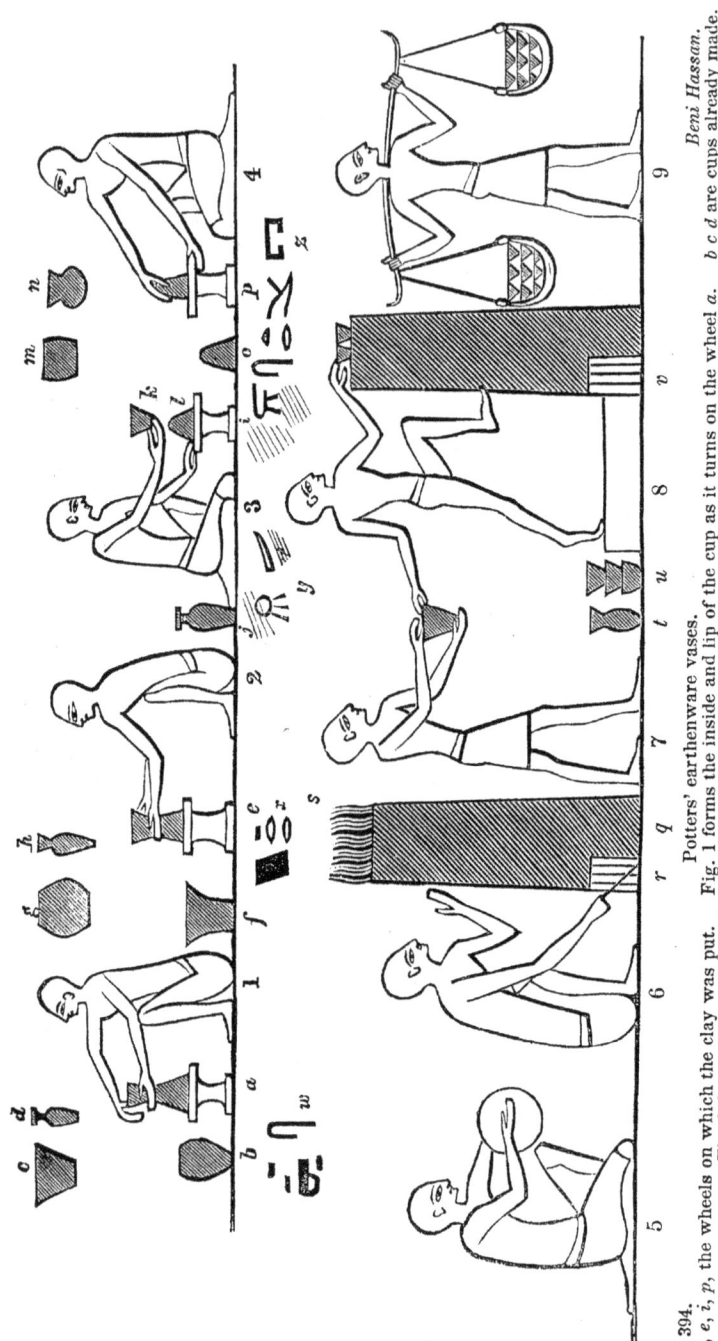

394. *Potters' earthenware vases.* *Beni Hassan.*

a, e, i, p, the wheels on which the clay was put. Fig. 1 forms the inside and lip of the cup as it turns on the wheel a. $b\ c\ d$ are cups already made. Fig. 2 forms the outside of the cup, indenting it with the hand at the base, preparatory to its being taken off. Fig. 3 has just taken off the cup from the clay l. Fig. 4 puts on a fresh piece of clay. Fig. 5 forms a round slab of clay with his two hands. Fig. 6 stirs and prepares the oven q. At s is the fire, which rises through the long narrow tube or chimney of the oven, upon the top of which the cups are placed to bake, as in v. Fig. 7 hands the cup to the baker 8. Fig. 9 carries away the baked cups from the oven.

monuments, which prove it was known previous to the arrival of Joseph, and consequently long before the foundation of Athens.

But Pliny's chapter of inventions abounds with errors of this kind, and serves to show how commonly the Greeks adopted the discoveries of other nations, particularly of Egypt and Phœnicia, and claimed them as their own: even the art of cutting stones is attributed to Cadmus of Thebes; and Thales of Miletus is said to have enlightened the Egyptians, under whom he had long been studying, by teaching them to measure the altitude of a pyramid, or other body, by its shadow, at the late period of 600 B.C. But we cannot suppose that the Greeks taught their instructors a discovery, of which men so skilful in astronomy and mathematics could not have been ignorant; and however superior they afterwards became in all branches of science, they were in their infancy long after the decline of Egypt.

The Egyptians displayed much taste in their gold, silver, porcelain, and glass vases, but when made of earthenware, for ordinary purposes, they were frequently devoid of elegance, and scarcely superior to those of England before the taste of Wedgewood substituted the graceful forms of Greek models for some of the unseemly productions of our old potteries. Though the clay of Upper Egypt was particularly suited to porous bottles, it could not be obtained of a sufficiently fine quality for the manufacture of vases like those of Greece and Italy; in Egypt, too, good taste did not extend to all classes, as in Greece; and vases used for fetching water from a well, or from the Nile, were of a very ordinary kind, far inferior to those carried by the Athenian women to the fountain of Kallirhoë.

The Greeks, it is true, were indebted to Egypt for much useful knowledge, and for many early hints in art, but they speedily surpassed their instructors; and in nothing, perhaps, is this more strikingly manifested than in the productions of the potter.

Carpenters and cabinet-makers were a very numerous class of workmen; and their occupations form one of the most important subjects in the paintings which represent the Egyptian trades.

Egypt produced little wood; and with the exception of the date and *dôm* palms, the sycamore, tamarisk, and acacias, few trees of native growth afforded timber either for building or for ornamental purposes.

The principal uses of the date and *dôm* trees have been already mentioned.*

For coffins, boxes, tables, doors, and other objects, which required large and thick planks, for idols and wooden statues, the sycamore was principally employed; and from the quantity discovered in the tombs alone, it is evident that the tree was cultivated to a great extent. It had the additional recommendation of bearing a fruit, to which the Egyptians were very partial; and a religious prejudice claimed for it, and the Persea, the name and rank of sacred fruit-trees. It is even now looked upon with favour; and when a foreigner is leaving the country, his Egyptian friends ask him if he has ever eaten any sycamore figs, and on his answering in the affirmative, express their delight at the prospect of his return, saying, " whoever has eaten sycamore figs is sure to come back to Egypt."

The tamarisk was preferred for the handles of tools, wooden hoes, and other things requiring a hard and compact wood; and of the acacia were made the planks and masts of boats, the handles of offensive weapons of war, and various articles of furniture. Large groves of this tree were cultivated in many parts of Egypt; especially in the vicinity of Memphis and Abydus; and besides its timber, the acacia was highly valued for the pods it produced, so useful for tanning, and for the gum, which exudes from the trunk and branches, now known under the name of gum Arabic. This tree is not less prized by the modern Egyptians, who have retained its name as well as its uses; *sont* being applied to this species of acacia, both in Arabic and the ancient Egyptian language.

Besides the *Sont*, or Acacia (Mimosa) Nilotica, the *Sellem, Sumr, Tulh, Fitneh, Lebbekh*, and other acacias, which grew in Egypt, were also adapted to various purposes; and some instances are met with of the wood of the *Egleeg*† or Balanites Ægyptiaca, and of different desert trees having been used by the Egyptian carpenters.

* Vol. i. p. 56. † Or *Eqlecq*.

FALSE WOODS.

For ornamental purposes, and sometimes even for coffins, doors, and boxes, foreign woods were employed; deal and cedar were imported from Syria; and part of the contributions exacted from the conquered tribes of Ethiopia and Asia consisted in ebony and other rare woods, which were annually brought by the chiefs, deputed to present their country's tribute to the Egyptian Pharaohs.

Boxes, chairs, tables, sofas, and other pieces of furniture were frequently made of ebony, inlaid with ivory; sycamore and acacia were veneered with thin layers, or ornamented with carved devices, of rare wood, applied, or let into them; and a fondness for this display suggested to the Egyptians the art of painting common boards, to imitate foreign varieties, so generally adopted in other countries at the present day.

The colours were usually applied, on a thin coating of stucco, laid smoothly upon the previously prepared wood, and the various knots and grains, painted upon this ground, indicated the quality of the wood they intended to counterfeit.

The usual tools* of the carpenter were the axe, adze, handsaw, chisels of various kinds (which were struck with a wooden mallet), the drill, and two sorts of planes (one resembling a chisel, the other apparently of stone, acting as a rasp on the surface of the wood, which was afterwards polished by a smooth body, probably also of stone†); and these, with the ruler,‡ plummet, and right angle,§ a leather bag containing nails, the hone, and the horn of oil, constituted the principal, and perhaps the only, implements he used.

Some of the furniture of their rooms, the work of the cabinetmaker, I have already noticed,‖ as well as the perfection to which they had arrived in the construction of the chairs and ottomans of their saloons; nor can I omit the mention of the art of dovetailing, already practised in the earliest Pharaonic ages, or the mode of applying two planks together in the same plane, by means of broad pins, or tongues, of hard wood. Of the former

---

* Woodcut 395. † Woodcuts 89, *fig.* 3, 392. ‡ Woodcut 396, *e.*
§ Woodcut 390, *part* 2, *fig. v*; and 396, *f.*
‖ In vol. i. p. 59 to 72, and 158 to 164.

112 THE ANCIENT EGYPTIANS. Chap. VII.

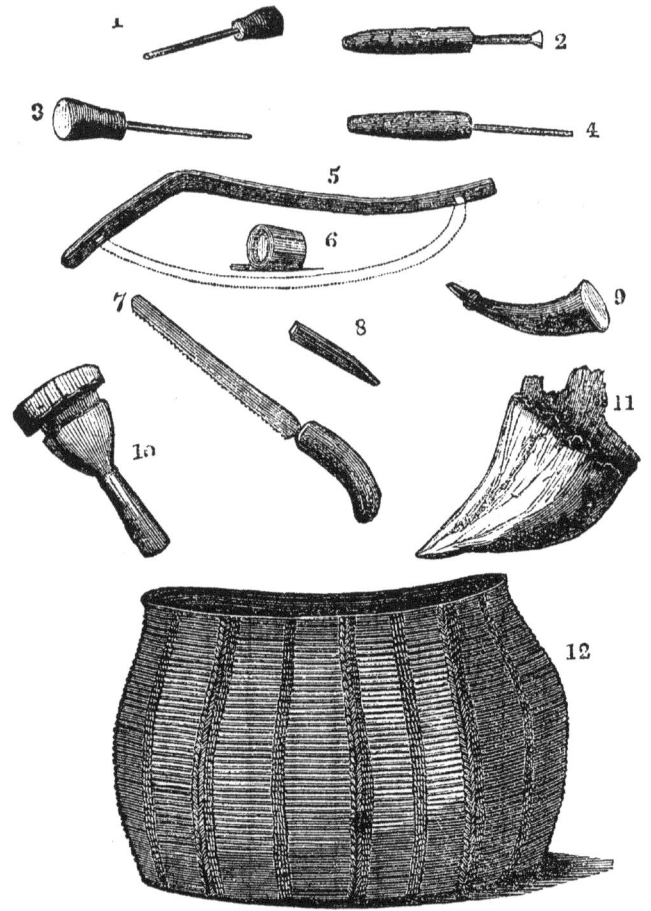

395. *In the British Museum.*
Figs. 1, 2, 3, 4. Chisels and drills.
5. Part of drill.
6. Nut of wood belonging to drill.
7, 8. Saws.
Fig. 9. Horn of oil.
10. Mallet.
11. Bag for nails.
12. Basket which held them.

numerous instances occur, both in large and small objects, and no illustration of it is required; the latter is peculiar, and shows the great care taken to make every thing durable, which characterizes all the works of the Egyptians.

When two boards are joined together by our modern carpenters, they fix small round pins horizontally into corresponding parts of the edges, which are then applied together, so as to form, as it were, a single piece; but the cautious Egyptian carpenter was not content with this; and having used flat pins for the purpose about two inches in breadth, he secured these again, after the boards had been put together, by round pins or wooden nails, driven vertically through the boards into each of the flat pins; and thus the possibility of the joint opening was effectually prevented, even should the glue, which was added as in our modern boxes, fail to hold them.

After the wood had been reduced to a proper size by the saw, the adze was the principal tool employed for fashioning it; and from the precision with which even the smallest objects are worked with it at the present day, by the unskilful carpenters of modern Egypt, we may form some idea of its use in the hands of their expert predecessors.

Many adzes, saws, and chisels have been found at Thebes. The blades are all of bronze, the handles of the acacia or the tamarisk; and the general mode of fastening the blade to the handle appears to have been by thongs of hide. It is probable that some of those discovered in the tombs are only models, or unfinished specimens; and it may have been thought sufficient to show their external appearance, without the necessity of nailing them, beneath the thongs; for those they worked with were bound in the same manner, though I believe them to have been also secured with nails. Some, however, evidently belonged to the individuals in whose tombs they were buried, and appear to have been used; and the chisels often bear signs of having been beaten with the mallet.

The drill is frequently represented in the sculptures. Like all the other tools, it was of the earliest date, and precisely similar to that of modern Egypt, even to the nut of the *dôm** in which it turned, and the form of its bow with a leathern thong.

The chisel was used for the same purposes, and in the same manner, as at the present day, and was struck with a wooden mallet, sometimes flat at the two ends, sometimes of circular or oval form, several of which last have been found at Thebes, and

---

* Wooodcuts 390, *part* 2, *fig. s*, and 395; and vol. i. p. 56.

114 THE ANCIENT EGYPTIANS. Chap. VII.

are in our European museums. The handles of the chisel were of acacia, tamarisk, or other compact wood; the blades of bronze; and the form of the points varied in breadth, according to the work for which they were intended.

The hatchet was principally used by boat-builders, and those who made large pieces of framework; and trees were felled with the same instrument.*

The mode of sawing timber was primitive and imperfect, owing to their not having adopted the double saw; and they were obliged to cut every piece of wood, however large, single-handed. In order, therefore, to divide a beam into planks, they placed it, if not of very great length, upright between two posts, firmly fixed in the ground, and being lashed to them with cords, or secured with pins, it was held as in a vice.†

Among the many occupations of the carpenter, that of veneering is noticed in the sculptures of Thebes as early as the time of the third Thothmes; and the application of a piece of rare wood of a red colour, to a yellow plank of more ordinary kind, is clearly pointed out. And in order to show that the yellow wood is of inferior quality, the workman is represented to have fixed his

---

* Woodcut 363, above in p. 18. † Woodcut 398, *a.*

adze carelessly in a block of the same colour, while engaged in applying them together. Near him are some of his tools, with a box or small chest, made of inlaid and veneered wood, of various hues; and in the same part of the shop are two other men, one employed in grinding something with a stone on a slab, and the other in spreading glue with a brush.

It might be conjectured that paint, or a varnish, were here represented; but the pot on the fire, the piece of glue with its concave fracture, and the workman before mentioned, applying the two pieces of wood together, decide the question, and attest the invention of glue nearly 3300 years ago. This is not, however, the only proof of its use at an early period, and several wooden boxes and coffins have been found, in which glue was employed to fasten the joints. It appears sometimes to be a fish glue.

Various boxes, shrines, articles of furniture, and other works of the cabinet-maker are frequently introduced in the paintings of Thebes, many of which present not inelegant forms, and are beautifully made. Several of the smaller objects, as boxes for trinkets and ointment, wooden spoons, and the like, have been mentioned among the furniture of their rooms; where I have also described a curious substitute for a hinge, in some of those discovered at Thebes.*

Many boxes had lids resembling the curved summit of a royal canopy,† and were ornamented with the usual cornice;‡ others had a simple flat cover; and some few a pointed summit, resembling the shelving roof of a house.§ This last kind of lid was divided into two parts, one of which alone opened, turning on two small pins at the base, on the principle of the doors of their houses and temples; and when necessary, the two knobs at the top‖ could be tied together and sealed.¶

When not veneered, or inlaid with rare wood, the sides and lid were painted, and those intended for the tombs, to be deposited there in honour of the deceased, had usually funereal

---

* In chap. iii. p. 158 to 164. † Woodcut 397, *figs.* 1, 2, 3, 6.
‡ *Fig.* 1. § *Figs.* 4, 5, 8.
‖ *Fig.* 4. ¶ *See* vol. i. p. 163.

116 THE ANCIENT EGYPTIANS. Chap. VII.

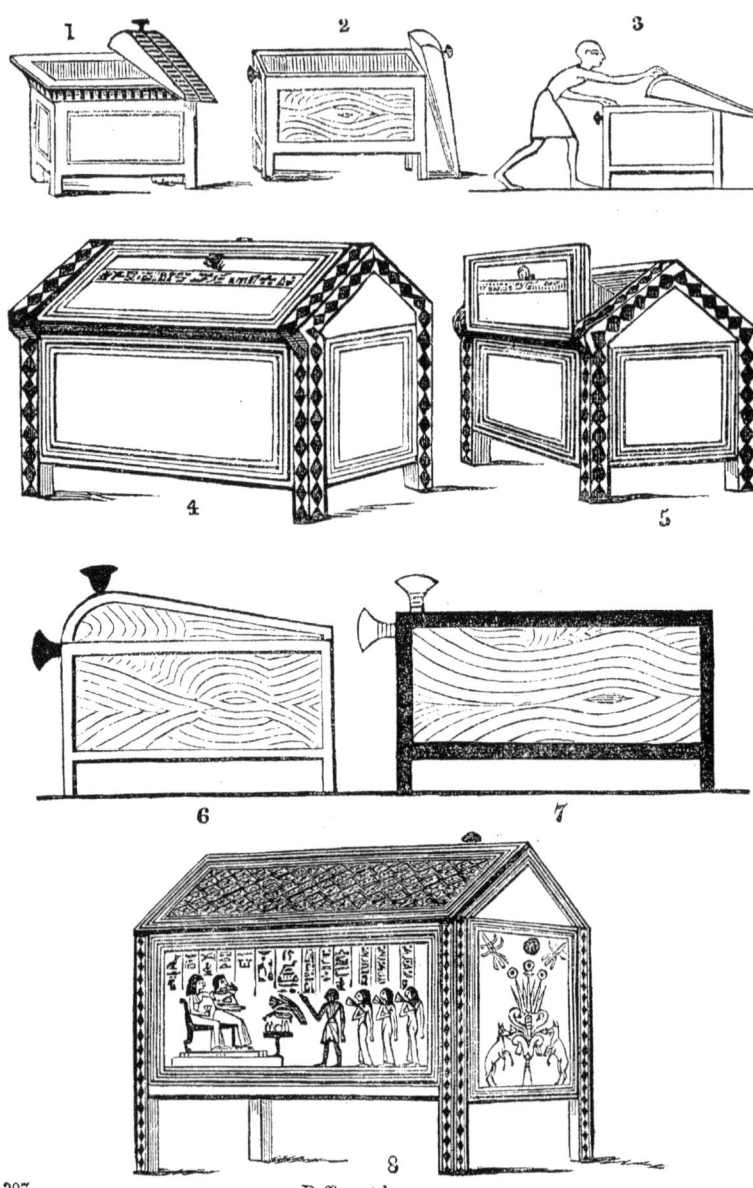

397. Different boxes.

Figs 1 and 2. Mode of placing the lid when the box was opened.
    3. Man opening a box, from a painting at Thebes.
    4 and 5. A painted box, showing how the lid opened.
    6 and 7. Boxes from the paintings of Thebes.
    8. Another painted box with a shelving lid, from Thebes, now at Alnwick Castle.

inscriptions, or religious subjects painted upon them, among which were offerings presented by members of their family.*

Several boxes have been found at Thebes; and in the British Museum is one remarkable for the brilliancy of the colours given to the ivory with which it is inlaid. The box is of ebony; the ivory, painted red and blue, is let into the sides and edges, and the lid is ornamented in the same manner. There is in this a substitute for a hinge, similar to the one before mentioned, except that here the back of the cross-bar, cut to a sharp edge along its whole extent, fits into a corresponding groove at the end of the box; and the two knobs are fixed in their usual place at the top and front.

The lids of many boxes were made to slide in a groove, like our small colour boxes;† others are fitted into the body, being cut away at the edges for this purpose; and some turned on a pin at the back, as I have shown in the long-handled boxes before mentioned.‡

In opening a large box they frequently pushed back the lid, and then either turned it sideways§ and left it standing across the breadth of the box, or suffered it to go to the ground; but in those of still larger dimensions, it was removed altogether and laid upon the floor. Others with a pointed top had a projection under what may be called the end, or corbel of the gables, on the side that opened, in order that the lid might fall down and lie out of the way, close to the side of the box, while the things were taken out of it.‖

With the carpenters may be mentioned the wheelwrights, the makers of coffins, and the coopers, and this subdivision of one class of artisans shows that they had systematically adopted the partition of labour.

The makers of chariots and travelling carriages were of the same class; but both carpenters and workers in leather were employed in their manufacture;¶ and chariots either passed through

---

* *Figs.* 4 and 8.
‡ Woodcuts 174, 175, and 178.
‖ Woodcut 397, *figs.* 4, 5.
† Woodcut 184, p. 163, vol. i.
§ Woodcut 397, *figs.* 1, 2, 3.
¶ Vol. i. p. 377

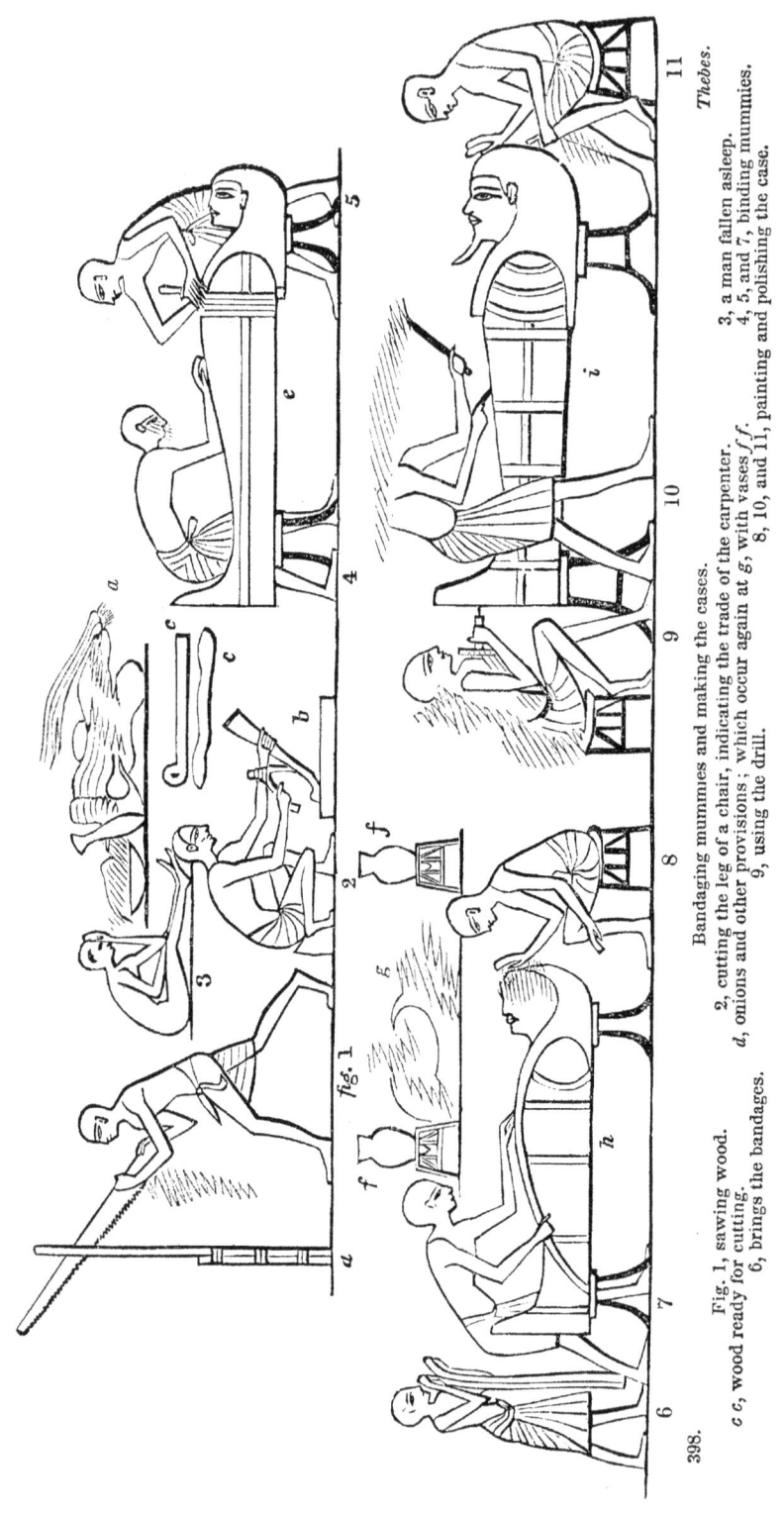

398. Bandaging mummies and making the cases. *Thebes.*

Fig. 1, sawing wood. 2, cutting the leg of a chair, indicating the trade of the carpenter. 3, a man fallen asleep. *c c*, wood ready for cutting. *d*, onions and other provisions; which occur again at *g*, with vases *f f*. 4, 5, and 7, binding mummies. 6, brings the bandages. 9, using the drill. 8, 10, and 11, painting and polishing the case.

the hands of both, or, which is more probable, chariot makers constituted a distinct trade.

Palanquins, canopies, and other wooden chests for travelling and religious purposes, were the work of cabinet makers or carpenters; but the makers of coffins were distinct from both of these. The undertakers, properly so called, were also a different class of people from these last, being attached to and even forming part of the sacerdotal order, though of an inferior grade. Indeed the ceremonies of the dead were so numerous, and so many persons were engaged in performing the several duties connected with them, that no particular class of people can be said to have had the sole direction in these matters; and we find that the highest orders of priests officiated in some, and in others those of a very subordinate station. Thus the embalmers were held in the highest consideration, while those who cut open the body, when the intestines were removed, are said to have been treated with ignominy and contempt. Those who swathed the body in bandages were called *Colchitæ* by the Greeks.

As in other trades, that of making coffins, or mummy cases, was a separate and distinct occupation, and it combined the work of the carpenter, the painter, and some others; while at the same time the coffin-maker included in his labours the manufacture of boxes, wooden figures, and other objects connected with funerals.

The boat-builders may be divided into two separate and distinct trades, one of which formed a subdivision of the carpenters; the other of the basket-makers, or the weavers of rushes and osiers, another very numerous branch.

The boats made by these last were a sort of canoe, or punt, used for fishing, and consisted merely of water plants or osiers, bound together with bands made of the stalks of the *common* papyrus. They were very light, and some so small that they could easily be carried from one place to another; and the Ethiopian boats, mentioned by Pliny, which were taken out of the water, and carried on men's shoulders past the rapids of the cataracts, were probably of a similar kind; though Strabo describes the boats at the cataracts of Syene passing the falls in perfect security, and exciting the surprise of the beholders, before whom the boatmen delighted in displaying their skill. These too are said by Celsius to have been made of the papyrus.

Papyrus boats are frequently noticed by ancient writers. Plutarch describes Isis going in search of the body of Osiris "through the fenny country in a bark made of the papyrus, whence it is supposed that persons using boats of this description are never attacked by crocodiles, out of fear and respect to the goddess;" and Moses is said to have been exposed in "an ark (or boat) of bulrushes, daubed with slime and with pitch." From this last we derive additional proof that the body of such boats was composed of rushes, which were bound together with the papyrus; and the mode of rendering them impervious to water is satisfactorily pointed out by the coating of pitch with which they were covered. Nor can there be any doubt that pitch was known in Egypt at that time, since we find it on objects which have been preserved of the same early date; and the Hebrew word *zift* is precisely the same as that used for "pitch" by the Arabs to the present day. It was also applied by the ancient Egyptians to "bitumen."

Pliny mentions boats "woven of the papyrus," the rind being made into sails, curtains, matting, ropes, and even into cloth; and observes elsewhere that the papyrus, the rush, and the reed, were all used for making boats in Egypt.

"Vessels of bulrushes" are again mentioned in Isaiah: Lucan alludes to the mode of binding or sewing them with bands of papyrus; and Theophrastus notices boats made of the papyrus,

Making a papyrus boat.   *Tomb at the Pyramids.*

and sails and ropes of the rind of the same plant. That small boats were made of these materials is certain; and the sculptures of Thebes, Memphis, and other places, abundantly show that they were employed as punts, or canoes, for fishing in all parts of Egypt during the inundation of the Nile, particularly in the lakes and canals of the Delta. And the "Memphite bark bound together with the papyrus," that Lucan describes, is figured in the Memphite sculptures, as well as on the monuments of Upper Egypt.

There was another kind, in one of which Strabo crossed the Nile to the island of Philæ, "made of thongs so as to resemble wicker-work;" but it does not appear from his account whether it was formed of reeds bound together with thongs, or was like those made in Armenia, and used for going down the river to Babylon, which Herodotus describes, of osiers covered with hides (like British coracles), and which are represented on the Nimroud marbles. Strabo also mentions another, used on the canals during the inundation, of still more simple construction, in which, if we might substitute, what is probable, earthenware bottles or gourds for shells, we should recognise a modern Egyptian custom.

The Armenian boats were merely employed for transporting goods down the current of the Euphrates, and on reaching Babylon were broken up, the hides being put upon the asses which had been taken on board for this purpose, and the traders returning home by land. "They were round, in the form of a shield, without either head or stern, the hollow part of the centre being filled with straw." "Some were large, others small, and the largest were capable of bearing 5000 talents weight." They were, therefore, very different from the boats reported by the same historian to have been made in Egypt for transporting goods up the Nile, which he describes as being built in the form of ordinary boats, with a keel and a mast and sails.

"The Egyptian boats of burthen," he says, "are made of a thorn wood, very similar to the lotus of Cyrene, from which a tear exudes, called gum. Of this tree they cut planks measuring about two cubits, and having arranged them like bricks, they build the boat in the following manner: They fasten the planks round firm long pegs, and, after this, stretch over the surface a series of girths, but without any ribs; and the whole is bound within by bands of papyrus. A single rudder is then put through the keel, and a mast of thorn-wood, and sails of the papyrus (rind), complete the rigging. These boats can only ascend the stream with a strong wind, unless they are towed by ropes from the shore; and, when coming down the river, they are provided with a hurdle made of tamarisk, sewed together with reeds, and a stone about two talents weight, with a hole in the centre. The hurdle is fastened to the head of the boat, and allowed to float on the water: the stone is attached to the stern, so that the former, carried down the river by the rapidity of the stream, draws after it the *baris* (for such is the name of these vessels), and the latter, dragged behind, and sinking into the water, serves to direct its course. They have many of these boats, some of which carry several thousand talents weight."

That boats of the peculiar construction he here describes were really used in Egypt is very probable; they may have been employed to carry goods from one town to another, and navigated in the manner he mentions; but we may be allowed to doubt their carrying several thousand talents, or many tons, weight; and we have the evidence of the paintings of Upper and Lower Egypt to show that the large boats of burthen were made of wooden planks, which men are seen cutting with saws and hatchets, and afterwards fastening together with nails and pins; and they were furnished with spacious cabins like those of modern Egypt. Those with planks, put together in the form of bricks, are also represented in the time of the 12th dynasty; but the use of the mallet and chisel, and the pins hammered into the holes to fasten the planks, show that they were not dependent on papyrus bands for their security; their construction was very like that of the modern Egyptian boats; and Herodotus has confounded the papyrus punt with the boat of burthen.

Pliny even goes farther than Herodotus, and speaks of papyrus vessels crossing the sea, and visiting the Isle of Taprobane* (Ceylon), which would throw the Chinese junk of modern days very far into the shade.

* Plin vi. 22.

But though punts and canoes of osiers, papyrus, or reeds, may have been used on some occasions, as they still are, on the Nile and the lakes of Egypt, we know that the Egyptians had strong and well-built vessels for the purposes of trade by sea, and for carrying merchandise, corn, and other heavy commodities on the Nile; and that, even if they had been very bold and skilful navigators, they would not have ventured to India, nor have defeated the fleets of Phœnicia, in their "paper vessels."

The sails, when made of the rind of the papyrus, were similar to those of the Chinese, which fold up like our Venetian blinds; but there is only one boat represented in the paintings, which appears to have sails of this kind, though so many are introduced there. It is of very early date; and we cannot readily believe that a people, noted for their manufactures of linen and other cloths, would have preferred so imperfect a substitute as the rind of a plant, especially as they exported sail-cloth to Phœnicia for that very purpose.*

The construction of the various boats used on the Nile varied, according to the purposes for which they were intended. The punts or canoes being either pushed with a pole, or propelled with a paddle,† had no mast, nor even rudder; and many of the small boats, intended merely for rowing, were unprovided with a mast or sails. They were also without the raised cabin, common in large sailing boats, and the rowers appear to have been seated on the flat deck, which covered the interior from the head to the stern, pushing instead of pulling the oars, contrary to the usual custom in boats of larger dimensions. The absence of a mast did not altogether depend on the size of the boat, since those belonging to fishermen, which were very small, were often furnished with a sail, besides three or four oars;‡ and some large boats, intended for carrying cattle and heavy goods, were sometimes without a mast.

In going up the Nile, they used the sail, whenever the wind

* Ezekiel xxvii. 7, In the lamentation of Tyre, " Fine linen, with broidered work from Egypt, was that which thou spreadest forth to be thy sail."
† *See* Contest of boatmen, woodcut 228, *fig.* 1.
‡ *See* Fishing scene, woodcut 420, part 1 *a*, in Chapter VIII.

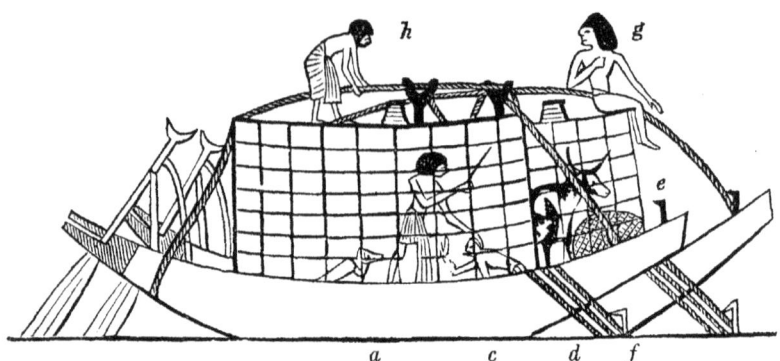

400. Boats for carrying cattle and goods on the Nile. *Thebes.*

a b, two boats, fastened to the bank by the ropes and pegs *f f*; in the cabin of one a man inflicts the bastinado on a boatman. He is one of the stewards of the estate, and is accompanied by his dog. In the other boat is a cow, and a net of hay or chopped straw (*e*), precisely the same as the *shenfeh* now used in Egypt.

was favourable; occasionally rowing, in those parts where the windings of the river brought it too much upon the bows; for it is probable that, like the modern Egyptians, they did not tack; and when the wind was contrary, or during a calm, they generally employed the tow-line, which was pulled by men on shore.

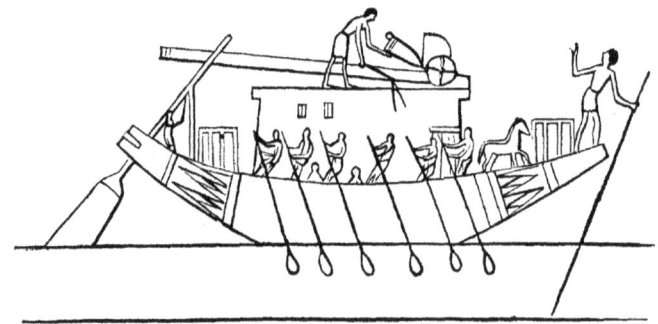

401. A boat with the mast and sail taken down, having a chariot and horses on board.
Eileithyias.

After they had reached the southernmost point of their journey up the stream, the sail was no longer considered necessary; and the mast and yards being taken down, were laid over the top of the cabin, or on a short, temporary mast, with a forked summit; precisely in the same way as at the present day, on board the *cangias*, and other masted rowing boats of Egypt. For as the wind generally blows from the N.W., it seldom happens that the sail can be used in going down the Nile, and in a strong wind the masts and rigging are so great an incumbrance, that the boat is unable to make much way against it with oars.

The heavy boats of burden, which from their great size cannot be propelled by oars, are suffered to retain their masts and sails, and float down the river sideways at the rate of the stream, advantage being taken of the wind whenever the bends of the river permit; and the large *germs*, used for carrying corn during the inundation, are only employed when the water is very deep, and are laid up the rest of the year, and covered with matting from the sun. These, therefore, form exceptions to the ordinary boats of the Nile, and may be considered similar to some represented in the sculptures of Tel el Amarna, which are fastened to the shore by several large ropes, and are shown, from the size of their cabins, the large awning in front for covering the goods they carried, and the absence of oars, to have been of unusual dimensions.

In the one given in the preceding wood-cut, from a tomb at Eileithyias, the size of the cabin, the horses taken on board with the chariot, and its height out of water, show that the common travelling boat was large and commodious; and we see that the cabin, as usual, was in the centre, with room enough on each side for the rowers to sit between it and the gunwale.

Large boats had generally one, small pleasure-boats two rudders at the stern. The former traversed upon a beam, between two projecting heads, a short pillar or mast supporting it, and acting as the centre on which it moved; the latter were nearly the same in principle, except that they turned on a bar, or in a ring, by which they were suspended to the gunwale at either side; and in both instances the steersman directed them by means of a rope fastened to the upper extremity. The rudders consisted of a long broad blade and still longer handle; evidently made in imitation of the oars, by which they originally steered their boats, before they had so far improved them as to adopt a fixed rudder; and in order to facilitate its motion upon the mast or pillar, and to avoid the friction of the wood, a piece of bull's hide was introduced, as is the custom in the modern boats, between the mast and yard.

The oar was a long round wooden shaft, to which a flat board, either oval, circular, or of diamond shape, was fastened; the same as still used on the Ganges, and in the Arabian Gulf. It turned either on a toll-pin, or in a ring, fastened to the gunwale of the boat; and the rowers sat on the deck, on benches, or on low seats, or stood or knelt to the oar, sometimes pushing it forwards, sometimes, and indeed more generally, pulling it, as is the modern custom in Egypt, and most other countries.

At the head of the boat a man usually stood, with a long pole in his hand, to sound every now and then, and prevent its running upon any of the numerous sandbanks in the river (which, from their often changing at the time of the inundation, are not always known to the most skilful pilot); a precaution adopted not always in time by the modern boatmen of the Nile.

That the ancient Egyptian boats were built with ribs, like those of the present day, is sufficiently proved by the rude models discovered in the tombs of Thebes. It is probable that they had very little keel, in order to enable them to avoid the sand-banks, and to facilitate their removal from them when they struck; and, indeed, if we may judge from the models, they appear to have been flat-bottomed. The boats now used on the Nile have a very small keel, particularly at the centre, where it is concave; so that when the head strikes, they put to the helm, and the hollow part clears the bank: except in those cases where the impetus is too great, or the first warning is neglected.

The sails of the ancient boats appear to have been always square, with one yard above; and none below in those of the oldest construction; this last having been introduced when they abandoned the double mast of early times. The square sail is still retained in Ethiopia, where it is furled by forcibly rolling up the lower yard in the sail; but in Egypt the only modern boats with square sails are a sort of lighter, employed for conveying stones from the quarries to Cairo and other places; and these have only a yard at the top. All other boats have *latine* or triangular-shaped sails, which, in order to catch the wind when the

Nile is low, are made of immense size : for, unless they reach above its lofty banks, they are often prevented from benefiting by a side wind at that season of the year; but the number of accidents which occur are a great objection to the use of such disproportionate sails.

The cabins of the Egyptian pleasure-boats were lofty and spacious; but even in the smallest they did not extend over the whole breadth of the boat, as they do in the modern cangias, and merely occupied the centre; the rowers sitting on either side, generally on a bench or stool. They were made of wood, with a door in front, or sometimes on one side, and they were painted within and without with numerous devices, in brilliant and lively colours. The same custom continued to the latest times, long after the conquest of the country by the Romans; and when the Arabs invaded Egypt in 638, under Amer, the general of the Caliph Omer, one of the objects which struck them with surprise was the gay appearance of the painted boats of the Nile.

The lotus was one of their favourite devices, as on their furniture, the ceilings of rooms, and other places, and it was very common on the blade of the rudder, where it was frequently repeated at both ends, together with the eye of Osiris. But the place considered peculiarly suited to the latter emblem was the bow of the boat; and the custom is still retained in some countries to the present day. In India and China it is very general; and we even see the small barks that ply in the harbour of Malta bearing the eye on their bows, in the same manner as the boats of ancient Egypt. The Egyptians, however, appear to have confined it to boats used in the funeral ceremonies.

Streamers were occasionally attached to the pole of the rudder, and a standard was erected near the head of the vessel; the latter generally a sacred animal, a sphinx, or some emblem connected with religion or royalty, like those belonging to the infantry; and sometimes the top of the mast bore a shrine, or feathers, the symbol of the deity to whose protection they committed themselves during their voyage.

There is a striking resemblance, in some points, between the boats of the ancient Egyptians and those of India; and the form of the stern, the principle and construction of the rudder, the cabins, the square sail, the copper eye on each side of the head, the line of small squares at the side, like false windows,* and the shape of the oars of boats used on the Ganges, forcibly call to mind those of the Nile, represented in the paintings of the Theban tombs.

The head and stern of the Egyptian pleasure-boats were usually ornamented with, or terminated in the shape of, a flower richly painted; in the boats of burden they were destitute of ornament, and simply rounded off; and I have met with two only in which there was any resemblance to a beak. But this was in Nile boats, and is a mode of construction common in those of the present day. Nor are the ships of war, represented at Medeenet Haboo, furnished with beaks.

At the head, a forecastle frequently projected above the deck, in which the man who held the fathoming pole sometimes stood, and which answered as a small lock-up box, like the *hôn* of modern Nile boats; and occasionally there was at the

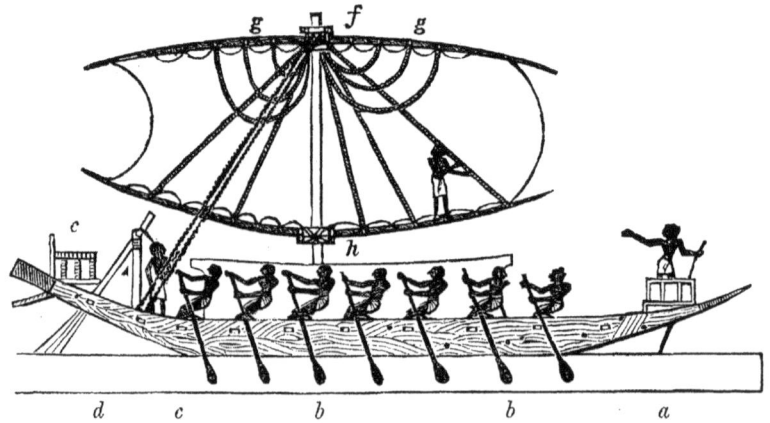

402. Boat of the Nile; showing how the sail was fastened to the yards, and the nature of the rigging. *Thebes.*

stern another of similar form, where the steersman sat.† They were both very generally adopted in the war galleys,‡ where they were found of great service: the archers profiting by these

* Woodcut 402. † Woodcut 402, *a* and *c*. ‡ Woodcut 351, vol. i. p. 412.

commanding positions to rake the enemy's decks, as they bore down upon a hostile galley.

There are no instances of boats with a rudder at both ends, said to have been used by some ancient nations; nor have any more than one mast and a single sail. Sometimes the rudder, instead of traversing in a groove, merely rested on the taffrel, and was suspended and secured by a rope, or band; but that imperfect method was confined to boats used in religious ceremonies on the Nile. The mallet and pegs for fastening the boat to the bank were kept in a particular place in the bows, as well as the landing plank, which was always in readiness, and under the surveillance of the man at the prow.

In some boats of burden, the cabin, or raised magazine, was very large, being used for carrying cattle, horses, and numerous stores; and it was sometimes made of open framework. As they often quitted these boats to fetch other cattle, or to put them ashore, a boy was left on board to take charge of the stores; but this was not the only precaution: a dog was also kept tied up in the magazine; and its utility was often shown when the idle boy either wandered away during the absence of his masters, or fell asleep; for either of which delinquencies he was, if found out, liberally treated to the stick.* Both the sleeping underling and the bastinado are common representations in the paintings.

Unlike the modern Egyptians, they paid great attention to the cleanliness of their boats, the cabins and decks being frequently washed and swept; and this the Theban artists thought of sufficient importance to be indicated in the sculptures.

Herodotus states that the mast was made of the acanthus (Acacia, or Mimosa, Nilotica); but the trunk and limbs of this tree are not sufficiently long or straight; and for that purpose they doubtless preferred the fir, with which they were well acquainted, great quantity of the wood being annually imported into Egypt from Syria. The planks, the ribs, and the keel were of the acacia, which, from its resisting the effect of water for a length of time, was found well adapted for this purpose, as is

* Woodcut 400.

fully proved by modern experience. The foot of the mast was let into a strong beam, which crossed the whole breadth of the boat; it was supported by and lashed to a knee, rising to a considerable height before it; and the many stout stays, fastened at the head, stern, and sides, sufficiently secured it, and compensated for the great pressure of the heavy yards and sail it carried. The sheets, halliards, and standing rigging, were all fastened "*within*" the gunwale, as at the present day, and the monuments confirm the statement of Herodotus respecting this peculiarity of the Egyptian boats.

In ships of war, the yard was allowed to remain aloft after the sail had been reefed; but in the boats of the Nile, which had a yard at the top and bottom of the sail, as soon as it was furled, they lowered the upper yard, and in this position it remained until they again prepared for their departure. To loosen the sail from the lower yard must have been a tedious operation, if it was bound to it with the many lacings represented in some of the paintings; but in these cases it may have been folded up between the two yards, as soon as the upper one was lowered, the whole being lashed together by an outer rope.

It is uncertain whether they used blocks or pulleys for raising and lowering the yards, or if the halliards merely passed through a smooth dead-sheave-hole near the top of the mast. The yards were evidently of very great size, and of two separate pieces, scarfed or joined together at the middle,[*] sometimes supported by five or six lifts, and so firmly secured that men could stand or sit upon them, while engaged in arranging the sail; and from the upper yards were suspended several ropes, resembling the *horses* of our square-rigged ships,[†] and perhaps intended for the same purpose when they furled the sail. They had also braces and sheets to the upper and lower yards, for trimming the sails; and each yard had its own halliards. Nor were the Egyptians ignorant of the pulley; and one has actually been found in Egypt, which is now in the museum of Leyden. It was apparently intended for drawing water from a well. The sides

---

[*] Woodcut 402 *h*.   [†] Woodcut 402 *gg*.

are of tamarisk wood, the roller of fir; and the rope, of *leef* or fibres of the date-tree, which belonged to it, was found at the same time. But it is uncertain whether they introduced the pulley into the rigging of their boats.

Many of the sails were painted with rich colours, or embroidered with fanciful devices, representing the emblem of the soul of the king, flowers, and various patterns; some were adorned with cheques, and others were merely striped, like those of the present day. This kind of cloth, of embroidered linen, appears to have been made in Egypt expressly for sails, and was bought by the Tyrians for that purpose; but its use was confined to the pleasure-boats of the grandees, or of the king himself, ordinary sails being white; and the ship in which Antony and Cleopatra went to the battle of Actium was distinguished from the rest of the fleet by its purple sails, which were the peculiar privilege of the admiral's vessel. The sail of the large ship of Ptolemy Philopater, mentioned by Atticus, was, in like manner, of fine linen, ornamented with a purple border. Nor was this custom of late introduction; and the most highly decorated sails are those represented in the tomb of the third Remeses, at Thebes.*

The devices, painted or embroidered upon them, depended on fancy, and the same monarch had ships with sails of different patterns; but the boats used in sacred festivals upon the Nile were probably decorated with appropriate symbols, according to the nature of the ceremony, or the deity in whose service they were engaged. The edges of the sails were furnished with a strong hem or border, also neatly coloured, serving to strengthen it, and prevent an injury, and a light rope was generally sewed round it for the same purpose.

Some of the Egyptian vessels were of very great size. Diodorus mentions one of cedar wood, dedicated by Sesostris to the god of Thebes, 280 cubits, or 420 feet long; another, built in much later times by Caligula in Egypt, to transport one of the obelisks to Rome, carried 120,000 pecks of lentils as ballast; and Ptolemy Philopater built one of forty banks of oars, which was 280 cubits (about 420 feet) long, and 48 (about 72 feet) in

* " See woodcut at the end of this chapter."

height, or 53 (80 feet) from the keel to the top of the poop, with a crew of 400 sailors, besides 4000 rowers, and near 3000 soldiers. Philopater had another he used on the Nile, upwards of 300 feet in length, and 30 cubits (45 feet) in breadth, and nearly 40 (60 feet) high; and Ptolemy Philadelphus had two of 30 banks, one of 20, four of 14, two of 12, fourteen of 11, thirty of 9, thirty-seven of 7, five of 6, seventeen of 5, and more than twice that number of 4 and 3 banks, with others of smaller size.

Of the origin of navigation no satisfactory conjecture can be offered, nor do we know to what nation to ascribe the merit of having conferred so important a benefit on mankind.

It is evident that the first steps were slow and gradual, and that the earliest attempts to construct vessels on the sea were rude and imperfect.

Ships of burden were originally mere rafts, made of the trunks of trees bound together, over which planks were fastened; which Pliny states to have been first used on the Red Sea; but he is wrong in limiting the era of ship-building to the age of Danaus, and in supposing that rafts alone were employed until that period. Rafts were adopted, even to carry goods, long after the invention of ships, as they still are for some purposes on rivers and other inland waters; but boats, made of hollow trees and various materials, covered with hides or pitch, were also of very early date, and to these may be ascribed the origin of planked vessels. Improvement followed improvement, and in proportion as civilization advanced, the inventive genius of man was called forth to push on an invention, so essential to those communities, where the advantages of commerce were understood; and numerous causes contributed to the origin of navigation, and the construction of vessels for traversing the sea.

Whatever may have been the date of those expeditions which colonized various parts of Greece and other countries, the people to whom the art of navigation was most indebted, who excelled all others in nautical skill, and who carried the spirit of adventure far beyond any nation of antiquity, were the Phœnicians, and these bold navigators even visited the coast of Britain in quest of tin.

The fleets of Sesostris, Amosis, and the Remeses, certainly date at a very remote age, and some Phœnician sailors, sent by Neco on a voyage of discovery, to ascertain the form of the African continent, actually doubled the Cape of Good Hope, about twenty-one centuries before the time of Bartholomew Diaz and Vasco de Gama; but it was not till the discovery of the compass that navigation became perfected, and the uncertain method of ascertaining the course by the stars gave place to the more accurate calculations of modern times.

After the fall of Tyre, and the building of Alexandria, Egypt became famous as a commercial country, and the emporium of the East; the riches of India, brought to Berenice, Myos-Hormos, and other ports on the Red Sea, passed through it, to be distributed over various parts of the Roman empire; and it continued to benefit by these advantages, until a new route was opened to India by the Portuguese, round the Cape of Good Hope.

It is difficult to explain how, at that early period, so great a value came to be attached to tin, that the Phœnicians should have thought it worth while to undertake a voyage of such a length, and attended with so much risk, in order to obtain it; even allowing that a high price was paid for this commodity in Egypt, and other countries, where, as at Sidon, the different branches of metallurgy were carried to great perfection. It was mixed with other metals, particularly copper, which was hardened by this alloy; it was employed, according to Homer, for the raised work on the exterior of shields, as in that of Achilles; for making greaves, and binding various parts of defensive armour; as well as for household and ornamental purposes; and it is remarkable, that the word *kassiteros*, used by the poet, is the same as the Arabic name *kasdeer*, by which the metal is still known in the East. It is also called *kastira* in Sanscrit.

We have no means of ascertaining the exact period when the Phœnicians first visited our coasts in search of tin; some have supposed about the year 400 or 450 before our era: but that this metal was employed many ages previously, is shown from the bronze vessels and implements discovered at Thebes, and other parts of Egypt. It cannot, however, be inferred that the mines of Britain were known at that remote period, since Spain and India may have furnished the Egyptians with tin; and the Phœnicians probably obtained it from these countries, long before they visited our distant coasts, and discovered the richness of their productive mines. It is still produced in small quantities in Gallicia and another part of northern Spain. Ezekiel says that the Tyrians received tin, as well as other metals, from Tarshish; and whether this was in India or not, there is sufficient evidence of the productions of that country having been known at the earliest times, as is proved by the gold of Ophir being mentioned in Job. For if Phœnician ships did not actually sail to India, its productions arrived partly by land through Arabia, partly through more distant marts, established midway from India by the merchants of those (as of later) days; and we have evidence of their having already found their way to Egypt, at the early period of Joseph's arrival in that country, from the spices which the Ishmaelites were carrying to sell there. And the amethyst, hæmatite, lapis lazzuli, and other objects discovered at Thebes, of the time of the third Thothmes, and succeeding Pharaohs, argue that the intercourse was constantly kept up.

The first mention of tin, though not the earliest proof of its use, is in connexion with the spoils taken by the Israelites from the people of Midian, in the year 1452 B.C., where they are commanded by Moses to purify " the gold and the silver, the brass, the *iron*, the *tin*, and the lead, by passing it through the fire ;" its combination with other metals is noticed by Isaiah, in the year 760 before our era, who alludes to it as an alloy mixed with a more valuable substance ;* Ezekiel† shows that it was used for this purpose in connexion with silver; and bronze, a compound of tin and copper, is found in Egypt of the time of the sixth dynasty, more than 2000 years B.C.

Strabo, Diodorus, Pliny, and other writers, mention certain islands discovered by the Phœnicians, which, from the quantity of tin they produced, obtained the name *Cassiterides*. Though their locality is not given correctly by them, it is evident they

---

* Isaiah, i. 25. † Ezek. xxii. 18, 20.

all allude to the cluster now known as the Scilly Isles; but these never produced tin, and the Phœnicians invented this story in order to conceal the fact of the mainland of Cornwall being the spot whence they obtained it. For, as Strabo says, the secret of their discovery was carefully concealed, and the Phœnician vessels continued to sail from Gades (Cadiz) in quest of this commodity, without its being known from whence they obtained it: though many endeavours were made by the Romans at a subsequent period to ascertain the secret, and to share the benefits of this lucrative trade.

So anxious, indeed, were the Phœnicians to retain their monopoly, that on one occasion, when a Roman vessel pursued a trader bound to the spot, the latter purposely steered his vessel on a shoal, preferring to suffer shipwreck, provided he involved his pursuers in the same fate, rather than disclose his country's secret; for which he was rewarded from the public treasury.

Pliny mentions a report of "white lead," or tin, being brought from certain islands of the Atlantic; yet he treats it as a "fable," and proceeds to state that it was found in Lusitania and Gallicia, and was the same metal known to the Greeks in the days of Homer by the name "*kassiteros*." Diodorus and Strabo, after noticing the tin of Spain and the Cassiterides, affirm that it was also brought to Massillia (Marseilles) from the coast of Britain; but this was probably after it had been long known to the Phœnicians, who still kept their secret; and it was doubtless through their means that the natives of Britain prevented other foreigners going direct to the mines, supplying them, as they did, with pigs of tin, carried to Vectis, or the Isle of Wight; the established depôt where the traders from the Continent were accustomed to purchase the metal. And this having become the established line of commerce probably led to the choice of the neighbouring port of Southampton, as the place whence the Pilgrims in later times crossed over to the Seine.

Spain, in early times, was to the Phœnicians what America, at a later period, was to the Spaniards; and no one can read the accounts of the immense wealth derived from the mines of that country, in the writings of Diodorus and other authors, without being struck by the relative position of the Phœnicians towards the ancient Spaniards, and the followers of Cortez or Pizarro towards the inhabitants of Mexico or Peru.

"The whole of Spain," says Strabo, "abounds with mines . . . . and in no country are gold, silver, copper, and iron in such abundance or of such good quality; even the rivers and torrents bring down gold in their beds, and some is found in the sand;" and the fanciful assertion of Posidonius, regarding the richness of the country in precious metals, surpassed the phantoms created in the minds of the conquerors of America.

The Phœnicians purchased gold, silver, tin, and other metals from the inhabitants of Spain and the Cassiterides, by giving in exchange earthenware vessels, oil, salt, bronze manufactures, and other objects of little value, like the Spaniards on their arrival at Hispaniola; and such was the abundance of silver, that after loading their ships with full cargoes, they stripped the lead from their anchors, and substituted the same weight of silver.

Among those bronze implements were very probably the beautiful swords, daggers, and spear-heads found in this country, buried with the ancient Britons, which are of such excellent workmanship and form, that they could only be the work of a highly-civilized and skilful people; and as they are neither of a Greek nor Roman type, it is difficult to attribute them to any other people than the Phœnicians.

A strong evidence of the skill of the Egyptians in working metals, and of the early advancement they made in this art, is derived from their success in the management of different alloys; which, as M. Goguet observes, is further argued from the casting of the golden calf, and still more from Moses being able to burn the metal and reduce it to powder; a secret which he could only have learned in Egypt. It is said in Exodus that "Moses took the calf which they had made, and burnt it in the fire, and ground it to powder, and strewed it upon the water, and made the children of Israel drink of it;" an operation which, according to the French *savant*, "is known by all who work in metals to be very difficult."

"Commentators' heads," he adds, "have been much perplexed

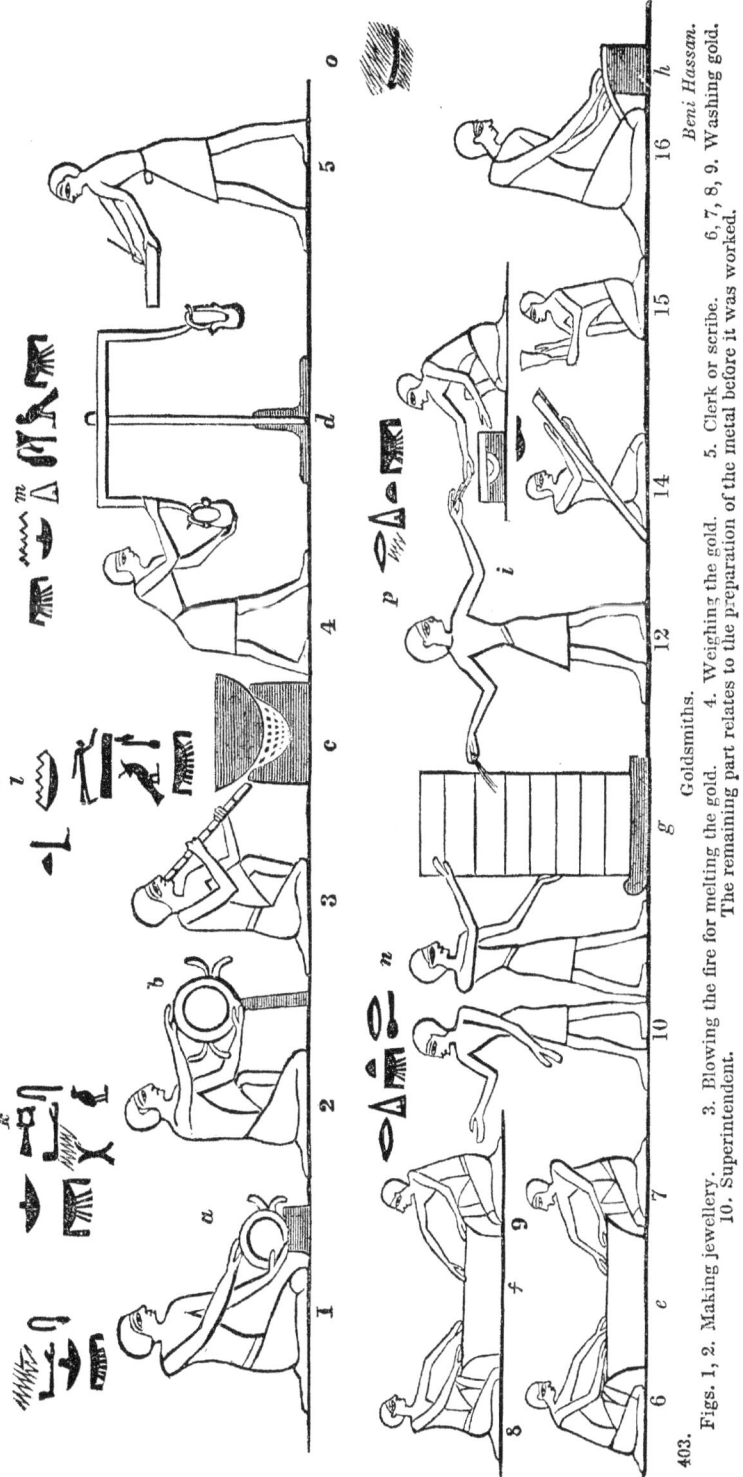

403. Figs. 1, 2. Making jewellery. 3. Blowing the fire for melting the gold. 4. Weighing the gold. 5. Clerk or scribe. 6, 7, 8, 9. Washing gold. 10. Superintendent. The remaining part relates to the preparation of the metal before it was worked.

Beni Hassan. Goldsmiths.

to explain how Moses burnt and reduced the gold to powder. Many have offered vain and improbable conjectures, but an experienced chemist has removed every difficulty upon the subject, and has suggested this simple process. In the place of tartaric acid, which we employ, the Hebrew legislator used natron, which is common in the East. What follows, respecting his making the Israelites drink this powder, proves that he was perfectly acquainted with the whole effect of the operation. He wished to increase the punishment of their disobedience, and nothing could have been more suitable; for gold reduced and made into a draught, in the manner I have mentioned, has a most nauseous taste."

The use of gold for jewellery and various articles of luxury dates from the most remote ages. Pharaoh having "arrayed" Joseph "in vestures of fine linen, put a gold chain about his neck;" and the jewels of silver and gold borrowed from the Egyptians by the Israelites at the time of their leaving Egypt (out of which the golden calf was afterwards made), suffice to prove the great quantity of precious metals wrought at that time into female ornaments. It is not from the Scriptures alone that the skill of the Egyptian goldsmiths may be inferred; the sculp-

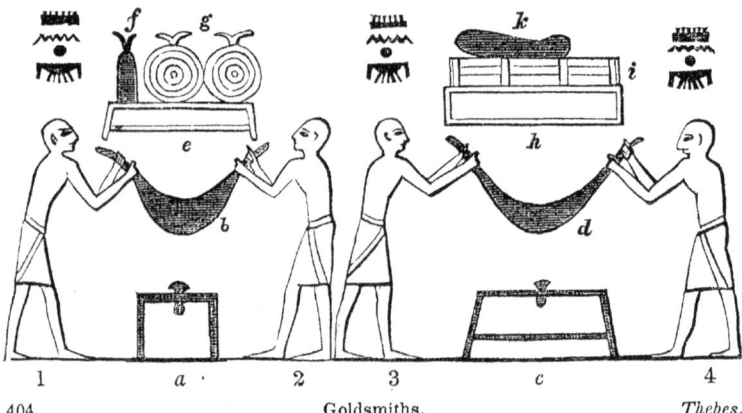

404. Goldsmiths. Thebes.
f g are articles of jewellery. The hieroglyphics read "goldsmith" or "worker in gold."

tures of Thebes and Beni Hassan afford their additional testimony, and the numerous gold and silver vases, inlaid work, and

CHAP. VII.   GOLD.   139

jewellery, represented in common use, show the great advancement they had made in this branch of art.

But gold was known in Egypt, and made into ornaments, long before; and the same mode of washing and working it is figured on the monuments of the fourth dynasty.

The engraving of gold, the mode of casting it, and inlaying it with stones, were evidently known at the same time; they are mentioned in the Bible, and numerous specimens of this kind of work have been found in Egypt.*

The origin of the sign signifying gold has been happily explained by Champollion as the *bowl* in which the metal was washed, the *cloth* through which it was strained, and the *dropping of the water*, united into one character, at once indicative of the process and the metal.

Much cannot, of course, be expected from the objects found in the excavated tombs, to illustrate the means employed in smelting the ore, or to disclose any of the secrets they possessed in metallurgy; and little is given in the paintings beyond the use of the blow-pipe, the forceps, and the mode of concentrating heat by raising cheeks of metal round three sides of the fire in which the crucibles were placed. Of the latter, indeed, there is no indication in these subjects, unless it be in a preceding woodcut (403, *fig. c*); but their use is readily suggested, and some which have been found in Egypt are preserved in the museum of Berlin. They are nearly five inches in diameter at the mouth, and about the same in depth, and present the

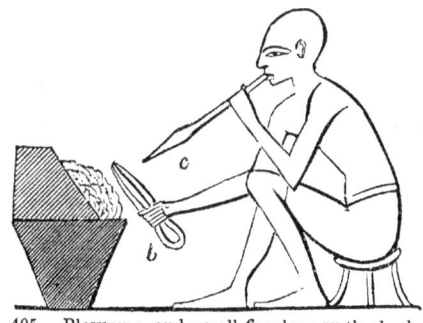
405. Blowpipe, and small fireplace with cheeks to confine and reflect the heat. *Thebes.*

ordinary form and appearance of those used at the present day.

At Beni Hassan, the process of washing the ore, smelting or fusing the metal with the help of the blow-pipe, and fashioning

* Exod. xxxii. 4; xxviii. 9 and 11.

it for ornamental purposes, weighing it, and taking an account of the quantity so made up, and other occupations of the goldsmith, are represented; but, as might be supposed, these subjects merely suffice, as they were intended, to give a general indication of the goldsmith's trade, without attempting to describe the means employed.

From the mention* of earrings and bracelets, and jewels of silver and gold, in the days of Abraham, it is evident that in Asia as well as in Egypt, the art of metallurgy was known at a very remote period; and workmen of the same countries are noticed by Homer† as excelling in the manufacture of arms, rich vases, and other objects inlaid or ornamented with metals. His account of the shield of Achilles proves the art of working the various substances of which it was made, copper, tin, gold, and silver, to have been well understood at that time, and the skill required to represent the infinity of subjects he mentions was such as no ordinary artisan could possess.

The ornaments in gold found in Egypt consist of rings, bracelets, armlets, necklaces, earrings, and numerous trinkets belonging to the toilet, many of which are of the time of Osirtasen I. and Thothmes III., about 3930, and 3290 years ago. Gold and silver vases, statues, and other objects of gold and silver, of silver inlaid with gold, and of bronze inlaid with the precious metals, were also common at the same time; and besides those manufactured in the country from the produce of their own mines, the Egyptians exacted an annual tribute from the conquered provinces of Asia and Africa, in gold and silver, and in vases made of those materials.

406.   Golden baskets, represented in the tomb of King Remeses III.   *Thebes.*

* Gen. xxiv. 47, 53.

† Hom. Iliad, xxiii. 741. A silver cup, the work of the Sidonians, Od. iv. 618, &c.; Iliad, ii. 872; vi. 236; xvii. 474.

There was great elegance in the form of many of the oldest Egyptian vases, especially those of gold and silver. Much taste was also displayed in other objects as well as in the devices which ornamented them, among which may be mentioned the golden basket in the tomb of Remeses III.

The gold mines of Egypt or of Ethiopia, though mentioned by Agatharchides and later writers, and worked even by the Arab Caliphs, long remained unknown, and their position has only been ascertained a few years since, by M. Linant and Mr. Bonomi. They lie in the Bisháree desert—the land of Bigah (or of the " Bugaitæ" mentioned in the inscription at Axum)—about seventeen or eighteen days' journey to the southeastward from Derow, which is situated on the Nile, a little above Kom Ombo, the ancient Ombos.

Those two travellers met with some Cufic funeral inscriptions there, which from their dates show that the mines were worked in the years 339 A.H. (951 A.D.), and 378 A.H. (989 A.D.); the former being in the fifth year of the Caliph Mostukfee Billah, a short time before the arrival of the Fatemites in Egypt, the latter in the fourteenth of El Azeéz, the second of the Fatemite dynasty.

They continued to be worked till a much later period, and were afterwards abandoned, the value of the gold barely covering the expenses; nor did Mohammed Ali, who sent to examine them and obtain specimens of the ore, find it worth while to reopen them.

The matrix is quartz: and so diligent a search did the Egyptians establish, throughout the whole of the deserts east of the Nile, for this precious metal, that I never remember to have seen a vein of quartz in any of the primitive ranges there, which had not been carefully examined by their miners; certain portions having been invariably picked out from the fissures in which it lay, and broken into small fragments. The same was done in later times by the Romans; and evidences of their searching for gold in quartz veins are even found in some parts of Britain.

The gold mines are said by Aboolfeda to be situated at El Allaga (or Ollagee); but Eshuranib (or Eshuanib), the principal place, is about three days' journey beyond Wadee Allaga according to Mr. Bonomi, to whom I am indebted for the following account of the mines. " The direction of the excavations depends on that of the strata in which the ore is found; and the position of the various shafts differs accordingly. As to the manner of extracting the metal, some notion may be given by a description of the ruins at Eshuranib, the largest station, where sufficient remains to explain the process they adopted. The principal excavation, according to M. Linant's measurement, is about 180 feet deep: it is a narrow oblique chasm, reaching a considerable way down the rock. In the valley near the most accessible part of the excavation are several huts, built of the unhewn fragments of the surrounding hills, their walls not more than breast high, perhaps the houses of the excavators or the guardians of the mine; and separated from them by the ravine or course of the torrent a group of houses, about three hundred in number, laid out very regularly in straight lines. In those nearest the mines lived the workmen who were employed to break the quartz into small fragments, the size of a bean, from whose hands the pounded stone passed to the persons who ground it in hand-mills, similar to those now used for corn in the valley of the Nile, made of a granitic stone; one of which is to be found in almost every house at these mines, either entire or broken.

" The quartz thus reduced to powder was washed on inclined tables, furnished with two cisterns, all built of fragments of stone collected there; and near these inclined planes are generally found little white mounds, the residue of the operation. Besides the numerous remains of houses in this station, are two large buildings, with towers at the angles, built of the hard blackish granitic, yet luminous, rock, that prevails in the district. The valley has many trees, and in a high part of the torrent bed is a sort of island, or isolated bank, on which we found many tombstones, some written in the ancient Cufic character, very similar to those at A'Souán."

Mr. Bonomi's account agrees very well with those given by Agatharchides and Diodorus, who both mention the great labour of extracting the gold, and separating it from the pounded stone by frequent washings; a process apparently represented in the tombs of the early time of the Osirtasens; and the descriptions of the old "diggings" have acquired additional interest from those of modern days.

But in Australia and California they are carried on under more auspicious circumstances than those of old, where the workers in the mines were principally captives taken in war, and men condemned to hard labour for crimes, or in consequence of offences against the government. They were bound in fetters, and obliged to work night and day, every chance of escape being carefully obviated by the watchfulness of the guards, who, in order that persuasion might not be used to induce them to relax in their duty, or feelings of compassion be excited for the sufferings of their fellow-countrymen, were foreign soldiers, ignorant of the Egyptian language.

Such was the system in the time of Diodorus; but it is uncertain whether it was introduced under the Ptolemies, or had already existed under the later Pharaohs. "The soil," says the historian, " naturally black, is traversed with veins of marble of excessive whiteness, surpassing in brilliancy the most shining substances; out of which the overseers cause the gold to be dug, by the labour of a vast multitude of people; for the kings of Egypt condemn to the mines notorious criminals, prisoners of war, persons convicted by false accusations, or the victims of resentment. And not only the individuals themselves, but sometimes even their whole families, are doomed to this labour, with the view of punishing the guilty, and profiting by their toil.

"The vast numbers employed in these mines are bound in fetters, and compelled to work day and night without intermission, and without the least hope of escape; for they set over them barbarian soldiers, who speak a foreign language, so that there is no possibility of conciliating them by persuasion, or the kind feelings which result from familiar converse.

"When the earth containing the gold is hard, they soften it by the application of fire, and when it has been reduced to such a state that it yields to moderate labour, several thousands (myriads) of these unfortunate people break it up with iron picks. Over the whole work presides an engineer, who views and selects the stone, and points it out to the labourers. The strongest of them, provided with iron chisels, cleave the marble-shining rock by mere force, without any attempt at skill; and in excavating the shaft below ground, they follow the direction of the shining stratum, without keeping to a straight line.

"In order to see in these dark windings, they fasten lamps to their foreheads, having their bodies painted, sometimes of one and sometimes of another colour, according to the nature of the rock; and as they cut the stone, it falls in masses on the floor, the overseers urging them to the work with commands and blows. They are followed by little boys, who take away the fragments as they fall, and carry them out into the open air. Those who are above thirty years of age are employed to pound pieces of the stone, of certain dimensions, with iron pestles in stone mortars, until reduced to the size of a lentil. The whole is then transferred to women and old men, who put it into mills arranged in a long row, two or three persons being employed at the same mill, and it is ground until reduced to a fine powder.

"No attention is paid to their persons; they have not even a piece of rag to cover themselves; and so wretched is their condition, that every one who witnesses it deplores the excessive misery they endure. No rest, no intermission from toil, are given either to the sick or maimed: neither the weakness of age nor women's infirmities are regarded; all are driven to their work with the lash, till, at last, overcome with the intolerable weight of their afflictions, they die in the midst of their toil. So that these unhappy creatures always expect worse to come than what they endure at the present, and long for death as far preferable to life.

"At length the masters take the stone thus ground to powder, and carry it away to undergo the final process. They spread it upon a broad table a little inclined; and, pouring water upon it, rub the pulverized stone until all the earthy matter is separated, which, flowing away with the water, leaves the heavier particles behind on the board. This operation is often repeated, the stone being rubbed lightly with the hand: they then draw up the useless and earthy substance with fine sponges, gently applied, until the gold comes out quite pure. Other workmen then take it away by weight and measure, and putting it with a fixed proportion of lead, salt, a little tin, and barley bran, into earthen crucibles well closed with clay, leave it in a furnace for five successive days and nights; after which it is suffered to cool. The crucibles are then opened, and nothing is found in them but the pure gold, a little diminished in quantity.

"Such is the method of extracting the gold on the confines of Egypt, the result of so many and such great toils. Nature, indeed, teaches that as gold is obtained with immense labour, so it is kept with difficulty, creating great anxiety, and attended in its use both with pleasure and grief."

In the early stages of society, when gold first began to be used, idols, ornaments, or other objects were made of the metal in its pure state, till, being found too soft, and too easily worn away, an alloy was added to harden it, at the same time that it increased the bulk of the valuable material. As men advanced in experience, they found that the great ductility of gold enabled them to cover substances of all kinds with thin plates of the metal, giving all the effect of the richness and brilliancy they admired in solid gold ornaments; and the gilding of bronze, stone, silver, and wood was speedily adopted.

The leaves so used were at first thick, but skill, resulting from experience, soon showed to what degree of fineness they could be reduced; and we find that in Egypt substances of various kinds were overlaid with fine gold leaf at a very remote period, even in the time of the first Osirtasen. Some things still continued to be covered with thick leaf, but this was from choice, and not in consequence of any want of skill in the workmen; and in the early age of Thothmes III. they were acquainted with the various methods of overlaying with gold leaf, gilding, inlaying, and beating gold into other metals, previously tooled with devices to receive it.

That the practice of applying it in leaf was common when the Israelites were in the country is evident from the direct mention of it in the Bible, the ark of shittim wood made by Moses being overlaid with pure gold; and the casting of the metal is noticed on the same occasion; nor can we doubt that the art was derived by the Jews from Egypt, or that the Egyptians had long before been acquainted with all those secrets of metallurgy, in which the specimens that remain prove them to have so eminently excelled.

The method devised by the Egyptians for beating out the leaf is unknown to us, but from the extreme fineness of some of that covering wooden and other ornaments found at Thebes, we may conclude it was done nearly in the same way as formerly in Europe, between parchment; and perhaps some membrane taken from the intestines of animals was also employed by them.

In Europe the skin of an unborn calf was at first substituted for the parchment previously used, but in the beginning of the 17th century, the German gold-beaters having obtained a fine pellicle from the entrails of cattle, found that they could beat gold much thinner than before, and this still continues to be used, and is known to us under the name of gold-beaters' skin. "About the year 1621," says Beckmann, " Merunne excited general astonishment when he showed that the Parisian gold-beaters could beat an ounce of gold into sixteen hundred leaves, which together covered a surface of one hundred and five square feet. But in 1711, when the pellicles discovered by the Germans came to be used in Paris, Réaumur found that an ounce of gold in the form of a cube, five and a quarter lines at most in length, breadth, and thickness, and which covered only a surface of about 27 square lines, could be so extended by the gold-beaters as to cover a surface of more than $1466\frac{1}{2}$ square feet. This extension, therefore, is nearly one half more than was possible about a century before."

Many gilt bronze vases, implements of various kinds, trinkets, statues, toys, and other objects, in metal and wood, have been discovered in the tombs of Thebes: the faces of mummies are frequently found overlaid with thick gold-leaf; the painted cloth, the wooden coffin, were also profusely ornamented in this manner, and sometimes the whole body itself of the deceased, previous to its being enveloped in the bandages. Not only were small objects appertaining to the service of the gods, and connected with religion, or articles of luxury and show, in the temples, tombs, or private houses, so decorated; the sculptures on the lofty walls of an adytum, the ornaments of a colossus, the doorways of a temple, and parts of numerous large monuments, were likewise covered with gilding, of which the wooden heifer which served as a sepulchre to the body of King Mycerinus's daughter, some of the mouldings in the temple of Kalabshi in Nubia, the statue of Minerva sent to Cyrene by Amasis, and portions of the Sphinx at the Pyramids, may be cited as instances.

Gold is supposed to have been used for money some time before silver. In Egypt it was evidently known before silver, this being called "white *gold;*" and it was there the representative of money; while in Hebrew, *kussuf*, "silver," signified "money," like "argent" in French. In neither case was the money coined in early times. Gold was perhaps first stamped by the Lydians; but the oldest known Greek coins are the silver ones of Ægina, with a tortoise on one side.

Much gold was used for ornamental purposes. Its richness, durability, and freedom from tarnish, led the ancients to employ it very generally, and to a greater extent than in modern times, when South America has given us the abundance, and the name, of "plate." Silver was chiefly confined to money; and the demand for gold in houses (*Plin.* xxxiii. 17), and in jewellery, left silver free for the currency, and for a few other purposes. But though gold was preferred, it is still singular that so few pieces of silver plate seem to have been made by the Greeks and Romans.

The Egyptian sculptures represent silver as well as gold vases and ornaments, in the time of the third Thothmes, and silver rings and trinkets have been found of the same epoch; but gold was the favourite metal in Egypt, as afterwards in Greece and Rome; and the rich frequently had ornamental works, statues, and furniture of solid gold. Those who could not afford them were satisfied to have bronze overlaid with gold, at first with a thick, in after times with a thin coating, until in time gold-beating brought the external appearance of gold within the reach of less wealthy people; and gold leaf in modern days covers the wooden ornaments of the humblest house. Now that gold is in greater abundance, we may look to its coming again into more general use, instead of silver, which sinks into the appearance of pewter by the side of that rich metal; and to its taking the place of some of our paltry imitations.

If the use of gold preceded that of silver, the latter was not long in following it; and the earliest authority, the Bible, mentions both at a remote age. Abraham was said to have been "very rich in cattle, in *silver*, and in gold;" Abimelech gave him a thousand pieces of the former; and the use of silver as money is distinctly pointed out in the purchase of the field of Ephron, with its cave, which Abraham bought for " four hundred shekels of silver, current money with the merchant." On this occasion, as usual, the price paid was settled by *weight*, which was the origin and meaning of the name *shekel*; and the custom of weighing money was retained among the Egyptians, Hebrews, and other Eastern people, till a late period. Indeed, until a government stamp, or some fixed value, was given to money, this could be the only method of ascertaining the price paid, and of giving satisfaction to both parties. Thus Joseph's brethren,

407.   *Kabbáneh* (Qabbáneh), or public weighers, and notaries.   *Thebes.*

CHAP. VII.   GOLD RING-MONEY.   149

when they discovered the money returned into their sacks, brought it back to Egypt, observing that it was "in full weight;" and the paintings of Thebes frequently represent persons in the act of weighing gold, on the purchase of articles in the market.

Egyptian money was in rings of gold and silver, a kind of currency that continues to this day in Sennaar and the neighbouring countries; but it is uncertain whether any of them had a government stamp to denote their purity or their value; and though so commonly represented, none have yet been found in the ruins or tombs of Thebes. They remind us of the "ring (*nuzm*) of gold" in Job (xlii. 11), given him with " a piece of money" by his friends.

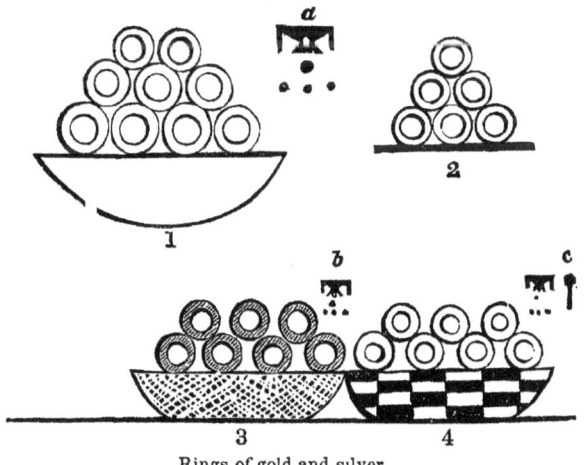

408.   Rings of gold and silver.   *Thebes.*

Gold when brought as tribute was often in bags, which were deposited in the royal treasury. These doubtless contained gold dust, which is mentioned by Job (xxviii. 6) as a well known form of that metal; and this is confirmed by "pure gold" being written over them. Though sealed, and warranted to contain a certain quantity, they were subjected to the usual ordeal of the scales by the cautious Egyptians. Money was sometimes kept ready weighed in known quantities for certain occasions, which, when intended as a present, or when the honesty of the person was beyond suspicion, did not require to be weighed; as when

Naaman gave "two talents of silver in two bags" to Gehazi (2 Kings v. 23; *see* Tobit ix. 5). The Egyptians had also unstamped copper money, called in the papyri "pieces of brass;" which, like the gold and silver, continued to be taken by weight even in the time of the Ptolemies; and it was only by degrees that the Greek coinage did away with the old imperfect system of weighing the price paid for every commodity.

But these princes were not the first who introduced coined money into Egypt: it had been current there during the Persian occupation of the country; and Aryandes, who was governor of Egypt under Cambyses and Darius, struck silver coins, in imitation of the gold Darics of his sovereign, for which act of presumption he was condemned to death.

They are supposed to be those with an owl, and the Egyptian sceptres of Osiris, the crook and flail, on the obverse; and an archer on a hippocampus, with a dolphin, on the reverse.

The art of stamping money in Asia began in the dominions of Lydia. Herodotus says the Lydians were "the first people who coined gold and silver for their use;" and if Ægina also claims the earliest coinage, this does not contradict Herodotus, as it was only the earliest in relation to Greece. The oldest coins that have been found are the *staters* of Lydia, which date even a little before the very ancient ones of Cyzicus. They are not of pure gold, but of *Electrum*, or three parts gold and one of silver: probably owing to the two metals having been found together, and first stamped in that state. They were mere lumps, or dumps, of a certain weight; often cracked at the edge from being suddenly flattened by the blow. They were impressed with a lion's head, or other emblem, on one side only. Similarly rude were the old Æginetan coins, with a tortoise on one side, and on the other the mark of the block on which the lump of metal was fixed while struck. These last were all of silver, none of gold; and the oldest coins of real gold were those of Darius.

Phidon, king of Argos, is said to have invented weights and measures (that is, in Greece), and to have established the silver coinage of Ægina B.C. 895: and though Pausanias thinks gold and silver money were unknown in the age of Polydorus, king of

Sparta (who died B.C. 724), the authority of the Parian Chronicle, and of Ælian, favour the earlier claims of Ægina. The coins of Syracuse and Magna Græcia date from 700 B.C.; having, like all others before 500 B.C., only a figure on one side; and the first silver coins of Athens were struck in 512 B.C. The gold Darics had only a figure on the obverse, representing an archer. They were coined about 500 B.C., and had not yet the round shape of later pieces, nor of the silver Darics, being 5-8ths of an inch long by 7-16ths. They were worth about 1*l.* 1*s.* 10*d.* each. These and other early coins therefore do not borrow their form from ring money, which may perhaps be traced in those of China.

Habit would naturally retain an original type for a long time; and sometimes even in Greece the archaic character of a coin was continued long after art had improved. Thus the old head of Minerva was repeated on the late Athenian drachm and tetradrachm, because strangers were accustomed to it in commerce, and the Athenians were satisfied to use the well-known Corinthian didrachm for the same reason, as all people on the Mediterranean still welcome the pillar dollar of Spain.

The tradition of *pecunia* being called from *pecus*, and of the ox or sheep having been at first a substitute for money, as in Greece and Rome, accords with a custom still common among some people, of making them the standard of valuation; in Darfoor and Kordofan a piece of cotton cloth is reckoned equal to a sheep; and in Job (xlii. 11), the name *Kesîteh* (or "lamb") is employed to signify a "piece of money." Homer also reckons the value of certain things as equal to an ox; and in Solon's time a sheep was equivalent "to a bushel and a half of corn."

If stamped money was not used by the ancient Egyptians, we have evidence of weights and measures having been invented by them long before the Greeks existed as a nation: and it is probable that they were known even in Greece previous to the time of Phidon. (*See below,* p. 239, *on the use of the precious metals.*)

One kind of balance used for weighing gold differed slightly from those of ordinary construction, and was probably more delicately formed. It was made, as usual, with an upright pole, rising from a broad base or stand, and a cross beam turning on a pin at its summit; but instead of strings suspending the scales, was an arm on either side, terminating in a hook, to which the gold was attached in small bags.*

Large scales were generally a flat wooden board, with four ropes attached to a ring at the extremity of the beam; and those of smaller size were of bronze, one and a half inch in diameter, pierced near the edge in three places for the strings.

The principle of the common balance was simple and ingenious; the beam passed through a ring suspended from a horizontal rod, immediately above and parallel to it, and when equally balanced, the ring, which was large enough to allow the beam to play freely, showed when the scales were equally poised, and had the additional effect of preventing the beam tilting, when the goods were taken out of one, and the weights suffered to remain in the other scale.† To the lower part of the ring a small plummet was fixed, and this being touched by the hand, and found to hang freely, indicated, without the necessity of looking at the beam, that the weight was just. The figure of a baboon was sometimes placed upon the top, as the emblem of the god Thoth, the regulator of measures, of time, and of writing, in his character of the moon; but there is no appearance of the goddess of Justice being connected with the balance, except in the judgment scenes of the dead.

The pair of scales was the ordinary and, apparently, only kind of balance used by the Egyptians; no instance of the steel-yard being met with in the paintings of Thebes, or of Beni Hassan: and the introduction of the latter is confined to a Roman era.

The Egyptians had another kind of balance, in which the equalization of the opposite weights was ascertained by the plummet; and this last, whose invention has been ascribed by Pliny to Dædalus, is shown to have been known and applied in Egypt at least as early as the time of the Osirtasens.

For ordinary purposes copper was most commonly used; arms, vases, statues, instruments, and implements of every kind, articles of furniture, and numerous other objects, were made of this metal hardened by an alloy of tin, and even chisels for cutting

* *See* woodcut 403, p. 136.   † *See* woodcut 407, p. 148.

stone, as well as carpenters' tools, and knives, were of bronze. It is generally allowed that copper or bronze was known long before iron, and though Tubal-Cain is said to have been "the instructor of every artificer in brass and *iron*," no direct mention is made of iron arms or tools till after the Exodus.

According to the Arundelian marbles, iron was known one hundred and eighty-eight years before the Trojan war, about 1370 years B.C., but Hesiod, Plutarch, and others limit its discovery to a much later period, after the capture of Troy. Homer, however, distinctly mentions its use:* and that there is little reason to doubt the *sideros* of the poet being iron, is shown by the simile, derived from the quenching of iron in water, which he applies to the hissing noise produced on piercing the eye of Polyphemus with the pointed stake, thus rendered by Pope:

> "And as when armourers temper in the ford
> The keen-edged poleaxe, or the shining sword,
> The red hot metal hisses in the lake,
> Thus in his eyeball hiss'd the plunging stake."

His "black *kyanus*" is also thought to be steel, as well as the *adamas* of Hesiod, who mentions the iron of the Idæi Dactyli in Crete; and the skill of the Chalybes in its manufacture dates from a very remote age. Among the earliest authorities for the use of iron may be cited the bedstead of Og, the King of Bashan, who is said to have lived about the year 1450 before our era; and Thrasyllus agrees with the Arundelian marbles in supposing iron to have been known before the Trojan war, or, indeed, one hundred and fourteen years previous to the foundation of Troy, 1537 before our era. On the other hand, it has been argued, that offerings of iron in the temples of Greece distinctly showed the value attached to that metal, as well as its limited use for ordinary purposes, and rings of iron were worn by the ancients, some of which have been found in the tombs of Egypt. But these last are of very late date, long after iron was commonly used, and I possess one of them, engraved with the figure of Harpocrates, which is of a Ptolemaic, or rather of

* Hom. Iliad, xxiii. 261, &c.

a Roman era, and which only claims some degree of interest from its bearing a device noticed by Pliny as becoming fashionable at Rome in his time.

That iron, as early as the days of Lycurgus, was held in little estimation, is shown by that legislator forbidding the introduction of gold and silver in his republic, and restricting the Spartans to the use of iron; and some notion may be formed of its value at that time by the assertion of Plutarch, that it required a cart drawn by two oxen to carry the small sum of ten minæ.

The Jews appear to have been acquainted with two kinds of iron previous to the Babylonish captivity; the *barzel*, which was in common use, and the northern iron, as well as steel: even as early as the days of Job iron was known; and Moses mentions an iron furnace.

One of the arguments against the early use of iron is the difficulty of smelting the ore, and of reducing it to a malleable state; and the various processes required to discover all its most useful properties render it less likely to be employed than a more ductile metal. Gold, silver, and copper were easily fused, and a single process sufficed to make them available for every purpose, the principal art required for fabricating implements of copper depending on the proper proportions and qualities of alloy introduced.

In the infancy of the arts and sciences, the difficulty of working iron might long withhold the secret of its superiority over copper and bronze; but it cannot reasonably be supposed that a nation so advanced, and so eminently skilled in the art of working metals as the Egyptians and Sidonians, should have remained ignorant of its use, even if we had no evidence of its having been known to the Greeks and other people; and the constant employment of bronze arms and implements is not a sufficient argument against their knowledge of iron, since we find the Greeks and Romans made the same things of bronze long after the period when iron was universally known.

Another argument, to show that bronze was used in Greece before iron, is derived from the word χαλκευς, " coppersmith," having in Greek the signification of "smith," whether applied to a worker of copper or iron. In Latin, on the contrary, *ferrum*, "an iron," is the word frequently applied to a sword; and some have hence argued the use of iron for those weapons, at the earliest period, among the Romans, which is confirmed by the treaty imposed upon them by Porsena, binding them not to use iron, except for agricultural implements. But long after iron was used by them, the Romans and Etruscans continued to make swords, daggers, spear-heads, and other offensive weapons of bronze, as well as their defensive armour; and the discovery of arms and tools of bronze ceases to argue an ignorance of iron.

To conclude, from the want of iron instruments, or arms, bearing the names of early monarchs of a Pharaonic age, that bronze was alone used, is neither just nor satisfactory, since the decomposition of that metal, especially when buried for ages in the nitrous soil of Egypt, is so speedy as to preclude the possibility of its preservation. Until we know in what manner the Egyptians employed bronze tools for cutting stone, the discovery of them affords no additional light, nor even argument, since the Greeks and Romans continued to make bronze instruments of various kinds so long after iron was known to them; and Herodotus mentions the iron tools used by the builders of the Pyramids.

Iron and copper mines are found in the Egyptian desert, which were worked in old times; and the monuments of Thebes, and even the tombs about Memphis, dating more than 4000 years ago, represent butchers sharpening their knives on a round bar of metal attached to their apron, which from its blue colour can only be steel; and the distinction between the bronze and iron weapons in the tomb of Remeses III., one painted red, the other blue, leaves no doubt of *both* having been used (as in Rome) at the same periods. In Ethiopia iron was much more abundant than in Egypt, and Herodotus states that copper was a rare metal there, though we may doubt his assertion of prisoners in that country having been bound with fetters of gold.

The speedy decomposition of iron would be sufficient to prevent our finding implements of that metal of an early period, and the greater opportunities of obtaining copper ore, added to the facility of working it, might be a reason for preferring the latter whenever it answered the purpose instead of iron. Bronze tools might also be made available for sculpturing and engraving stone; though there is great difficulty in accounting for their use in mines and quarries, where the stone was frequently hewn with them; as Agatharchides informs us in his account of the gold mines, and as was evidently done in cutting the limestone rock of the tombs at Thebes; a bronze chisel having been found amidst the chippings of the stone, where it had been accidentally left by the workmen.

The hieroglyphics on obelisks and other granitic monuments are sculptured with a minuteness and finish which is surprising, even if they had used steel as highly tempered as our own.

Some are cut to the depth of more than two inches, the edges and all the most minute parts of the intaglio presenting the same sharpness and accuracy; and I have seen the figure of a king in high relief, reposing on the lid of a granite coffin, which was raised to the height of nine inches above the level of the surface. What can be said, if we deny to men who executed such works as these the aid of steel, and confine them to bronze implements? Then, indeed, we exalt their skill in metallurgy far beyond our own, and indirectly confess that they had devised a method of sculpturing stone of which we are ignorant. In vain should we attempt to render copper, by the addition of certain alloys, sufficiently hard to sculpture granite, basalt, and stones of similar quality. No one who has tried to perforate or cut a block of Egyptian granite will scruple to acknowledge that our best steel tools are turned in a very short time, and require to be re-tempered; and the labour experienced by the French engineers, who removed the obelisk of Luxor from Thebes, in cutting a space less than two feet deep along the face of its partially decomposed pedestal, suffices to show that, even with our excellent modern implements, we find considerable difficulty in doing what to the Egyptians would have been one of the least arduous tasks. The use of tools on granite is thus described by Sir R. Westmacott:

"Granite, as most hard materials of that nature, being generally worked with a pick of various strength, until reduced to a surface, the duration of the tool depends on its form; the more obtuse, the longer it will work, remaining longer cold. In *jumping* (as it is termed) holes for the admission of bolts into fractured parts of granite, the tools are usually of strong tempered iron, about three quarters of an inch in diameter, which resist the heat sometimes half an hour, seldom longer. One man holds, and turns, or moves the tool, whilst the other strikes it with a heavy hammer, the hole being supplied with water. Tools of less diameter are formed of steel, but these will not resist more than 300 strokes, when the points fly, and require to be fresh battered. Sculptors generally use tools formed of blistered steel, or of cast steel, the finer sort highly tempered by immersing them, when heated to a proper degree, into cold water."

Some have imagined that the granite, being somewhat softer at the time it is taken from the quarry, was more easily sculptured when the Egyptians put up the obelisks than at present, and thus satisfy themselves that the labour was considerably less; but this argument is entirely overthrown by the fact of other sculptures having been frequently added, one hundred, and one hundred and fifty, years after the erection of a monument, as in the lateral lines of hieroglyphics on obelisks, which are sometimes found more deeply cut and more beautifully executed than those previously sculptured. Others have suggested that the stone being stunned, as it is termed, in those places were it was to be sculptured, yielded more readily to the blow of the chisel; but neither is this sufficient to produce the effect proposed, nor an advantage exclusively enjoyed by the ancient Egyptians.

Thus, then, the facility they possessed in sculpturing granite is neither attributable to any process for bruising the crystals, nor to its softer state on coming from the quarry, and we have still to discover the means they employed with such wonderful success.

The hieroglyphics on the obelisks are rather engraved than sculptured; and, judging from the minute manner in which they are executed, we may suppose they adopted the same process as engravers, and even in some instances employed the wheel and drill. That they were acquainted with the use of emery powder is not at all improbable, since, being found in the islands of the Archipelago, it was within their reach; and if this be admitted, we can account for the admirable finish and sharpness of the hieroglyphics on granitic and basaltic monuments, and explain the reason of their preferring tools of bronze to those of harder and more compact steel; for it is evident the powder enters more readily into the former, and its action upon the stone is increased in proportion to the quantity retained by the point of the chisel; whence we now prefer tools of soft iron to hard steel for the same purpose.

As far as the sculpture or engraving of hieroglyphics, this explanation might suffice for their preference of bronze implements; but when we find tools used in *quarries* made of the same metal, we are unable to account for it, and readily express our surprise how they could render a bronze chisel capable of hewing stone. We know of no means of tempering copper, under any form or united with any alloys, for such a purpose. The addition of tin or other metals to harden it, if exceeding certain proportions, renders it too brittle for use; and that such is not the case is evident from the above-mentioned chisel I found at Thebes, which contains very little alloy, 100 parts being 94·0 copper,

$$5\cdot 9 \text{ tin,}$$
$$0\cdot 1 \text{ iron,}$$
$$\overline{100\cdot 0};$$

and its point is instantly turned by striking it against the very stone it was once used to cut. And yet, when found, the summit was turned over by the blows it had received from the mallet, while the point was intact, as if it had recently left the hands of the smith who made it.

It is hard to say how it could have been used for cutting stone, and unless some medium was employed, as a sheath of steel or other protection to its point, the Egyptians must have possessed certain secrets in hardening or tempering copper with which we are totally unacquainted. The size of this chisel is $9\frac{1}{4}$ inches in length; its diameter at the summit is 1 inch, and the point is 7-10ths of an inch in its greatest width: its weight 1 lb. 12 oz., and in general form it resembles those now used by the masons of modern Europe.

The skill of the Egyptians in compounding metals is abundantly proved by the vases, mirrors, arms, and implements of bronze, discovered at Thebes, and other parts of Egypt; and the numerous methods they adopted for varying the composition of bronze, by a judicious admixture of alloys, are shown in the many qualities of the metal. They had even the secret of giving to bronze, or brass, blades a certain degree of elasticity, as in the dagger of the Berlin Museum; which probably depended on the mode of hammering the metal, and the just proportions of peculiar alloys. (*See* vol. i. p. 148.)

Another remarkable feature in their bronze is the resistance it offers to the effect of the atmosphere; some continuing smooth and bright, though buried for ages, and since exposed to the damp of European climates. They had also the secret of covering the surface with a rich patina of dark or light green, or other colour, by applying acids to it; as was done by the Greeks and Romans, and as we do to the iron guns on board our men-of-war.

The colour of their bronze depended on the alloys. It generally had from twelve to twenty parts tin to eighty or eighty-five copper. When half tin it had a whitish appearance; and some Roman bronze was of a "liver colour," probably like our urns. Lackered brass has even been found, of Roman time. Yellow brass was a compound of zinc and copper; and a white and finer kind had a mixture of silver, which was used for mirrors, and is one quality of the so-called "Corinthian brass." Another, which was yellow, and very like gold in appearance, was partly made of that metal with copper; and its beauty has been proved by the discovery of a cup, still capable of receiving some portion of its original polish.

In Egypt, as in Greece, bronze ornaments were often gilt, but statues were preferred plain, or inlaid, or damascened with gold or silver. Those of the Navarchai were, therefore, said by Plutarch to be blue from exposure to the air; and Pliny thinks the large colossus of Nero improved by the gilding having been scraped off, in spite of the scratches caused by the operation.

It is not known at what period they began to cast statues and other objects in bronze, or how long the use of beaten copper preceded the art of casting in that metal. No light is thrown on this point by the earlier paintings, nor is there any representation in later times, among the many subjects connected with the trades, arts, and occupations of the Egyptians, which relates to this process: one of the many proofs that no argument against the existence of a custom ought to be derived from the circumstance of its not being indicated on the monuments.

Many bronzes have been found, evidently, from their style, of a very early period. A cylinder with the name of Papi, of the sixth dynasty, has every appearance of having been cast; and other bronze implements of the same age bear still stronger evidence of having come from a mould; all of which date more than two thousand years before our era.

Pausanias, in speaking of the art of casting metal, says the people of Pheneum in Arcadia pretended that Ulysses dedicated a statue of bronze to Neptune Hippius, in order that he might recover the horses he had lost, through the intervention of the Deity; "indeed," he adds, "they showed me an inscription on the pedestal of the statue offering a reward to any person who should find and take care of the animals; but I do not give credit to the whole of their statement, and no one can persuade me that Ulysses erected a *bronze* statue to Neptune. The art of fusing metal and casting it in a mould was not yet known; a statue was made in those days like a dress, successively, and in pieces, not at one time, or in a single mass, as I have already shown in speaking of the statue of Jupiter, surnamed the Most High. In fact, the first who cast statues were Rhœcus the son of Philæus, and Theodorus the son of Telecles, both natives of Samos; the latter the same who engraved the beautiful emerald in the ring of Polycrates."

The Samians were noted at an early period for their skill in this branch of art; and before the foundation of Cyrene, or B.C. 630, they made a bronze vase, ornamented with griffins, supported on three colossal figures of the same metal, for the temple of Juno. The art was also known at a very remote period in Italy.

Among the Etruscans, bronze statues were common before the foundation of Rome; and Romulus is said to have placed a statue of himself, crowned by Victory, in a four-horsed car of bronze, which had been captured at the taking of Camerium.

Pliny attributes the discovery of gold and the secret of smelting it to Cadmus, who is supposed to have gone to Greece 1493 years before our era; but this, like most of the inventions mentioned by him, was long before known to the Egyptians; and we may apply the same remark to the supposed discovery of Rhœcus and Theodorus.

It is uncertain whether the Egyptians possessed the art of damascening or inlaying iron with gold, since, owing to the speedy decomposition of that metal, nothing made of iron has been preserved of a remote era; but we may conclude, from their inlaying bronze in this manner, that it was not unknown to them.

Some have supposed that Glaucus of Chios was the inventor of this art, and that the stand of his silver vase presented to the temple of Delphi by Alyattes, king of Lydia, which, according to Herodotus, was the most beautiful of all the offerings there, was made of iron inlaid with gold. But the description given of it by Pausanias will scarcely sanction this opinion, as he states " it consisted of several plates of iron, adjusted one over the other in the form of steps, the last, that is, those of the summit, curving a little outwards. It had the form of a tower, large at the base, and decreasing upwards, and the pieces of which it was composed were not fastened either with nails or pins, but simply soldered together."

The Greeks, however, were not ignorant of damascening, and if the stand of Alyattes' vase was not so inlaid, it is certain they possessed the art, and ornamented goblets and other objects in that manner. The process was very simple: the iron was carved with various devices, and the narrow lines thus hollowed out were filled with gold or with silver, which in some instances may have been soldered, but in others was simply beaten in with the hammer, the surface being afterwards filed and polished.

The term damascening, though generally confined to iron or steel so inlaid (owing to its having been borrowed from the specimens of this work in the modern sword blades of Damascus), may with equal propriety be extended to any metal; and numerous instances of bronze inlaid with gold and silver occur in statues, scarabæi, and various ornamental objects discovered at Thebes and other places. Hard stones were also engraved in the same manner, and the intaglio filled with gold or silver beaten into it; a process commonly adopted at the present day by the Turks, and other Eastern people, in their *hookahs* or *nârgilehs*, and in the stone ornaments of their amber mouth-pieces.

The art of soldering metals had long been practised in Egypt before the time of Glaucus; and it is curious to find gold and bronze vases, made apparently in the same manner as the stand of that mentioned by Pausanias, represented at Thebes, in the tribute brought from Asia to the third Thothmes, and consequently dating many centuries previous to the Chian artist. They are shown to have been composed of plates of metal, imbricated, or overlapping each other, as Pausanias describes, and sometimes bound at intervals with bands of metal. Instances occur in the same sculptures of gold vases with stands formed of similar plates, which are interesting also from the elegance of their forms.

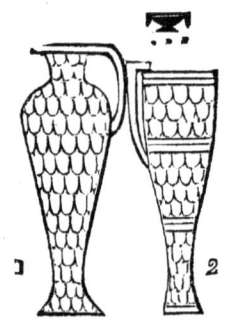
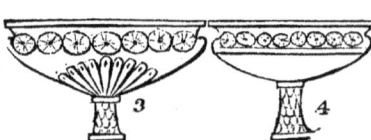

409. Vases of the time of Thothmes III., imbricated, or ornamented with plates of metal. Thebes.

In coarser work, or in those parts which were out of sight, the Egyptians soldered with lead, but we are ignorant of the time when it was first used for that purpose, though it could only have been after the discovery of tin; for, as Pliny justly observes, "lead can only be united by the addition of tin, nor is this last efficient without the application of oil." The oldest specimen of metal soldered with lead with which I am acquainted is the sistrum of Mr. Burton: its date, however, is uncertain; and though, from the style of the figures engraved upon it, we may venture to ascribe to it a Pharaonic age, the exact period when it was made cannot be fixed.

In early ages, before men had acquired the art of smelting ore, and of making arms and implements of metal, stones of various kinds were used, and the chasseur was contented with the pointed flint with which nature had provided him. The only effort of his ingenuity was to fix it in some kind of handle, or at the extremity of a reed, in order to make the knife, or the arrow; and we still witness the skill which some savage people of the present day display in constructing those rude weapons.

The Egyptians, at a remote period, before civilization dawned upon them, adopted the same; and we find that stone-tipped arrows continued to be occasionally used for hunting long after the metal head had been commonly adopted, and after the arts had arrived at the state of perfection in which they appear subsequently to the accession of the 18th dynasty. Long habit had reconciled them to the original reed shaft with its head of flint, and even to arrows made with a point of hard wood inserted into them, which were also the remnant of a primæval custom. Those, however, who preferred them of a stronger kind, adopted arrows of wood tipped with bronze heads; and these were considered more serviceable, and were almost invariably used in war.

The same prejudice in favour of an ancient and primitive custom retained the use of stone knives for certain purposes connected with religion among the Egyptians; and Herodotus tells us it was usual to make an incision in the body of the deceased, when brought to be embalmed, with an Ethiopic stone. This name, in all instances where the stone is said to be used for cutting, evidently signifies flint, which is shown by its frequent employment for that purpose among many people, and by our finding several flint knives in the tombs of Thebes. In other cases, the Ethiopic stone, mentioned by Herodotus, is evidently granite, so called from being common in Ethiopia; and it is possible that the flint received that name from its *black* colour.

The stone knives found in the excavations and tombs, many of which are preserved in our European museums, are generally of two kinds; one broad and flat like the blade of a knife, the other narrow and pointed at the summit, several of which are preserved in the Berlin Museum (*fig.* 1). These last are supposed to have been used for making the incision in the side of the body, for the purpose of removing the intestines, preparatory to the embalming process already mentioned; and, considering how strongly men's minds are prepossessed in favour of early habits connected with religion, and how scrupulous the Egyptians were, above all people, in permitting the introduction of new customs in matters relating to the gods, we are not surprised that they should have retained the use of these primitive instruments in a ceremony of so sacred a nature as the embalming of the dead.

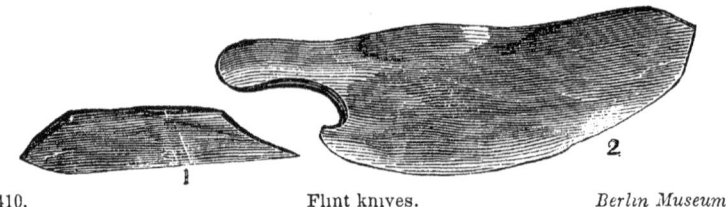

410.   Flint knives.   *Berlin Museum.*

The difference in the type of the metal implements of the Egyptians and early European people is very marked. The former continued always to use flat blades of metal for adzes and hatchets; those of Italy, Greece, the Tyrol, Gaul, Britain, Ireland, and other parts of Europe, gradually changed the form of the flat blade (which had succeeded to the stone hammer and hatchet), and gave it projecting sides, then a transverse ridge in the centre to prevent the slipping of the wooden handle fitted *upon* it, and to withstand the shock of a blow; and at length they made it into a metal socket, with which the wood was shod. The mode of fastening the metal to the handle was the same in Europe as in Egypt, which was with thongs of hide (as is still done in the South Sea Islands and other places); but our various forms of celtes, or "hatchets," were unknown to, and are readily distinguished from the tools of, the Egyptians.

Besides the various trades already noticed, were public weighers and common notaries, answering to the *kabbáneh* of modern Egypt. The business of the former was to ascertain the exact weight of everything they were called upon to measure, in the public street or market, where they temporarily erected their scales, and where the law compelled them to adjust the sale of each commodity with the strictest regard to justice, without favouring either the buyer or seller. All things sold by weight were submitted to this test, and the value of the money paid for them was settled by the same unquestionable criterion.

A scribe or notary marked down the amount of the weight, whatever the commodity might be; and this document, being given or shown to the parties, completely sanctioned the bargain, and served as a pledge that justice had been done them.

The same custom is still retained by the modern Egyptians, the scales of the public *ḳabbáneh* in the large towns being a criterion to which no one can object; and the weight of meat, vegetables, honey, butter, cheese, wood, charcoal, and other objects, having been ascertained, is returned in writing on the application of the parties.

The notaries were merely public writers, like the modern *katebs* of Egypt, or the *scrivani* of Italy, who for a small trifle compose and pen a petition to government, settle accounts, and write letters, or other documents not requiring the priest or the lawyer, for those who are untaught, or too idle to do so for themselves. These persons, however, must not be confounded with the "royal" or "priestly scribes"—men of high rank, of the military or sacerdotal class; and they were only on a par with the shop-keepers and master tradesmen, most of whom learnt to write; while the working-men were contented to occupy their time in acquiring a knowledge of the art to which they were brought up.

Certain persons were also employed in the towns of Egypt, as at the present day in Cairo and other places, to pound various substances in large stone mortars; and salt, seeds, and other things were taken in the same manner by a servant to these shops, whenever it was inconvenient to have it done in the house. The pestles they used, as well as the mortars themselves, were precisely similar to those of the modern Egyptians; and their mode of pounding was the same; two men alternately raising ponderous metal pestles with both hands, and directing

411. Pounding various substances in stone mortars, with metal pestles. *Thebes.*
a g i, mortars.   *d d*, pestles.   Figs. 1 and 2, alternately raising and letting fall the pestles into the mortar.   Figs. 3 and 4, sifting the substance after it is pounded; the coarser parts, *h*, being returned into the mortar to be again pounded.

their falling point to the centre of the mortar, which is now generally made of a large piece of granite, or other hard stone, scooped out into a long narrow tube, to little more than half its depth. When the substance was well pounded, it was taken out and passed through a sieve, and the larger particles were again returned to the mortar, until it was sufficiently and equally levigated; and this, and the whole process here represented, so strongly resemble the occupation of the public pounders at Cairo, that no one, who has been in the habit of walking in the streets of that town, can fail to recognize the custom, or doubt of its having been handed down from the early Egyptians, and retained without alteration to the present day.

The occupation of the cooper was comparatively limited in Egypt, where water and other liquids were carried, or kept, in skins and earthenware jars; and wooden barrels were little suited to its arid climate. Barrels were not, therefore, in common use there; and the skill of the cooper was only required to make wooden measures for grain, which were bound with hoops of wood or metal, and resembled in principle those used by the modern Egyptians for the same purpose, though in form some approached nearer to the small barrels, or kegs, of modern Europe.

Boats with coloured and embroidered sails. *Tomb of Remeses III. Thebes.*

Cattle during the Inundation in the Delta.

CHAPTER VIII.

THE FIFTH CLASS—PASTORS, POULTERERS, SHOPS, FOWLERS, FISHERMEN, LABOURERS, BRICKMAKERS, AND COMMON PEOPLE—JEWS—PEOPLE GIVING AN ACCOUNT OF THEIR MODE OF LIVING—LAWS—JUDGES—CRIMES AND PUNISHMENTS—THIEVES—DEBTORS—SALES AND DEEDS—MARRIAGES—PARENTS—LAWGIVERS—PROVINCES AND GOVERNORS—REVENUES—GOLD—MENSURATION—THREE SEASONS — INTERCALATION — SOTHIC YEAR — LAND MEASURES — CUBIT — WEIGHTS AND MEASURES.

THE fifth class was composed of pastors, poulterers, fowlers, fishermen, labourers, brickmakers, and common people. The pastors were divided into oxherds, shepherds, goatherds, and swineherds; but even among them a gradation of rank was observed; and those who tended the herds and flocks while grazing were inferior in position to the managers of stock in the farmyard, who prepared provender for them when the Nile covered the lands. Those too who understood the veterinary art and took care of the sick cattle were men of skill and intelligence, who held a higher post among the pastors. But they were all looked upon by the Egyptian aristocracy as people who followed a disgraceful employment; and it is therefore not surprising that Pharaoh should have treated the Israelites with that contempt which it was usual for the Egyptians to feel towards "shepherds;" or that Joseph should have warned his brethren, on their arrival, of this aversion of the Egyptians, and of their considering every shepherd an abomination. rd from his recommending them to request they might dwell the land of Goshen, we may conclude it was with a view to avoid, as much as possible, those who were not shepherds like themselves, or to obtain a settlement in the land peculiarly adapted for pasture. It is also probable that much of Pharaoh's cattle was kept there, since the monarch gave orders that if any of those strangers were remarkable for skill in the management of herds, they should be selected to overlook his own cattle, after they were settled in the land of Goshen. This part of the country received at a later time the name of *Bucolia;* and the northern part of the Delta, with the lands lying to the east of the Damietta branch of the Nile, are still preferred for grazing cattle.

The hatred borne against shepherds by the Egyptians was not owing solely to their contempt for that occupation; this feeling originated in another and a far more powerful cause—the occupation of their country by a pastor race, who had committed great cruelties during their possession of the country. And as if to prove how much they despised every order of pastors, the artists, both of Upper and Lower Egypt, delighted on all occasions in caricaturing their appearance.

The swineherds were the most ignoble, and, of all the Egyptians, the only persons who are said not to have been permitted to enter a temple; and even if this statement is exaggerated, it tends to show with what contempt they were looked upon by the individuals from whom Herodotus received his information, and how far they ranked beneath any others of the whole order of pastors. Indeed (as I have before stated), the same is still the case in India, where the swineherds are the very lowest class, and are so despised that no others will associate with them.

The skill of these people in rearing animals of different kinds was the result, says Diodorus, of the experience they had inherited from their parents, and subsequently increased by their own observation; and the spirit of emulation, which is natural to all men, constantly adding to their stock of knowledge, they introduced many improvements unknown to other people. Their sheep were twice shorn, and twice brought forth lambs in the cour of year; and though the climate was the chief cause of these phenomena, the skill and attention of the shepherd were also necessary; nor, if the animals were neglected, would unaided nature alone suffice for their continuance.

170	THE ANCIENT EGYPTIANS.	Chap. VIII.

But of all the discoveries to which any class of Egyptians attained, the one that the historian considered most worthy of admiration was their artificial process of hatching the eggs of fowls and geese, which has been continued to the present day by their Copt successors. The modern process, like that of ancient times, is this: they have ovens expressly built for the purpose; and persons are sent round to the villages to collect the eggs from the peasants, which, being given to the rearers, are all placed on

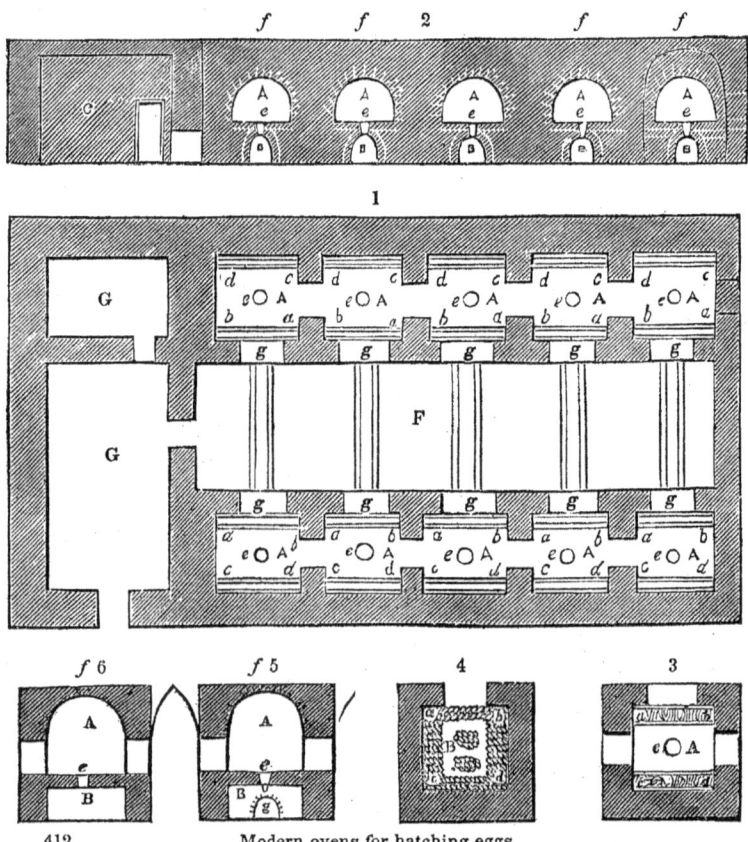

412. Modern ovens for hatching eggs.

Fig. 1. Plan of the building, showing the form of the upper rooms A A, the entrance-room G G, and the passage F. At *a a* are the fires; *e e* the aperture communicating with the oven.
2. Section of the same, showing the upper rooms A and B.
3. Plan of upper room, in which the fires are placed at *a b* and *c d*.
4. Lower room in which the eggs are placed.
5, 6. Sections from the back and front of the upper and lower rooms A and B.

mats, strewed with bran, in a room about eleven feet square, with a flat roof, and about four feet high, over which is another chamber of the same size, with a vaulted roof, and about nine feet high; a small aperture in the centre of the vault (at f), admitting light during the warm weather, and another (e) of larger diameter, immediately below, communicating with the oven through its ceiling. By this also the man descends to observe the eggs; but in the cold season both are closed, and a lamp is kept burning within; another entrance at the front part of the oven, or lower room, being then used for the same purpose, and shut immediately on his quitting it. By way of distinction, I call the vaulted (A) the upper room, and the lower one (B) the oven. In the former are two fires, in the troughs $a\,b$ and $c\,d$, which, based with earthen slabs, three quarters of an inch thick, reach from one side to the other, against the front and back walls. These fires are lighted twice a day: the first dies away about midday; and the second, lighted at 3 P.M., lasts until 8 o'clock. In the oven, the eggs are placed on mats strewed with bran, in two corresponding lines to, and immediately below, the fires $a\,b$ and $c\,d$, where they remain half a day. They are then removed to $a\,c$ and $b\,d$, and others (from two heaps in the centre) are arranged at $a\,b$ and $c\,d$ in their stead; and so on, till all have taken their equal share of the warmest positions, to which each set returns again and again, in regular succession, till the expiration of six days.

They are then held up, one by one, towards a strong light; and if the eggs appear clear, and of a uniform colour, it is evident they have not succeeded; but if they show an opaque substance within, or the appearance of different shades, the chickens are already formed, and they are returned to the oven for four more days, their positions being changed as before. At the expiration of the four days they are removed to another oven, over which, however, are no fires. Here they lie for five days in one heap, the apertures (e,f) and the door (g) being closed with tow to exclude the air; after which they are placed separately about one or two inches apart, over the whole surface of the mats, which are sprinkled with a little bran. They are at this time continually turned, and shifted from one part of the mats to another, during six or seven days, all air being carefully excluded; and are constantly examined by one of the rearers, who applies each singly to his upper eyelid. Those which are cold prove the chickens to be dead, but warmth greater than the human skin is the favourable sign of their success.

At length the chicken, breaking its egg, gradually comes forth: and it is not a little curious to see some half exposed and half covered by the shell; while they chirp in their confinement, which they show the greatest eagerness to quit.

The total number of days is generally twenty-one, but some eggs with a thin shell remain only eighteen. The average of those that succeed is two thirds, which are returned by the rearers to the proprietors, who restore to the peasants one half of the chickens, the other being kept as payment for their expenses.

The size of the building depends, of course, on the means or speculation of the proprietors; but the general plan is usually the same, being a series of eight or ten ovens and upper rooms, on either side of a passage about 100 feet by 15, and 12 in height. The thermometer in any part is not less than 86° or 88° Fahr.; but the average heat in the ovens does not reach the temperature of fowls, which is 104°.

Excessive heat or cold are equally prejudicial to this process; and the only season of the year at which they succeed is from the 15th of Imsheer (23rd of February) to the 15th of Baramoodeh (24th of April), beyond which time they can scarcely reckon upon more than two or three in a hundred.

The great care bestowed by the shepherds on the breed of sheep was attended with no less important results; and the selection of proper food for them at particular seasons, and the mode of treating them when ill, was their constant study. Indeed, their skill in curing animals was carried to the greatest perfection; and Cuvier's discovery of the left *humerus* of a mummied ibis fractured and reunited, evidently through the intervention of human art, fully confirms the fact.

Those who exercised the veterinary art were of the class of

413. Herdsmen and poulterers treating sick animals and geese. *Beni Hassan.*

Fig. 1. Feeding a sick goose.
2. In the original, this figure shows more skill in the drawing than is usual in Egyptian sculpture.
3. Feeding an oryx.
4, 5. Treatment of goats. The foreleg is tied up to prevent the animal rising while the medicine is administered to it.
7. Forces a ball of medicated food, taken from the vase before him, into the ox's mouth.

174 THE ANCIENT EGYPTIANS. Chap. VIII.

shepherds. They took the utmost care of the animals, providing them with proper food, which they gave them with the hand, and preparing for them whatever medicine they required, which they forced into their mouths. Their medical aid was not confined to oxen and sheep; it extended also to the oryx, and other animals of the desert they tamed or bred in the farmyard; and the poulterers bestowed the same care on the geese and fowls.

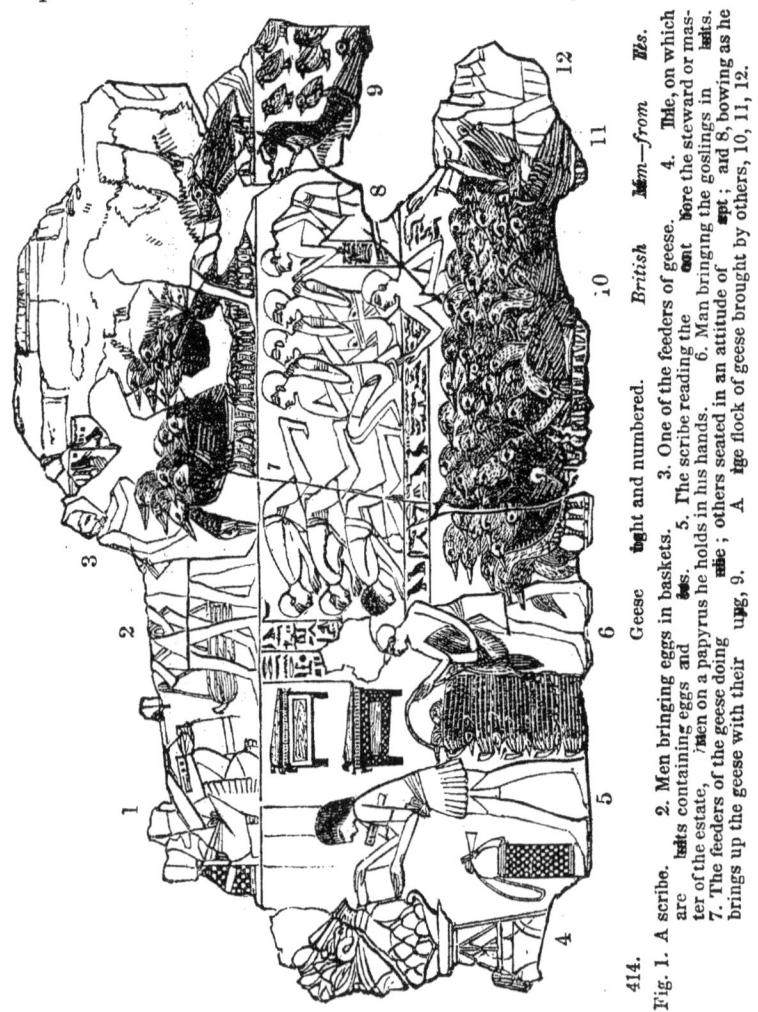

414.
Fig. 1. A scribe. 2. Men bringing eggs in baskets. 3. One of the feeders of geese. 4. One, on which are baskets containing eggs and fowls. 5. The scribe reading the account bore the steward or master of the estate, Men on a papyrus he holds in his hands. 6. Man bringing the goslings in baskets. 7. The feeders of the geese doing the; others seated in an attitude of respect; and 8, bowing as he brings up the geese with their young, 9. A large flock of geese brought by others, 10, 11, 12.

Geese tight and numbered. British Mum—from His.

And such was their attention to the habits of different animals, and the patient treatment of them, that the wildest and most timid were rendered so tame as to be driven, like the sheep and goats; and the wild geese and other birds were brought to the stewards, whenever an inventory was made of the live stock on the estate.

The pastors were a class apart from the agriculturists, and were held in disrepute, partly from the nature of their occupation, partly from the prejudices of the Egyptians against all herdsmen. But this did not extend to the farmers who bred cattle or sheep; it was confined to the poor people who kept them; and as if to show how degraded a class they were, they are represented, as at Beni Hassan and the tombs near the Pyramids, lame, or deformed, dirty, unshaven, and even of a ludicrous appearance; and often clad in dresses made of matting, similar in quality to the covering thrown over the backs of the oxen they are tending.

415. A deformed oxherd. *Tombs near the Pyramids.*

They generally lived in sheds made of reeds, deriving a scanty nourishment from the humblest and coarsest food; but they were overlooked by other persons of a superior condition among the pastoral class. There were also overseers of the shepherds, who regulated everything respecting the stock—which were to graze in the field, which to be stall-fed; and their duty was also to give reports at certain periods to the scribes attached to the steward's office, who examined them preparatory to their being presented to the owner of the estate. In these nothing was omitted; and every egg was noted in the account, and entered with the chickens and goslings. And in order to prevent

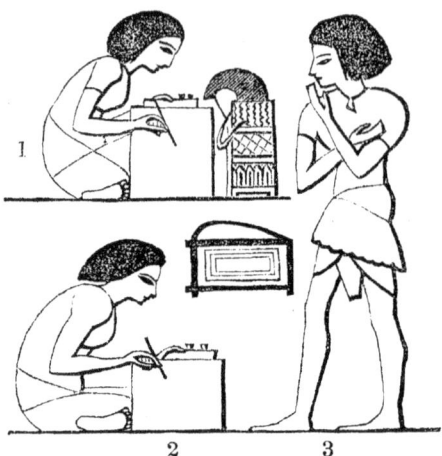

416.   Giving an account to two scribes of the stock on the estate.   *Thebes.*
Before fig. 1 is the sachel, and above fig. 2 the box for holding writing implements and papyri. They are writing on boards: in their left hands are the inkstands with black and red ink.

any connivance, or a question respecting the accuracy of a report, two scribes received it from the superintendents at the same moment. Everything was done in writing. Bureaucratie was as consequential in Egypt as in modern Austria, or France; scribes were required on every occasion, to settle public or private questions; no bargain of consequence was made without the vouchure of a written document; and the sale of a small piece of land required sixteen witnesses. Either the Egyptians were great cheats, or a very cautious people—probably both; and they would have been in an agony of mind to see us so careless, and so duped in many of our railway and other speculations.

The shepherds on the estate were chosen by the steward, who ascertained their character and skill before they were appointed to their various duties; and Pharaoh in like manner commanded Joseph, who was superintendent " over all the land of Egypt," to select from among his brethren such as were skilful in the management of the flocks or herds, and " make them rulers over his cattle."

There was also the honorary office of " superintendent of the

CHAP. VIII. SHEPHERDS APPOINTED TO THEIR POST. 177

herds;" but this was very different from the duty of any one in the class of shepherds: it was a high and distinguished post, being held by persons of rank belonging to the priestly and military classes, who were called "superintendents of the cattle

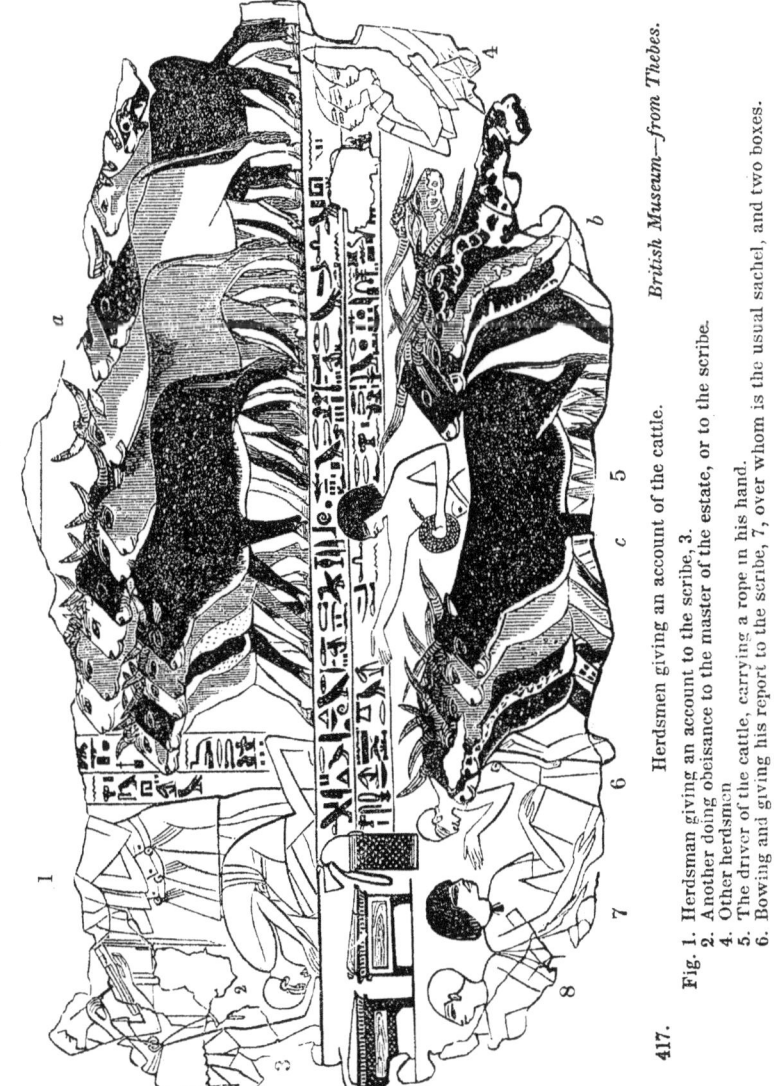

417. Fig. 1. Herdsman giving an account to the scribe, 3.
2. Another doing obeisance to the master of the estate, or to the scribe.
4. Other herdsmen
5. The driver of the cattle, carrying a rope in his hand.
6. Bowing and giving his report to the scribe, 7, over whom is the usual sachel, and two boxes.

Herdsmen giving an account of the cattle.   British Museum—from Thebes.

of the 'king," or " of some god ;" and one of the former, named Honofr, whose wife was one of the sacred women of Amun, is mentioned in a very beautiful papyrus in the British Museum.

The cattle were brought into a court attached to the steward's house, or into the farmyard, and counted by the superintendent in the presence of the scribes; and the bastinado was freely administered if any fraud was detected, or if any shepherd had neglected the flocks committed to his care.

In the accompanying woodcut the numbers written over the animals correspond to the report made to the steward, who, in the presence of the master of the estate, receives it from the overseer, or the head shepherd. First come the oxen, over which is the number 834, then cows 220, goats 3234, asses 760, rams 974; followed by a man carrying the young lambs in baskets slung upon a pole. The steward leaning on his staff, and accompanied by what was then a fashionable dog, "with a curly tail," stands on the left of the picture; and in another place the scribes are making out the statements presented to them by the different persons employed on the farm. The tomb where this subject occurs is at the Pyramids, dating upwards of 4000 years ago, when the Egyptians had already the same customs as at a much later period. How long before this they had reached this state of civilization; had laid aside their arms; had decimal as well as duodecimal calculation, and the reckoning by units, tens, hundreds, and thousands, it is impossible to determine; but these, as well as the use of squared stone, even granite, and many other arts, were known to them before the Pyramids were built.

Many birds which frequented the interior and skirts of the desert, and were highly prized for the table, were caught by the fowlers, as the partridge, *gutta* (*pterocles*, or sand-grouse), bustard, and quail; and water-fowl of different descriptions, which abounded in the Valley of the Nile, afforded endless diversion to the sportsman, and profit to those who gained a livelihood by their sale.

Fowling was a favourite amusement of all classes; and the

NUMBERS OVER CATTLE. 179

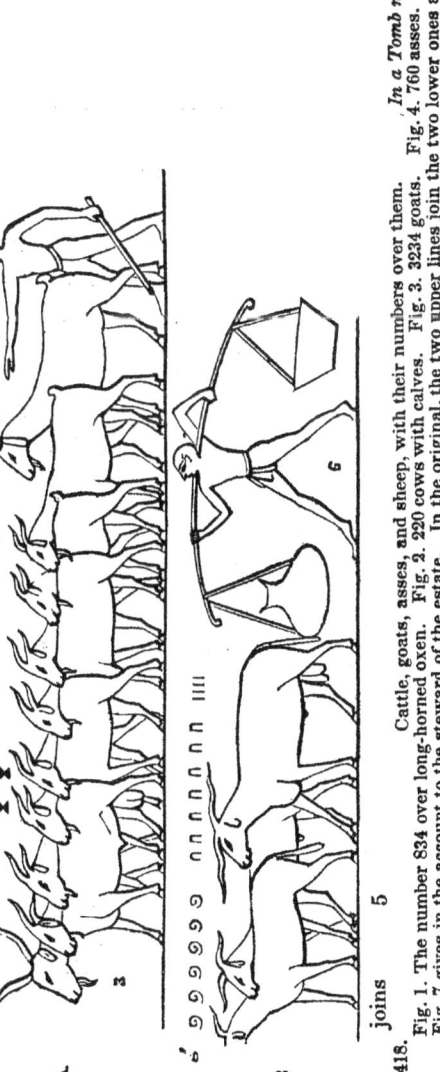

418. Cattle, goats, asses, and sheep, with their numbers over them. *In a Tomb near the Pyramids.* Fig. 1. The number 834 over long-horned oxen. Fig. 2. 220 cows with calves. Fig. 3. 3234 goats. Fig. 4. 760 asses. Fig. 5. 974 sheep. Fig. 7 gives in the account to the steward of the estate. In the original, the two upper lines join the two lower ones at A and B.

fowlers and fishermen were subdivisions of one of the classes into which the Egyptians were divided. They either caught the birds in large clap-nets or in traps; and they sometimes shot them with arrows, or felled them with a throw-stick, as they flew in the thickets. (*See* vol. i. p. 234 to 236.)

The trap was generally made of net-work, strained over a frame. It consisted of two semicircular sides or flaps, of equal sizes, one or both moving on the common bar, or axis, upon which they rested. When the trap was set, the two flaps were kept open by means of strings, probably of catgut, which, the moment the bait that stood in the centre of the bar was touched, slipped aside, and allowed the two flaps to collapse, and thus secured the bird.

Another kind, which was square, appears to have closed in the same manner; but its construction was different, the framework

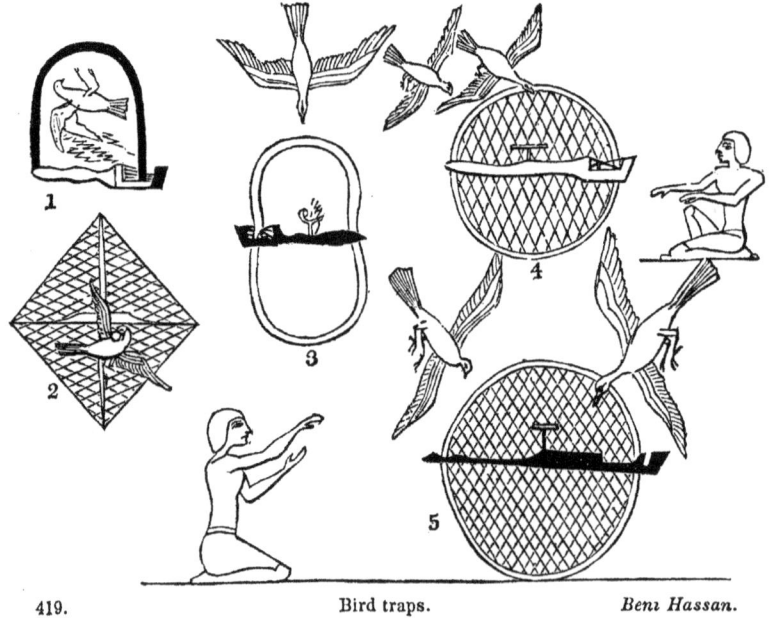

419.   Bird traps.   *Beni Hassan.*

Fig. 1. Trap closed, and the bird caught in it; the net-work of it has been effaced, as also in fig. 3. The other traps are open.

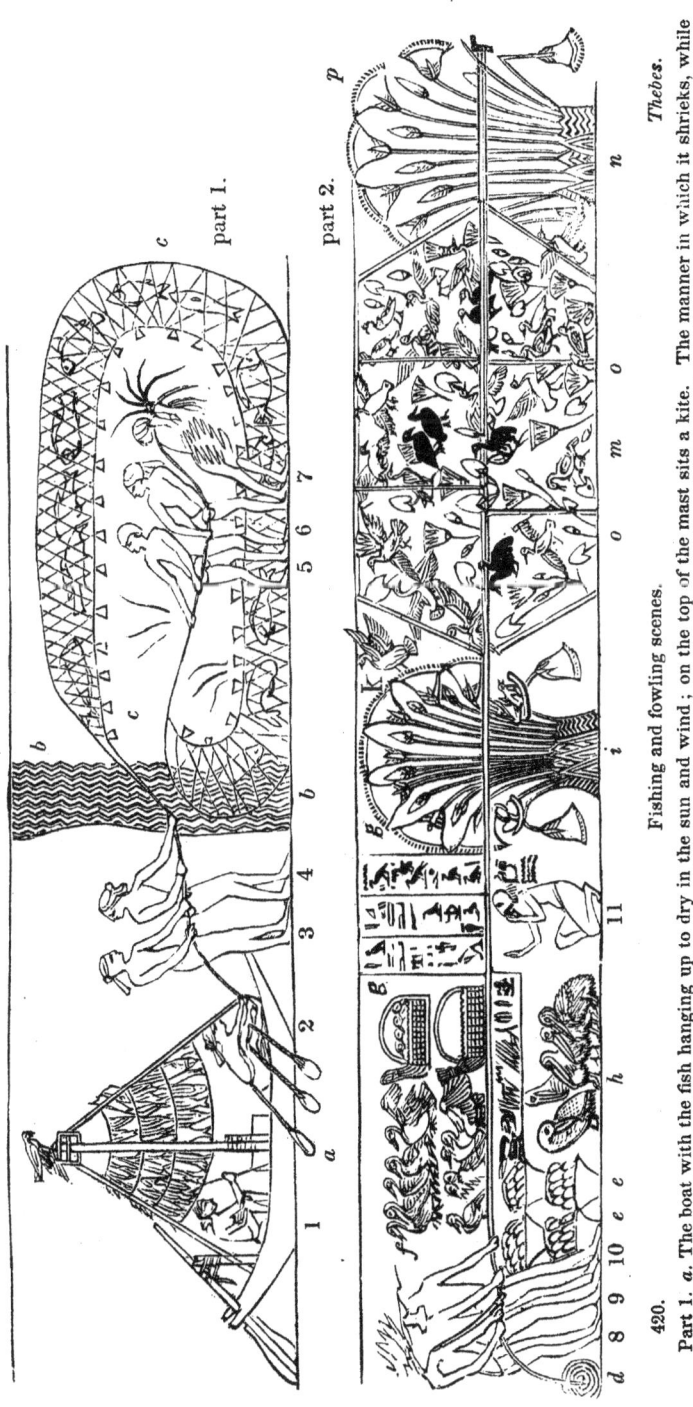

420. Fishing and fowling scenes. *Thebes.*

Part 1. *a.* The boat with the fish hanging up to dry in the sun and wind; on the top of the mast sits a kite. The manner in which it shrieks, while waiting for the entrails of the fish, as they are thrown out, is very characteristically shown in the original painting. The boat is supposed to be close to the shelving bank to which they are dragging the net. The water is represented by zigzag lines at *b*, which, to prevent confusion, I have not continued over the net.

Part 2. Figs. 8, 9, 10, pull the rope that the net may collapse; 11 makes a sign with his hand to keep silence and pull; at *p* the rope is fixed; at *f, g, i, e,* are geese and baskets of their young and eggs; *h* are pelicans; *i* and *n*, papyrus plants.

running across the centre, and not, as in the others, round the edges of the trap.

And so skilful were they in making traps, that they were strong enough to hold the hyæna; and in the one which caught the robber in the treasury of Rhampsinitus, the power of the spring, or the mechanism of the catch, was so perfect that his brother was unable to open it, or release him.

Similar in ingenuity, though not in strength, were the nets made by the convicts banished to Rhinocolura by Actisanes, which, though made of split straws, were yet capable of catching many of the numerous quails that frequented that desert region at a particular period of the year.

The clap-net was of different forms, though on the same general principle as the traps. It consisted of two sides or frames, over which the network was strained; at one end was a short rope, which they fastened to a bush, or a cluster of reeds, and at the other was one of considerable length, which, as soon as the birds were seen feeding in the area within the net, was pulled by the fowlers, causing the two sides to collapse.*

As soon as they had selected a convenient spot for laying down the net, in a field or on the surface of a pond, the known resort of numerous wild fowl, they spread open the two sides or flaps, and secured them in such a manner that they remained flat upon the ground until pulled by the rope. A man, crouched behind some reeds growing at a convenient distance from the spot, from which he could observe the birds as they came down, watched the net, and enjoining silence by placing his hand over his mouth, beckoned to those holding the rope to keep themselves in readiness till he saw them assembled in sufficient numbers, when a wave of his hand gave the signal for closing the net.

The Egyptian mode of indicating silence is evidently shown, from these scenes, to have been by placing "the hand on their mouth" (as in Job, xxix. 9), not, as generally supposed, by approaching the forefinger to the lips; and the Greeks erroneously concluded that the youthful Harpocrates was the deity of silence,

* Woodcut 420, part 2.

NETS. SIGN FOR SILENCE. 183

from his appearing in this attitude; which, however humiliating to the character of a deity, was only illustrative of his extreme

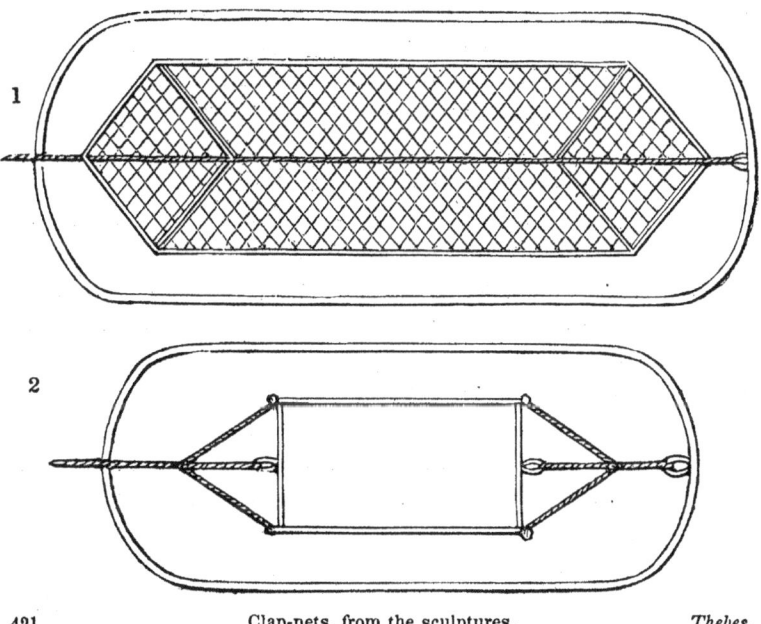

421. Clap-nets, from the sculptures. *Thebes.*

youth, and of a habit common to children in every country, whether of ancient or modern times.

The poulterers may be divided into two grades—the rearers, and those who sold poultry in the market; the former living in the country and villages, the latter in the towns. They fed them for the table; and besides the number required for private consumption, a great many were exclusively fattened for the service of the temple, as well as for the sacred animals, and for the daily rations of the priests and soldiers, or others who lived at the government expense. The birds were principally geese, ducks, teal, quails, and some small birds, which they were in the habit of salting, especially in Lower Egypt, where they ate "all sorts of birds and fish, not reckoned sacred, either roasted or boiled." For besides geese and pigeons, which abounded in Egypt, many of the wading tribe—the ardea and several others —were esteemed for the table, and even introduced among the choice offerings to the gods. But the favourite was the *Vulpanser* of the Nile, known to us as "the Egyptian goose," which, with some others of the same genus, were tamed and kept like ordinary poultry. Those in a wild state, having been caught in the large clap-nets, were brought to the poulterers, who salted and potted them in earthenware jars; and others were put up in the shops for immediate sale. Like other rearers of animals, the poulterers paid great attention to the habits of wild geese, which were tamed to feed in flocks, like our turkeys; and they had doubtless perceived that, besides warmth, chickens require to have their food constantly within reach; perhaps even buried, that they may exercise their natural habit of scratching it up; and not to have a great quantity after long intervals.

The form and character of the various shops depended on the will, or the particular trade of the person they belonged to; and many no doubt sat and sold in the streets, as at the present day. The poulterers suspended geese and other birds from a pole, or on nails, in front of the shop, over which an awning was stretched to keep off the sun; and many of the shops resembled our stalls, being open in front, with the goods exposed on shelves, or hanging from the inner wall, as is still the custom in the *bazárs* of eastern towns.

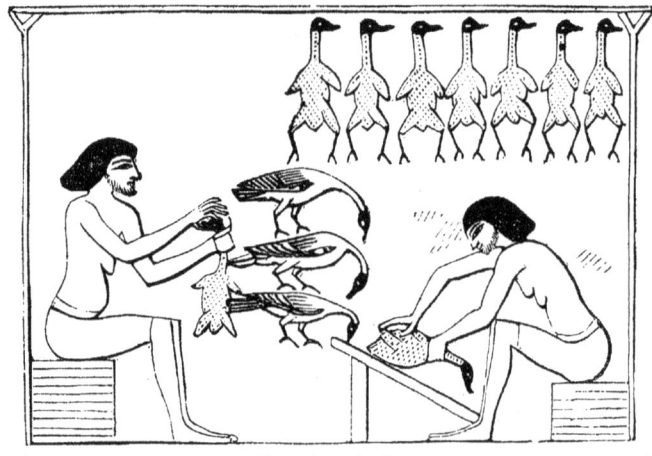

422.   A poulterer's shop.   *Thebes.*

CHAP. VIII. POULTERERS' SHOPS. 185

The distribution of labour seems to have been as well understood by the Egyptians as in modern times; one plucked, another opened and trussed, and a third potted, or hung up the birds; and the same variety of offices was allotted to different individuals in other trades. Part of the occupation of poulter-

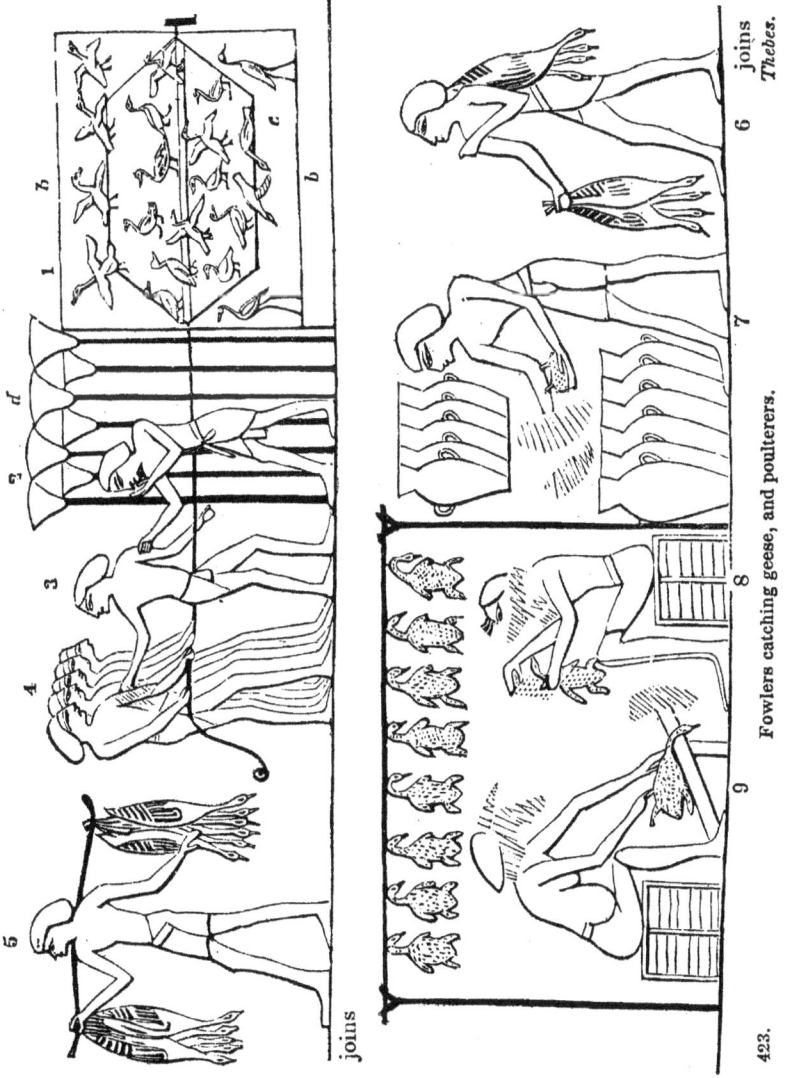

Fowlers catching geese, and poulterers.

ers was to collect eggs of wild birds; and whenever these could be procured, they were carefully collected and submitted to the management of the rearers, like those of tame fowl. The same care was taken to obtain the young of gazelles, and other wild animals of the desert, whose meat was reckoned among the dainties of the table; and by paying proper attention to their habits, they were enabled to collect many head of antelopes, which formed part of the herds of the Egyptian nobles. And in order to give an idea of the pains they took in rearing these timid animals, and to show the great value of the possessions of the deceased, they are introduced with the cattle, in the sculptures of the tombs.

Those who were fishermen by trade, and gained a livelihood by it, generally used the net in preference to the line; though on some occasions they employed the latter, seated or standing on the bank. But these last were poor people who could not afford the expense of nets; and the use of their very simple line was mostly confined, as at the present day, to those who depended on skill or good luck for a precarious subsistence. If we may believe Ælian—that most unsophisticated fish, the Thrissa of the Lake Mareotis, "was caught by singing to it,

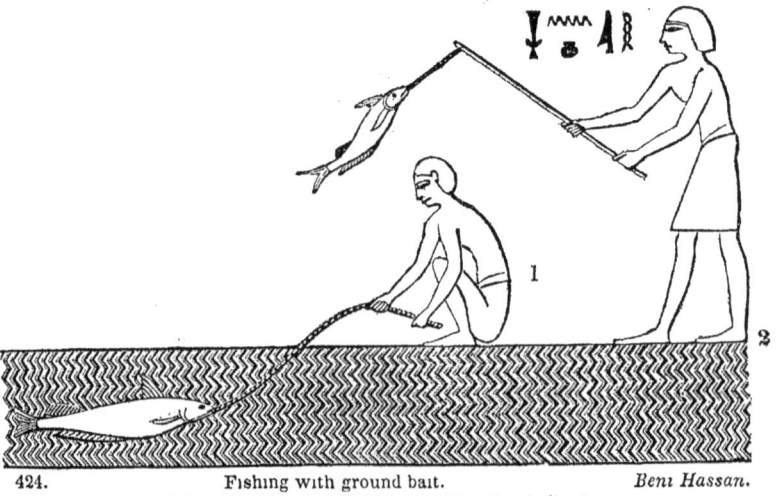

424.   Fishing with ground bait.   *Beni Hassan.*
These fish are the *Shilbeh,* or rather the *Arábrab.*

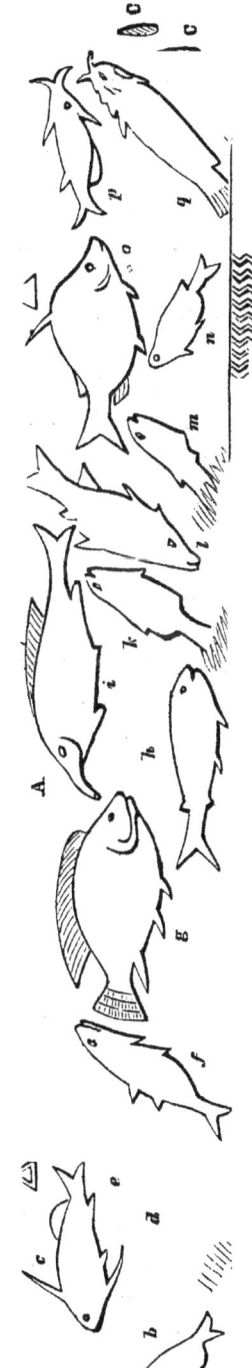

A A. The net.   B B. The floats.   C C. The leads.

Fishing with a drag-net. *Tomb near the Pyramids.*

and by the sound of *crotala* (clappers) made of shells;" and so musically inclined was this species, and so sharp in hearing sounds even out of its own element, that, " dancing up, it leapt into the nets spread for the purpose, giving great and abundant sport." Indeed, if Plato and others are to be trusted, the Egyptians not only caught, but tamed fish, with the same facility as land animals.

Fishermen mostly used the net. It was of a long form, like the common drag-net, with wooden floats on the upper, and leads on the lower side;* but though it was sometimes let down from a boat, those who pulled it generally stood on the shore, and landed the fish on a shelving bank. The leads were occasionally of an elongated shape, hanging from the outer cord or border of the net; but they were most usually flat, and, being folded round the cord, the opposite sides were beaten together; a satisfactory instance of which is seen in the ancient net preserved in the Berlin Museum; and this method continues to be adopted by the modern Egyptians.

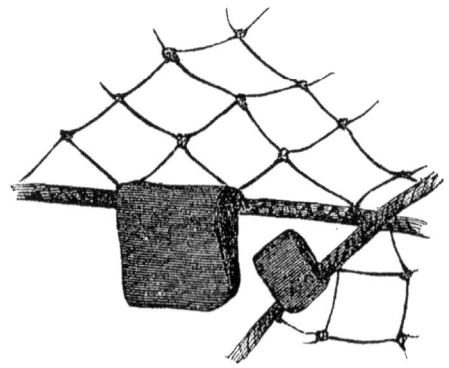

426.	Leads, with part of a net.	*Berlin Museum.*

Besides the ordinary Egyptian net, they sometimes used a smaller kind, for catching fish in shallow water, furnished with a pole on either side, to which it was attached, exactly similar to one now used in India; and the fisherman, holding one of the poles in either hand, thrust it below the surface of the water, and

* *See* woodcut 425.

awaited the moment when a shoal of small fry passed over it. And this, or a smaller landing-net, secured the large fish, which had been wounded with the spear, or entangled with the hook.

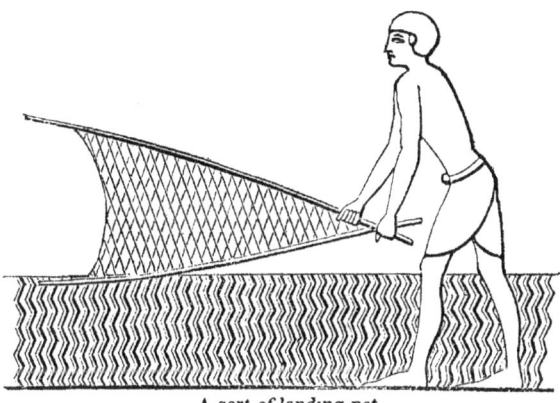

427. A sort of landing-net. Thebes.

When they employed the drag-net, and even when they pulled it to the shore, a boat sometimes attended, in which the fish were deposited as soon as caught; those intended for immediate use, to be eaten fresh, being sent off to market when the day's sport was finished, and the others being opened, salted, and hung up to dry in the sun.*

Some were cut in half, and, suspended on ropes, were left to dry in the sun and the open air; sometimes the body was simply laid open with a knife from the head to the tail, the two sides being divided as far as the back bone; and many were contented with taking out the intestines, and removing the head and tip of the tail, and exposing them, when salted, to the sun.

When caught, the small fish were generally put into baskets, but those of a larger kind were suspended to a pole, borne by two or more men over their shoulders, or were carried singly in the hand, slung at their back, or under the arm; all which methods are adopted by the modern fishermen at the Cataracts of A'Souán, and in other parts of the country.

Great was the consumption of fish in Egypt, as we know from

* Woodcuts 420, 428.

the sculptures and other good authority; the "fishers" of the Nile, and "they that cast angle into the brooks," "they that spread nets," and they "that make sluices and ponds for fish," are mentioned in the Bible;* and the Israelites remembered with regret "the fish which (they) did eat in Egypt freely."† They were eaten either fresh or salted; and at a particular month of the year, on the 9th day of the first month (Thoth), every person was obliged, by a religious ordinance, to eat a fried fish before the door of his house, with the exception of the priests, who were contented to burn it on that occasion.‡

Some fish were particularly prized for the table, and preferred as being more wholesome, as well as superior in flavour to others; among which we may mention the *búlti*,§ the *kishr*,‖ the *benni*,¶ the *shall*,** the *shilbeh*,†† and *arábrab*, the *byad*,‡‡ the *karmoot*,§§ and a few others; but it was unlawful to touch those which were sacred, as the oxyrhinchus, the phagrus, and the lepidotus: and the inhabitants of the city of Oxyrhinchus objected even to eat any fish caught by a hook, lest it should have been defiled by the blood of one they held so sacred.

The oxyrhinchus was probably the *mizdeh*, a mormyrus remarkable among the fish of the Nile for its pointed nose, as the word *oxyrhinchus* implies; and a prejudice is still felt

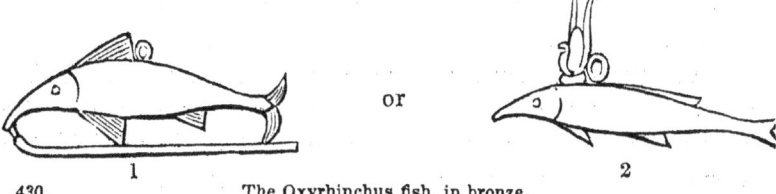

430.   The Oxyrhinchus fish, in bronze.

against it in some parts of Upper Egypt. Indeed, *mızdeh* is not very unlike the Coptic name of the city of (Oxyrhinchus) Mge. It is often represented in the sculptures and in bronze; and in the temple of the Great Oasis this fish is accompanied by the name of Athor, or Venus, showing it to have been one of her emblems.

431.   At the Oasis.

* Isaiah, xix. 8, 10.
† Numb. xi. 5.
‡ Plut. de Is. s. 7.
§ Or *booltee*, Labrus Niloticus.
‖ Perca Nilotica.
¶ Cyprinus Benni, or C. Lepidotus.
** Silurus Shall.
†† The Silurus Schilbe Niloticus.
‡‡ Silurus Bajad.
§§ Silurus Carmuth.

The phagrus was the eel; and the reason of its sanctity, like that of the former, was owing to its being unwholesome; and the best way of preventing its being eaten was to assign it a place among the sacred animals of the country.

The lepidotus is still uncertain; from its name it was a scaly fish; and representations of it in bronze are not uncommon,

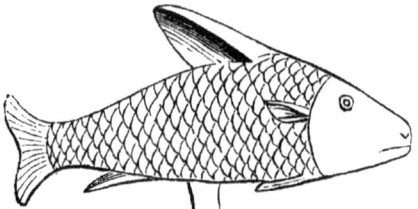

432.   Bronze Lepidotus (in my possession).

which show it to be the Cyprinus Lepidotus or Benni; though the *Kishr*, the *bulti*, and the *Kelb el Bahr* or *Salmo Dentex* (all wholesome, and the best of the insipid fish of the Nile) have each been invited to accept the name. It might reasonably be supposed that the *Raad*, or Electric fish of the Nile, would be one of the most sacred and forbidden for food; and it seems not to be represented among those caught in the ancient fishing scenes. It is a small fish; and the one I saw measured little more than a foot long, by 4 inches in depth. But it had the power of giving a very strong shock. It is the Melapterurus Electricus; and may have been the ancient *Latus*.

The name *Raad*, "thunder," is very remarkable, since the modern Egyptians are quite ignorant of the cause of its peculiar powers, and if it was borrowed by them from their predecessors, the question naturally arises, were they acquainted with electricity?

Like the sacred quadrupeds, they were not all regarded with the same reverence in different parts of the country; and the people of Cynopolis were in the habit of eating the oxyrhinchus, which "was the origin of a civil war between the two cities, till both sides, after doing each other great mischief, were severely punished by the Romans."

Besides the fish cured, or sent to market for the table, a very

ABUNDANCE OF FISH.

great quantity was set apart expressly for feeding the sacred animals and birds—as the cats, crocodiles, ibises, and others; and some of the large reservoirs, attached to the temples, were used as well for keeping fish as for the necessary ablutions of the devout, and for various purposes connected with religion.

The quantity of fish in Egypt was a very great boon to the poor classes, and when the Nile overflowed the country the inhabitants of the inland villages benefited by this annual gift of the river, as the land did by the fertilizing mud deposited upon it. The canals, ponds, and pools, on the low lands, continued to abound in fish, even after the inundation had ceased, and it was then that their return to the Nile was intercepted by closing the mouth of the canals. The same happens at the present day; and so numerous are they, that the tax upon the profits now paid annually by the poor peasants to the Turkish government on the fish of a small canal amounts to 21*l.*

The revenue from the fisheries was much larger in old times; though we may not believe that "while the water retired from the Lake Mœris (which Ælian quaintly calls the 'fish harvest'), the royal treasury received daily a talent of silver (supposed to be 193*l.* 15*s.* English), and during the other six months, when the water flowed from the Nile into the lake, 20 *minæ*" (about 64*l.* 12*s.*). The sum said to have been derived from this source was given as a dowry to the queen, for the purchase of jewels, ointment, and other things connected with her toilet—a very liberal provision, being upwards of 94,000*l.* a year; and when this formed only a portion of the pin-money of the Egyptian queens, who also received the revenues of the town of Anthylla, famous for its wines, they had no reason to complain of the allowance they enjoyed.

Though the fish of the Nile were a great benefit, their quality was not such as would satisfy modern taste, being insipid, and often muddy in flavour; but the Egyptians, like many others who live on rivers, were not connoisseurs in fish; and those of the sea were scarcely known to them, though the waters of the Mediterranean and the Arabian Gulf might have afforded them many excellent kinds. The sea was looked upon by them with abhorrence; political reasons had led the government in old times to increase that aversion; and prejudice prevented their appreciating the good things it contained, which might have raised their taste above the carp-and-tench-level of their inexperience.

Of the various kinds of labourers few are worthy of notice, except the brick-makers; and their employment derives considerable interest from the detailed notice of it in the Bible, according as it does so remarkably with the Egyptian paintings. Brick-making, a mere manual occupation, with nothing to stimulate the clever workman to improvement, was only followed by the meanest of the community, who had not even the satisfaction of working for themselves; for bricks were a government monopoly, and the pay for a tale of them was a small remuneration for this laborious drudgery in mud.

The use of crude bricks baked in the sun was universal throughout the country for private and for many public buildings, and the dry climate of Egypt was peculiarly suited to those simple materials. They had the recommendation of cheapness, and even of durability; and those made 3000 years ago, whether with or "without straw," are even now as firm and fit for use as when first put up in the reigns of the Amunophs and Thothmes, whose names they bear. When made of the Nile mud, or alluvial deposit, they required straw to prevent their cracking; but those formed of clay (now called *Háybeh*) taken from the torrent beds on the edge of the desert, held together without straw; and crude brick walls frequently had the additional security of a layer of reeds or sticks placed at intervals to act as binders. The courses of bricks were also disposed occasionally in horizontal curves, or a succession of concave and convex lines, throughout the length of the wall; and this undulating arrangement was even adopted in stone, especially in quays by the river side.

Burnt bricks were not used in Egypt, and, when found, they are known to be of Roman time. Enclosures of gardens, or granaries, sacred circuits surrounding the courts of temples, walls of fortresses and towns, dwelling-houses and tombs, and even some few of the temples themselves, were of crude brick, with stone columns and gateways; and so great was the demand, that the government, foreseeing the profit to be obtained from a monopoly of them, undertook to supply the public at a moderate price, thus preventing all unauthorized persons from engaging in their manufacture. And, in order more effectually to obtain their end, the seal of the king, or of some privileged person, was stamped upon the bricks at the time they were made; and bricks so marked are found both in public and private buildings; some having the ovals of a king, and some the name and titles of a priest or other influential person. Those which bear no characters either formed part of a tale, of which the first only were stamped, or were from the brick-fields of individuals, who had obtained a license from government to make them for their own consumption.

The employment of numerous captives, who worked as slaves, would in any case have enabled the government to sell the bricks at a lower price than those persons who had recourse solely to free labour; so that, without the necessity of a prohibition, they must soon have become an exclusive manufacture; and we find that, independent of native labourers, a great many foreigners were constantly engaged in the brick-fields at Thebes, and other parts of Egypt. The Jews, of course, were not excluded from this drudgery; and, like the captives detained in the Thebaï, they were condemned to the same labour in Lower Egypt. They not only erected granaries, treasure cities, and many public monuments for the Egyptian monarch, but the materials used in building them were the work of their hands; and the number of persons constantly employed in making bricks may be readily accounted for by the extensive supply required, and kept by the government for sale.

To meet with Hebrews in the sculptures cannot reasonably be expected, since the remains in that part of Egypt where they lived have not been preserved; but it is curious to discover other foreign captives occupied in the same manner, overlooked by similar "taskmasters,"* and performing the very same labours as the Israelites described in the Bible; and no one can look at

* *Figs.* 3 and 6 in woodcut 433.

196   THE ANCIENT EGYPTIANS.   Chap. VIII.

433.   Foreign captives employed in making bricks at Thebes.   *Thebes.*
Fig. 1. Man returning after carrying the bricks.   Figs. 3, 6. Taskmasters.   Figs. 4, 5. Men carrying bricks.
Figs. 7, 9, 12, 13. Digging and mixing the clay, or mud.   Figs. 8, 16. Making bricks with a wooden mould. *d, h.*

the paintings of Thebes, representing brick-makers, without a feeling of the highest interest. That the scene in the accompanying wood-cut is at the capital of Upper Egypt is shown by the hieroglyphics, which state that the "bricks" (*tôbi*) are made for a building at "Thebes" (*fig.* 9, *e*); and this occurrence of the word implying bricks, similar both in modern Arabic* and ancient Coptic, gives an additional value to the picture.

It is not very consistent, nor logical, to argue, that because the Jews made bricks, and the persons here introduced are so engaged, these must necessarily be Jews, since the Egyptians and their captives were constantly required to perform the same task; and the great quantity made at all times is proved by the number of buildings, which still remain, constructed of those materials. And a sufficient contradiction is given to that conclusion, by their being said to be working at Thebes, where the Jews never were, and by the names of various Asiatic captives of the time being recorded in the same tomb, among which no mention is made of Jews.

With regard to the features of foreigners resembling the Jews, it is only necessary to observe that the Egyptians adopted the same character for all the inhabitants of Syria, as may be seen in the sculptures of Karnak and other places, where those people occur, as well as in one of the sets of figures in Belzoni's tomb; and the brick-makers, far from having what is considered the very Jewish expression found in many of those figures, have not even the long beard, so marked in the people of Syria and the prisoners of Sheshonk (Shishak). They are represented as a white people, like others from Asia introduced into the paintings, and some have blue eyes and red hair, which are also given to the people of Rot-ñ-n in this same tomb. Indeed, if I were disposed to think them Jews, I should rather argue it from many of these figures *not* having the large nose and dark eyes and hair we consider as Jewish types; for some of these brick-makers are painted yellow, with blue eyes and small beards. Others are red, with a *rétroussé* nose. (*Woodcut* 434, *fig.* 2.)

These last may be Egyptians, or people of Pount who are re-

* "Tob" or "toob," in Arabic "a brick:" in Coptic "tôbi."

434.   Two of the Brick-makers.   *Thebes.*

presented bringing tribute in the same tomb. The fact of some having small beards, others merely the "stubble-field" of an unshaven chin, might accord with Jews as well as with the Rot-ṅ-n, or other northern races; but their making bricks at Thebes, and the name of Jews not being mentioned in the whole tomb, are insuperable objections.

And here I may mention a remarkable circumstance, that the Jews of the East to this day often have red hair and blue eyes, with a nose of delicate form and nearly straight, and are quite unlike their brethren of Europe; and the children in modern Jerusalem have the pink and white complexions of Europeans. The Oriental Jews are at the same time unlike the other Syrians in features; and it is the Syrians who have the large nose that strikes us as the peculiarity of the western Israelites. This prominent feature was always a characteristic of the Syrians; but not of the ancient, nor of the modern, Jews of Judæa; and the Saviour's head, though not really a portrait, is evidently a traditional representation of the Jewish face, which is still traceable at Jerusalem. No real portrait of him was ever handed down; and Eusebius, of Cæsarea, pronounced the impossibility of obtaining one for the sister of Constantine; but the character of the Jewish face would necessarily be known in those early days (in the 4th century), when the first representations of Him were attempted; and we should be surprised to find any artist abandon the style of features thus agreed upon for ages, and represent the Saviour with those of our western Jews. Yet this would be perfectly correct if the Jews of his day had those features; and such would have been, in that case, His traditional portrait.

I had often remarked the colour and features of the Jews in the East, so unlike those known in Europe, and my wish to ascertain if they were the same in Judæa was at length gratified by a visit to Jerusalem, where I found the same type in all those really of eastern origin; and the large nose is there an invariable proof of mixture with a western family. It may be difficult to explain this great difference in the eastern and western face (and the former is said to be also found in Hungary); but the subject is worthy of investigation, as is the origin of those Jews now living in Europe, and the early migrations that took place from Judæa long before the Christian era. These would be more satisfactory than mere speculations on the Lost Tribes.

The occupations of the common people in Egypt were carefully watched by the magistrate, and no one was allowed to live an idle life, useless to himself and to the community. It was thought right that the industrious citizen should be encouraged, and distinguished from the lazy or the profligate; and in order to protect the good and detect the wicked, it was enacted that every one should at certain times present himself before the magistrates, or provincial governors, and give in his name, his place of abode, his profession or employment, and the mode in which he gained his livelihood, the particulars being duly registered in the official report. The time of attendance was fixed, and those from the same parish proceeded in bodies to the appointed office, accompanied by their respective banners, and each individual being introduced singly to the registering clerks, gave in his statement and answered the necessary questions. In approaching these functionaries, they adopted the usual forms of respect before a superior, making a profound bow, one hand falling down to the knee, the other placed over the mouth to keep the breath from his face. The same mark of deference was expected from every one, as a token of respect to the court, on all occasions; when accused before a magistrate, and when attending at the police office to prefer a complaint, or to vindicate his character from an unjust imputation; and when a culprit sought to deprecate punishment, or to show great deference before a superior, he frequently placed one hand across his breast to the opposite shoulder.

435. Persons coming to be registered. Thebes.
436. Brought before the scribes. Thebes.

The custom of giving an account of their occupations was not of late introduction; it was adopted in old times; and the above representations are of the time of the 18th dynasty. It appears that they not only enrolled their names and gave in the various particulars required of them, but were obliged to have a passport from the magistrates; and this may possibly be the paper presented in the preceding woodcut to the scribe; for a document of that kind was required for every ship quitting a port, and all the precautions respecting a man's mode of life would have been useless if he could leave his town for another part of the country without some notice being required on his departure, and some vouchure being shown by him on his arrival at a new place of abode. The tiresome system of passports is exactly what the scrutiny of the cautious " paternal government" of Egypt would have invented; their formula may be recognized in the description of persons, who were parties to the sale of estates, and other private or public contracts; and in a deed of the time of Cleopatra Cocce and Ptolemy Alexander I., written in Greek, and relating to the sale of a piece of land at Thebes, five individuals are thus described: " Pamonthes, aged about forty-five, of middle size, dark complexion, and handsome figure, bald, round faced, and straight nosed; Snachomneus, aged about twenty, of middle size, sallow complexion, round faced, and straight nosed; Semnuthis Persineï, aged about twenty-two, of middle size, sallow complexion, round faced, flat nosed, and of quiet demeanour; and Tathlyt Persineï, aged about thirty, of middle size, and sallow complexion, round faced, and straight nosed—the four being children of Petepsais, of the leather-cutters of the Memnonia; and the Nechutes the less, the son of Asos, aged about forty, of middle size, sallow complexion, cheerful countenance, long face, and straight nose, with a scar upon the middle of his forehead."

During this examination before the magistrates, if excesses were found to have been committed by any one, in an irregular course of life, he was sentenced to the bastinado; but a false statement, or the proof of being engaged in unlawful pursuits, entailed upon him the punishment of a capital crime.

Another, and a fuller account of his conduct was required in the Confession, which the soul of every Egyptian was doomed to make at his death, before he could receive his last passport to eternal happiness.

The laws of the Egyptians were partly a compilation from decisions of learned judges in noted cases; as in some modern countries, and as with the Bedouins, who are guided by precedents and the opinion of their *ḳádis*, handed down from past times, rather than by the fixed law of the Koran. They had also a grand code of laws and jurisprudence, known as the celebrated " Eight Books of Hermes," which it was incumbent on those high-priests called " prophets" to be thoroughly versed in, and which the king, who held that office, was also required and entitled to know. It was not only in Egypt that the kings were judges; it was usual in many eastern countries to intrust the laws and their administration to them; and Xenophon, who ascribes the origin of the custom in Asia to Cyrus, says that those who wished to present petitions to the king attended at the gate of the palace.* It was probably from a similar custom that the Turkish title " the Sublime Porte" (or " lofty gate") was derived; and the same idea is contained in the common Oriental expression *Ana fee bab Allah*, " I am waiting at God's gate" (for help), in cases of complete distress.

We are acquainted with few of the laws of the ancient Egyptians; but the superiority of their Legislature has always been acknowledged as the cause of the duration of an empire, which lasted with the same form of government for a much longer period than the generality of ancient states. Indeed the wisdom of that people was proverbial, and was held in such consideration by other nations, that we find it taken by the Jews as the standard to which superior learning† in their own country was willingly compared; and Moses had prepared himself for the duties of a legislator by becoming versed " in all the wisdom of the Egyptians."

Besides their right of enacting laws, and of superintending all affairs of religion and the state, the kings administered justice to their subjects on those questions which came under their immediate cognizance, and they were assisted in the management of state affairs by the advice of the most able and distinguished members of the priestly order. With them the monarch consulted upon all questions of importance relating to the internal administration of the country; and previous to the admission of

---

* *Comp.* 2 Sam. xix. 8, and Esther, and other parts of the Bible.

† Of Solomon; 1 Kings, iv. 30.

Joseph to the confidence of Pharaoh, the opinion of his ministers was asked as to the expediency of the measure.*

His edicts appear to have been issued in the form of a *firmán*, or written order, like the Hot e' Sheréef, "handwriting of the Descendant of the Prophet" (or the Turkish Sultan), and like the royal commands in all Oriental countries; and from the expression used by Pharaoh in granting power to Joseph, we may infer that the people who received his order adopted the same Eastern mode of acknowledging their obedience and respect for the sovereign, now shown to a *firmán*; the expression in the Hebrew† being, "according to thy word shall all people *kiss*" (be ruled), and evidently alluding to the custom of *kissing* the signature attached to those documents. They were also expected to "bow the knee‡" in the presence of the monarch and chiefs of the country, and even to prostrate themselves to the ground, as Joseph's brethren did before him.

Causes of ordinary occurrence were decided by those who held the office of judges; and the care with which persons were elected to this office is a proof of their regard for the welfare of the community, and of their earnest endeavours to promote the ends of justice. None were admitted to it but the most upright and learned individuals; and, in order to make the office more select, and more readily to obtain persons of known character, ten only were chosen from each of the three cities— Thebes, Memphis, and Heliopolis; a body of men, says Diodorus, by no means inferior either to the Areopagites of Athens, or to the senate of Lacedæmon.

These thirty individuals constituted the bench of judges; and at their first meeting they elected the most distinguished among them to be president, with the title of Arch-judge. His salary was much greater than that of the other judges, as his office was

* Gen. xli. 38, "And Pharaoh said unto his servants (ministers), Can we find such a one as this is?" Gen. l. 7, "The elders of his (Pharaoh's) house." And Isaiah, xix. 11, "The wise counsellors of Pharaoh."
† Gen. xli. 40.
‡ Gen. xli. 43. The word *abrek*, אברך, is very remarkable, as it is used to the present day by the Arabs, when requiring a camel to *kneel* and receive its load, and is derived from *rúkbeh*, the "knee." Hence, too, *báraka*, a "blessing," from "kneeling" in prayer.

more important, and the city to which he belonged enjoyed the privilege of returning another judge, to complete the number of the thirty from whom he had been chosen. They all received ample allowances from the king, in order that, possessing a sufficiency for their maintenance and other necessary expenses, they might be above the reach of temptation, and be inaccessible to bribes; for it was considered of primary importance that all judicial proceedings should be regulated with the most scrupulous exactitude, sentences pronounced by authorized tribunals always having a decided influence, either salutary or prejudicial, on the affairs of common life. They felt that precedents were thereby established, and that numerous abuses frequently resulted from an early error, which had been sanctioned by the decision of some influential person; and for this reason they weighed the talents, as well as the character, of the judge.

The first principle was, that offenders should be discovered and punished, and that those who had been wronged should be benefited by the interposition of the laws, since the least compensation which can be made to the oppressed, and the most effectual preventive of crime, are the speedy discovery and exposure of the offender. On the other hand, if the terror which hangs over the guilty in the hour of trial could be averted by bribery or favour, nothing short of distrust and confusion would pervade all ranks of society; and the spirit of the Egyptian laws (as Diodorus shows) was not merely to hold out the distant prospect of rewards and punishments, nor simply threaten the future vengeance of the gods, but to apply the more persuasive stimulus of present retribution.

Besides the care taken by them that justice should be administered according to the real merits of the case, and that before their tribunals no favour or respect of persons should be permitted, another very important regulation was adopted, that justice should be gratuitously administered; and it was consequently accessible to the poor as well as to the rich. The very spirit of their laws was to give protection and assistance to the oppressed, and everything that tended to promote an unbiassed judgment was peculiarly commended by the Egyptian sages.

GODDESS OF JUSTICE. THUMMIM.

When a case was brought for trial, it was customary for the arch-judge to put a golden chain round his neck, to which was suspended a small figure of Truth, ornamented with precious

437.   The goddess of Truth and Justice.   *Thebes.*

stones. This was, in fact, a representation of the goddess who was worshipped under the double character of Truth and Justice, and whose name, Thmei, appears to have been the origin of the Hebrew Thummim — a word, according to the Septuagint translation, implying "truth," and bearing a further analogy in its plural termination. And what makes it more remarkable is that the chief priest of the Jews, who, before the election of a king, was also the judge of the nation, was alone entitled to wear this honorary badge; and the Thummim, like the Egyptian figure, was studded with precious stones of various colours. The goddess was represented "hav-

438.   The goddess of Truth, "with her eyes closed."   *Thebes.*

ing her eyes closed," purporting that the duty of a judge was to weigh the question according to the evidence he had heard, and to trust rather to his mind than to what he saw, and was intended to warn him of that virtue which the Deity peculiarly enjoined: an emblematic idea, very similar to "those statues at Thebes of judges without hands, with their chief or president at their head having his eyes turned downwards," signifying, as Plutarch says, "that Justice ought neither to be accessible to bribes, nor guided by favour and affection."

It is not to be supposed that the president and the thirty judges above mentioned were the only house of judicature in the country; each city, or capital of a nome, had no doubt its own "County court," for the trial of minor and local offences; and it is probable that the assembly returned by the three chief cities resided wherever the royal court was held, and performed many of the same duties as the senates of ancient times. And that this was really the case appears from Diodorus mentioning the thirty judges and their president, represented at Thebes in the sculptures of the tomb of Osymandyas.

The president, or arch-judge, having put on the emblem of Truth, the trial commenced, and the eight volumes which contained the laws of the Egyptians were placed close to him, in order to guide his decision, or to enable him to solve a difficult question, by reference to that code, to former precedents, or to the opinion of some learned predecessor. The complainant stated his case. This was done in writing; and every particular that bore upon the subject, the mode in which the alleged offence was committed, and an estimate of the damage, or the extent of the injury sustained, were inserted.

The defendant then, taking up the deposition of the opposite party, wrote his answer to each of the plaintiff's statements, either denying the charge, or endeavouring to prove that the offence was not of a serious nature; or, if obliged to admit his guilt, suggesting that the damages were too high, and incompatible with the nature of the crime. The complainant replied in writing, and the accused having brought forward all he had to say in his defence, the papers were given to the judges; and if no witnesses could be produced on either side, they decided upon the question according to the deposition of the parties. Their opinion only required to be ratified by the president, who then proceeded, in virtue of his office, to pronounce judgment on the case; and this was done by touching the party who had gained the cause with the figure of Truth. They considered that this mode of proceeding was more likely to forward the ends of justice, than when the judges listened to the statements of pleaders; eloquence having frequently the effect of fascinating the mind, and tending to throw a veil over guilt, and to pervert truth. The persuasive arguments of oratory, or those artifices which move the passions and excite the sympathy of the judges, were avoided; and thus neither did an appeal to their feelings, nor the tears and dissimulation of an offender, soften the just rigour of the laws. And while ample time was afforded to each party to proffer or to disprove an accusation, no opportunity was given to the offender to take advantage of his opponent, but poor and rich, ignorant and learned, honest and dishonest, were placed on an equal footing; and it was the case, rather than the persons, upon which the judgment was passed.

The laws of the Egyptians were handed down from the earliest times, and looked upon with the greatest reverence. They had the credit of having been dictated by the gods themselves, and Thoth (Hermes, Mercury, or the Divine Intellect) was said to have framed them for the benefit of mankind.

The names of many of the earliest monarchs and sages, who had contributed to the completion of their code, were recorded and venerated by them; and whoever, at successive periods, made additions to it, was mentioned with gratitude as a benefactor of his country.

Truth or justice was thought to be the main cardinal virtue among the Egyptians, inasmuch as it relates more particularly to others; prudence, temperance, and fortitude being relative qualities, and tending chiefly to the immediate benefit of the individual who possesses them. It was, therefore, with great earnestness that they inculcated the necessity of fully appreciating it; and falsehood was not only considered disgraceful, but when it entailed an injury on any other person was punishable by law. A calumniator of the dead was condemned to a severe punishment; and a false accuser was doomed to the same sentence which would have been awarded to the accused, if the offence had been proved against him; but to maintain a falsehood by an oath was deemed the blackest crime, and one which, from its complicated nature, could be punished by nothing short of death. For they considered that it involved two distinct crimes—a contempt for the gods, and a violation of faith towards man; the former the direct promoter of every sin, the latter destructive of all those ties which are most essential for the welfare of society.

The wilful murder of a freeman, or even of a *slave*, was punished with death, from the conviction that men ought to be restrained from the commission of sin, not on account of any distinction of station in life, but from the light in which they viewed the crime itself; while at the same time it had the effect of showing, that if the murder of a slave was deemed an offence deserving of so severe a punishment, they ought still more to shrink from the murder of one who was a compatriot and a free-born citizen.

In this law we observe a scrupulous regard to justice and humanity, and have an unquestionable proof of the great advancement made by the Egyptians in the most essential points of civilization. Indeed, the Egyptians considered it so heinous a crime to deprive a man of life, that to be the accidental witness of an attempt to murder, without endeavouring to prevent it, was a capital offence, which could only be palliated by bringing proofs of inability to act. With the same spirit they decided, that to be present when any one inflicted a personal injury on another, without interfering, was tantamount to being a party, and was punishable according to the extent of the assault; and every one who witnessed a robbery was bound either to arrest, or, if that was out of his power, to lay an information, and to prosecute the offenders; and any neglect on this score being proved against him, the delinquent was condemned to receive a stated number of stripes, and to be kept without food for three whole days.

Although, in the case of murder, the Egyptian law was inexorable and severe, the royal prerogative might be exerted in favour of a culprit, and the punishment was sometimes commuted by a mandate from the king. Sabaco, indeed, during the fifty years of his reign, " made it a rule not to punish his subjects with death," whether guilty of murder or any other capital offence, but, " according to the magnitude of their crimes, he condemned the culprits to raise the ground about the town to which they belonged. By these means the situations of the different cities became greatly elevated above the reach of the inundation, even more than in the time of Sesostris;" and either on account of a greater proportion of criminals, or from some other cause, the mounds of Bubastis were raised considerably higher than those of any other city.

The same laws that forbade a master to punish a slave with death took from a father every right over the life of his offspring; and the Egyptians deemed the murder of a child an odious crime, that called for the direct interposition of justice. They did not, however, punish it as a capital offence, since it appeared inconsistent to take away life from one who had given it to the child, but preferred inflicting such a punishment as would induce grief and repentance. With this view they ordained that the corpse of the deceased should be fastened to the neck of its parent, and that he should be allowed to pass three whole days and nights in its embrace, under the surveillance of a public guard.

But parricide was visited with the most cruel of chastisements; and conceiving, as they did, that the murder of a parent was the most unnatural of crimes, they endeavoured to prevent its occurrence by the marked severity with which it was avenged. The criminal was therefore sentenced to be lacerated with sharpened reeds, and after being thrown on thorns he was burnt to death.

When a woman was guilty of a capital offence, and judgment had been passed upon her, they were particularly careful to ascertain if the condemned was in a state of pregnancy, in which case her punishment was deferred till after the birth of the child, in order that the innocent might not suffer with the guilty, and thus the father be deprived of that child to which he had at least an equal right.

But some of their laws regarding the female sex were cruel and unjustifiable; and even if, which is highly improbable, they succeeded by their severity in enforcing chastity, and in putting an effectual stop to crime, yet the punishment rather reminds us of the laws of a barbarous people than of a wise and civilized state. A woman who had committed adultery was sentenced to lose her nose, upon the principle that, being the most conspicuous feature, and the chief, or, at least, an indispensable ornament of the face, its loss would be most severely felt, and be the greatest detriment to her personal charms; and the man was condemned to receive a bastinado of one thousand blows. But if it was proved that force had been used against a free woman, he was doomed to a cruel mutilation.

The object of the Egyptian laws was to preserve life, and to reclaim an offender. Death took away every chance of repentance, it deprived the country of his services, and he was hurried out of the world when least prepared to meet the ordeal of a future state. They, therefore, preferred severe punishments, and, except in the case of murder, and some crimes which appeared highly injurious to the community, it was deemed unnecessary to sacrifice the life of an offender.

In military as well as civil cases, minor offences were generally punished with the stick; a mode of chastisement still greatly in vogue among the modern inhabitants of the valley of the Nile, and held in such esteem by them, that, convinced of (or perhaps by) its efficacy, they relate "its descent from heaven as a blessing to mankind."

If an Egyptian of the present day has a government debt or tax to pay, he stoutly persists in his inability to obtain the money till he has withstood a certain number of blows, and considers himself compelled to produce it; and the ancient inhabitants, if not under the rule of their native princes, at least in the time of the Roman emperors, gloried equally in the obstinacy they evinced, and the difficulty the governors of the country experienced in extorting from them what they were bound to pay;

CHAP. VIII.   BASTINADO.   211

whence Ammianus Marcellinus tells us, "an Egyptian blushes if he cannot show numerous marks on his body that evince his endeavours to evade the duties."

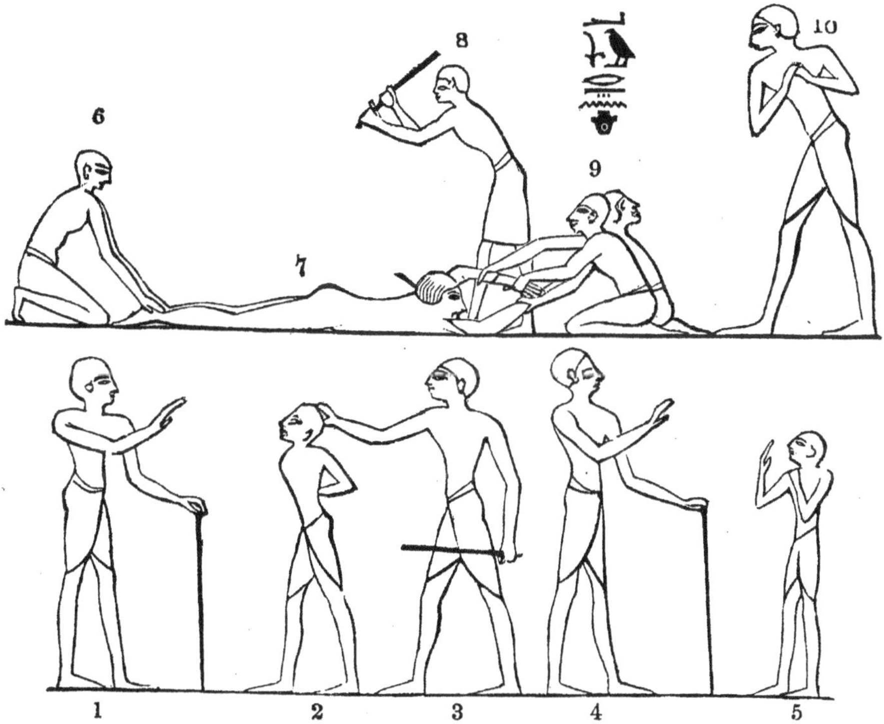

439.   The bastinado.   *Beni Hassan.*

The bastinado was inflicted on both sexes, as with the Jews. Men and boys were laid prostrate on the ground, and frequently held by the hands and feet while the chastisement was administered; but women, as they sat, received the stripes on their back, which was also inflicted by the hand of a man. Nor was it unusual

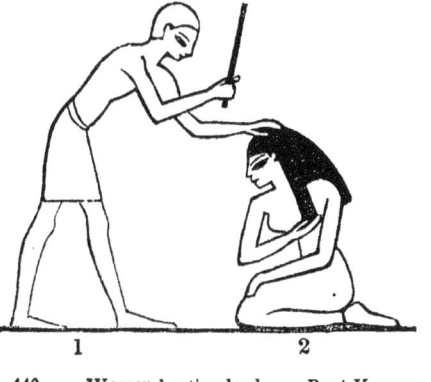

440.   Women bastinadoed.   *Beni Hassan.*

for the superintendents to stimulate labourers to their work by the persuasive powers of the stick, whether engaged in the field or in handicraft employments; and boys were sometimes

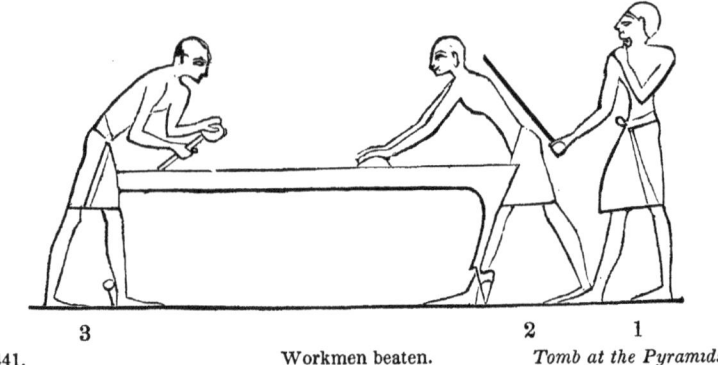

441.   3   Workmen beaten.   2   1
                                    Tomb at the Pyramids.

beaten without the ceremony of prostration, the hands being tied behind their back while the punishment was applied.

It does not, however, appear to have been from any respect to the person that this less usual method was adopted; nor is it probable that any class of the community enjoyed a peculiar privilege on these occasions, as among the modern Moslems, who, extending their respect for the Prophet to his distant descendants of the thirty-sixth and ensuing generations, scruple to administer the stick to a *Sheréef* until he has been politely furnished with a mat on which to prostrate his guilty person. Among other amusing privileges in modern Egypt is that conceded to the grandees, or officers of high rank. Ordinary culprits are punished by the hand of persons usually employed on such occasions; but a Bey, or the governor of a district, can only receive his chastisement from the hand of a Pasha, and the aristocratic *daboss* (mace) is substituted for the vulgar stick. This is no trifling privilege: it becomes fully *impressed* upon the sufferer, and renders him, long after, sensible of the peculiar honour he has enjoyed; nor can any one doubt that an iron mace, in form not very unlike a chocolate-mill, is a *distingué* mode of punishing men who are proud of their rank.

Having noticed the pertinacity of the modern Egyptians in

resisting the payment of their taxes, I shall introduce the following story as remarkably illustrative of this fact. In the year 1822, a Copt Christian, residing at Cairo, was arrested by the Turkish authorities for the non-payment of his taxes, and taken before the Kehia, or deputy of the Pasha. "Why," inquired the angry Turk, "have you not paid your taxes?"—"Because," replied the Copt, with a pitiable expression, perfectly according with his tattered appearance, "I have not the means." He was instantly ordered to be thrown upon the floor, and bastinadoed. He prayed to be released, but in vain: the stick continued without intermission, and he was scarcely able to bear the increasing pain. Again and again he pleaded his inability to pay, and prayed for mercy: the Turk was inexorable; and the torments he felt at length overcame his resolution: they were no longer to be borne. "Release me," he cried, "and I will pay directly."—"Ah, you Giower! go." He was released, and taken home, accompanied by a soldier, and the money being paid, he imparted to his wife the sad tidings. "You coward! you fool!" she exclaimed; "what! give them the money on the very first demand! I suppose, after five or six blows, you cried, 'I will pay, only release me;' next year our taxes will be doubled through your weakness; shame!"—"No, my dear," interrupted the suffering man, "I assure you I resisted as long as it was possible; look at the state I am in before you upbraid me. I paid the money, but they had trouble enough for it; for I obliged them to give me at least a hundred blows before they could get it." She was pacified; and the pity and commendation of his wife, added to his own satisfaction in having shown so much obstinacy and courage, consoled him for the pain, and, perhaps, in some measure, for the money thus forced from him.

Hanging was the customary mode of punishment, in ancient Egypt, for many capital crimes; and the prisoners were kept "bound" in prison till their fate was decided, whether it depended on the will of the sovereign, or the decision of the judges. These places of confinement were under the immediate superintendence, and within the house, of the chief of the police, or "captain of the guard," "an officer of Pharaoh," who was probably the captain of the watch, like the *Zábut* of the modern Egyptian police.*

The character of some of the Egyptian laws was quite consonant with the notions of a primitive age. The punishment was directed more particularly against the offending member: and adulterators of money, falsifiers of weights and measures, forgers of seals or signatures, and scribes who altered any signed documents by erasures or additions, without the authority of the parties, were condemned to lose both their hands.

But their laws do not seem to have sanctioned the gibbet, or the exposure of the body of an offender; for the conduct of Rhampsinitus, in the case of the robbery of his treasure, is mentioned by Herodotus as a singular mode of discovering an accomplice, and not as an ordinary punishment; if, indeed, the whole story is not the invention of a Greek *cicerone*.

Thefts, breach of trust, and petty frauds were punished with the bastinado; but robbery and house-breaking were sometimes considered capital crimes, and deserving of death, as is evident from the conduct of the thief when caught by the trap in the treasury of Rhampsinitus, and from what Diodorus states respecting Actisanes. This monarch, instead of putting robbers to death, instituted a novel mode of punishing them, by cutting off their noses, and banishing them to the confines of the desert, where a town was built, called Rhinocolura, from the peculiar nature of their punishment; and thus, by removing the bad, and preventing their corrupting the good, he benefited society, without depriving the criminals of life, at the same time that he punished them severely for their crimes, by obliging them to live by their labours, and derive a precarious sustenance from quails, or whatever they could catch in that barren region. Commutation of punishment was the foundation of this part of the convict system of Egypt, and Rhinocolura was their Norfolk Island, where a sea of sand separated the worst felons from those guilty of smaller crimes; who were transported to the mines in the desert, and condemned to work for various terms, according to their offence.

* Gen. xxix. 1, 20; xl. 3, 22.

BASTINADO. 215

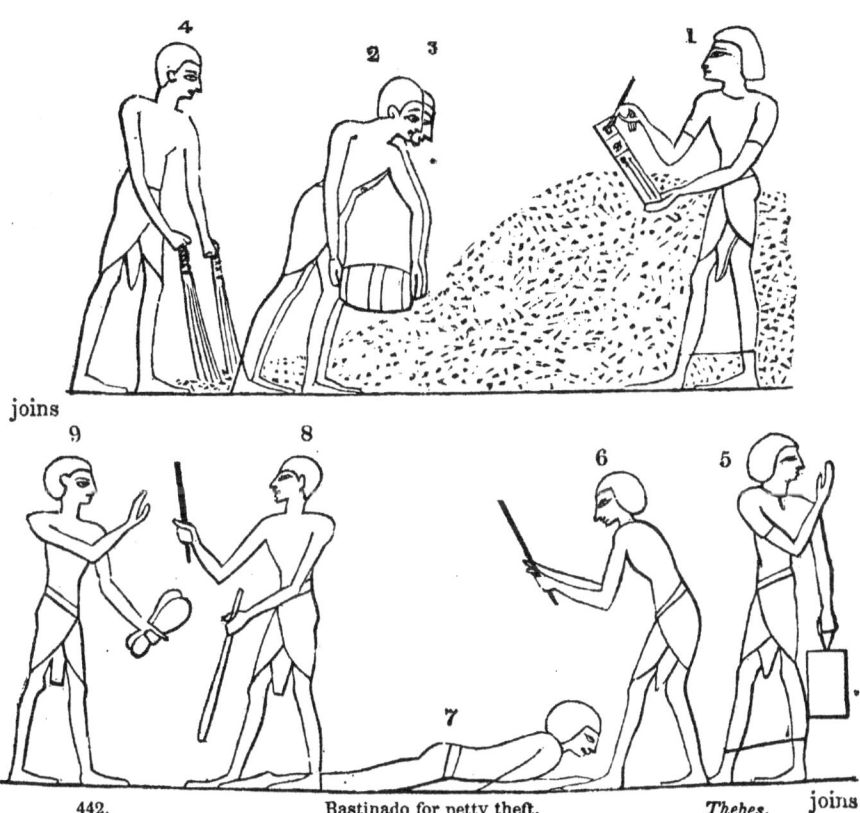

442.   Bastinado for petty theft.   *Thebes.*

Blindly following the old-fashioned notion of merely *punishing* for offences committed, the Egyptian government had never thought of *preventing* crime by educating the youth of the poor, and checking the supply of future criminals by thwarting vice in embryo; they did, however, attempt it in some degree by preventing idleness, and requiring each to account for his mode of life; and they could scarcely be expected in those early days to have arrived at a system we have only just adopted, and which has been so ably carried out in Scotland. Our next problem, on the return of criminals to society, when transportation shall have ceased, has yet to be solved; and we shall be fortunate if we excel the Egyptians as far in this as in the case of juvenile offenders.

The Egyptians had a singular custom respecting theft and burglary. Those who followed the *profession* of thief gave in their names to the chief of the robbers, and agreed that he should be informed of everything they might thenceforward steal, the moment it was in their possession. In consequence of this, the owner of the lost goods always applied by letter to the chief for their recovery : and having stated their quality and quantity, the day and hour when they were stolen, and other requisite particulars, the goods were identified, and, on payment of one quarter of their value, they were restored to the applicant, in the same state as when taken from his house.

For being fully persuaded of the impracticability of putting an entire check to robbery, either by the dread of punishment, or by any method that could be adopted by the most vigilant police, they considered it more for the advantage of the community that a certain sacrifice should be made in order to secure the restitution of the remainder, than that the law, by taking on itself to protect the citizen and discover the offender, should be the indirect cause of greater loss. And that the Egyptians, like the Indians, and I may say the modern inhabitants of the Nile, were very expert in the art of stealing, we have abundant testimony from ancient authors.

It may be asked, what redress could be obtained if goods were stolen by thieves who failed to enter their names on the books of the chief; but it is evident that there could be few of those private speculators, since by their interfering with the interests of all the *profession*, the detection of such egotistical persons would have been certain ; and thus all others were effectually prevented from robbing, save those of the privileged class.

The salary of the chief was not merely derived from his own demands upon the goods stolen, or from any voluntary contribution of the robbers themselves, but was probably a fixed remuneration granted by the government, as one of the chiefs of the police ; nor is it to be supposed that he was any other than a respectable citizen, and a man of integrity and honour. The same may be said of the modern " *shekh* of the thieves" at Cairo, where this very ancient office is still retained.

LAWS ON DEBT AND USURY.

The great confidence reposed in the public weighers rendered it necessary to enact suitable laws in order to bind them to their duty; and considering how much public property was at their mercy, and how easily bribes might be taken from a dishonest tradesman, the Egyptians inflicted a severe punishment as well on the weighers as on the shop-keepers, who were found to have false weights and measures, or to have defrauded the purchaser in any other way; and these, as well as the scribes who kept false accounts, were punished (as before stated) with the loss of both their hands; on the principle, says Diodorus, that the offending member should suffer; while the culprit was severely punished, that others might be deterred from the commission of a similar offence.

As in other countries, their laws respecting debt and usury underwent some changes, according as society advanced, and as pecuniary transactions became more complicated.

Bocchoris (who reigned in Egypt about the year 800 B.C., and who, from his learning, obtained the surname of Wise), finding that in cases of debt many causes of dispute had arisen, and instances of great oppression were of frequent occurrence, enacted that no agreement should be binding unless it was acknowledged by a written contract; and if any one took oath that the money had not been lent him, that no debt should be recognized, and the claims of the suing party should immediately cease. This was done, that great regard might always be had for the name and nature of an oath, at the same time that, by substituting the unquestionable proof of a written document, the necessity of having frequent recourse to an oath was avoided, and its sanctity was not diminished by constant repetition.

Usury was in all cases condemned by the Egyptian Legislature; and when money was borrowed, even with a written agreement, it was forbidden to allow the interest to increase to more than double the original sum. Nor could the creditors seize the debtor's person: their claims and right were confined to the goods in his possession, and such as were really his own, which were comprehended under the produce of his labour, or what he had received from another individual to whom they lawfully belonged. For the person of every citizen was looked upon as the property of the state, and might be required for some public service, connected either with war or peace; and, independent of the injustice of subjecting any one to the momentary caprice of his creditor, the safety of the country might be endangered through the avarice of a few interested individuals.

This law, which was borrowed by Solon from the Egyptian code, existed also at Athens; and was, as Diodorus observes, much more consistent with justice and common sense than that which allowed the creditor to seize the person, while it forbade him to take the ploughs and other implements of husbandry. For if, continues the historian, it is unjust thus to deprive men of the means of obtaining subsistence, and of providing for their families, how much more unreasonable must it be to imprison those by whom the implements were used!

To prevent the accumulation of debt, and to protect the interests of the creditor, another remarkable law was enacted by Asychis, which, while it shows how greatly they endeavoured to check the increasing evil, proves the high respect paid by the Egyptians to the memory of their parents, and to the sanctity of their religious ceremonies. By this it was pronounced illegal for any one to borrow money without giving in pledge the body of his father, or the tomb of his ancestors; and, if he failed to redeem so sacred a deposit, he was considered infamous; and, at his death, the celebration of the accustomed funeral obsequies was denied him, and he could not enjoy the right of burial either in that tomb or in any other place of sepulture; nor could he inter his children, or any of his family, as long as the debt was unpaid, the creditor being put in actual possession of the family tomb.

In the large cities of Egypt, a fondness for display, and the usual allurements of luxury, were rapidly introduced; and considerable sums were expended in furnishing houses, and in many artificial caprices. Rich jewels and costly works of art were in great request, as well among the inhabitants of the provincial capitals, as at Thebes and Memphis: they delighted in splendid equipages, elegant and commodious boats, numerous attendants, horses, dogs, and other requisites for the chase; and, besides, their houses, their villas, and their gardens, were laid out with no ordinary expense. But while the funds arising from extensive farms, and the abundant produce of a fertile soil, enabled the rich to indulge extravagant habits, many of the less wealthy envied the enjoyment of those luxuries which fortune had denied to them; and, prompted by vanity, and a silly desire of imitation, so common in civilized communities, they pursued a career which speedily led to an accumulation of debt, and demanded the interference of the Legislature; and it is probable that a law, so severe as this must have appeared to the Egyptians, was only adopted as a measure of absolute necessity, in order to put a check to the increasing evil.

The necessary expenses of the Egyptians were remarkably small, less, indeed, than of any people; and the food of the poorer classes was of the cheapest and most simple kind. Owing to the warmth of the climate, they required few clothes, and young children were in the habit of going without shoes, and with little or no covering to their bodies; and so trifling was the expense of bringing up a child, that, as Diodorus affirms, it never need cost a parent more than 20 drachms (13 shillings English), until arrived at man's estate. It was, therefore, luxury, and the increasing wants of an artificial kind, which corrupted the manners of the Egyptians, and rendered such a law necessary for their restraint; and we may conclude that it was mainly directed against those who contracted debts for the gratification of pleasure, or with the premeditated intent of defrauding an unsuspecting creditor.

In the mode of executing deeds, conveyances, and other civil contracts, the Egyptians were peculiarly circumstantial and minute; and the great number of witnesses is a singular feature in those documents. In the time of the Ptolemies, sales of property commenced with a preamble, containing the date of the king in whose reign they were executed; the name of the president of the court, and of the clerk by whom they were written, being also specified. The body of the contract then followed.

It stated the name of the individual who sold the land, the

description of his person, an account of his parentage, profession, and place of abode, the extent and nature of the land, its situation and boundaries, and concluded with the name of the purchaser, whose parentage and description were also added, and the sum for which it was bought. The seller then vouched for his undisturbed possession of it; and, becoming security against any attempt to dispute his title, the name of the other party was inserted as having accepted it, and acknowledged the purchase. The names of witnesses were then affixed; and, the president of the court having added his signature, the deed was valid. Sometimes the seller formally recognized the sale in the following manner: " All these things have I sold thee: they are thine; I have received their price from thee, and will make no demand upon thee for them from this day; and if any person disturb thee in the possession of them, I will withstand the attempt; and, if I do not otherwise repel it, I will use compulsory means," or, " I will indemnify thee."

But, in order to give a more accurate notion of the form of these contracts, I shall introduce a copy of the whole of one of them, as given by Dr. Young, and refer the reader to others occurring in the same work. " Translation of the enchorial papyrus of Paris, containing the original deed relating to the mummies: ' This writing dated in the year 36, Athyr 20, in the reign of our sovereigns Ptolemy and Cleopatra his sister, the children of Ptolemy and Cleopatra the divine, the gods Illustrious: and the priest of Alexander, and of the Saviour gods, of the Brother gods, of the (Beneficent gods), of the Father-loving gods, of the Illustrious gods, of the Paternal god, and of the Mother-loving gods, being (as by law appointed): and the prize-bearer of Berenice the Beneficent, and the basket-bearer of Arsinoë the Brother-loving, and the priestess of Arsinoë the Father-loving, being as appointed in the metropolis (of Alexandria); and in (Ptolemais) the royal city of the Thebaïd? the guardian priest for the year? of Ptolemy Soter, and the priest of King Ptolemy the Father-loving, and the priest of Ptolemy the Brother-loving, and the priest of Ptolemy the Beneficent, and the priest of Ptolemy the Mother-loving; and the priestess of Queen Cleopatra, and the priestess of the Princess Cleopatra, and the priestess of Cleopatra, the (queen) mother, deceased, the Illustrious; and the basket-bearer of Arsinoë the Brother-loving (being as appointed): declares: The Dresser? in the temple of the Goddess, Onnophris, the son of Horus, and of Senpoëris, daughter of Spotus? ("aged about forty, lively"), tall ("of a sallow complexion, hollow-eyed, and bald"); in the temple of the goddess to (Horus) his brother? the son of Horus and of Senpoëris, has sold, for a price in money, half of one third of the collections for the dead "priests of Osiris?" lying in Thynabunum . . . in the Libyan suburb of Thebes, in the Memnonia . . . likewise half of one third of the liturgies: their names being, Muthes, the son of Spotus, with his children and his household; Chapocrates, the son of Nechthmonthes, with his children and his household; Arsiesis, the son of Nechthmonthes, with his children and his household; Petemestus, the son of Nechthmonthes; Arsiesis, the son of Zminis, with his children and his household; Osoroëris, the son of Horus, with his children and his household; Spotus, the son of Chapochonsis, surnamed? Zoglyphus (the sculptor), with his children and his household: while there belonged also to Asos, the son of Horus and of Senpoëris, daughter of Spotus? in the same manner one half of a third of the collections for the dead, and of the fruits and so forth . . . he sold it on the 20th of Athyr, in the reign of the King ever-living, to (complete) the third part: likewise the half of one third of the collections relating to Peteutemis, with his household, and . . . likewise the half of one third? of the collections and fruits for Petechonsis, the bearer of milk, and of the . . . place on the Asian side, called Phrecages, and . . . the dead bodies in it: there having belonged to Asos the son of Horus one half of the same: he has sold to him in the month of . . . the half of one third of the collections for the priests of Osiris? lying in Thynabunum, with their children and their households: likewise the half of one third of the collections for Peteutemis, and also for Petechonsis, the bearer of milk, in the place Phrecages on the Asian side: I have received for them their price in silver . . . and gold; and I make no further demand on thee for them from the present day . . . before the authorities . . . (and if any one shall disturb thee in the possession of them, I will resist him, and, if I do not succeed, I will indemnify thee?) . . . Executed and confirmed. Written by Horus, the son of Phabis, clerk to the chief priests of Amonrasonther, and of the contemplar? Gods, of the Beneficent gods, of the Father-loving gods, of the Paternal god, and of the Mother-loving gods. Amen.

" ' Names of the witnesses present:
  ERIEUS, the son of Phanres Erieus.
  PETEARTRES, the son of Peteutemis.
  PETEARPOCRATES, the son of Horus.
  SNACHOMNEUS, the son of Peteuris.
  SNACHOMES, the son of Psenchonsis.
  TOTOES, the son of Phibis.
  PORTIS, the son of Appollonius.
  ZMINIS, the son of Petemestus.
  PETEUTEMIS, the son of Arsiesis.
  AMONORYTIUS, the son of Pacemis.
  HORUS, the son of Chimnaraus.
  ARMENIS (rather Arbais), the son of Zthenaetis.
  MAESIS, the son of Mirsis.
  ANTIMACHUS, the son of Antigenes.
  PETOPHOIS, the son of Phibis.
  PANAS, the son of Petosiris.' "

In this, as in many other documents, the testimony required is very remarkable, sixteen witnesses being thought necessary for the sale of a moiety of the sums collected on account of a few tombs, and for services performed to the dead, the total value of which was only 400 pieces of brass; and the name of each person is introduced, in the true Oriental style, with that of his father. Nor is it unreasonable to suppose that the same precautions and minute formulas were observed in similar transactions during the reign of the Pharaonic kings, however great may have been the change introduced by the Ptolemies and Romans into the laws and local government of Egypt.

Of the marriage contracts of the Egyptians we are entirely ignorant, nor do we even find the ceremony represented in the paintings of their tombs. We may, however, conclude that they were regulated by the customs usual among civilized nations; and, if the authority of Diodorus can be credited, women were indulged with greater privileges in Egypt than in any other country. He even affirms that part of the agreement entered into at the time of marriage was, that the wife should have control over her husband, and that no objection should be made to her *commands*, whatever they might be; but, though we have sufficient to convince us of the superior treatment of women among the Egyptians, as well from ancient authors as from the sculptures that remain, it may fairly be doubted if those indulgences were carried to the extent mentioned by the historian, or that command extended beyond the management of the house, and the regulation of domestic affairs.

It is, however, remarkable that the royal authority and supreme direction of affairs were intrusted without reserve to women, as in those states of modern Europe where the Salic law has not been introduced; and we not only find examples in Egyptian history of queens succeeding to the throne, but Manetho informs us that the law, according this important privilege to the other sex, dated as early as the reign of Binothris, the third monarch of the second dynasty.

In primitive ages, the duties of women were very different from those of later and more civilized periods, and varied, of course, according to the habits of each people. Among pastoral tribes, they drew water, kept the sheep, and superintended the herds as well as flocks. As with the Arabs of the present day, they prepared both the furniture and the woollen stuffs of which the tents themselves were made, ground the corn, and performed other menial offices. They were also engaged, as in ancient Greece, in weaving, spinning, needlework, embroidery, and other sedentary occupations within doors. The Egyptian ladies in like manner employed much of their time with the needle; and the sculptures represent many females weaving and using the spindle. But they were not kept in the same secluded manner as those of ancient

Greece, who, besides being confined to certain apartments in the house, most remote from the hall of entrance, and generally in the uppermost part of the building, were not even allowed to go out of doors without a veil, as in many Oriental countries at the present day. The Egyptians treated their women very differently, as the accounts of ancient authors and the sculptures sufficiently prove. At some of the public festivals women were expected to attend—not alone, like the Moslem women at a mosque, but in company with their husbands or relations; and Josephus states that on an occasion of this kind, " when it was the custom for women to go to the public solemnity, the wife of Potiphar, having pleaded ill health in order to be allowed to stay at home, was excused from attending," and availed herself of the absence of her husband to talk with Joseph. (*See* vol. i. p. 4, 144.)

That it was the custom of the Egyptians to have only one wife, is shown by Herodotus and the monuments, which present so many scenes illustrative of their domestic life; and Diodorus is wrong in supposing that the laity were allowed to marry any number, while the priests were limited to one. (*See* vol. i. p. 5.)

But a very objectionable custom, which is not only noticed by Diodorus, but is fully authenticated by the sculptures both of Upper and Lower Egypt, existed among them from the earliest times, the origin and policy of which it is not easy to explain—the marriage of brother and sister—which Diodorus supposes to have been owing to, and sanctioned by, that of Isis and Osiris; but as this was purely an allegorical fable, and these ideal personages never lived on earth, his conjecture is of little weight; nor does any ancient writer offer a satisfactory explanation of so strange a custom.

In the time of the Patriarchs, as in the case of Abraham and Sarah, and among the Athenians, it was lawful to marry a sister by the father's side, not, however, if born of the same mother; but that this restriction was not observed in Egypt, we have sufficient evidence from the marriage of several of the Ptolemies.

Though the Egyptians confined themselves to one wife, they, like the Jews and other Eastern nations, both of ancient and modern times, scrupled not to admit other inmates to their *hareem*, most of whom appear to have been foreigners, either taken in war, or brought to Egypt to be sold as slaves. They became members of the family, like those in Moslem countries at the present day, and not only ranked next to the wives and children of their lord, but probably enjoyed a share of the property at his death. These women were white or black slaves, according to the countries from which they were brought; but, generally speaking, the latter were employed merely as domestics, who were required to wait upon their mistress and her female friends. The former, likewise, officiated as servants, though they of course held a rank above the black slaves.

The same custom prevailed among the Egyptians regarding children, as with the Moslems and other Eastern people, no distinction being made between their offspring by a wife or any other woman, and all equally enjoying the rights of inheritance; for, since they considered a child indebted to the father for its existence, it seemed unjust to deny equal rights to all his progeny.

In speaking of the duties of children in Egypt, Herodotus declares, that if a son was unwilling to maintain his parents, he was at liberty to refuse, but that a daughter, on the contrary, was compelled to assist them, and, on refusal, was amenable to law. But we may question the truth of this statement; and, drawing an inference from the marked severity of filial duties among the Egyptians, some of which we find distinctly alluded to in the sculptures of Thebes, we may conclude that in Egypt much more was expected from a son than in any civilized nation of the present day; and this was not confined to the lower orders, but extended to those of the highest ranks of society. And if the office of fan-bearer was an honorable post, and the sons of the monarch were preferred to fulfil it, no ordinary show of humility was required on their part; and they walked on foot behind his chariot, bearing certain insignia over their father during the triumphal processions which took place in commemoration of his victories, and in the religious ceremonies over which he presided.

It was equally a custom in the early times of European history that a son should pay a marked deference to his parent; and no prince was allowed to sit at table with his father, unless through his valour, having been invested with arms by a foreign sovereign, he had obtained that privilege; as was the case with Alboin, before he succeeded his father on the throne of the Lombards. The European nations were not long in altering their early habits, and this custom soon became disregarded; but a respect for ancient institutions, and those ideas, so prevalent in the East, which reject all love of change, prevented the Egyptians from discarding the usages of their ancestors; and we find this and many other primitive customs retained, even at the period when they were most highly civilized.

In the education of youth they were particularly strict; and "they knew," says Plato, "that children ought to be early accustomed to such gestures, looks, and motions as are decent and proper, and not to be suffered either to hear or learn any verses and songs than those which are calculated to inspire them with virtue; and they consequently took care that every dance and ode introduced at their feasts and sacrifices should be subject to certain regulations." They particularly inculcated respect for old age; and the fact of this being required even towards strangers, argues a great regard for the person of a parent; for we are informed that, like the Israelites and the Lacedæmonians, they required every young man to give place to his superiors in years, and even, if seated, to rise on their approach.

Nor were these honours limited to their lifetime: the memory of parents and ancestors was revered through succeeding generations: their tombs were maintained with the greatest respect; liturgies were performed by their children, or by priests at their expense; and we have previously seen what advantage was taken of this feeling in the laws concerning debt.

Guided by the same principle, the Egyptians paid the most marked respect to their monarch, as the father of his people. He was obeyed with courteous submission, his will was tantamount to a law, and such implicit confidence did they place in his judgment that he was thought incapable of error. He was the representative of the Divinity on earth: the Gods were supposed to communicate through him their choicest benefits to man; and they believed that the sovereign power had been delegated to him by the will of the Deities themselves. They entertained a strong feeling of gratitude for the services done by him to the state; and the memory of a monarch who had benefited his subjects was celebrated after death with the most unbounded honours. "For of all people," says Diodorus, "the Egyptians retain the highest sense of a favour conferred upon them, deeming it the greatest charm of life to make a suitable return for benefits they have received;" and from the high estimation in which the feeling of gratitude was held among them, even strangers felt a reverence for the character of the Egyptians. Through this impulse, they were induced to solemnize the funeral obsequies of their kings with the enthusiasm described by the historian; and to this he partly attributes the unexampled duration of the Egyptian monarchy. (*See* vol. i. p. 314.)

It is only doing justice to the modern Egyptians to say that gratitude is still a distinguishing trait of their character; and this is one of the many qualities inherited by them, for which their predecessors were remarkable; confirming what I have before stated, that the general peculiarities of a people are retained, though a country may be conquered, and nominally peopled by a foreign race. (*See* vol. i. p. 2, 3.)

Another remarkable feature of the Egyptian laws was the sanctity with which old edicts were upheld. They were closely interwoven with the religion of the country, and said to be derived from the Gods themselves; whence it was considered both useless and impious to alter such sacred institutions. Those innovations only were introduced by their monarchs which were loudly called for by circumstances; and we neither read of any attempts on the part of the people to alter or resist the laws, nor on that of their rulers to introduce a more arbitrary mode of government.

The Egyptians were particularly remarkable for their great love for their country, which is also inherited by their successors. They considered it to be under the immediate protection of the Gods, and the centre of the world; they even called it the "world" itself; and it was thought to be the favoured spot where all created beings were first generated, while the rest of the earth was barren and uninhabited.

But as society advanced, it necessarily happened that some alterations were required, either in the reformation of an existing code, or in the introduction of additional laws; and among the different legislators of the Egyptians are particularly noticed the names of Mnevis, Sasyches, Sesostris, Bocchoris, Asychis, Amasis, and even the Persian Darius. The great merit of the first of these seems to have consisted in inducing the people to conform to those institutions which he pretended to have received from Hermes, the Egyptian Mercury; "an idea," says Diodorus, "which has been adopted with success by many other ancient lawgivers, who have inculcated a respect for their institutions, through the awe that is naturally felt for the majesty of the Gods." The additions made by Sasyches chiefly related to matters of religious worship; and Sesostris, in addition to numerous regulations of a military nature, is said to have introduced some changes into the agricultural system. He divided all the land of Egypt, with the exception of that which belonged to the priests and soldiers, into squares of equal areas, assigning to each peasant his peculiar portion, or a certain number of these *arouras*, for which he annually paid a fixed rent; and having instituted a yearly survey of the lands, any deficiency, resulting from a fall of the bank during the inundation, or other accidental causes, was stated in the returns, and deducted for in the government demands. Of the laws of Bocchoris and Asychis respecting debt, I have already spoken; and the former is said to have introduced many others relating to the kings, as well as to civil contracts and commerce, and to have established several important precedents in Egyptian jurisprudence. (*See above*, p. 217, 218.)

Amasis was particularly eminent for his wisdom, and for the many salutary additions he made to the laws of his country. He remodelled the system of provincial government, defining the duties of the monarchs with peculiar precision; and his conduct in the management of affairs was so highly approved by the people, that their respect for him was scarcely inferior to that shown to his most glorious predecessors. Nor was Darius, though a Persian, and of a nation justly abhorred by the Egyptians,* denied those eulogiums which the mildness of his government, and the introduction of laws tending to benefit the country, claimed for him; and they even granted him the title of Divus, making him partaker of the same honours which were bestowed on the native princes. But the Ptolemies in after times abrogated some of the favourite laws of the country; and though much was done by them, in repairing the temples, and in executing very grand and useful works, and though several of those sovereigns courted the good will of the Egyptians, yet their name became odious, and Macrobius has stigmatized their sway with the title of " tyranny."

After the king and council, the judges or magistrates of the capital held the most distinguished post; and next to them may be considered the nomarchs, or governors, of districts.

The whole of Egypt was divided into nomes, or districts, the total of which, in the time of Sesostris, amounted to thirty-six; afterwards increased to fifty-three.

The limits of Egypt were the Mediterranean to the north, and Syene, or the Cataracts, to the south; and the cultivated land east and west of the Nile contained within this space, or between the latitude 31° 37′ and 24° 3′, was all that constituted the original territory of the Pharaohs; though the Mareotis, the Oases, the Nitriotis, and even part of Libya, were attached to their dominions, and were considered part of the country.

The main divisions of Egypt were " the Upper and Lower regions;" and this distinction, which had been maintained from the earliest times, was also indicated by a difference in the dialects of the language. Thebes and Memphis enjoyed equal rank as capitals of Egypt; and every monarch at his coronation assumed the title of " lord of the two regions," or " the two worlds." But a change afterwards took place in the division of the coun-

* Though Cambyses was so execrated, his conduct was at first conciliatory; and a monument in the Louvre proves that he confirmed the leading men in their offices, and did not interfere with their customs until the Egyptians became turbulent.

try, and the northern portion was subdivided into the two provinces of Heptanomis and Lower Egypt. The latter extended from the sea to the head of the Delta, and advancing to the natural boundary of the low lands, which is so strongly marked by the abrupt ridge of the modern Mokuttum, it included the city of Heliopolis within its limits.

Heptanomis, or Middle Egypt, extended thence to the Theban castle, which marked the frontier a few miles above Tanis, and which appears to have occupied the site of the present town of Dahroot; and its name, Heptanomis, was derived from the seven nomes, or districts, it contained, which were those of Memphis, Aphroditopolis, Crocodilopolis, or Arsinoë, Heracleopolis, Oxyrhinchus, Cynopolis, and Hermopolis.

The limits of the Thebaïd remained the same, and extended to the cataracts of Syene; but it appears that the Oases were all attached to the province of Heptanomis. The chief towns of the three provinces were Thebes, Memphis, and Heliopolis, the same from which the bench of judges was elected.

According to Diodorus, the celebrated Sesostris was the first who divided the country into nomes; but it is more reasonable to suppose that long before his time, or at least before that of Remeses the Great, or even of Osirtasen, all necessary arrangements for the organization of the provinces had already been made, and that this was one of the first plans suggested for the government of the country.

The office of nomarch was at all times of the highest importance, and to his charge was committed the management of the lands, and all matters relating to the internal administration of the district. He regulated the assessment and levying of the taxes, the survey of the lands, the opening of the canals, and all other agricultural interests of the country, which were under the immediate superintendence of certain members of the priestly order; and, as his residence was in the chief town of the nome, all causes respecting landed property, and other accidental disputes, were referred to him, and adjusted before his tribunal. The division of the country into thirty-six parts, or nomes, continued to be maintained till a late period, since in Strabo's time the number was still the same; ten, says the geographer, being assigned to the Thebaï, ten to the Delta, and sixteen to the intermediate province, though some changes were afterwards introduced both in the nomes and provinces of Egypt. The nomes, he adds, were subdivided into local governments, and these again into minor jurisdictions; and we may conclude that the three offices of nomarchs, toparchs, and the third or lowest grade, answered to those of bey, kashef, and kẏmaḳám of the present day. The distinctive appellation of each nome, in later times at least, was derived from the chief town, where the governor resided, and the rank of each nomarch depended on the extent of his jurisdiction. But of the condition of Egypt in the early period of its history little is known, owing to the scanty information obtained by those Greeks who visited it, or to the loss of their writings, as well as to the jealousy of the Egyptians towards foreigners, to whom little or nothing was imparted respecting the institutions and state of the country.

They prevented all strangers from penetrating into the interior; and if any Greek was desirous of becoming acquainted with the philosophy of their schools, he was tolerated, rather than welcomed, in Egypt; and those who traded there were confined to the town of Naucratis, in the same manner that Europeans are now obliged to live in the Frank quarter of a Turkish or a Chinese city. And when, after the time of Amasis and the Persian conquest, foreigners became better acquainted with the country, its ancient institutions had begun to lose their interest, and the Egyptians mourned under a victorious and cruel despot. Herodotus, it is true, had ample opportunity of examining the state of Egypt during his visit to the country; but he has failed to give us much insight into its laws and institutions.

Strabo mentions some of the offices which existed in Egypt in his time; but, though he asserts that many of them were the same as under the Ptolemies, we are by no means certain that they answer to those of an earlier period. " Under the eparch," says the geographer, " who holds the rank of a king, is the dicæodotes, that is, the lawgiver or chancellor, and another officer, who is called the privy-purse, or private accountant, whose business it is to take charge of everything that is left without an owner, and which falls of right to the emperor. These two are also attended by freedmen and stewards of Cæsar, who are intrusted with affairs of greater or less magnitude. . . . . But of the natives who are employed in the government of the different cities, the principal is the exégétés, or expounder, who is dressed in purple, and is honoured according to the usages of the country, and takes care of what is necessary for the welfare of the city; the register, or writer of commentaries; the archidicastes, or chief judge; and, fourthly, the captain of the night."

From all that can be collected on this subject, we may conclude, that in early times, after the king, the senate, and others connected with the court, the principal persons employed in the management of affairs were the judges of different grades, the rulers of provinces and districts, the government accountants, the chief of the police, and those officers immediately connected with the administration of justice, the levying of taxes, and other similar employments; and that the principal part of them were chosen either from the sacerdotal or military class.

During the reigns of the latter Ptolemies, considerable abuses crept into the administrative system: intrigues, arising out of party spirit and conflicting interests, corrupted men's minds; integrity ceased to be esteemed: every patriotic feeling became extinguished: the interests of the community were sacrificed to the ambition of a successful candidate for a disputed throne; and the hope of present advantage blinded men to future consequences. New regulations were adopted to suppress the turbulent spirit of the times: the government, no longer content with the mild office of protector, assumed the character of chastiser of the people; and Egypt was ruled by a military force, rendered doubly odious, from being, in a great measure, composed of foreign mercenaries. The military class had lost its consequence, its privileges were abolished, and the harmony once existing between it and the people was entirely destroyed. Respect for the wisdom of the sacerdotal order, and the ancient institutions of Egypt, began to decline; and the influence once possessed by the priests over the public mind could only be traced in the superstitious reverence shown by fanatics to the rites of a religion, now much corrupted and degraded by fanciful doctrines; and if they retained a portion of their former privileges, by having the education of youth intrusted to them, as well as the care of the national records, the superintendence of weights and measures, the surveying of the lands, and the equal distribution of the annual payments, they lost their most important offices —the tutelage and direction of the councils of government, and the right of presiding at the courts of justice.

The provincial divisions of Egypt varied at different times, particularly after the Roman conquest. The country, as already stated, consisted originally of two parts, Upper and Lower Egypt; afterwards of three—the Thebaid; Heptanomis, or Middle Egypt; and the Delta, or Lower Egypt; but Heptanomis, in the time of Arcadius, the son of Theodosius the Great, received the name of Arcadia; and the eastern portion of the Delta, about the end of the fourth century, was formed into a separate province called Augustamnica, itself divided into two parts. The Thebaid was also made to consist of Upper and Lower, the line of separation passing between Panopolis and Ptolemaïs Hermii.

Under the Romans, Egypt was governed by a præfect, or eparch, aided by three officers, who superintended the departments of justice, revenue, and police throughout the country, the inferior charges being chiefly filled by natives; and over each of the provinces a military governor was appointed, who was subordinate to the præfect in all civil affairs, though frequently intruding on his jurisdiction, when it was necessary to use military coercion in the collection of the taxes. But as the condition of Egypt under the Ptolemies and Romans is not directly connected with the manners and customs of the ancient Egyptians, it is unnecessary to describe the changes that took place during their rule.

Judging from the sculptures of Thebes, the tribute annually received in early times by the Egyptians, from nations they had subdued in Asia and Northern Ethiopia, was of immense value, and tended greatly to enrich the coffers of the state; and the quantity of gold in dust, rings, and bars, and silver in rings and ingots, copper, iron, lead, and tin (?), the various objects of luxury, vases of glass, porcelain, gold, silver, and other metals, ivory, ebony, and different woods, precious stones, horses, dogs, oxen, wild animals, trees, seeds, fruits, bitumen, incense, gums, perfumes, spices, and other foreign productions there described, perfectly accord with the statements of ancient authors. And though they are presented to the king, as chief of the nation, we may conclude they formed part of the public revenue, and were not solely intended for his use; especially in a country where royalty was under the restraint and guidance of salutary laws, and where the welfare of the community was not sacrificed to the caprice of a monarch.

According to Strabo, the taxes, even under Ptolemy Auletes, the father of Cleopatra, the most negligent of monarchs, amounted to 12,500 talents, or between three and four millions sterling; and the constant influx of specie resulting from commercial intercourse with foreign nations, who purchased the corn and manufactures of Egypt, during the very careful administration of its native sovereigns, necessarily increased the riches of the country, and greatly augmented the revenue at that period.

Among the exports were yarn, fine linen cloth, and embroidered work, purchased by the Tyrians and Jews; chariots and horses, bought by the merchants of Judæa in the time of Solomon at 600 and 150 shekels of silver; and other commodities, produced or manufactured in the country.*

The Egyptians also derived important advantages from their intercourse with India and Arabia; and the port of Philoteras, which, there is reason to believe, was constructed at a very remote period, long before the Exodus of the Israelites, was probably the emporium of that trade. It was situated on the western coast of the Red Sea, in latitude 26° 9′; and though small, the number of ships its basin would contain sufficed for a constant traffic between Egypt and Arabia, no periodical winds there interfering with the navigation at any season of the year.

* 2 Chron. i. 16, 17; 1 Kings, x.; and Ezek. xxvii. 7.

It is not probable that they had a direct communication with India at the same early epoch, but they were supplied through Arabia with the merchandise of that country; and even an indirect trade was capable of opening to them a source of immense wealth. And that the productions of India did actually reach Egypt, we have positive testimony from the tombs of Thebes.

The Scripture history shows the traffic established by Solomon with India, through the Red Sea, to have been of very great consequence, producing, in one voyage, no less than 450 talents of gold;* and to the same branch of commerce may be ascribed the main cause of the flourishing condition of Tyre itself. And if the Egyptian trade was not so direct as that of Solomon and the Tyrians, it must still be admitted that *any* intercourse with India at so remote a period would have been highly beneficial to the country, since it was enjoyed with little competition, and consequently afforded increased advantages.

The other harbours in this part of the Arabian Gulf—Myos Hormos, Berenice, Arsinoë, Nechesia, and Leucos Portus—were built in later times; and the lucrative trade they enjoyed was greatly increased after the conquest of Egypt by the Romans, 120 vessels annually leaving the coast of Egypt for India, at midsummer, about the rising of the dog-star, and returning in the month of December or January. " The principal objects of Oriental traffic," says Gibbon, " were splendid and trifling: silk (a pound of which was esteemed not inferior in value to a pound of gold), precious stones, and a variety of aromatics." When Strabo visited Egypt, the Myos Hormos seems to have superseded Berenice, and all the other maritime stations on the coast; and indeed it possessed greater advantages than any other, except Philoteras and Arsinoë, in its overland communication with the Nile. Yet Berenice, in the later age of Pliny, was again preferred to its rival. From both ports the goods were taken on camels by an almost level road across the desert to Coptos, and thence distributed over different parts of Egypt; and, in the time of the Ptolemies and Cæsars, those

* 2 Chron. viii. 18; 1 Kings, ix. 26.

particularly suited for exportation to Europe went down the river to Alexandria, where they were sold to merchants who resorted to that city at a stated season.

At a subsequent period, during the reigns of the Arab Caliphs, Apollinopolis, Parva, or Koos succeeded Coptos as the rendezvous of caravans from the Red Sea; and this town flourished so rapidly, in consequence of the preference it enjoyed, that in Aboolfeda's time it was second only to Fostat, the capital of Egypt; until it ceded its place to Keneh, as Myos Hormos was destined to do in favour of Kossayr. Philoteras, however, continued to be resorted to after the Arab conquest; and it was during the reigns of the Egyptian caliphs that the modern Kossayr took the place of that ancient port.

The Myos Hormos, called also Aphrodité, stood in latitude 27° 22′, upon a flat coast, backed by low mountains, distant from it about three miles, where a well, the Fons Tadnos, supplied the town and ships with water. The port was more capacious than those of Berenice and Philoteras; and though exposed to the winds, it was secure against the force of a boisterous sea. Several roads united at the gates of the town, from Berenice and Philoteras on the south, from Arsinoë on the north, and from Coptos on the west; and stations supplied those who passed to and from the Nile with water and other necessaries.

Berenice owed its foundation to Ptolemy Philadelphus, who called it after the name of his mother, the wife of Lagus or Soter. The town was extensive, and was ornamented with a small but elegant temple of Serapis; and though the harbour was neither deep nor spacious, its position in a receding gulf tended greatly to the safety of the vessels lying within it, or anchored in the bay. A road led thence direct to Coptos, furnished with the usual stations, or *hydreumas;* and another, which also went to the emerald mines, joined, or rather crossed it, from Apollinopolis Magna.

Arsinoë, which stood at the northern extremity of the Red Sea, near the modern town of Sooez, was founded by the second Ptolemy, and so named after his sister. Though vessels anchored there rode secure from the violence of the sea, its exposed situation, and the dangers they encountered in working up the narrow extremity of the gulf, rendered its position less eligible for the Indian trade than either Myos Hormos or Berenice; and had it not been for the convenience of establishing a communication with the Nile by a canal, and the shortness of the journey across the desert in that part, it is probable it would not have been chosen for a sea-port.

The small towns of Nechesia and the Leucos Portus were probably of Roman date, though the natural harbours they possess may have been used at a much earlier period. Their positions are still marked by the ruins on the shore, in latitude 24° 54′ and 25° 37′, where I discovered them in 1826, while making a survey of this part of the coast from Sooez to Berenice. The former stands in, and perhaps gave the name to, the Wadee Nukkaree; the latter is called E'Shoona, or "the Magazine," and, from being built of very *white* limestone, was readily indicated by the Arabs when I inquired of them the site of the White Harbour.

Many other ports, the "Portus multi" of Pliny, occur along the coast, particularly between Berenice and Kossayr; but though they all have landmarks to guide boats in approaching their rocky entrances, which are openings in the coral reefs, none of them have any remains of a town, or the vestiges of habitations.

The principal objects introduced in early times into Egypt, from Arabia and India, were spices and various Oriental productions, required either for the service of religion or the purposes of luxury; and a number of precious stones, lapis lazzuli, and other things brought from those countries, are frequently discovered in the tombs of Thebes, bearing the names of Pharaohs of the 18th dynasty. The mines of their own desert did, indeed, supply the emeralds they used; and these were worked as early, at least, as the reign of Amunoph III., at the beginning of the 15th century B.C., but many other stones must have come from India; and some plants, as the Nymphæa Nelumbo, seem to have been introduced from that country.

Though we cannot ascertain the amount or exact quality of the various imports, of the goods re-exported from Egypt, or the proportion which these last bore to the internal consumption, it is reasonable to conclude that every article of luxury was a source of revenue to the government; and that both native and foreign productions coming under this denomination, whether exported or sold in Egypt, tended to enrich the state, to which they belonged, or paid a duty.

That the riches of the country were immense, is proved by the appearance of the furniture and domestic utensils, and by the great quantity of jewels of gold, and silver, precious stones, and other objects of luxury in use among them in the earliest times; their treasures became proverbial throughout the neighbouring states,* and a love of pomp and splendour continued to be the ruling passion of the Egyptians till the latest period of their existence as an independent state.

The wealth of Egypt was principally derived from taxes, foreign tribute, monopolies, commerce, mines, and, above all, from the productions of a fruitful soil. The wants of the poorer classes were easily satisfied; the abundance of grain, herbs, and esculent plants afforded an ample supply to the inhabitants of the valley of the Nile, at a trifling expense, and with little labour; and so much corn was produced in this fertile country, that after sufficing for the consumption of a very extensive population, it offered a great surplus for the foreign market, and afforded considerable profit to the government, being exported to other countries, or sold to the traders who visited Egypt for commercial purposes.

The gold mines of the Bisharee desert were in those times very productive; and, though we have no positive notice of their first discovery, there is reason to believe they were worked at the earliest periods of the Egyptian monarchy. The total of the annual produce of the gold and silver mines (which Diodorus, on the authority of Hecatæus, says, was recorded in the tomb of Osymandyas at Thebes, apparently a king of the 19th dynasty) is stated to have been 3200 myriads, or 32 millions of *minæ*

---

* "Greater riches than the treasures in Egypt."—Ep. Heb. xi. 26. "The pomp of Egypt."—Ezek. xxii. 12. *Comp.* also the jewels of silver and gold which the Jews borrowed from the Egyptians. Exod. xii. 35.

Chap. VIII. GOLD AND SILVER OF THE ANCIENTS. 239

—a weight of that country, called by the Egyptians *mn* or *mna*, 60 of which were equal to one talent. The whole sum amounted to 133 millions of our money; but it was evidently exaggerated.

The position of the silver mines is unknown; but the gold mines of Allaga* (already mentioned), and other quartz "diggings," have been discovered, as well as those of copper, lead, iron, and emeralds, all of which are in the desert near the Red Sea; and the sulphur, which abounds in the same districts, was not neglected by the ancient Egyptians.

The abundance of gold and silver in Egypt and other ancient countries, and the sums reported to have been spent, accord well with the reputed productiveness of the mines in those days; and, as the subject has become one of peculiar interest, it may be well to inquire respecting the quantity and the use of the precious metals in ancient times. They were then mostly confined to the treasuries of princes, and of some rich individuals; the proportion employed for commercial purposes was small, copper sufficing for most purchases in the home market; and nearly all the gold and silver money (as yet uncoined) was in the hands of the wealthy few. The manufacture of jewellery and other ornamental objects took up a small portion of the great mass; but it required the wealth and privilege of royalty to indulge in a grand display of gold and silver vases, or similar objects of size and value.

The mines of those days, from which was derived the wealth of Egypt, Lydia, Persia, and other countries, afforded a large supply of the precious metals; and if most of them are now exhausted, or barely retain evidences of the treasures they once gave forth, there can be no doubt of their former productiveness; and it is reasonable to suppose that gold and silver abounded in early times, in those parts of the world which were first inhabited, as they did in countries more recently peopled. They may never have afforded at any period the immense riches of a California or an Australia, yet there is evidence of their having been sufficiently distributed over various parts of the old world.

For though Herodotus (iii., 106) says that the extremities of

* In chap. vii. p. 141.

the earth possess the greatest treasures; those extremities may approach or become the centre, *i. e.*, of civilization, when they arrive at that eminence which all great countries in their turn seem to have a chance of reaching; and Britain, the country of the greatly coveted tin, once looked upon as separated from the rest of mankind, is now one of the commercial centres of the world. The day, too, may come when Australia and California will be rivals for a similar distinction; and England, the rendezvous of America in her contests with Europe, will yield its turn to younger competitors.

The greatest quantity of gold and silver in early times was derived from the East; and Asia and Egypt possessed abundance of those metals. The trade of Colchis, and the treasures of the Arimaspês and Massagetæ, coming from the Ural (or from the Altai) Mountains, supplied much gold at a very early period, and Indian commerce sent a large supply to Western Asia. Spain, the Isle of Thasos, and other places, were resorted to by the Phœnicians, particularly for silver; and Spain, for its mines, became the "*El Dorado*" of those adventurous traders.

The mines of the Eastern desert, the tributes from Ethiopia and Central Africa, as well as from Asia, enriched Egypt with gold and silver; but it was long before Greece (where in heroic times the precious metals were scarcely known) obtained a moderate supply of silver from her own mines; and gold only became abundant there after the Persian war.

Thrace and Macedonia produced gold, as well as other countries, but confined it to their own use, as Ireland employed the produce of its mines; and as early Italy did, when its various small states were still free from the Roman yoke; and though the localities from which silver was obtained in more ancient times are less known, it is certain that it was used at a very remote period; and (as before stated) it was commonly employed in Abraham's time for mercantile transactions.

Gold is mentioned on the Egyptian monuments of the 4th dynasty, and silver was probably of the same early time; but gold was evidently known in Egypt before silver, which is consistent

CHAP. VIII. PROPORTIONS OF GOLD AND SILVER.

with reason, gold being more easily obtained than silver, and frequently near the surface or in streams. (*See above*, p. 147.)

The relative value and quantity of the precious metals in the earliest times, in Egypt and Western Asia, are not known; and even if a greater amount of gold were found mentioned in a tribute, this could be no proof of the silver being more rare, as it might be merely intended to show the richness of the gifts. In the tribute brought to Thothmes III. by the southern Ethiopians and three Asiatic people, the former present scarcely any silver, but great quantities of gold in rings, ingots, and dust. The Asiatic people of Pount bring two baskets of gold rings, and one of gold dust in bags, a much smaller amount of gold than the Ethiopians, and no silver; those of Kufa or Kaf, more silver than gold, and a considerable quantity of both made into vases of handsome and varied shapes; and the Rot-ñ-n (apparently living on the Euphrates) present rather more gold than silver, a large basket of gold and a smaller one of silver rings, two small silver and several large gold vases, which are of most elegant shape, as well as coloured glass or porcelain cups, and much incense and bitumen. The great Asiatic tribute to the same king at Karnak speaks in one place of 100 ingots (or pounds weight?) of gold and silver, and afterwards of 401 of silver; but the imperfect preservation of that record prevents our ascertaining how much gold was brought, or the relative proportions of the two metals.

M. Léon Faucher, indeed, suggests that "the value of silver in some countries originally equalled, if it did not exceed, that of gold . . . and the laws of Menes state that gold was worth two and a half times more than silver. . . . Everywhere, except in India, between the fifth and sixth centuries B.C., the relative value of gold and silver was 6 or 8 to 1, as it was in China and Japan at the end of the last century." In Greece it was, according to Herodotus, as 13 to 1; afterwards, in Plato's and Xenophon's time, and more than 100 years after the death of Alexander, as 10 to 1, owing to the quantity of gold brought in through the Persian war; when the value of both fell so much, that in the time of Demosthenes it was five times less than at the death of Solon.

The relative price of gold and silver continued for a long time at 10 to 1 (Liv. xxxviii. 11), except when occasional events altered the equilibrium by an increase of one of those metals; as when the taking of Syracuse, and the plunder of the treasury by Julius Cæsar, reduced the proportions to 7 and 9 to 1. But these sudden changes, as Humboldt says, were owing to the less general commercial relations of the world, and they could not have happened with the rapidity of communication in the present day.

Under the empire, the produce of the silver mines of Asia, Thrace, and Spain again raised the value of gold, and the proportions were 18 to 1 in the time of Theodosius II.; but the skill required for working silver was so deficient during the Middle Ages and in the sixteenth century, that they were brought to 11 and 12 to 1. Before the discovery of America, they were 11 and 10 to 1 in England; and, after great fluctuations, they were in Newton's time 16 to 1, becoming at length about $14\frac{1}{4}$ to 1; which may again be altered by the modern discoveries of California and Australia, unless another Potosi affords fresh supplies of silver. But owing to the constant export of gold, the extent of trading operations, the rapidity of communication throughout the world, and the quantity required to keep up the equilibrium after restoring the deficiency in many countries, a long time must elapse before the effects of these new gold supplies on the general circulation will be felt, or the value of gold be sensibly altered beyond its relative proportion to silver.

Though it may not be possible to arrive at any satisfactory conclusion respecting the quantity of gold and silver taken from the mines, employed in objects of art and luxury, or in circulation as money in Egypt and other countries, I shall introduce a few facts, derived from the accounts of ancient authors, relating to the amount of wealth amassed, and the purposes to which those precious metals were applied. I shall also show some of the fluctuations that have taken place in the supply of them at various periods, and shall endeavour to establish a comparison between the quantity said to have been in use in ancient and modern times.

When we read of the enormous wealth amassed by the Egyptian and Asiatic kings, or the plunder by Alexander and the Romans, we wonder how so much could have been obtained; for, even allowing for considerable exaggeration in the accounts of early times, there is no reason to disbelieve the private fortunes of individuals at Rome, and the sums squandered by them, or even the amount of some of the tributes levied in the East. Of ancient cities, Babylon is particularly cited by Herodotus and others for its immense wealth. Diodorus (ii. 9) mentions a golden statue of Jupiter at Babylon 40 feet high, weighing 1000 Babylonian talents; another of Rhea, of equal weight, having two lions on its knees, and near it silver serpents of 300 talents each; a standing statue of Juno weighing 800 talents, holding a snake, and a sceptre set with gems; as well as a golden table of 500 talents weight, on which were two cups weighing 300 talents, and two censers each of 300 talents weight, with three golden bowls, one of which, belonging to Jupiter, weighed 1200 talents, the others each 600; making a total of at least 6900 talents, reckoned equal to 11,000,000 sterling. And the golden image of Nebuchadnezzar, 60 cubits, or 90 feet, high, at the same ratio would weigh 2250 talents.

David, who had not the Indian and Arabian trade afterwards obtained by Solomon, left for the building of the temple 100,000 talents of gold and 1,000,000 of silver;* and the sum given by him of his "own proper good," "over and above all prepared for the holy house," was "3000 talents of gold" and "7000 of refined silver;" besides the chief men's contributions† of 500 talents and 10,000 drachms of gold, 10,000 talents of silver, and an abundance of brass, iron, and precious stones.

The annual tribute of Solomon‡ was 666 talents of gold, besides that brought by the merchants, and the present from the Queen of Sheba of 120 talents; and the quantity of gold and silver used in the temple and his house was extraordinary. Mr. Jacob, in his valuable work on the precious metals, has noticed many of these immense sums, collected in old times. Among them are the tribute of Darius, amounting to 9880 talents of silver and 4680 of gold, making a total of 14,560, estimated at

* 1 Chron. xxii. 14. † 1 Chron. xxix. 3, 4, 7.
‡ 2 Chron. ix. 13; 1 Kings, x. 14.

about 3¼ millions sterling; the sums taken by Xerxes to Greece; the wealth of Crœsus; the riches of Pytheus, king of a small territory in Phrygia, possessing gold and silver mines, who entertained the army of Xerxes, and gave him 2000 talents of silver and 4,093,000 staters of gold (equal to 4,770,000 pounds of our money, or, according to Larcher, 3,600,000); the treasures acquired by Alexander in Susa and Persia, exclusive of that found in the Persian camp and in Babylon, said to have amounted to 40,000 or 50,000 talents; the treasure of Persepolis, rated at 120,000 talents; that of Pasagarda at 6000; and the 180,000 talents collected at the capture of Ecbatana; besides 6000 which Darius had with him, and were taken by his murderers. " Ptolemy Philadelphus is stated by Appian to have possessed treasure to the enormous amount of 740,000 talents;" either " 178 millions, or at least a quarter of that sum;" and fortunes of private individuals at Rome show the enormous wealth they possessed. " Crassus had in lands 1,614,583*l*., besides as much more in money, furniture, and slaves; Seneca, 2,421,875*l*.; Pallas, the freedman of Claudius, an equal sum; Lentulus, the augur, 3,229,166*l*.; Cæc. Cl. Isidorus, though he had lost a great part of his fortune in the civil war, left by his will 4116 slaves, 3600 yoke of oxen, 257,000 other cattle, and in ready money 484,375*l*. Augustus received by the testaments of his friends 32,291,666*l*. Tiberius left at his death 21,796,875*l*., which Caligula lavished away in less than one year; and Vespasian, at his succession, said that to support the state he required *quadrigenties millies*, or 322,916,666*l*. The debts of Milo amounted to 565,104*l*. J. Cæsar, before he held any office, owed 1300 talents, 251,875*l*.; and when he set out for Spain after his prætorship, he is reported to have said that ' Bis millies et quingenties sibi deesse, ut nihil haberet,' or ' that he was 2,018,229*l*. worse than nothing.' When he first entered Rome, in the beginning of the civil war, he took out of the treasury 1,095,979*l*., and brought into it at the end of it 4,843,750*l*.; he purchased the friendship of Curio, at the commencement of the civil war, by a bribe of 484,373*l*., and that of the consul L. Paulus by 1500 talents, about 279,500*l*.; Apicius wasted on luxurious living 484,375*l*.; Caligula laid out on a supper 80,729*l*.; and the ordinary expense of Lucullus for a supper in the Hall of Apollo was 50,000 drachms, or 1614*l*. The house of Marius, bought of Cornelia for 2421*l*., was sold to Lucullus for 16,152*l*.; the burning of his villa was a loss to M. Scaurus of 807,291*l*.; and Nero's golden house must have cost an immense sum, since Otho laid out in furnishing a part of it 403,645*l*."* But though Rome was greatly enriched by conquest, she never obtained possession of the chief wealth of Asia; and the largest quantity of the precious metals was always excluded from the calculations of ancient writers.

The whole revenue of the Roman Empire under Augustus is " supposed to have been equal to 40 millions of our money;" and at the time of his death (A.D. 14) the gold and silver in circulation throughout the empire is supposed to have amounted to 358,000,000*l*., which, at a reduction of 1 grain in 360 every year for wear, would have been reduced by the year A.D. 482 to 87,033,099*l*.; and when the mines of Hungary and Germany began to be worked, during the seventh and ninth centuries, the entire amount of coined money was not more than about 42 at the former, and 33 or 34 millions sterling at the latter, period; so that if no other supply had been obtained, the quantity then circulating would long since have been exhausted.

" The loss by wear on silver" is shown by Mr. Jacob " to be four times that of gold;" that on our shillings is estimated at more than one part in a hundred annually; and " the smaller the pieces, the greater loss do they suffer by abrasion." " The maximum of durability of gold coins seems to be fixed at 22 parts, in 24, of pure gold with the appropriate alloys. When the fineness ascends or descends from that point, the consumption by abrasion is increased." It is from its ductility that gold wears so much less than silver; and many ancient gold coins (as those of Alexander and others), though evidently worn by use, nearly retain their true weight, from the surface being partly transferred into the adjacent hollows, and not entirely rubbed off as in silver.

The quantity of the precious metals formerly used for the

* Adams' Roman Antiquities, p. 438–440.

purposes of luxury, greatly diminished after the decline of the Roman empire, and in the Middle Ages they were sparingly employed except for coinage; ornamental work in gold and silver, mostly executed by first-rate artists, being confined to men of rank, till the opening of new mines added to the supply, which was afterwards increased by the abundant treasures of America; and the quantity applied to ornamental purposes then began to vie with that of olden times. M. Léon Faucher even calculates the annual abstraction of the precious metals from circulation by use for luxury, disasters at sea, and export, at 5 millions sterling, in Europe and the United States.

The silver from the American mines exported to Europe in 100 years, to 1630, gave an addition to the currency of 1 million sterling annually, besides that used for other purposes, or re-exported; and from 1630 to 1830, from $1\frac{1}{2}$ to 2 millions annually, an increase in the quantity used for currency having taken place, as well as in that exported to India, and employed for purposes of luxury. Humboldt states the whole quantity of gold from the American mines, up to 1803, to be 162 millions of pounds in weight, and of silver 7178 millions, or 44 of silver to 1 of gold.

Again, the total value of gold produced during three centuries to 1848, including that from Russia, has been estimated at 565 millions; and the total annual quantity of gold, before the discovery of the Californian fields, has been reckoned at about 10,000,000*l*. That from California and Australia already amounts yearly to 34,000,000*l*. (or 3 2-5ths times as much as previously obtained), and is still increasing; but though far beyond the supply afforded by the discovery of America, the demand made upon it by the modern industry of man, together with the effect of rapid communication, and of the extension of trade, as well as by the great deficiency of gold in the world, will prevent its action being felt in the same way as when the American supply was first obtained; and still less will be the effect now, than it would have been in ancient times, if so large and sudden a discovery had then been made. For, as Chevalier says, "Vast as is the whole amount of gold in the world, it sinks into insignificance when contrasted with the aggregate product of other branches of human industry. If they increase as fast as the gold, little or no alteration will take place in its value, which depends on the relation between it and the annual production of other wealth."

According to another calculation, all the gold now in the world is supposed to be equal to about 682 millions; but the whole amount of either of the two precious metals in old times is not easily ascertained, nor can any definite comparison be established between their former and present value. And still less in Egypt, than in Greece and Rome; no standard of calculation being obtainable from the prices of commodities there, or from any other means of determining the value of gold and silver.

In the infancy of her existence as a nation, Egypt was contented with the pursuits of agriculture; but in process of time, the advancement of civilization and refinement led to numerous inventions, and to improvements in the ordinary necessaries of life, and she became at length a great manufacturing country, famed amongst foreigners for the excellence of her fine linen, her cotton and woollen stuffs, cabinet work, porcelain, glass, and numerous branches of industry. That the Egyptians should be more known abroad for their manufactures, than for those occupations which related solely to themselves, might be reasonably expected, in consequence of the exportation of the commodities in which she excelled, and the ignorance of foreigners respecting the internal condition of a country from which they were excluded by the jealousy of the natives; though, judging from the scanty information imparted to us by the Greeks, who in later times had opportunities of examining the valley of the Nile, it appears that we have as much reason to blame the indifference of strangers who visited the country, as the exclusiveness of the Egyptians.

There are fortunately other sources of information, which give an insight into many of their pursuits; and, independent of what may be gleaned from Herodotus and Diodorus, the paintings, in the tombs of Thebes and Lower Egypt, show the experience they had acquired in the management of their lands and herds, and the different duties connected with husbandry, as well as their progress in various arts, and even in scientific knowledge.

In considering the state of agriculture in Egypt, we ought not to confine its importance to the direct and tangible benefits it annually conferred upon the people, by the productiveness of the soil; the influence it had on the manners, and scientific acquirements, of the people is no less obvious; and to the peculiar nature of the Nile, and the effects of its inundation, has been reasonably attributed the early advancement of the Egyptians in geometry and mensuration. Herodotus, Plato, Diodorus, Strabo, Clemens of Alexandria, Iamblichus, and others, ascribe the origin of geometry to changes which annually took place from the inundation, and to the consequent necessity of adjusting the claims of each person respecting the limits of the lands; and, though Herodotus may be wrong in limiting the commencement of those observations to the reign of Sesostris, his remark tends to the same point, and confirms the general opinion that this science had its origin in Egypt.

It is reasonable to suppose, that as the inundation subsided, litigation often occurred between neighbours respecting the limits of their unenclosed fields; and the fall of a portion of the bank, carried away by the stream during the rise of the Nile, frequently made great alterations in the extent of land near the river side; a mode of determining the quantity which belonged to each individual was therefore very necessary, both for settling disputes with a neighbour, and for ascertaining the tax due to government. But it is difficult to fix the period when the science of mensuration commenced; if we have ample proofs of its being known in the time of Joseph, this does not carry us far back into the ancient history of Egypt; and there is evidence of geometry and mathematics having already made nearly the same progress at the earliest period of which any monuments remain, as in the later era of the Great Remeses.

Besides the mere measurement of superficial areas, it was of the highest importance to agriculture, and to the interests of the peasant, to distribute the benefits of the inundation in due proportion to each individual, that the lands which were low might not enjoy the exclusive advantages of the fertilizing water, by constantly draining it from those of a higher level. For this purpose they were obliged to ascertain the various elevations of the country, and to construct accurately levelled canals and dykes; and if it be true that Menes, their first king, turned the course of the Nile into a new channel he had made for it, we have a proof of their having, long before his time, arrived at considerable knowledge in this branch of science, since so great an undertaking could only have been the result of long experience.

These dykes were succeeded or accompanied by the invention of sluices, and all the mechanism appertaining to them; the regulation of the supply of water admitted into plains of various levels, the report of the exact quantity of land irrigated, the depth of the water, and the time it continued upon the surface, which determined the proportionate payment of the taxes, required much scientific skill; and the prices of provisions for the ensuing year were already ascertained by the unerring prognostics of the existing inundation. Hence they were led to make minute observations respecting the increase of the Nile during that season: Nilometers, for measuring its gradual rise or fall, were constructed in various parts of Egypt, and particular persons were appointed to observe each daily change, and to proclaim the favourable or unfavourable state of this important phenomenon. On these reports depended the time chosen for opening the canals, whose mouths were closed until the river rose to a fixed height; upon which occasion grand festivities were proclaimed throughout the country, in order that every person might show his sense of the great benefit vouchsafed by the Gods to the land of Egypt. The introduction of the waters of the Nile into the interior, by means of these canals, was allegorically construed into the union of Osiris and Isis; the instant of cutting away the dam of earth which separated the bed of the canal from the Nile was looked forward to with the utmost anxiety, and many omens were consulted in order to ascertain the auspicious moment for this important ceremony.

Superstition added greatly to the zeal of a credulous people. The Deity, or presiding Genius, of the river was propitiated by suitable oblations, both during the inundation, and about the period when it was expected; and Seneca tells us, that on a particular fête the priests threw presents and offerings of gold into the river near Philæ, at a place called the Veins of the Nile, where they first perceived the rise of the inundation. It was reasonable that the grand and wonderful spectacle of the inundation should excite in them feelings of the deepest awe for the divine power, to which they were indebted for so great a blessing; and a plentiful supply of water was supposed to be the result of the favour of the Gods, as a deficiency was attributed to their displeasure, punishing the sins of an offending people.

On the inundation depended all the hopes of the peasant; it affected the revenue of the government, both by its influence on the scale of taxation, and by the greater or less profits on the exportation of grain and other produce; and it involved the comforts of all classes. For in Upper Egypt no rain fell to irrigate the land; it was a country which did not look for showers to advance its crops; and if "these fell in Lower Egypt, they were confined to that district, and heavy rain was a prodigy in the Thebaïd." But though, speaking generally, it may be said not to rain there, heavy storms did occasionally fall in the vicinity of Thebes, as is proved by the appearance of the deep ravines worn by water in the hills, about the tombs of the kings, probably, as now, after intervals of fifteen or twenty years; and modern experience shows that slight showers fall at Thebes about five or six times a year; in Lower Egypt much more frequently; and at Alexandria almost as often as in the south of Europe.

The result of a favourable inundation was not confined to tangible benefits; it had the greatest effect on the mind of every Egyptian by long anticipation; the happiness arising from it, as the regrets on the appearance of a scanty supply of water, being far more sensibly felt than in countries which depend on rain for their harvest, where future prospects are not so soon foreseen. The Egyptian, on the other hand, was able to form a just estimate of his crops even before sowing the seed, or preparing the land for its reception.

Other remarkable effects may likewise be partially attributed to the interest excited by the expectation of the rising Nile; and the accurate observations required for fixing the seasons, and the period of the annual return of the inundation, contributed greatly to the early study of astronomy in the valley of the Nile. The precise time when these and other calculations were first made by the Egyptians, it is impossible now to determine, but from the height of the inundation being already recorded in the reign of the kings of the 12th dynasty, we may infer that constant observations had been made, and Nilometers constructed, even before that early period; and astronomy, geometry, and other sciences are said to have been known in Egypt in the time of the hierarchy which preceded the accession of their first king, Menes.

We cannot, however, from the authority of Diodorus and Clemens of Alexandria, venture to assert that the books of Hermes, which contained the science and philosophy of Egypt, all date before the reign of Menes; the original work, by whomsover it was composed, was probably very limited and imperfect; and the famous books of Hermes were not all written at the same period, like the Jewish collection of poems received under the name of David's Psalms, some of which date after the Babylonish captivity. Nor was Thoth, Hermes, or Mercury a real personage, but (as I have before stated) a deified form of the divine intellect, which, being imparted to man, had enabled him to produce this effort of genius, and the only argument in favour of the high antiquity of any portion of this work is the tradition of the people, supported by the positive proof of the great mathematical skill of the Egyptians in the time of Menes, by the change he made in the course of the Nile. It may also be inferred from their advancement in the arts and sciences at this early period, that many ages of civilization had preceded the accession of their first monarch.

At all events, we may conclude that to agriculture and the peculiar nature of the river, the accurate method adopted by the Egyptians in the regulation of their year is to be attributed; that by the return of the seasons so decidedly marked in Egypt, they were taught to correct those inaccuracies, to which an approximate calculation was at first subject; and that thus the calendar, which could not long be suffered to depend on the vague length of a solar revolution, was necessarily brought round to a fixed period.

It is highly probable that the Egyptians, in their infancy as a nation, divided their year into twelve lunar months; the twenty-eight years of Osiris's reign being derived, as Plutarch says, from the number of days the moon takes to perform her course round the earth; and it is worthy of remark, that the hieroglyphic signifying " month" was represented by the crescent of the moon, as is abundantly proved from the sculptures and the authority of Horapollo. From this we also derive another very important conclusion—that the use of hieroglyphics was of a far more remote date than is generally supposed, since they existed previous to the adoption of solar months.

The substitution of solar for lunar months was the earliest change in the Egyptian year. It was then made to consist of twelve months of thirty days each, making a total of 360 days; but as it was soon discovered that the seasons were disturbed, and no longer corresponded to the same months, five additional days were introduced at the end of the last month, Mesoré, in order to remedy the previous defect in the calendar, and to insure the returns of the seasons to fixed periods.

The twelve months were Thoth, Paopi, Athor, Choeak, Tobi, Mechir, Phamenoth, Pharmuthi, Pachons, Paoni, Epep, Mesoré: and the year being divided into three seasons, each period comprised four of these months. That containing the first four was styled the season of the " plants;" the next *perhaps* of the " manifestation," or " appearance of the inundation;" and the last season of the " tanks of water," which had been laid up when the Nile subsided. The 1st of Thoth, in the time of Julius Cæsar, fell on the 29th of August; and Mesoré, the last month, began on the 25th of July, as may be seen in the accompanying woodcut, where I have introduced the modern names given them by the Copts, who still use them in preference to the lunar months of the Arabs; and, indeed, the Arabs themselves are frequently guided by the Coptic months in matters relating to agriculture, particularly in Upper Egypt.

THE EGYPTIAN YEAR.

1st Season.

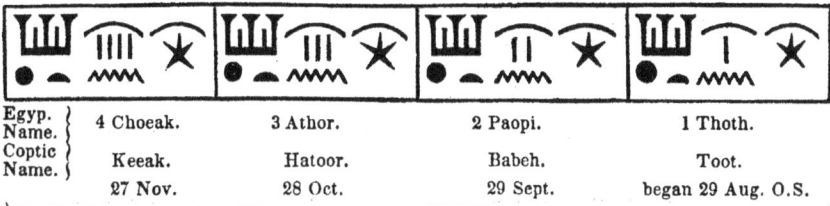

Egyp. Name.	4 Choeak.	3 Athor.	2 Paopi.	1 Thoth.
Coptic Name.	Keeak.	Hatoor.	Babeh.	Toot.
	27 Nov.	28 Oct.	29 Sept.	began 29 Aug. O.S.

2nd Season.

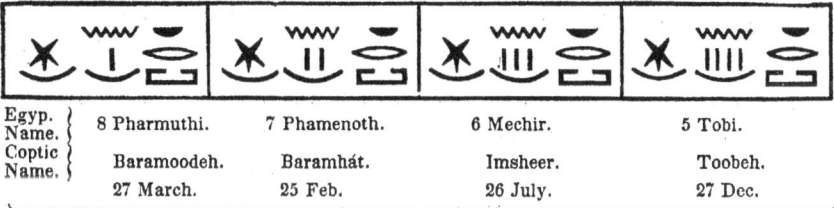

Egyp. Name.	8 Pharmuthi.	7 Phamenoth.	6 Mechir.	5 Tobi.
Coptic Name.	Baramoodeh.	Baramhát.	Imsheer.	Toobeh.
	27 March.	25 Feb.	26 July.	27 Dec.

3rd Season.

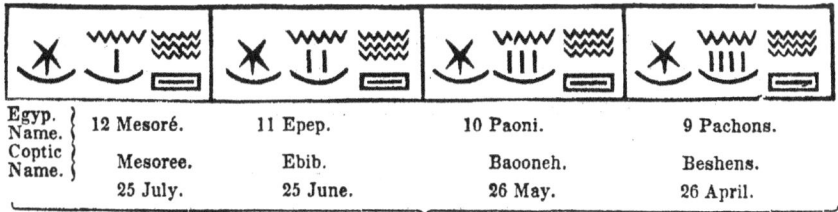

Egyp. Name.	12 Mesoré.	11 Epep.	10 Paoni.	9 Pachons.
Coptic Name.	Mesoree.	Ebib.	Baooneh.	Beshens.
	25 July.	25 June.	26 May.	26 April.

443.   The 12 Egyptian Months.

A people who gave any attention to subjects so important to their agricultural pursuits, could not long remain ignorant of the deficiency which even the intercalation of the five days left in the adjustment of the calendar; and though it required a period of 1461 years for the seasons to recede through all the twelve months, and to prove by the deficiency of a whole year the imperfection of this system, yet it would be obvious to them, in the lapse of a very few years, that a perceptible alteration had taken place in the relative position of the seasons; and the most careless observation would show that in 120 years, having lost a whole month, or thirty days, the rise of the Nile, the time of sowing and reaping, and all the periodical occupations of the peasant, no longer coincided with the same month. They therefore added a quarter day to remedy the defect, making every fourth year to consist of 366 days; which, though still subject to a slight error, was a sufficiently accurate approximation; and the length of each year was computed from one heliacal rising of the Dog-star to another. It was therefore called the "Sothic year;" and Censorinus says "it was termed by the Greeks 'κυνικον,' by the Latins 'canicularem,' because its commencement is taken from the rising of the Dog-star on the first day of the month, called by the Egyptians Thoth." But that day was not made the beginning of the year *because* Sothis rose heliacally upon it; the Sothic period was fixed *when* it coincided with it; and the beginning of the year, or the first of Thoth, was, perhaps, originally at a very different season; though they even pretended in later times that the commencement of the Sothic period corresponded with the beginning of the world. Some have supposed that the name Thoth was formerly applied to the first day alone, and not to the month itself.

That the five days, called of the Epact, were added at a most remote period, may readily be credited; and so convinced were the Egyptians of this, that they referred it to the fabulous times of their history, wrapping it up in the guise of allegory; and it is highly probable that the intercalation of the quarter day, or one day in four years, was also of very early date. The first direct notice of the five days is on a box at Turin of the time of Amunoph III.; but M. de Rougé has shown they were used in the 12th dynasty, and that the fête of Sothis was celebrated at the same period.

The Sothic period, as is well known, was fixed in the year 1322 before our era, when the Egyptians had ascertained by observation that 1460 Sothic were equal to 1461 solar years, the seasons having in that time passed through every part of the year, and returned again to the same point. They thus established a standard for adjusting their calendar, under the name of the Sothic period; and though for ordinary purposes, as the dates of their kings and other events, they continued to use the vague year of 365 days, every calculation could thus be corrected, by comparing the time of this last with that of the Sothic or sidereal year. When the idea first occurred to them is unknown; but the oath imposed on the Egyptian kings "that they would not intercalate any month or day, but that the sacred year of 365 days should remain as instituted in ancient times," evidently had for its object the employment of both the years for a counter-reckoning in present and past records; and as the Sothic period was fixed in 1322 B.C. from observations, it is evident that these must have been continued during the time that elapsed up to that year, which would throw back the beginning of their observations to a very remote age. The king in whose reign the Sothic period was fixed is said to be Menophres; but the name he is known by on the monuments has not yet been ascertained, though he seems to have lived about the beginning of the 19th dynasty.

The astronomical subjects and various data to be derived from the monuments will doubtless some day clear up most essential points relating to Egyptian Chronology; and though we must sometimes depend upon conjecture, it is satisfactory, considering the general uncertainty of history, to have arrived at a fair approximation in Egyptian dates. Those I have ventured to assign to the Pharaohs only pretend to a similar approximation; but the rising of Sothis in the reign of Thothmes III, now calculated by the learned M. Biot to correspond to between 1464 and 1424 B.C., shows that my placing his reign from 1495 to 1456 B.C. only differed from his real date by about 30 years.

The pursuits of agriculture did not prevent the Egyptians from arriving at a remarkable pre-eminence as a manufacturing nation; and that they should successfully unite the advantages of an agricultural and a manufacturing country is not surprising, when we consider that in those early times the competition of other manufacturing countries did not interfere with their market; and though Tyre and Sidon excelled in various manufactures, many branches of industry brought exclusive advantages to the Egyptian workman. Even in the flourishing days of the

Phœnicians, Egypt exported linen to other countries, and she probably enjoyed at all times an entire monopoly in this, and every article she manufactured, with the caravans of the interior of Africa.

The Egyptian land measure was the aroura (or arura), a square of 100 cubits, covering an area of 10,000 cubits, and like our acre solely employed for measuring land. It contained 29,184 square feet English (the cubit being full 20½ inches), and was little more than ¾ of an English acre. The other measures of Egypt were the schœne, equal to 60 stades in length, which served like the stade of Greece, the parasang of Persia, and the more modern mile, for measuring distance; the cubit, which Herodotus says was equal to that of Samos; and the palm and digit, which were parts of the cubit. Though the stade was often used by Greek writers in giving measurements in Egypt, it was not an Egyptian measure; and, generally speaking, it was equal to 600 Greek feet. They also mention the plethrum in giving the length of some buildings, as the Pyramids; but this was properly a Greek square measure, containing 10,000 square feet. When used as a measure of length, it was estimated at 100 feet; though, if Herodotus's measurement of the Great Pyramid be correct, it could not complete 100 of our feet, as he gives the length of each face 8 plethra. But little reliance can be placed on his measurements, since in this he exceeds the true length; and to the face of the third Pyramid he only allows 3 plethra, which, calculating the plethrum at 100 feet, is more than half a plethrum short of the real length—each face, according to the measurement of Colonel Howard Vyse, being 354 feet.

The total length of each face of the Great Pyramid when entire I believe to have been 754 or 755 feet, which would be exactly 440 cubits; but neither this, nor the courts of the temples, the statues, and other monuments can be depended upon for the exact length of that Egyptian measure.

Happily, other data of a less questionable nature are left us for this purpose, and the graduated cubit in the Nilometer of Elephantine, and the wooden cubits discovered in Egypt, suffice to establish its length, without the necessity of conjecture.

Some have supposed that the Egyptian cubit varied at different periods, and that it consisted at one time of 24, at another of 32 digits; or that there were two cubits of different lengths—one of 24 digits or 6 palms, the other of 32 digits or 8 palms, employed for different purposes. Some have maintained, with M. Girard, that the cubit used in the Nilometer of Elephantine consisted of 24 digits, others that it contained 32; and numerous calculations have been deduced from these conflicting opinions, respecting the real length of the cubit. But a few words will suffice to show the manner in which that cubit was divided, the number of its digits, and its real length; and respecting the supposed change in the cubit used in the Nilometers of Egypt, I shall only observe, that people far more prone to innovation than the Egyptians would not readily tolerate a similar deviation from long-established custom; and it is obvious that the greatest confusion would have been caused throughout the country, and that agriculture would have suffered incalculable injuries, if the customary announcement of a certain number of cubits for the rise of the Nile had been changed, through the introduction of a cubit of a different length.

The Nilometer in the island of Elephantine is a staircase between two walls descending to the Nile, on one of which is a succession of graduated scales containing one or two cubits, accompanied by inscriptions recording the rise of the river at various periods, during the rule of the Cæsars. Every cubit is divided into fourteen parts, each of 2 digits, giving 28 digits to the cubit; and the length of the cubit is 1 ft. 8⅝ in., or 165 eighths, which is 1 ft. 8·625 in. to each cubit, and 0·736 in. to each digit.

The wooden cubit, published by M. Jomard, is also divided into 28 parts or digits, and therefore accords, both in its division, and, as I shall show, very nearly in length, with the cubit of Elephantine. In this last we learn, from the inscriptions accompanying the scales, that the principal divisions were palms and digits; the cubit being 7 palms or 28 digits; and the former in like manner consisted of 7 palms or 28 digits. The ordinary division, therefore, of the cubit was as follows:

258   THE ANCIENT EGYPTIANS.   Chap. VIII.

The Cubit in the Nilometer of Elephantine.			Feet.	Inches.
1 digit			0	0·736
4	1 palm		0	2·946
28	7	1 cubit	1	8·625

The full division of the wooden Egyptian cubits, which have been found, appears to be :

Parts of the Cubit.							Cubit of the Nilometer.	Cubit of Memphis according to Jomard.
							Inches English.	Inches English.
1-16 of a digit							0·04603	0·04569
16	1 digit						0·7366	0·73115
	2	1 condyle					1·4732	1·4623
	4	2	1 palm				2·9464	2·9247
	5	..	..	1 hand			3·6830	3·6557
	6	..	.	..	1 *kubdeh*, or fist with thumb erect		4·4196	4·3869
	8	.	2	..	..	1 dichas, or 2 palms	5·8928	5·8494
	11	..	..	..	..	..	1 *fitr* or forefinger span	8·1026	8·0428
	13	..	..	..	..	..	1 *shibr*, spithamé, or full span	9·5758	9·5051
	28	..	7	..	..	..	1 cubit	20·6250	20·47291

There is no indication of a foot, and the 15 last digits are solely occupied with fractional parts, beginning with a 16th, and ending in ½ a digit, from which we may conclude that the smallest measurement in the Egyptian scale of length was the 16th of a digit, or the 26th of an inch.

The lengths of different Egyptian cubits are :

	Millimètres.		English Inches.
Cubit in the Turin Museum, according to my measurement	522 4-10	or	20·5730
The same, according to M. Jomard	522 7-10	"	20·5786
Another, he gives	523	"	20·6180
Another	524	"	20·6584
M. Jomard's cubit of Memphis	520	"	20·4729
Cubit of Elephantine, according to M. Jomard	527	"	20·7484
The same, according to my measurement	...	"	20·6250
Part of a cubit found by me at A'Souán	apparently about		21·0000
The cubit at the Pyramids, according to Mr. Perring	....		20·6280
Mr. Harris's cubit from Thebes	....		20·6500

The careless manner in which the graduation of the scales of the Nilometer at Elephantine has been made by the Egyptians, renders the precise length of its cubit difficult to determine; but as I have carefully measured all of them, and have been guided by their general length as well as by the averages of the whole, I am disposed to think my measurement as near the truth as possible; and judging from the close approximation of different wooden cubits, whose average M. Jomard estimates at 523·506 millimètres, we may conclude that they were all intended to represent the same measures, strongly arguing against the supposition of different cubits having been in use, one of 24 and others of 28 and 32 digits; and indeed, if at any time the Egyptians employed a cubit of a different length, consisting of 24 digits, it is not probable that it was used in their Nilometers, for architectural purposes, or for measuring land.

And if, when cited from ancient authors, I have calculated the cubit at $1\frac{1}{2}$ foot, this is only because custom has reconciled us to that approximate measurement.

The principal Egyptian measures of weight were the talent and the mina; the former called in Coptic *ginshôr*, the latter *emna* or *amna*, and in the hieroglyphics *men* or *mna*.

The talent is supposed to have contained 60 minæ, and the mina 100 drachms, as in Greece; but the uncertainty about their real value is so great, that the talent has been reckoned at 114 or 113, at 91, $86\frac{3}{4}$, or even 65 lbs. Troy; and the mina in the same proportion. It seems really to have been about 40 lbs. Troy, and the mina $16\frac{1}{2}$ ounces.

The mina, *mna*, or *men*, is often mentioned on the monuments, and from their reckoning upwards of 2000 minæ (as of " *sift,*" *zift*, or bitumen), it was evidently used for large quantities, where we should rather have expected the talent, and was, like our pound, the standard weight. The name is quite Egyptian, and of a more common form than any other in the language; and it is found applied to weights at least as early as the 18th dynasty, followed by a square, indicative of a " weight." It seems also to be related to the Arabic word *mana*, " to count" (and the " *mna*," " mene," of Daniel), from which Al-manach is supposed to be derived.

The weights represented, when they are engaged in weighing gold and silver and other commodities, are in the form of a whole ox, a bull's head, and a conical mass, as well as the square representing the mina; and the three first seem to be the whole, the half, and another subdivision of the talent, or 60, 30, and 20 or 10 minæ. The adoption of the bull for the talent may have originated in the original mode of bartering, and accords with Homer's reckoning the bull as a standard of value. Indeed it is said to have represented a talent. Thus the *pecunia* of the Romans was taken from *pecus*.

The Egyptians had also a measure, or weight, apparently of the same name, *mn* or *mna*, used for gold and silver, and followed by a similar square sign; which Mr. Birch supposes to have been divided like our pound into 16 parts or ounces, no higher number having been found than 15. These have also a square sign after them, determinative of weight, and are called *kit* or *kiti*, the Coptic name of the drachma and didrachma.

The idea of the mina being equivalent to our pound seems to be confirmed by the weights, in the form of lions and ducks, brought by Mr. Layard from Nimroud* (now in the British Museum); as the most perfect of the large ducks, which was ½ a talent, or 30 minæ, weighs little more than 484 ounces, or 40 lbs. troy and 4 ozs. Each mina is therefore 16¼ ounces; and the close approximation in the weight of the lions and ducks shows they represented the same quantity.

Of the Egyptian measures of capacity one was small, answering to the modern *mid*, or nearly 2½ pecks English; another larger, also used for measuring grain, distinguished by the king's crook that surmounts it, which, as M. de Rougé suggests, may point to its value fixed by royal authority; or be a royal, *i.e.* a large measure. It may, perhaps, be the origin of the modern Egyptian *ardéb* (the *ertób* of the Copts, and the Medish artaba), equal nearly to 5 English bushels; and the smaller one is shown to be the one employed for measuring grain when taken to, or from, the

---

* See Layard's Nineveh and Babylon, p. 601. In the woodcut he gives, p. 602, the supposed ring on the back of the crouched lion is only the same conical weight seen in the scales.

granary; being the standard like the modern *mid*, which in size and shape it so much resembled. This name is very like the Latin *modius*.

The modern ardéb contains 8 *mid*; and the latter 4 *reftów*, or 3 *roob*; and according to another calculation, the ardéb is made to consist of 6 *waybeh*, a name answering to the *ouôpi* of the Copts, which was equal to 4 *roob*. The half ardéb, or mid, was called also *koros* in Coptic.

There was another measure used both for liquids, as wine, and for dry substances, as incense and bitumen, which had likewise a name very like *mn* or *mina*.

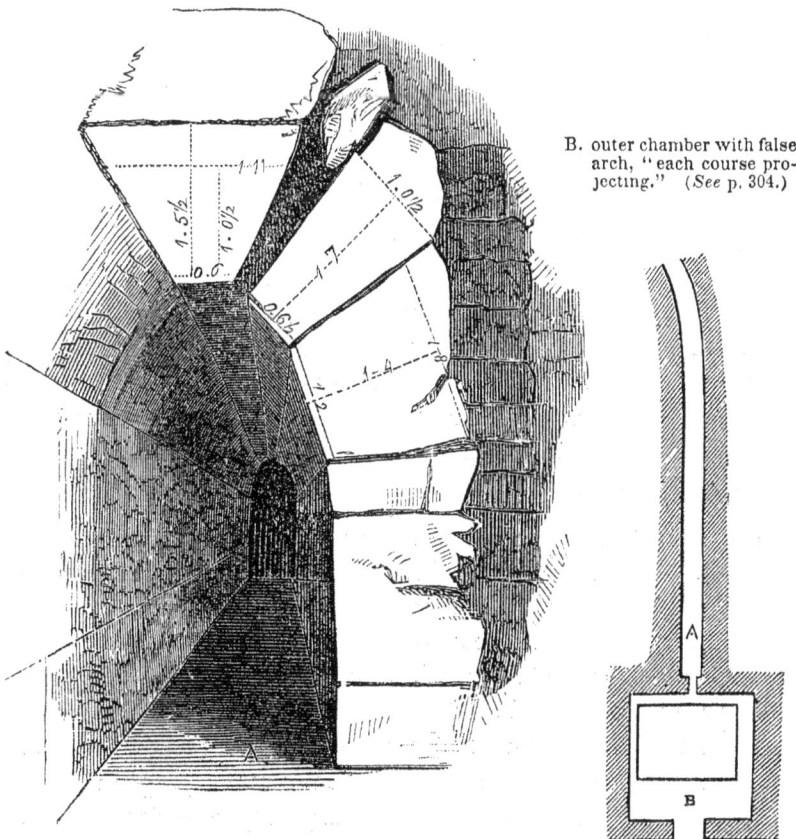

B. outer chamber with false arch, "each course projecting." (*See* p. 304.)

N. Arch at Tusculum, in Italy (built while the Kings ruled at Rome?).

O. View of the modern town of Manfaloót, showing the height of the banks of the Nile in summer. In the mountain range, opposite Manfaloót, are the large crocodile mummy caves of Maábdeh.

CHAPTER IX.

EGYPTIAN ART—REMAINS OF NINEVEH—HUMAN FIGURE—DRAWING AND PAINTING—ARCHITECTURE—ORDERS OF ARCHITECTURE—SOME DEVICES COPIED FROM NATURE—TOO GREAT SYMMETRY AVOIDED—USE OF LARGE STONES—ANTIQUITY OF THE ARCH—BRICKS—PROGRESS OF ARCHITECTURE—USE OF LIMESTONE—COLOSSI—MONOLITHS—MACHINERY—MASONS—EARLY EGYPTIAN INVENTIONS—DRESSES—WIGS—DRESSES OF WOMEN—ORNAMENTS—OINTMENTS—MIRRORS—DOCTORS—MAGIC.

The interest that attaches to Egyptian art is from its great antiquity. We see in it the first attempts to represent what in after times, and in some other countries, gradually arrived, under better auspices, at the greatest perfection; and we even trace in it the germ of much that was improved upon by those who had a higher appreciation of, and feeling for, the beautiful. For, both in ornamental art, as well as in architecture, Egypt exercised in early times considerable influence over other people less advanced than itself, or only just emerging from barbarism; and the various conventional devices, the lotus flowers, the sphinxes, and other fabulous animals, as well as the early Medusa's head, with a protruding tongue, of the oldest Greek pottery and sculptures, and the ibex, leopard, and, above all, the (Nile) "goose and sun," on the vases, show them to be connected with, and frequently directly borrowed from, Egyptian fancy. It was, as it still is, the custom of people to borrow from those who have attained to a greater degree of refinement and civilization than themselves; the nation most advanced in art led the taste; and though some had sufficient invention to alter what they adopted, and to render it their own, the original idea may still be traced whenever it has been derived from a foreign source. Egypt was long the dominant nation, and the intercourse established at a very remote period with other countries, through commerce or war, carried abroad the taste of this the most advanced people of the time; and so general seems to have been the fashion of their ornaments, that even the Nineveh marbles present the winged globe, and other well-known Egyptian emblems, as established elements of Assyrian decorative art. This fact would suffice to disprove the early date of the marbles hitherto discovered, which are, in fact, of a period comparatively modern in the history of Egypt; and recent discoveries have fully justified the opinion I ventured to express, when they were first brought to this country: 1°, that they are not of archaic style, and that original Assyrian art is still to be looked for; 2°, that they give evidences of the decadence, not the rise, of art; and, 3°, that they have borrowed much from Egypt, long the dominant country in power and art, and will be found to date within 1000 B.C. This, however, is far from lessening their importance; for the periods they chiefly illustrate— those of Shalmaneser and Sennacherib, so closely connected with Hebrew history—give an interest to them, which the oldest monuments of Assyria would fail to possess.

While Greece was still in its infancy, Egypt had long been the leading nation of the world; she was noted for her magnificence, her wealth, and power, and all acknowledged her preeminence in wisdom and civilization. It is not, therefore, surprising that the Greeks should have admitted into their early art some of the forms then most in vogue; and though the wonderful taste of that gifted people speedily raised them to a point of excellence, never attained by the Egyptians or any others, the rise and first germs of art and architecture must be sought in the valley of the Nile. In the oldest monuments of Greece, the sloping or pyramidal line constantly predominates; the columns in the oldest Greek order are almost purely Egyptian, in the proportions of the shaft, and in the form of its shallow flutes without fillets; and it is a remarkable fact, that the oldest Egyptian columns are those which bear the closest resemblance to the Greek Doric.

Though great variety was permitted in objects of luxury, as furniture, vases, and other things depending on caprice, the Egyptians were forbidden to introduce any material innovations into the human figure, such as would alter its general character; and all subjects connected with religion retained to the last the same conventional type. A god in the latest temple was of the same form as when represented on monuments of the earliest date; and King Menes would have recognized Amun, or Osiris, in a Ptolemaic or a Roman sanctuary. In sacred subjects the law was inflexible; and religion, which has frequently done so much for the development and direction of taste in sculpture, had the effect of fettering the genius of Egyptian artists. No improvements, resulting from experience and observation, were admitted in the mode of drawing the human figure; to copy nature was not allowed; it was therefore useless to study it, and no attempt was made to give the proper action to the limbs. Certain rules, certain models had been established by the priesthood; and the faulty conceptions of ignorant times were copied and perpetuated by every successive artist. For, as Plato and Synesius say, the Egyptian sculptors were not suffered to attempt anything contrary to the regulations laid down regarding the figures of the gods; they were forbidden to introduce any change, or to invent new subjects and habits; and thus the art, and the rules which bound it, always remained the same.

Egyptian bas-relief appears to have been, in its origin, a mere copy of painting, its predecessor. The first attempt to represent the figures of gods, sacred emblems, and other subjects consisted in drawing, or painting, simple outlines of them on a flat surface, the details being afterwards put in with colour; but in process of time these forms were traced on stone with a tool, and the intermediate space between the various figures being afterwards cut away, the once level surface assumed the appearance of a bas-relief. It was, in fact, a pictorial representation on stone, which is evidently the character of all the bas-reliefs on Egyptian monuments, and which readily accounts for the imperfect arrangement of their figures.

Deficient in conception, and, above all, in a proper knowledge of grouping, they were unable to form those combinations which give true expression; every picture was made up of isolated parts, put together according to some general notions, but without harmony or preconceived effect. The human face, the whole body, and everything they introduced, were composed in the same manner, of separate members placed together one by one, according to their relative situations: the eye, the nose, and other features composed a face; but the expression of feelings and passions was entirely wanting; and the countenance of the king, whether charging an enemy's phalanx in the heat of battle, or peaceably offering incense in a sombre temple, presented the same outline and the same inanimate look. The peculiarity of the front view of an eye, introduced in a profile, is thus accounted for: it was the ordinary representation of that feature added to a profile, and no allowance was made for any change in the position of the head.

It was the same with drapery: the figure was first drawn, and the drapery then added, not as a part of the whole, but as an accessory; they had no general conception, no previous idea of the effect required to distinguish the warrior or the priest, beyond the impressions received from costume, or from the subject of which they formed a part; and the same figure was dressed according to the character it was intended to perform. Every portion of a picture was conceived by itself, and inserted as it was wanted to complete the scene; and when the walls of the building, where a subject was to be drawn, had been accurately ruled with squares, the figures were introduced, and fitted to this mechanical arrangement. The members were appended to the body, and these squares regulated their form and distribution, in whatever posture they might be placed.

As long as this conventional system continued, no great change could take place, beyond a slight variation in the proportions, which at one period became more elongated, particularly in the reign of the second Remeses; but still the general form and character of the figures continued the same, which led to the remark of Plato, "that the pictures and statues made ten thousand years ago, are in no one particular better or worse than what they now make." And taken in this limited sense—that no nearer approach to the beau ideal of the human figure, or its real character, was made at one period than another—his remark is true, since they were always bound by the same regulations, which prohibited any change in these matters, even to the latest times, as is evident from the sculptures of the monuments erected after Egypt had long been a Roman province. All was still Egyptian, though of bad style; and if they then attempted to finish the details with more precision, it was only substituting ornament for simplicity; and the endeavour to bring the proportions of the human figure nearer to nature, with the retention of its conventional type, only made its deformity greater, and showed how incompatible the Egyptian was with any other style.

The proportions of the human figure did not, as I have just said, continue always the same. During the 4th and other early dynasties, it differed from that of the Augustan age of the 18th and 19th; and another change took place under the Ptolemies. The chief alteration was in the height of the knee from the ground, which was higher during the 18th and 19th than in the ancient and later periods. The whole height of the figure in bas-reliefs and paintings was then divided into nineteen parts; and the wall having been ruled in squares, according to its intended size, all the parts of it were put in according to their established positions, the knee, for instance, falling on the sixth line. But the length of the foot was not, as in Greece, the standard from which they reckoned; for, being equal to 3 spaces, it could not be taken as the base of 19, though the height of the foot being 1 might

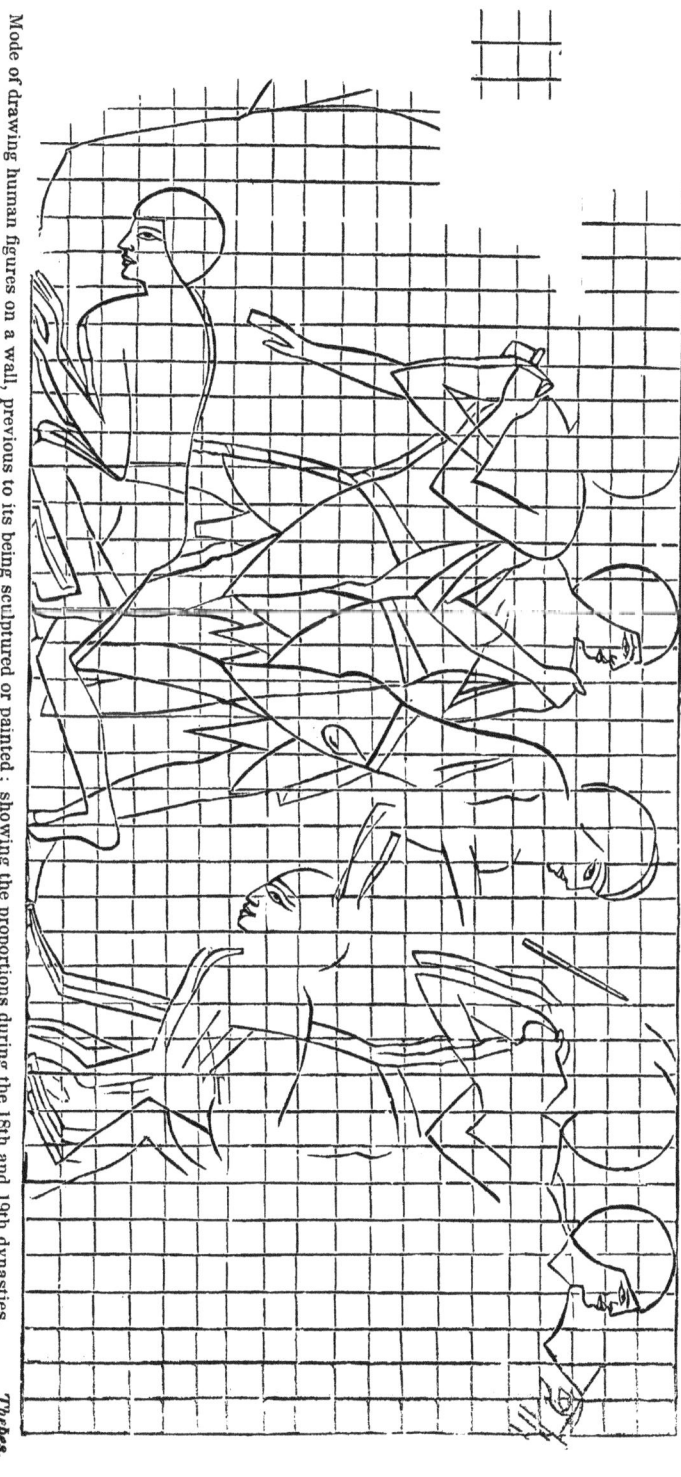

Mode of drawing human figures on a wall, previous to its being sculptured or painted; showing the proportions during the 18th and 19th dynasties.

Thebes.

answer for the unit. (*See* Müller's Ancient Art, p. 392, on Greek forms.)

In the composition of modern paintings three objects are required: one main action, one point of view, and one instant of time, and the proportion and harmony of the parts are regulated by perspective; but in Egyptian sculptures these essentials were disregarded: every thing was sacrificed to the principal figure; its colossal dimensions pointed it out as a centre to which all the rest was a mere accessory; and, if any other was made equally conspicuous, or of equal size, it was still in a subordinate station, and only intended to illustrate the scene connected with the hero of the piece.

In the paintings of the tombs greater license was allowed in the representation of subjects relating to private life, the trades, or the manners and occupations of the people; and some indication of perspective in the position of the figures may occasionally be observed; but the attempt was imperfect, and, probably, to an Egyptian eye, unpleasing; for such is the force of habit, that even where nature is copied, a conventional style is sometimes preferred to a more accurate representation.

In the battle scenes on the temples of Thebes, some of the figures representing the monarch pursuing the flying enemy, despatching a hostile chief with his sword, and drawing his bow, as his horses carry his car over the prostrate bodies of the slain, are drawn with much spirit; and the position of the arms gives a perfect idea of the action which the artist intended to portray; still, the same imperfections of style, and want of truth, are observed; there is action, but no sentiment, expression of the passions, nor life in the features; it is a figure ready formed, and mechanically *varied* into movement; and whatever position it is made to assume, the point of view is the same : the identical profile of the human body with the anomaly of the shoulders seen in front. It is a description rather than a representation.

But in their mode of portraying a large crowd of persons they often show great cleverness; and, as their habit was to avoid uniformity, the varied positions of the heads give a truth to the subject without fatiguing the eye. Nor have they any symmetrical arrangement of figures, on opposite sides of a picture, such as we find in some of the very early paintings in Europe.

In the representation of animals, they appear not to have been restricted to the same rigid style; but genius once cramped can scarcely be expected to make any great effort to rise, or to succeed in the attempt; and the same union of parts into a whole, the same preference for profile, and the same stiff action, are observable in these as in the human figure. Seldom did they attempt to draw the face in front, either of men or animals; and when this was done, it fell far short of the profile, and was composed of the same juxtaposition of parts. It must, however, be allowed, that in general the character and form of animals were admirably portrayed; the parts were put together with greater truth; and the same conventionality was not maintained, as in the shoulders and other portions of the human body. Nor will I deny that great life and animation are given to the antelope, and many wild beasts, in the hunting scenes of the Theban tombs.

The mode of representing men and animals in profile is primitive, and characteristic of the commencement of art: the first attempts made by an uncivilized people are confined to it; and until the genius of artists bursts forth, this style continues to hold its ground. From its simplicity it is readily understood; the most inexperienced perceive the object intended to be represented, and no effort is required to comprehend it. Hence it is that, though few combinations can be made under such restrictions, those few are perfectly intelligible, the eye being aware of the resemblance to the simple exterior; and the modern uninstructed peasant of Egypt, who is immediately struck with and understands the paintings of the Theban tombs, if shown an European drawing, is seldom able to distinguish men from animals; and no argument will induce them to tolerate foreshortening, the omission of those parts of the body concealed from his view by the perspective of the picture, or the introduction of shadows, particularly on the human flesh.

Bas-relief may be considered the earliest style of sculpture. It originated in those pictorial representations which were the primæval records of a people anxious to commemorate their victories, the accession or the virtues of a king, and other events connected with their history. These were the first purposes to which the imitative powers of the mind were applied; but the progress was slow, and the infant art (if it may be so called) passed through several stages ere it had the power of portraying real occurrences, and imitating living scenes. The rude outlines of a man holding a spear, a sword, or other weapon, or killing a wild animal, were first drawn, or scratched, upon a rock, as a sort of hieroglyphic; but in process of time the warrior and a prostrate foe were attempted, and the valour of the prince who had led them to victory was recorded by this simple group.

As their skill increased, the mere figurative representation was extended to that of a descriptive kind, and some resemblance of the hero's person was attempted; his car, the army he commanded, and the flying enemies, were introduced; and what was at first scarcely more than a symbol, aspired to the more exalted form and character of a picture. Of a similar nature were all their historical records; and these pictorial illustrations were a substitute for written documents. Rude drawing and sculpture, indeed, long preceded letters, and we find that even in Greece, to describe, draw, engrave, and write, were expressed by the same word, γραφειν.

The want of letters, and the inability to describe an individual, his occupations, or his glorious actions, led them in early ages to bury with the body some object which might indicate the character of the deceased. Thus, warriors were interred with their arms; artisans with the implements they had used; the oar was placed over the sailor; and *pateræ*, and other utensils connected with his office, or the emblems of the deity in whose service he had been employed, were deposited in the sepulchre of a priest. In those times a simple mound was raised over chieftains, sometimes with a rough stone pillar placed upon it, but no inscription; and even, at a later period, when they intended to show the occupations of the deceased, an allegorical emblem was often engraved on the levelled surface of the stone, and the implements continued to be buried with them after writing was invented.

Poetry and songs also supplied the want of writing to record the details of events; and tradition handed down the glorious achievements of a conqueror, and the history of past years, with the precision and enthusiasm of national pride. The poetry was recited to the sound of music; whence the same expression often implied the "ode" and the "song;" and as laws were recorded in a similar manner, the word νομος signified, as Aristotle observes, both a "law" and a "song."

Man *attempted* sculpture long before he *studied* architecture: a simple hut, or a rude house, answered every purpose as a place of abode, and a long time elapsed before he sought to invent what was not demanded by necessity.

Architecture is a creation of the mind; it has no model in nature, and it requires great imaginative powers to conceive its ideal beauties, to make a proper combination of parts, and to judge of the harmony of forms altogether new and beyond the reach of experience. But the desire in man to imitate and to record what has passed before his eyes—in short, to transfer the impression from his own mind to another, is natural in every stage of society; and however imperfectly he may succeed in representing the objects themselves, his attempts to indicate their relative position, and to embody the expression of his own ideas, are a source of the highest satisfaction.

As the wish to record events gave the first, religion gave the second impulse to sculpture. The simple pillar of wood or stone, which was originally chosen to represent the Deity, afterwards assumed the human form, the noblest image of the power that created it; though the *Hermæ* of Greece were not, as some have thought, the origin of statues, but were borrowed from the mummy-shaped gods of Egypt.

Pausanias thinks that "all statues were in ancient times of wood, particularly those made in Egypt;" but this must have been at a period so remote as to be far beyond the known history of that country; though it is probable that when the arts were in their infancy, the Egyptians were confined to statues of that kind; and they occasionally erected wooden figures in their temples, even till the times of the latter Pharaohs.

Long after men had attempted to make out the parts of the

figure, statues continued to be very rude; the arms were placed directly down the side to the thighs, and the legs were united together; nor did they pass beyond this imperfect state in Greece until the age of Dædalus. Fortunately for themselves and for the world, the Greeks were allowed to free themselves from old habits; while the Egyptians, at the latest periods, continued to follow the imperfect models of their early artists, and were for ever prevented from arriving at excellence in sculpture: and though they made great progress in other branches of art, though they evinced considerable taste in the forms of their vases, their furniture, and even in some architectural details, they were for ever deficient in ideal beauty, and in the mode of representing the natural positions of the human figure.

In Egypt, the prescribed automaton character of the figures effectually prevented all advancement in the statuary's art; the limbs being straight, without any attempt at action, or, indeed, any indication of life: they were really *statues* of the person they represented, not the person "living in marble;" in which they differed entirely from those of Greece. No statue of a warrior was sculptured in the varied attitudes of attack and defence; no wrestler, no *discobolus*, no pugilist exhibited the grace, the vigour, or the muscular action of a man; nor were the beauties, the feeling, and the elegance of female forms displayed in stone: all was made to conform to the same invariable model, which confined the human figure to a few conventional postures.

A sitting statue, whether of a man or woman, was represented with the hands placed upon the knees, or held across the breast; a kneeling figure sometimes supported a small shrine or sacred emblem; and when standing, the arms were placed directly down the sides of the thighs, one foot (and that always the left) being advanced beyond the other, as if in the attitude of walking, but without any attempt to separate the legs.

The oldest Egyptian sculptures on all large monuments were in low relief, and, as usual at every period, painted (obelisks and everything carved in hard stone, some funereal tablets, and other small objects, being in intaglio); and this style continued in vogue until the time of Remeses II., who introduced intaglio very generally on large monuments; and even his battle scenes at

Karnak and the Memnonium are executed in this manner. The reliefs were little raised above the level of the wall; they had generally a flat surface, with the edges softly rounded off, far surpassing the intaglio in effect; and it is to be regretted that the best epoch of art, when design and execution were in their zenith, should have abandoned a style so superior, which, too, would have improved in proportion to the advancement of that period.

Intaglio continued to be generally employed until the accession of the 26th dynasty, when the low relief was again introduced; and in the monuments of Psammitichus and Amasis are numerous instances of the revival of the ancient style. This was afterwards universally adopted, and a return to intaglio on large monuments was only occasionally attempted, in the Ptolemaic and Roman periods.

The intaglio introduced by Remeses may perhaps be denominated *intaglio rilievato*, or relieved intaglio. The sides of the *incavo*, which are perpendicular, are cut to a considerable depth, and from that part to the centre of the figure (or whatever is represented) is a gradual swell, the centre being frequently on a level with the surface of the wall. On this all the parts of dress, features, or devices are delineated and painted, and even the perpendicular sides are ornamented in a corresponding manner, by continuing upon them the adjoining details.

In the reign of Remeses III. a change was made in the mode of sculpturing the intaglios, which consisted in carving the lower side to a great depth, while the upper face inclined gradually from the surface of the wall till it reached the innermost part of the intaglio; its principal use was for the hieroglyphics, in order to enable a person standing immediately beneath, and close to the wall on which they were sculptured, to distinguish and read them; and the details upon the perpendicular sides, above mentioned, had the same effect.

It was a peculiarity of style not generally imitated by the successors of Remeses III., and hieroglyphics bearing this character may serve to fix the date of monuments, wherever they are found, to the age of that monarch. After his reign no great encouragement appears to have been given to the arts; the subjects represented on the few monuments of the epoch intervening between his death and the accession of the 26th dynasty are principally confined to sacred subjects, in which no display of talent is shown; and the records of Sheshonk's victories at Karnak are far from partaking of the vigour of former times, either in style, or in the mode of treating the subject.

After the accession of the 26th dynasty some attempt was made to revive the arts, which had been long neglected; and, independent of the patronage of government, the wealth of private individuals was liberally employed in their encouragement. Public buildings were erected in many parts of Egypt, and beautified with rich sculpture; the city of Saïs, the royal residence of the Pharaohs of that dynasty, was adorned with the utmost magnificence; and extensive additions were made to the temples of Memphis, and even to those of the distant Thebes.

The fresh impulse thus given to art was not without effect; the sculptures of that period exhibit an elegance and beauty which might even induce some to consider them equal to the productions of an earlier age; and in the tombs of the Assaseef, at Thebes, are many admirable specimens of Egyptian art. To those, however, who understand the true feeling of this peculiar school, it is evident, that though in minuteness and finish they are deserving of the highest commendation, yet in grandeur of conception and in boldness of execution they fall far short of the sculptures of Sethos and the second Remeses.

The skill of the Egyptian artists in drawing bold and clear outlines is, perhaps, more worthy of admiration than anything connected with this branch of art; and in no place is the freedom of their drawing more conspicuous than in the figures in the unfinished part of Belzoni's tomb at Thebes. It was in the drawing alone that they excelled, being totally ignorant of the correct mode of colouring a figure; and their painting was not an imitation of nature, but merely the harmonious combination of certain hues, which they well understood. Indeed, to this day the harmony of positive colours is thoroughly felt in Egypt and the East; and it is strange to find the little perception of it in Northern Europe, where theories take upon themselves to explain to the mind what the eye has not yet learnt, as if a grammar could be written before the language is understood.

Drawing was always a principal point in ancient art. The Greeks made it their great study, knowing how it improved the accuracy of the eye and the management of the hand, as well as the perception of the beautiful; and the most extraordinary correctness must have been acquired to enable Apelles to draw the line within that of Protogenes.

The neglect that drawing has experienced in England is now, we may hope, in a fair way of being remedied; for to many a real *line* has been almost unknown; and while the French have persevered so successfully in drawing, we have seldom been alive to its importance, occasionally excusing ourselves from the trouble by some such subterfuge as "there is no outline in nature." How often, indeed, is a line made up of a few dotted strokes; and many a youth, as yet unacquainted with the proper use of a pencil, thinks that the brush will at once enable him to acquire excellence in art!

Of the quality of the pencils used by the Egyptians for drawing and painting, it is difficult to form any opinion. Those generally employed for writing were a reed or rush, many of which have been found with the tablets or inkstands belonging to the scribes; and with these, too, they probably sketched the figures in red and black upon the stone or stucco of the walls. To put in the colour, we may suppose that brushes of some kind were used; but the minute scale on which the painters are represented in the sculptures prevents our deciding the question.

Habits among men of similar occupations are frequently alike, even in the most distant countries; and we find it was not unusual for an Egyptian artist, or scribe, to put his reed pencil behind his ear, when engaged in examining the effect of his painting, or listening to a person on business, like a clerk in the counting-house of an European town.

Painters and scribes deposited their writing implements in a box with a pendent leather top, which was tied up with a loop or thong; and a handle or strap was fastened to the side, to enable them to carry it more conveniently. Their ordinary wooden inkstand was furnished with two or more cavities for holding the colours, and a tube in the centre for the pens or reeds;

445. A scribe writing on a tablet. *c* and *d* are two cases for carrying writing materials.
Thebes.

446. Scribe with his inkstand upon the table. One pen is put behind his ear, and he is writing with another.
Thebes.

and certain memoranda were frequently written on the back of it, when a large piece of papyrus, or the wooden slab, was not at hand. An idle moment was often occupied in making rough sketches on a piece of stone or on some other common material; and subjects of greater size were drawn in a happy mood of fancy upon a papyrus: for the Egyptians (as I have already said) were addicted to caricature, and some papyri in the British and other museums show that even religious subjects were not exempt from it; and one in the Turin collection presents a severe libel on the taste and conduct of women.

Of painting, apart from sculpture, and of the excellence to

PAINTING ON PANEL.

which it attained in Egypt, we can form no accurate opinion, nothing having come down to us of a Pharaonic period, or of that epoch when the arts were at their zenith in Egypt; but that, already, in the time of Osirtasen, they painted on panel, is shown by one of the subjects at Beni Hassan, where two artists are engaged in a picture representing a calf, and an antelope overtaken by a dog. The painter holds his brush in one hand, and

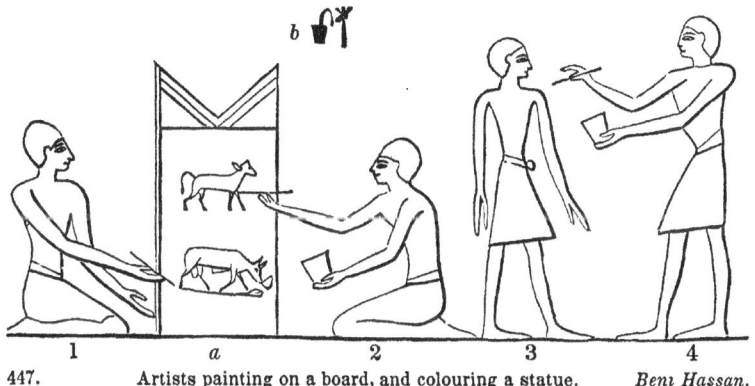

447.   Artists painting on a board, and colouring a statue.   *Beni Hassan.*

his palette or saucer of colour in the other; but, though the boards stand upright, there is no indication of a contrivance to steady or support the hand. The Greeks drew and painted in the same manner without that help.

Mention is made of an Egyptian painting by Herodotus, who tells us that Amasis sent a portrait of himself to Cyrene, probably on wood, and in profile; for the full face is rarely represented either in their paintings or bas-reliefs. The faces of the kings in the tombs and temples of Egypt are unquestionably portraits, but they are always in profile; and the only ones in full face are on wood, and of late time. Two of these are preserved in the British Museum, but they are evidently Greek, and date, perhaps, even after the conquest of Egypt by the Romans. It is therefore vain to speculate on the nature of their painting, or their skill in this branch of art; and, though some of the portraits taken from the mummies may prove that encaustic painting with wax and naphtha was adopted in Egypt, the time when it was first known there is uncertain, nor can we conclude, from a specimen of Greek time, that the same was practised in a Pharaonic age.

Fresco painting was entirely unknown in Egypt; and the figures on walls were always drawn and painted after the stucco was quite dry. But they sometimes coated the colours with a transparent varnish, which was also done by the Greeks; and the wax said by the younger Pliny to have been used for this purpose, on the painted exterior of a house at Stabia, may have been a substitute for the usual varnish, which last would have been far more durable under a hot Italian sun.

Pliny states, in his chapter on inventions, that "Gyges, a Lydian, was the earliest painter in Egypt; and Euchir, a cousin of Dædalus according to Aristotle, the first in Greece; or, as Theoprastus thinks, Polygnotus the Athenian." But the painting represented in Beni Hassan evidently dates before any of those artists. Pliny, in another place, says, "the origin of painting is uncertain: the Egyptians pretend that it was invented by them 6000 years before it passed into Greece; a vain boast, as every one will allow." It must, however, be admitted, that all the arts (however imperfect) were cultivated in Egypt long before Greece existed as a nation; and the remark he afterwards makes, that painting was unknown at the period of the Trojan war, can only be applied to the Greeks, as is shown by the same unquestionable authority at Beni Hassan, dating about 900 years before the time usually assigned to the taking of Troy.

It is probable that the artists, in Egypt, who painted on wood, were in higher estimation than mere decorators, as was the case in Greece, where "no artists were in repute but those who executed pictures on wood, for neither Ludius nor any other wall painter was of any renown." The Greeks preferred movable pictures, which could be taken away in case of fire, or sold if necessary; and, as Pliny says, "there was no painting on the walls of Apelles' house" (or "no painting by Apelles on the walls of a house"). The painting and decoration of buildings was another and an inferior branch of art. The pictures were put up in temples, as the works of great masters in later times in churches; but they were not dedications, nor solely connected with sacred subjects; and the temple was selected as the place of security, as it often was as a repository of treasure. They had also picture galleries in some secure place, as in the Acropolis of Athens.

Outline figures on walls were in all countries the earliest style of painting; they were in the oldest temples of Latium; and in Egypt they preceded the more elaborate style, that was afterwards followed by bas-relief and intaglio. In Greece, during the middle period, which was that of the best art, pictures were painted on wood by the first artists; and Raoul-Rochette thinks that if any of them painted on walls, this was accidental; and the finest pictures, being on wood, were in after times carried off to Rome. This removal was lamented by the Greeks "as a spoliation;" which having left the walls bare, accounts for Pausanias saying so little about pictures in Greece. Historical compositions were of course the highest branch of art, though many of the greatest Greek artists, who seem to have excelled in all styles, often treated inferior subjects, and some (as in later times) combined the two highest arts of sculpture and painting.

In the infancy of art, figures were represented in profile; but afterwards they were rare in Greece; and art could not reach any degree of excellence until figures in a composition had ceased to be in profile; and it was only in order to conceal the loss of an eye that Apelles gave one side of the face in his portrait of Antigonus.

The oldest paintings were also, as Pliny admits, *monochrome*, or painted of one uniform colour, like those of Egypt; and, indeed, statues in Greece were at first of one colour, doubtless red like those of the Egyptians, Romans, and Etruscans. For not only bas-reliefs were painted, which, as parts of a coloured building, was a necessity, but statues also; and as art advanced they were made to resemble real life. For that statue by Scopas, of a Bacchante, with a disembowelled fawn, whose cadaverous hue contrasted with the rest, at once shows that it was *painted*, and not of a *monochrome* colour; and the statues of Praxiteles, painted for him by Nicias, would not have been preferred by that sculptor to his other works if they had merely been stained red.

The blue eyes of Minerva's statue; the inside of her shield painted by Pannæus, and the outside by Phidias (originally a painter himself), could only have been parts of the whole coloured figure; Pannæus assisted in painting the statue of Olympian Jupiter; and ivory statues were said to have been prevented turning yellow by the application of colour.

If the artists of Greece did not paint on walls, it was not from any mistaken pride, since even the greatest of them would paint statues not of their own work; and those in modern days who study decorative art will do well to remember that to employ superior taste in ornamental composition is no degradation, and that the finest specimens of decorative work in the Middle Ages were executed by the most celebrated artists.

Egyptian architecture evidently derived much from the imitation of different natural productions, as palm-trees, and various plants of the country; but Egyptian columns were not borrowed from the wooden supports of the earliest buildings. Columns were not introduced into the interior of their houses until architecture had made very great progress; the small original temple, and the primitive dwelling, consisted merely of four walls; and neither the column nor its architrave were borrowed from wooden constructions, nor from the house. And though the architrave was derived in Egypt, as elsewhere, from constructed buildings, that member originated in the *stone* beam, reaching from pillar to pillar, in the temples. And if the square stone pillar was used in the quarry, the stone architrave was unknown to the Egyptians, until they found reason to increase the size of, and add a portico to, their temples. And that the portico was neither a necessary, nor an original, part of their temples, is plainly shown by the smaller sanctuaries being built, even at the latest times, without it. Some members of Egyptian architecture, it is true, were derived from the woodwork of the primitive house or temple, as the overhanging cornice, and the torus that runs up the ends of the walls, which it separates from the cornice; the former being the projecting roof of palm branches, and the other the framework of reeds bound together, which secured the mud (or bricks) composing the walls.

The early houses of Egypt were of mud; and the *masses* of that material, used in making their walls, afterwards led to the simple invention of *large* sun-baked bricks. The flat roof was palm-beams, covered with branches of the same tree, and a thick coating of mud laid upon them completed the whole. But it was not till luxury had been introduced that the column performed a part in an Egyptian mansion; and the temple of early Egypt was a simple quadrangular chamber. (*See a complete Temple in Frontispiece, Vol. I.*)

Square pillars were the first used; and their presence in the old temples is consistent with the fact of their having been the first kind adopted there. They are found in some of the earliest constructed porticoes, and in the peristyles of the old peripteral temples. This square pillar originated in the stone quarry, where too it appears without any architrave; a mere mass, often rather irregular, left to support the roof; and when in after times large tombs and temples were excavated in the rock, they in their turn borrowed from constructed monuments; and the pillar was no longer permitted to support the roof, without the intervening architrave.

Thus, then, constructed buildings were indebted to the quarry for the pillar, and rock-hewn monuments derived from the former the architrave and plinth. The same spirit of imitation also led to the introduction of square dentils over an architrave, as in the façade of a tomb at Beni Hassan; and the ceiling of one of the rock tombs at the Pyramids imitating the palm-beams of a house, is another proof that the two borrowed from each other. In these, the rock monuments imitated timber roofs; but this was long after columns and architraves had been used in temples, and architecture was then only dependent for new features on caprice or taste.

As painted decoration preceded sculpture, the ornaments (in later times carved in stone) were at first represented in colour; and the mouldings of Egyptian monuments were then merely painted on the flat surfaces of the walls and pillars. The next step was to chisel them in relief. The lotus blossom, the papyrus head, water-plants, the palm-tree, and the head of a goddess, were among the usual ornaments of a cornice or a pillar; and these favourite devices of ancient days continued in after times to be repeated in relief, when an improved style of art had substituted sculpture for the mere painted representation. But when the square pillar had been gradually converted into a polygonal shape, the ornamental devices not having room enough upon its narrow *facettes*, led to the want and invention of another form of column; and from that time a round shaft was surmounted by the palm-tree capital, or by the blossom, or the bud of the papyrus; which had hitherto only been painted, or represented in relief, upon the flat surfaces of a square pillar. Hence the origin of new orders differing so widely from the polygonal column.

It is a curious fact that both the Egyptians and the Greeks began with the same simple polygonal column, the severe grandeur of which we admire in both styles of architecture. Those at Beni Hassan are 3 feet 4 inches in diameter, and 16 feet $8\frac{1}{2}$ inches high.* They have sixteen faces or grooves, each about eight inches wide, and so light and elegant that their depth does not exceed half an inch; and one of the faces, which is not hollowed into a groove, is left for the introduction of a column of hieroglyphics. The old and new orders continued, for some time, to divide the taste of the early Egyptian architects; until at length, when the size and height of Egyptian buildings had increased beyond the scale adapted to the old polygonal shaft, the more elongated style of the new columns superseded the use of their rival; and in the later periods of the native dynasties, these, with the varieties that grew out of them, were employed, to the entire exclusion of the older order.

It is uncertain when the new columns were invented; but the water-plant capital, with the blossom and bud of the lotus and the papyrus, and probably also the palm-tree column, were used at least as early as the 6th dynasty; and the most elegant of the water-plant columns are those in the tombs of Beni Hassan, where they were used contemporaneously with the polygonal and fluted order. A capital, resembling a bunch of flax, or other flowers, is also represented in early paintings supporting wooden canopies.

* *See* Woodcut 449.

NEW ORDERS OF COLUMNS.

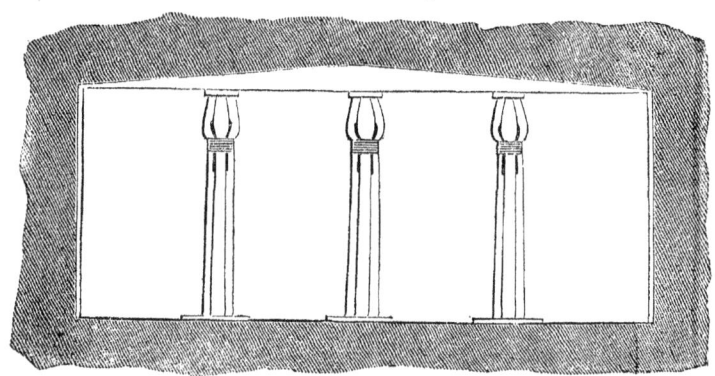

448. Section of one of the *southern* grottoes of Beni Hassan.

The palm-tree and water-plant columns were not therefore in imitation of the wooden support of the early roof; they owed their origin to the devices painted, and afterwards sculptured, on the face of the square pillar, which was carved into a round shaft and capital to imitate the shape of the plant itself; and the binding together of a number of water-plants, to form a column, was evidently not taken from a similar frail support, but was a fanciful caprice, borrowed from the *ornaments* of the old pillar.

The formation of the polygonal and circular fluted column was evidently owing to the four corners of the square pillar having been first cut off for convenience. This converted it into an octagonal shaft; and in course of time, the eight sides having been again subdivided, the number was increased to 12, 16, 20, and 32; and these flat *facettes* being hollowed into grooves, presented the actual form of the fluted column. It was doubtless from this, the oldest Egyptian order, that the Greeks borrowed their Doric shaft; and it is not impossible that the Doric capital may even have been taken from that of the water-plant column, since by removing the upper part, and bringing down the abacus, it gives the very shape of the Doric capital.* The annuli also round the neck of that early Greek column seem also to be taken from the bands tied round the cluster of water-plants, which are an anomaly in a single shaft where there is *nothing to bind*.

The Egyptian column, like that of Greece, was constructed of

* Woodcut 449, *figs*. 5 and 6.

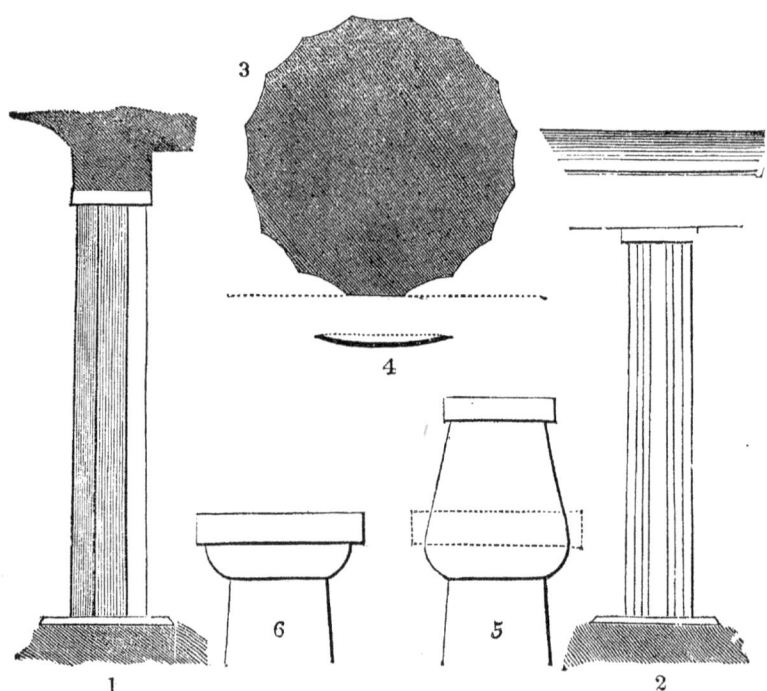

449. Fig. 1. Columns in the portico of the northern grottoes of Beni Hassan.
2. Columns of the interior.
3. Horizontal section of fig. 2, showing the grooves.
4. One of the grooves on a larger scale.
5. An Egyptian capital, which seems to have been the origin of the Doric, fig. 6.

several pieces; but it consisted of half (not of whole) drums, with the joint placed alternately one way and the other, each two at right angles with those next below and above them, sometimes secured by dovetailed cramps. Whole drums were never used, except in a few small granite shafts; and the only columns of a single piece were of that stone, which were also of moderate dimensions, and nearly confined to temples in the Delta.

Nor were the Egyptian drums secured or adjusted with the precision of those in the Parthenon, and other Greek buildings, by means of a cramp and socket in the centre, round which the upper drums were turned, till the two moistened surfaces had been ground together, and their edges made to fit with the greatest nicety, leaving a slightly concave space around the cramp.

CHAP. IX.   ORDERS OF COLUMNS.   285

Egyptian columns may be classed in eight *orders*, as in the accompanying wood-cut, where, being drawn to the same scale, their respective dimensions are shown. For though columns of the same order vary very much in different buildings, an average proportion may be assigned to them; which, indeed, is all that can be done in those of Greece, though they varied less than in Egyptian architecture. In point of antiquity, the first was certainly the square pillar; then the polygonal and round fluted column of the second order; and soon afterwards the third and fourth came into use. But the fourth and fifth, though used long before, were not common till the 18th dynasty, and the fourth assumed a larger size than any other, as at Karnak and Luxor. The sixth, though mostly in Ptolemaic and Roman temples, dates at least as early as the 18th dynasty; as does the eighth, which

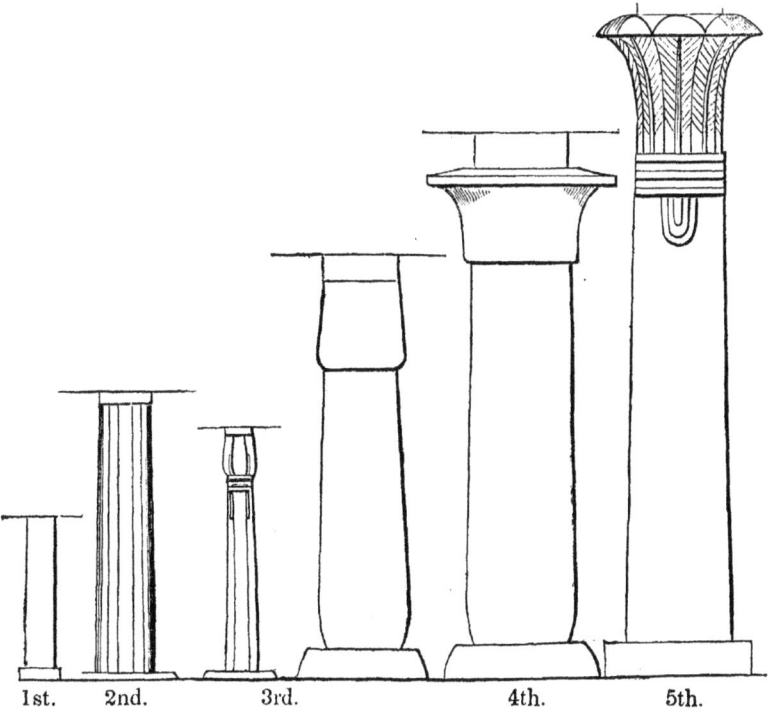

450.   The five first orders of columns; to the same scale.

6th.   7th, or Composite.   8th, or Osiride.

450 a.   The remaining three orders of columns, and the *scale*.

is, in fact, the square pillar, with a figure attached, and the evident original of the Caryatide of Greece; but the seventh is limited to the age of the Ptolemies, and has an endless variety in the form and ornaments of its capital. It was, however, quite Egyptian, and in no way indebted to Greek taste for its introduction. Of the same kind were the columns described by Athenæus (v. 103), with circular capitals, set round with rose-like ornaments, or with flowers and interlaced leaves, some of which were made of the long tapering form used in their houses, to which he also alludes. There was also a pilaster surmounted by a cow's head.

The figure attached to the square pillar was that of the king, in the form of Osiris, whence I have given it the name of

"Osiride pillar." But it did not support any member of the building; the sacred person of a king could not be subjected to such a degradation, and it was merely ornamental. Not so the figures, and heads, of captives made to support thrones, tables, or various parts of architecture; and vanquished chiefs performed the duties of consoles over the window-sills in the palace of the third Remeses in Thebes, as they decorated the sandals and thrones of other Pharaohs.

451. Heads of enemies once supporting something now removed. *Thebes.*

The oldest existing monuments in the world are the Pyramids and the tombs about them, which date as far back as the 4th, and perhaps 3rd, dynasty, and show at what a remote period sculpture and the use of squared stone in horizontal courses were practised in Egypt. The employment of squared granite blocks, and the beauty of the masonry in the interior of the Pyramids (which has not been surpassed, if even equalled, at any subsequent age), also prove the degree of skill the Egyptians had reached at a time long anterior to the building of the walls of Tiryns, and, consequently, to the rudest attempts in masonry in Italy or Greece. How long they took to arrive at that perfection it is difficult to determine; but the period between the builders of the Pyramids and the reign of Tosorthrus, the second king of the 3rd dynasty, said by Manetho to have first used squared stone, is evidently much too short; and we may conclude that it was known to them, as well as the engineering skill required for changing the course of the Nile, even before the reign of Menes.

Another very remarkable invention of those early times was the glazed tiles used for lining the walls of a chamber in the pyramid of Sakkára, and bearing the name of a king of the 3rd or 4th dynasty, the employment of which in wainscoting Egyptian rooms is mentioned by Athenæus (v. 104). He describes them of a white and black colour, here and there intermixed with slabs of alabaster; but they made them of various hues; and those at Sakkára are blue and white.

For their devices the Egyptians frequently selected objects which were favourites with them, as the lotus and other flowers, and these, as well as various animals or their heads, were adopted to form a cornice, particularly in their houses and tombs, or to ornament fancy articles of furniture and of dress. In this they committed an error, which the Greeks, with a finer perception of taste and adaptability, rightly avoided. These refined people knew that in architecture conventional devices had a much more pleasing effect than objects merely copied from nature; for, besides the incongruity of an actual representation of flowers to compose mouldings and other decorative parts of architecture, the *imperfect* imitation in an *unsuitable* material has a bad effect. To represent figures on buildings in their proper and dignified places belongs to sculpture, which then exercises its talent in the way eminently suited to it, and it is the province of art to imitate nature both in sculpture and painting. But neither the works of the sculptor should be degraded by being made merely decorative, nor should decorative design attempt to pass beyond its own sphere. The latter remark applies equally to embroidery and household furniture: even tapestry goes out of its own province when it invades that of painting; and our worsted work mistakes its capabilities when it represents men and other natural objects in staircase outlines, and transfers them from their proper place, a picture, to its conventional squares.

The Greeks preferred taking the sentiment of natural objects to making a direct copy of them when intended for ornament, and it is evident that their elegant honeysuckle moulding would lose all its beauty if it were converted into a close representation of the real flower and its leaf-bud. There is a pleasure in the variety arising from harmonious combination applied to ornament, which could never be obtained to the same extent by the mere imitation of natural objects; and the custom of depending solely on the latter is the result of poverty of invention, and the refuge of a mind deficient in talent and taste. Such was their perception of beauty that the Greeks at once saw it wherever it was to be found; and they presented the *sentiment* of it to the eye, thus relieving the spectator from the common-place inquiry about the exact representation of an object—generally, too, in a position where it would have no right to be found. They did the same in copying from " the Barbarian;" and when they perceived in any of his devices the germ of the beautiful, they adopted, or adapted, it, making it, with a small modification, what it was capable of being; and when thus remodelled, it became their own.

And well might we in modern times imitate their example, instead of striving to make what is merely *new*, and thinking more of originality than excellence. It would be no discredit if we knew how to borrow and improve, like the Greeks; and when we can do this, we may hope to have an object of taste recommended to us, not because it is the " *newest*," but because it is the " *best*," and to cease to be guided by fashion in our selection.

We have abundant proofs of the length of time that the same devices, and the same subjects, for decorative purposes, continued to be used by the Greeks. They remained favourites because they were elegant; and many of the fancy ornaments, in trinkets and furniture, continued the same also among the Egyptians for ages, who, at the same time, did not reject any novelty if worthy of adoption; and they even admitted many alterations, unknown to their ancestors, in the architecture of the temple and the tomb. But neither they nor the Greeks committed the error of preferring any work of taste because it was new, or not of native growth; and we who in England too often refuse due honour to " a prophet in his own country," would do ourselves more credit by showing a full appreciation of the exquisite designs of a Flaxman, than by seeking some far inferior production of a foreign hand. To combine, like the Greeks, excellence in sculpture with decorative taste is the highest merit, and those who possess them both will know how to combine them for architectural purposes; but many people, and, above all, the Arabs, have shown how decorative art may be fully effective, even without the assistance of its more exalted companion. Who indeed can look at the endless variety and exquisite beauty of Saracenic ornaments without appreciating them? and the harmony produced by those combinations affords the same gratification to the eye that music does to the ear.

It must, however, be allowed, that the Egyptians did not always confine themselves to the mere imitation of natural objects for ornament, and their ceilings and cornices offer numerous graceful fancy devices, among which are the *guilloche*, miscalled Tuscan border, the *chevron*, and the scroll pattern. These are even met with in a tomb of the time of the ·6th dynasty; they were therefore known in Egypt many years before they were adopted by the Greeks; and the most complicated form of the guilloche covered a whole Egyptian ceiling, upwards of a thousand years before it was represented on those comparatively late objects found at Nineveh.

Not only the tomb and house, but all parts of the temple, were coloured, both within and without, and this variety served as a relief to the otherwise sombre appearance of the massive straight walls of the exterior. Colour was an essential part of Egyptian architecture, and some of the mouldings and other details were made out solely by it, without any sculptured indication of them, as was often done on the monuments of Greece. The ceilings of Egyptian temples were painted blue and studded with stars, to represent the firmament (as in early European churches); and on the part over the central passage, through which the king and the religious processions passed, were vultures and other emblems, the winged globe always having its place over the doorways. The whole building, as well as its sphinxes and other accessories, were richly painted; and though a person unaccustomed to see the walls of a large building so decorated, might suppose the effect to be far from pleasing, no one who understands the harmony of colours will fail to admit that they perfectly understood their distribution and proper combinations, and that an Egyptian temple was greatly improved by the addition of painted sculptures.

The introduction of colour in architecture was not peculiar to the Egyptians; it was common to the Etruscans, and even to the Greeks; and the mention made of it by ancient authors is confirmed by its having been found on the monuments of Sicily and Greece.

In the temple of Theseus at Athens, vestiges of colours are seen on the ground of the frieze, on the figures themselves, and on the ornamental details. The Parthenon presents remains of painting on some members of the cornice; many coloured devices remain on the upper part of the walls in the interior, and the ground of the frieze, containing the reliefs of the Panathenaic procession, was blue. The Propylæa of the Acropolis and the Choragic monument of Lysicrates also offer traces of colour, as did the Ionic temple on the Ilissus; and vestiges of red, blue, and green have been discovered on the metopes of a temple at Selinus in Sicily. In one of these, the figure of Minerva has the eyes and eyebrows painted; her drapery and the girdle of Perseus are also ornamented with coloured devices; and the whole ground of this, and of two other metopes, is red.

Red and blue seem to have been generally used for the ground; and these two, with green and yellow, were the principal colours introduced in Greek architecture, many members of which were also gilt, as the shields, guttæ, and other prominent details; but many suppose that the shafts of columns were always white, and that the coloured parts were confined to the entablature and pediment.

In Egyptian buildings, indeed, it sometimes happened that the shafts of columns were merely covered with white stucco, without any ornament, and even without the usual line of hieroglyphics; and the same custom of coating certain kinds of stone with stucco was common in Greece. The Egyptians put this layer of stucco, or paint, over stone, whatever its quality might be; and we are surprised to find the beautiful granite of obelisks, and other monuments, concealed in a similar manner; but it was occasionally allowed to retain its own red hue, the sculptures being painted green, or sometimes blue, red, and other colours.

Whenever they employed sandstone, it was absolutely necessary to cover it with a surface of a smoother and less absorbent nature, to prevent the colour being too readily imbibed by so porous a stone; and a coat of calcareous composition was laid on before the paint was applied. When the subject was sculptured, either in relief or intaglio, the stone was coated, after the figures were cut, with the same substance, to receive the final colouring; and it had the additional advantage of enabling the artist to finish the figures and other objects with a precision and delicacy in vain to be expected on the rough and absorbent surface of sandstone.

They sometimes coated the inside walls of a sanctuary, a tomb, or a house, with granite, or some other kind of stone, or stained them to imitate it; and the adytum of the temple of Osiris at Abydus was lined with Oriental alabaster. They also used, for interiors of houses and tombs, the black and white tiles already mentioned (which were similar to those afterwards made by the Arabs and the Dutch); and cased the exterior of a limestone or sandstone building with granite; and a great portion of the third pyramid was covered with this "Ethiopian stone of various hues," which still remains.

Their colours were principally blue, red, green, black, yellow, and white. The red was an earthy bole; the yellow an iron ochre; the green was a mixture of a little ochre with a pulverulent glass, made by vitrifying the oxides of copper and iron with sand and soda; the blue was a glass of like composition without the ochreous addition; the black was bone or ivory black, and the white a very pure chalk. They were mixed with water, and apparently a little gum, to render them tenacious and adhesive. With the Egyptians the favourite combination of colour was red, blue, and green; when black was introduced, yellow was added to harmonize with it; and in like manner they sought for every hue its congenial companion. They also guarded against the false effect of two colours in juxtaposition, as of red and blue, by placing between them a narrow line of white or yellow. They had few mixed colours, though purple, pink, orange, and brown are met with, and frequently on papyri. The blue, which is very brilliant, consists of fine particles of blue glass, and may be considered equivalent to our smalt; it seems to be the same that Vitruvius describes, which he supposes to have been first made at Alexandria; and it also agrees with the artificial *kyanus* of Theophrastus, invented in Egypt, which he says was laid on thicker than the native (or lapis lazzuli). The thickness of the blue on the ceilings in Belzoni's tomb confirms his remark. The green is also a glass in powder, mixed with particles of colourless glass, to which it owes its brightness.

Gilding was employed in the decoration of some of the ornamental details of the building, and was laid on a purple ground, to give it greater richness; an instance of which may be seen in the larger temple at Kalabshee, in Nubia. It was sparingly employed, and not allowed to interfere, by an undue quantity, with the effect of the other colours, which they knew well how to introduce in their proper proportions; and such discords as light green and strawberry-and-cream were carefully avoided.

The Egyptians showed considerable taste in the judicious arrangement of colours for decorative purposes; they occasionally succeeded in *form*, as in the shapes of many of their vases, their furniture, and their ornaments; and they had still greater knowledge of *proportion*, so necessary for their gigantic monuments; but though they knew well how to give to their buildings the effect of grandeur, vastness, and durability, they had little idea of the beautiful, and were far behind the Greeks in the appreciation of form. It is, however, rare to find any people who combine colour, form, and proportion; and even the Greeks occasionally failed to attain perfection in their beautiful vases, some of which are faulty in the handles and the foot.

For knowledge of proportion, no people in later times have equalled the Italians. It is most remarkable in their public buildings; where, though perfection of form may be sometimes wanting, the first impressions arising from harmony of proportion conceal the faults that afterwards become apparent to the eye, and show the importance of a thorough knowledge of it.

We are now making a laudable effort to disseminate taste among the whole community; the Great Exhibition of 1851 has, among other good effects, made people think a little more for themselves; and a revival of architecture, as well as of mediæval ornament, has directed the eye to better models than those of Georgian times. And as we have no prescribed rules like those of the Egyptians, and no Louis XIV. and XV. splendid monstrosities, to give us preconceived notions in favour of the utter decomposition of an outline, there is no reason and no excuse for taste not flourishing, and not pervading even those least alive to it.

But it is not by mere patronage of the great that art and taste are to be made to flourish in a country; all must be made sensible of the charm and the effect they produce, and the feeling for them must become general. Encouragement may be advantageously given, and their progress may be greatly advanced by such praiseworthy assistance; but for a people to attain to excellence in them, the masses, and particularly the middle classes, must learn how to appreciate what is good, and how to discountenance the bad. It was the general taste in Greece that made the arts flourish—they were intelligible to all; and many a column, or other portion of a public edifice, was raised at the combined expense of several poor subscribers. It is an error to suppose that the religion of Greece had peculiarly the tendency to encourage the fine arts. Christian story abounds in noble subjects, with many feelings of a far more exalted kind than those portrayed by the Greeks; and historical compositions are not confined to any one people, nor to any age. To make art and taste flourish and endure, they must be generally encouraged; and it is not to the grandees of any country, who condescendingly permit their names to appear at the head of a list of patrons, that these must trust; and to obtain any good result, the judgment of the public must be cultivated. It is vain for any artists or artisans to excel in painting, sculpture, or ornamental art, if the taste of the country is deficient, and if busts or portraits are more prized than fine statues or good historical compositions; and how often, when good works are produced in decorative art, is the talented inventor obliged to discontinue them, because he finds no encouragement! He " must live;" and he is, therefore, compelled to satisfy the demands of the purchasers, by making something more consonant with their bad taste.

It is, therefore, with great satisfaction that we now look forward to the effect of the schools of design, and the well-directed energies of those who have such important objects in view; and when taste becomes general, we shall cease to have committees sanctioning what is bad. Indeed, it might always be better to submit the selection of works of art to a single individual of sound judgment, who should be, and feel that he was, *responsible*, than to leave it to the doubtful decision of a number—some indifferent, some who never attend, some put there for their name alone, none individually responsible, and many glad to shift the blame or the trouble upon some very active member, who, often being the most busy, and tiresome in the inverse ratio of his talents, gets his own way in opposition to less assuming and more capable men.

Another great impediment to the extension of taste is the notion that beauty of design is only to be sought in expensive ornamental objects, and those connected with the arts; but so long as it is confined to them, and not introduced into all the ordinary utensils of common life, it will be possessed by few, and will be a sort of exotic plant. Beauty of form and proportion, exquisite detail, and high finish, are found in the vases and commonest objects among the Greeks; they were afterwards prized by the Romans, and looked upon as rarities by them as by modern collectors; but among those who originated them they were appreciated by all "Arts of production" must not be independent of the arts of design—they must go together; and as the commonest lamp, strainer, or other things used for ordinary purposes, were beautiful in Greece, so must they be with those who strive to arrive at similar refinement. It is not by making what is elegant dear to the purchaser that art and taste will flourish; this is an impediment, not an encouragement to them; and until the beautiful is within the reach of all, and appreciated by all, it is vain to hope for excellence in any country.

The sculptures of an Egyptian temple mostly represented the king making offerings to the Triad of the city, and to the principal deities worshipped there; the king's name, who erected or enlarged the building, was frequently repeated in the dedications upon the architraves, as well as on the ornamental cornices and other places; and as it was his right to make the offerings in the temple, he alone was represented pouring out libations, and making sacrifices before the gods. On the outer walls similar subjects were repeated; but in the large temples, especially of the capital, the chief places both of the outer and inner walls were occupied by battle scenes, representing the victories obtained by the monarch over the enemies of Egypt; and upon the great towers of the façade he was portrayed routing them in battle, or in the act of smiting the captive "Heads," or "chiefs, of the Gentiles," in the presence of the great deity of the place.

Among the peculiarities of Egyptian architecture, one of the most important is the studied avoidance of uniformity in the arrangement of the columns and many of the details. Of these, some are evident to the eye, others are only intended to have an influence on the general effect, and are not perceptible without careful examination. Thus the capitals of the columns in the great hall at Karnak are at different heights, some extending lower down the shaft than others, evidently with a view to correct the sameness of symmetrical repetition, and to avoid fatiguing the sight with too much regularity. This is not to be perceived until the eye is brought on a level with the lower part of the capitals; and its object was only effect, like that of many curved lines introduced in a Greek temple, as at the Parthenon.

But the Egyptians often carried their dislike of uniformity to an extreme, beyond even what is justified by the study of variety Where they avoided that extreme, their motive was legitimate; and it is remarkable that they were the first people whose monuments offer instances of that diversity, which forms so essential a characteristic of Saracenic and Gothic architecture.

This feeling increased, rather than diminished, after the accession of the Ptolemies; and intercourse with the Greeks had not the effect of inducing the Egyptians to adopt any of the notions of symmetry which prevailed in their monuments. Those, therefore, who imagine that the great variety then in vogue, from the juxtaposition of columns of different orders, was introduced by the Ptolemies, attribute it to a very improbable cause; for if any change had been introduced by the Greeks, it would have been that of greater uniformity; and the arrangement of columns, each with a different capital in the same portico, is evidently the result of Egyptian taste. It shows the same progress which our decorated made from the more simple, but still varied, character of our early pointed style. The decorated and flamboyant each grew out of its predecessor; but no one looks for their origin in a *different* style of architecture; and in like manner, the more ornamental column and the more *varied* arrangements of the details, in later Egyptian buildings, arose out of the old Egyptian style, and did not certainly proceed from the *uniformity* of Greek taste.

Our perpendicular style, though really derived from its varied predecessors, did undergo a change, and one that at last deprived it of the principal characteristic of the pointed style; it even admitted by degrees an incipient taste for greater uniformity (which about a century later Europe unequivocally welcomed back, by a return to classic architecture); and though it did not positively fraternize with the renaissance, it lost that great feature—variety, which peculiarly distinguished its Gothic parent. In one part overloaded with fretwork, in another with an endless repetition of monotonous lines, it strove to make rich what it ceased to make beautiful; and at last departed so far from the Gothic type, that one portion of a perpendicular edifice cast in metal might almost serve to construct the rest.

Egyptian architecture was at first simple, as was the Greek, and both had the severe fluted column, which, as I have shown, originated in the still more simple square pillar of an Egyptian quarry. The Greeks varied their style by the introduction of the Ionic, and a basket capital with leaves, which by degrees took the form of the Corinthian; borrowing from the Ionic, and from the basket capital of Egypt, and varying the ornaments, as they had before modified the volutes, for these were also derived from the Egyptian columns attached to the canopies of the kings. But here the variety ended; or at least they did not go the length of the

Egyptians in placing columns of different orders one by the other in the same portico. This was confined to the taste of Egyptian (and of the later Gothic) architects. And though the original Egyptian column was so simple, no foreign influence introduced the change: it was of native growth; and the water-plant and other columns, as I have already shown, date from the time of the earliest periods before the invasion of the Shepherds. Their formation, too, was consistent with the style of their decoration.

But while the architecture of the Egyptians and that of the Greeks had some points of resemblance in certain details, their general character was essentially distinct; and the Egyptian flat roof had a totally different effect from the pediment, or gable, of a Greek temple. The plans of their sacred buildings were also quite dissimilar, and the circular form of the early Greek tomb was unknown in Egypt. The Egyptians, too, a cautious people, made durability their chief object, and they never sought for that beauty, to which the Greeks were so successful in attaining. If certain nations, like individuals, are gifted with peculiar talents, none have been favoured with the same variety as the Greeks; and all their habits and feelings were eminently suited to the development of taste. Not so those of the Egyptians, who, independently of the restrictions imposed upon them, were deficient in the requisites for that purpose. They wanted the imaginative faculty of the Greeks; they thought chiefly of carrying out a particular object; and their speculative powers led to abstruse theories, not to the ideal conceptions required for excellence in art.

With regard to the pyramidal or sloping line in Egyptian buildings, it is scarcely necessary to say that its object was greater solidity; and its use is one of many arguments against the opinion that Egyptian temples had their origin in excavated monuments; for it is evident that the pyramidal line can neither be required, nor be consistently introduced, in the walls of a rock temple, and wherever the sloping line does occur there, it is merely in the ornamental mouldings, and is one more evidence of the imitation of a constructed monument. Another misconception respecting Egyptian architecture is that they *began* with *large* buildings *because* the mountains gave them the power of excavating to any depth, and extending the front to any length, which is disproved by the fact that the oldest sanctuaries were of very *small* dimensions; *large* monuments were erected *before large* rock temples were made; and the mere irregular quarry (opened solely to supply materials) did not bear any resemblance to the plan or general character of a temple. The attempt, too, to account for the use of large blocks, from the "facility of transport" in a level country, and the preference given by the Greeks to smaller or shorter architraves, from the difficulty of conveying them from the quarries in a hilly country, is equally unsatisfactory, and is far from being consistent with the positions of many early Greek temples, and with what may be observed in other countries, since we find that in the mountainous districts of Syria heavier blocks were used than in the temples of Egypt.

If the employment of large blocks were thus to be accounted for, it would be difficult to explain how the Syrians acquired the habit, or obtained the experience, which enabled them to move the enormous stones at Baalbek, far heavier than any in Egypt, being upwards of 60 feet long by 9 broad and 12 feet thick. Some stones in the walls of Jerusalem are more than 20 feet in length; and massive columns, of a single piece, were raised in temples on the mountain summits of Syria. It was therefore as common a practice to use large blocks in the mountainous Syria as in the level Egypt; so that neither the great breadth of the Egyptian, nor the narrowness of Greek, or any other intercolumniations, can be accounted for by the facility, or difficulty, of transporting long blocks of stone to serve as architraves. Nor was size originally a condition in the edifices of the Egyptians. They began, as did the Greeks, with small monuments, which increased in scale with the increase of wealth and the advancement of art; and though, as their taste was developed, the Egyptians preferred monuments of large size, the origin of this preference must not too hastily be attributed to the facility of transporting the blocks, nor even to the convenience of obtaining materials near at hand, since the granite quarries of Syene were upwards of 130 miles from Thebes, or five times as much from Memphis, and the monoliths of that material erected in the Delta were conveyed more than 800 miles. The same hasty conclusion has been made about the largest colossi being peculiar to Egypt. But that of Olympian Jove was 60 feet high; that of Apollo, mentioned by Pausanias, was 30 cubits, or 45 feet; and the colossus of Rhodes, measuring 105 feet, far exceeded any in Egypt.

The arch was employed in Egypt at a very early period; and crude brick arches were in common use in roofing tombs at least as early as Amunoph I., in the 16th century before our era. And since I first discovered one at Thebes bearing his name, others have been found of the age of Thothmes III. (his fourth successor) and of Remeses V. It even seems to have been known in the time of the 12th dynasty, judging from the representation of what appear to be vaulted granaries at Beni Hassan.

That it should have originated in a country where wood was rare is consistent with probability; and it has been conjectured that the chambers in the large brick pyramids near Memphis were arched. Those at Thebes, of a rather later period, were so roofed; nor is it unreasonable to suppose that in the other large ones they had the same construction; and the superiority over the stone pyramids, boasted in the inscription upon that of Asychis, has been supposed to consist in its vaulted chambers. It is also evident that in the time of Osirtasen the vaulted ceilings of rock-tombs were made in imitation of arches; and the arch seems to have been particularly used in sepulchral monuments.

The earliest stone arches are of the time of a Psammitichus, in the 7th century before our era. One of these is at Sakkára, but from the thin slabs of stone forming its roof, it is a far less satisfactory instance of the arch than some of those near the pyramids of Geezeh of the same date; though an arch being of stone is no stronger proof of its existence than are those of brick at Thebes, which are on the same principle, the bricks (like the stones) radiating to a common centre. For it is not necessary that an arch should be of any particular material; nor does the principle of the arch depend on its having a keystone; and arches, both round and pointed, are found at all ages without it. The same is the case in Egypt, and the small chapels before the pyramids of Ethiopia have instances of round and pointed arches, with and without the keystone.

Many crude brick arches, of different dates, exist in Thebes, besides the small pyramids* already alluded to, some of which are of very beautiful construction. The most remarkable are the doorways of the enclosures surrounding the tombs in the Assaseéf, which are composed of two or more concentric semicircles of brick, as well constructed as any of the present day. They are of the time of Psammitichus and other princes of the 26th dynasty, immediately before the invasion of Cambyses. All the bricks radiate to a common centre: they are occasionally pared off at the lower part, to allow for the curve of the arch, and sometimes the builders were contented to put in a piece of stone to fill up the increased space between the upper edges of the bricks. In those roofs of houses or tombs, which were made with less care, and required less solidity, the bricks were placed longitudinally, in the direction of the curve of the vault, and the lower ends were then cut away considerably, to allow for the greater opening between them; and many were grooved at the sides, in order to retain a greater quantity of mortar between their united surfaces.

Though the oldest stone arch, whose age has been positively ascertained, dates only in the time of the second Psammitichus,† we cannot suppose that the use of stone was not adopted by the Egyptians, for that species of construction, previous to his reign; even if none of the arches of the Pyramids in Ethiopia should prove to be anterior to his era. Nor does the absence of the arch in temples, and other large buildings, excite our surprise, when we consider the style of Egyptian monuments; and no one who understands the character of their architecture could wish for its introduction. In some of the small temples of the Oasis, the Romans attempted this innovation, but the appearance of the chambers so constructed fails to please; and the introduction of an imitation of the arch into a building at Abydus, bearing the name of Sethi, or Osirei, was owing to its being a sepulchral monument. Here the roof is formed of single blocks of stone

* One is introduced into woodcut 452, *fig.* 1. † Vignette P., Chap X.

reaching from one architrave to the other, which, instead of being placed in the usual manner, stand upon their edges, in order to allow room for hollowing out an arch in their thickness; but its effect is by no means good. (*Woodcut* 452, *fig.* 3.)

Like the Egyptians, the Greeks abstained from introducing the arch into their monuments, being unsuited to a style already formed; an objection not felt by the Romans, who modified what they borrowed, so far as to adopt the arch, and break through the horizontal line of Greek architecture, thus establishing the first elements of the vertical of later times; and the great benefits conferred by the arch in covering large spaces, where crowded assemblies were to meet, are well demonstrated by a comparison of our churches, and the Great Hall of Karnak, with its forest of columns to support the roof. But the Greeks were not ignorant of the arch; instances of it still remain; and Posidonius claims its invention for Democritus, who was born B.C. 460. The arched tunnel of brick under the Euphrates at Babylon, mentioned by Diodorus, also shows that it was known at a remote age in other countries as well as in Egypt. (*See also Vignette N., end of Chap. VIII.*)

Another imitation of the arch occurs in a building at Thebes. Here, however, a reason may perhaps be given for its introduction, in addition to its being a tomb, and not bound to accord with the ordinary rules of architecture laid down for Egyptian temples. The chambers lie under a friable rock, and are cased with masonry, to prevent the fall of its crumbling stone; but instead of being roofed on the principle of the arch, they are covered with a number of large blocks, placed horizontally, one projecting beyond that immediately below it, till the uppermost two meet in the centre, the interior angles being afterwards rounded off to form the appearance of a vault.

This building dates in the 15th century B.C., consequently many years after the Egyptians had been acquainted with the art of vaulting; and the reason of their preferring such a mode of construction probably arose from their calculating the great difficulty of repairing an injured arch in this position, and the consequences attending the decay of a single block; nor can any one suppose, from the great superincumbent weight applied to

TRUE AND FALSE ARCHES.

452. Fig. 1. Vaulted rooms and doorway of a crude brick pyramid at Thebes.
2. An imitation of an arch at Thebes.
3. Another at Abydus.
4. Mode of commencing a quarry.

the *haunches*, that this style of building is devoid of strength, and of the usual durability of an Egyptian fabric, or pronounce it ill suited to the purpose for which it was erected.

This was either an imitation of an arch, or a method of older times used before its invention; and we have other instances, in Italy, of false and true arches being employed contemporaneously, by people well acquainted with the principle of forming *voussoirs* with stones radiating to a common centre.

The first deviation from the mode of roofing with flat stones was what is called the pent-shaped roof, formed by the application of two sets of stones, inclined towards each other, at an angle of about 100°, as over the entrance to the Great Pyramid and the roof of the Queen's chamber. The next was when the space was covered over with slabs of small dimensions, each course projecting beyond the one below it, until the uppermost ones approached each other near enough for the remaining space to be covered by a single stone. These two, used at the same time in the Great Pyramid, were also employed by the early Greeks; and they may be considered the first steps towards the want, and invention, of the arch. And this seems to confirm the notion of the boasted superiority of the brick pyramid having consisted in supplying this desideratum. Bricks certainly led to its invention; and thus small materials have contributed to the greatest variety in construction at different periods: witness groined arches, as well as long-and-short-work, opus incertum, round towers, and various peculiarities of brickwork. In the earliest arches, the bricks were placed lengthways towards each other; and not only many of the oldest tombs at Thebes have their roofs so constructed, but the stones forming the arches at the pyramids of Gebel Berkel are placed in the same manner. This, however, was afterwards abandoned; and the beautiful brick arches of the Assaseéf at Thebes resemble those of modern times.

The same longitudinal arrangement of the bricks again occurs in the pointed arches of the early Christians in Egypt; and they give evidence of being a first essay of a new principle. Doubtful as to the power of an arch of this form, they only used it at first to cover passages, and other small spaces; and many consisted only of 1, 2, or 3 very long bricks in height, with a portion of one placed between the two uppermost ones as a key. They are, however, remarkable from their antiquity, being about the 7th century of our era; and though a much older pointed arch is found at Gebel Berkel, as well as in Italy, and the pointed arch seems to be *imitated* in the time of the 18th dynasty, that style of building does not seem to have come into common use in the East much before the 9th century. But it was then very general, and though some dream of pointed arches having been invented in Europe, from the intersection of two round arches, we may be sure that the East gave us the first notion of the new principle, and that we derived it from the Saracens, as they composed their architecture from the Byzantine and Persian styles, and the earliest pointed *architecture*, if not the first pointed arches, should be looked for in Asia Minor and about Constantinople. As the Greeks instructed the Romans, the Byzantine Christians worked for the Saracens, and gave them the first notions of a style, which they afterwards modified according to their views. The cupola introduced a new feature into the mosk, whose original simple courts, and small round arches, were humble imitations of Roman buildings; the golden mosaics of Byzantium, themselves descended from the "golden vaults" of Imperial Rome, decorated the walls and arched ceilings of Damascus houses, as they enriched the apses of Italian basilicas; and the Byzantine or Romanesque style spread its influence over Europe and the East. But the stream of taste was diversified according to the ground over which it flowed. As yet one general system was not acknowledged, as in later times, when Gothic architecture was the same, with slight variations, throughout Europe; each people at first made their own selection in the principles or the mouldings they imitated; in England the rude Saxon, with its long-and-short-work—the common house construction even before the age of Justinian; the more decorated Norman; and the Italian Lombard style, were all indebted to the Roman and the Byzantine; and from the arrival of a fresh element from the East, itself of cognate origin, arose the pointed style of Western Europe. Such was the progress of architecture from the earliest times; each system borrowing, adopting, or recasting the component parts of its predecessor, according to the wants, climate, materials, or taste of the new country of its growth.

The most ancient buildings in Egypt were constructed of limestone, hewn from the mountains bordering the valley of the Nile to the East and West, extensive quarries of which may be seen at El Māsara, Nesleh Shekh Hassan, El Maabdeh, and other places; and that it was used long before sandstone, is proved by the tombs of the pyramids, as well as those monuments themselves, and by the vestiges of old substructions and ruins in Upper Egypt. Limestone continued to be occasionally employed for building even after the accession of the 12th dynasty; but so soon as the durability of sandstone was ascertained, the quarries of Silsilis were opened, and those materials were universally adopted, and preferred for their even texture, and the ease with which they were wrought.

The extent of the quarries at Silsilis was very great; and it is not by the size and scale of the monuments of Upper Egypt alone that we are enabled to judge of the stupendous works executed by the ancient Egyptians; these would suffice to prove the character they bore, were the gigantic ruins of Thebes and other cities no longer in existence; and safely may we apply the expression, used by Pliny in speaking of the porphyry quarries, to those of Silsilis, " they are of such extent, that masses of any dimensions might be hewn from them."

In opening a new quarry, when the stone could not be taken from the surface of the rock, and it was necessary to cut into the lower part of its perpendicular face, they pierced it with a horizontal shaft, beginning with a square trench, and then breaking away the stone left in the centre (as indicated in woodcut 452, *fig*. 4, by the space B), its height and breadth depending of course on the size of the stones required. They then cut the same around C, and so on to any extent in a horizontal direction, after which they extended the work downwards, in steps, taking away E, and leaving D for the present, and thus descending as far as they found convenient, or the stone continued good. They then returned, and cut away the steps D, F, and all the others, reducing each time one step in depth, till at last there remained at x a perpendicular wall; and when the quarries were of very great horizontal extent, pillars were left at intervals to support the roof.

453.   Removing a stone from the quarries of El Māsara.

In one of the quarries at El Māsara, the mode of transporting the stone is represented. It is placed on a sledge, drawn by oxen, and is supposed to be on its way to the inclined plane that led to the river, vestiges of which may still be seen a little to the south of the modern village.

Sometimes, and particularly when the blocks were large and ponderous, men were employed to drag them, and those condemned to hard labour in the quarries, as a punishment, were required to assist in moving a certain number of stones, according to the extent of their offence, ere they were liberated; which seems to be proved by this expression, "I have dragged 110 stones for the building of Isis at Philæ," in an inscription at the quarries of Gertassy in Nubia. In order to keep an account of their progress, they frequently cut the initials of their name, or some private mark, with the number, on the rock whence the stone was taken, as soon as it was removed: thus, C. XXXII., PD. XXXIII.; PD. XXXIIII., and numerous other signs occur at the quarries of Fateereh.

All large blocks were taken from the quarry on sledges; and in a grotto behind E'Dayr, a Christian village between Antinoë and El Bersheh, is the representation of a colossus, which a number of men are employed in dragging with ropes—a subject doubly interesting from being of the early age of Osirtasen II., and one of the very few paintings which throw any light on the method employed by the Egyptians for moving weights.

It is not necessary that the colossus should have been hewn in the hill of El Bersheh; and this picture, though it refers to what *really happened*, may also represent one of the occupations of the Egyptians, like the trades, gardening-scenes, and other subjects. At all events, the statue could not have been placed in the tomb, as some suppose, being too large for the doorway; and traces of it must have remained.

One hundred and seventy-two men, in four rows, of forty-three each, pull the ropes attached to the front of the sledge; and grease is poured from a vase by a person standing on the pedestal of the statue, in order to facilitate its progress as it slides over the ground, which was probably covered with a bed of planks, though they are not indicated in the painting. (*See Frontispiece.*)

Some of the persons employed in this laborious duty appear to be Egyptians, the others are foreign slaves, who are clad in the costume of their country; and behind are four rows of men, who, though only twelve in number, may be intended to represent the "superintendents," and the set which relieved the others when fatigued.

Below are persons carrying vases of the liquid, or perhaps water, for the use of the workmen, and some implements connected with the transport of the statue, followed by taskmasters with their wands of office. On the knee of the figure stands a man who claps his hands to the measured cadence of a song, to mark the time and insure their simultaneous draught; for it is evident that, in order that the whole power might be applied at the same instant, a sign of this kind was necessary; and the custom of singing at their work was usual in every occupation of the Egyptians, as it now is in that country, in India, and many other places. Nor is it found a disadvantage among the modern sailors of Europe, when engaged in pulling a rope, or in any labour which requires a simultaneous effort. Above are seven companies of soldiers, *unarmed*, holding green twigs in their hands.

The height of the statue was 13 cubits, $19\frac{1}{2}$ ft., or really 22ft. $2\frac{1}{2}$ in., and of lime or freestone, as the colour and the hieroglyphics inform us. It was bound to the sledge by double ropes, which were tightened by means of long pegs placed between them, and twisted round until completely braced; and, to prevent injury from the friction of the ropes, a compress of leather, lead, or other substance was introduced at the part where they touched the statue.

It is singular that the position of the ring to which all the ropes were attached for moving the mass was confined to one place at the front of the statue, and did not extend to the back part of the sledge; but this was owing to the shortness of the body; and, when of great length, it is probable that ropes were fixed at intervals along the sides, in order to give an opportunity of applying a greater moving power. For this purpose, in blocks of very great length (as the columns at Fateereh, which are about 60 ft. long, and $8\frac{1}{2}$ ft. in diameter), certain pieces of stone were left projecting from the sides, like the trunnions of a gun, to which several ropes were attached, each pulled by its own set of men.

Small blocks of stone were sent from the quarries by water to their different places of destination in boats, or rafts; and if any land-carriage was required, they were placed on sledges and rollers; but those of very large dimensions were dragged the whole way by men, overland, in the manner here represented. The immense weight of some shows that the Egyptians were well acquainted with mechanical powers, and the mode of applying a locomotive force with the most wonderful success; and the use of grease for large weights, in preference to rollers, is consistent with modern experience.

The obelisks transported from the quarries of Syene, at the first cataracts, in latitude 24° 5′ 23″, to Thebes and Heliopolis, vary in size from seventy to ninety-three feet in length. They are of one single stone; and the largest in Egypt, which is that of the great temple at Karnak, I calculate to weigh about 297 tons. This was brought about 138 miles from the quarry to where it now stands, and those taken to Heliopolis passed over a space of more than 800 miles. The power, however, to move the mass was the same, whatever might be the distance, and the mechanical skill which transported it five, or even one, would suffice for any number of miles.

In examining the ruins of western Thebes, and reading the statements of ancient writers regarding the stupendous masses of granite conveyed by this people for several hundred miles, our surprise is greatly increased. We find in the plain of Koorneh two colossi of Amunoph III., of a single block each, forty-seven feet in height, which contain about 11,500 cubic feet, and are made of a stone not known within several days' journey of the place; and at the Memnonium is another of Remeses II., which, when entire, weighed upwards of 887 tons, and was brought from A'Souán to Thebes, a distance, as before stated, of more than 130 miles. This is certainly a surprising weight, and we cannot readily suggest the means adopted for its transport, or its passage of the river; but the monolithic temple, said by Herodotus to have been taken from Elephantine to Buto, in the Delta, was still larger, and far surpassed in weight the pedestal of Peter the Great's statue at St. Petersburgh, which last is calculated at about 1200 tons.

He also mentions a monolith at Saïs, of which he gives the

following account: "What I admire still more is a monument of a single block of stone, which Amasis transported from the city of Elephantine. Two thousand men, of the class of boatmen, were employed to bring it, and were occupied three years in this arduous task. The exterior length is twenty-one cubits (31½ ft.); the breadth fourteen (21 ft.); and the height eight (12 ft.); and, within, it measures eighteen cubits twenty digits (28 ft. 3 in.) in length; twelve (18 ft.) in breadth; and five (7½ ft.) in height. It *lies* near the entrance of the temple, not having been admitted into the building, in consequence, as they say, of the engineer, while superintending the operation of dragging it forward, having sighed aloud, as if exhausted with fatigue, and impatient of the time it had occupied; which being looked upon by Amasis as a bad omen, he forbade its being taken any further. Some, however, state that it was in consequence of a man having been crushed beneath it, while moving it with levers."

Herodotus's measurement is given as it lay on the ground; his length is properly its height, and his height the depth, from the front to the back; for, judging from the usual form of these monolithic monuments, it was doubtless like that of the same king at Tel-et-Mai, the dimensions of which are 21 ft. 9 in. high, 13 ft. broad, and 11 ft. 7 in. deep; and internally 19 ft. 3 in., 8 ft., and 8 ft. 3 in.

The weight of the Saïte monolith cannot certainly be compared to that of the colossus of Remeses; but when we calculate the solid contents of the temple of Latona at Buto, our astonishment is unbounded; and we are perplexed to account for the means employed to move a mass which, supposing the walls to have been only 6 ft. thick (for Herodotus merely gives the external measurement of forty cubits, or 60 ft. in height, breadth, and thickness), must have weighed upwards of 6000, or, at the lowest computation, of 5000 tons.

The skill of the Egyptians was not confined to the mere moving of immense weights; their wonderful knowledge of mechanism is shown in the erection of obelisks, and in the position of large stones, raised to a considerable height, and adjusted with the utmost precision; sometimes, too, in situations where the space will not admit the introduction of the inclined plane. Some of the most remarkable are the lintels and roofing stones of the large temples; and the lofty doorway leading into the grand hall of assembly, at Karnak, is covered with sandstone blocks, 40 ft. 10 in. long., and 5 ft. 2 in. square.

In one of the quarries at A'Souán (Syene) is a granite obelisk, which, never having been finished or separated from the rock, remains in its original place. The depth of the quarry is so small, and the entrance to it so narrow, that it would have been impossible for them to turn the stone, in order to remove it by that opening; they had therefore to lift it out of the hollow in which it had been cut; and this was the case with all the other shafts previously hewn in the same quarry. Such instances as these suffice to prove the wonderful mechanical knowledge of the Egyptians; and we may question whether our engineers could raise weights with the same facility, without using some of those modern appliances, which were quite unknown to that ancient people.

Pliny mentions several obelisks of very large dimensions, some of which were removed to Rome, where they now stand.

The Egyptians naturally looked on those monuments with feelings of veneration, being connected with their religion, and the glorious memory of their monarchs ; and at the same time perceived that, in buildings constructed as their temples were, the monotony of numerous horizontal lines required a relief of this kind; but the same feelings cannot influence others, and few motives can be assigned for their removal to Europe, beyond the desire of possessing what requires great difficulty to obtain.

I will not pretend to say that the ancient Romans committed the same strange outrage to taste as their modern successors, who have destroyed the effect of the most graceful part of these monuments, by crowning the apex, which should of course terminate in a point, with stars, rays, or other whimsical additions; and, however habit may have reconciled the eye to such a monstrosity, every one who understands the beauty of form, and the harmony of lines, must observe and regret the incongruity of balls and weather-cocks on our own spires.

Pliny says, that the first Egyptian king who erected an obelisk was Mitres, who held his court at Heliopolis, the city of the Sun, to whom they were there dedicated, as to Amun at Thebes. Many others were raised by different monarchs, and "Ramises" made one 99 feet in height, " on which he employed 20,000 workmen." "And, fearing lest the engineer should not take sufficient care to proportion the power of the machinery to the weight he had to raise, he ordered his son to be bound to the apex, more effectually to guarantee the safety of the monument."

The same writer describes a method of transporting obelisks from the quarries down the river, by lashing two flat-bottomed boats together, side by side, which were admitted into a trench, cut from the Nile to the place where the stone lay, laden with a quantity of ballast exactly equal to the weight of the obelisk; which, so soon as they had been introduced beneath the transverse block, was all taken out; and the boats rising, as they were lightened, bore away the obelisk in lieu of their previous burden. But we are uncertain if this method was adopted by the Egyptians; and though he mentions it as the invention of one Phœnix, he fails to inform us at what period he lived.

No insight is given into the secrets of their mechanical knowledge from the sculptures, or paintings of the tombs, though so many subjects are there introduced. Our information connected with this point is confined to the use of levers, and a sort of crane, which last is mentioned by Herodotus, in describing the mode of raising the stones from one tier to another, when they built the Pyramids. He says it was made of short pieces of wood; an indefinite expression, conveying no notion either of its form or principle; and every stone was raised to the succeeding tier by a different machine.

Diodorus tells us that machines were not invented at that early period, and that the stone was raised by mounds or inclined planes; but we may be excused for doubting his assertion, and thus be relieved from the effort of imagining an inclined plane five hundred feet in perpendicular height, with a proportionate base.

Whatever may have been the means employed, they evidently had acquired great facility in moving large blocks; and this was

CHAP. IX.   MASONS AND STATUARIES.   313

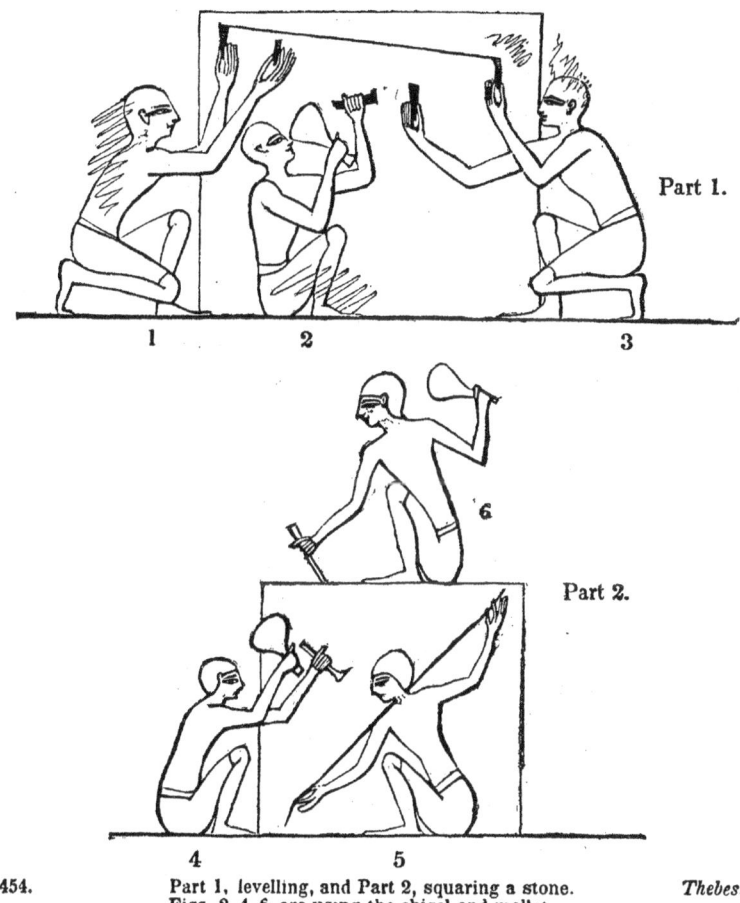

454.   Part 1, levelling, and Part 2, squaring a stone.   *Thebes.*
Figs. 2, 4, 6, are using the chisel and mallet.

often a temptation to a later king to appropriate the monuments of a predecessor in embellishing a temple. Thus Tirhakah took the two lions of Amunoph III. from Soleb (the *name* of which place they bear) to Gebel Birkel; which was an easy task, when obelisks were transplanted from Memphis and Heliopolis to Alexandria, and afterwards to Rome; and Amunoph's lions have at last found a place in the British Museum.

It is true that the occupations of the mason and the statuary are sometimes alluded to in the paintings; the former, however,

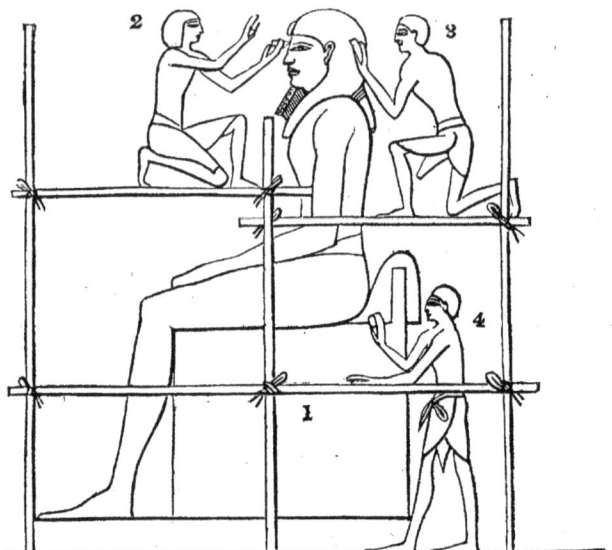

455.   Large sitting colossus of granite, which they are polishing

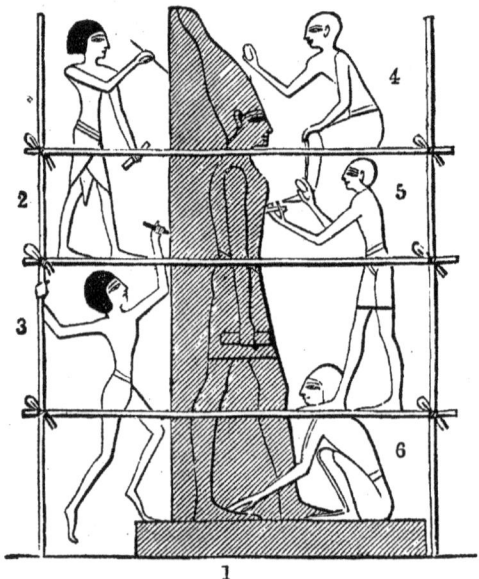

456.   Standing figure of a king, and, like the former, painted to represent granite. Figs. 4, 6, are polishing it; and figs. 2 and 3 painting and sculpturing the hieroglyphics at the back. *Thebes.*

are almost confined to the levelling or squaring a stone, and the use of the chisel. Some are represented polishing and painting statues of men, sphinxes, and small figures; and two instances occur of large granite colossi, surrounded with scaffolding, on which men are engaged in chiselling and polishing the stone; the painter following the sculptor to colour the hieroglyphics he had engraved at the back of the statue. (*Woodcut* 455, *fig.* 2.)

The usual mode of cutting large blocks from the quarries was by a number of metal wedges, which were struck at the same instant along its whole length; sometimes, however, they seem to have been of highly dried wood, which, being driven into holes previously cut for them by a chisel, and then saturated with water, split the stone by their expansion; and the troughs frequently found along the whole line of the holes, where the wedges were inserted, argue strongly in favor of this opinion.

Such a method could only be adopted when the wedges were in a horizontal position, upon the upper surface of the stone; but those put into the sides were impelled by the hammer only.

To separate the lower part of a ponderous mass from the rock, we may suppose they cut under it, leaving long pieces here and there to support it, like beams, which traversed its whole depth from the front to the back; and then, having introduced wooden rafters into the open spaces which were cleared away, they removed the remainder of the stone, and the block rested on the wood. This was also the process in the quarry at Baalbek.

Some have imagined that they used the same means now practised in India, of lighting a fire along the whole length of the mass, in the direction where they intended it should split; and then pouring water upon it, cracked the stone in that part by its sudden action; but this is very doubtful, and the presence of the holes for the wedges sufficiently proves the method they usually employed.

Among the remarkable inventions of a remote era among the Egyptians may be mentioned bellows and siphons. The former were used at least as early as the reign of Thothmes III., being represented in a tomb bearing the name of that Pharaoh. They consisted of a leather bag, secured and fitted into a frame, from which a long pipe extended for carrying the wind to the fire. They were worked by the feet, the operator standing upon them, with one under each foot, and pressing them alternately, while he pulled up each exhausted skin with a string he held in his hand. In one instance we observe from the painting, that when the man left the bellows, they were raised, as if full of air; and this would imply a knowledge of the valve. (*Woodcut* 457, *k, o.*)

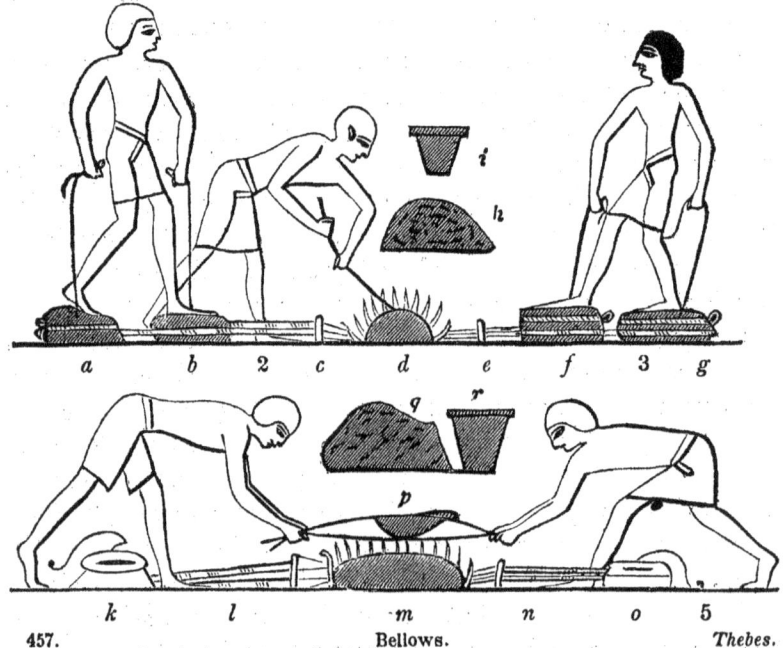

457.   Bellows.   Thebes.

a, b, k, o, the leather case.   *c, e, l, n,* the pipes conveying the wind to the fire.   *d, m,* the fire.   *h, q,* charcoal.   *k* and *o* are raised as if full of air.

It is uncertain when bellows were first invented; the earliest contrivance of this kind was probably a mere reed or pipe, which we find used by goldsmiths in the age of Osirtasen, and also at a late period, after the invention of bellows; and the tubes of these last appear even in the time of Thothmes III. to have been simply of reed, tipped with a metal point, to resist the action of the fire.

The first step was to add the sack containing the air; and

various improvements succeeded each other in the form and principle of the bellows : there are, however, no means of ascertaining the period when they assumed their present form ; and the merit of the late invention of *wooden* bellows is still disputed. Strabo ascribes the bellows to Anacharsis, but with the evident conviction that these (the double anchor), and the potter's wheel, were of an age far anterior to the Scythian philosopher, which is fully proved by the paintings of Thebes.

The ordinary hand-bellows now used for small fires in Egypt are a sort of a bag made of the skin of a kid, with an opening at one end (like the mouth of a common carpet-bag), where the skin is sewed upon two pieces of wood ; and these being pulled apart by the hands, and closed again, the bag is pressed down, and the air thus forced through the pipe at the other end. It is, perhaps, an ancient invention, but I find no indication of it in the paintings.

The bellows with sides of wood, made at the present day, are a more perfect construction than these last, or the foot-bellows of the time of Thothmes. They are supposed to have been known to the Greeks, though I confess the

"——— taurinis follibus auras
 Accipiunt redduntque"

of Virgil is rather calculated to convey the idea of bellows made of ox leather without wooden sides.

Siphons are shown to have been invented in Egypt at least as early as the reign of Amunoph II., in the 15th century before our era; and they again occur in the paintings of the third Remeses. In a tomb at Thebes, bearing the name of Amunoph, their use is unequivocally pointed out by one priest pouring a liquid into some vases, and the other drawing it off, by applying the siphon to his mouth, and thence to a large vase ; and it is not improbable that they owed their invention to the necessity of allowing the Nile water to deposit its thick sediment in vases, which could not be moved without again rendering it turbid, whether by inclining the vessel, or dipping a cup into it with the hand. They seem to be of a pliant material, from their bending (at *f*, and perhaps at *g*, in Woodcut 458).

458. Siphons used about the year 1430 B.C. Thebes.
1 pours a liquid into vases from the cup *b*, and 2 draws it off by the siphons *a*.

Julius Pollux says they were used for tasting wine; and Heron of Alexandria, the first writer of consequence who mentions them, and who lived under Ptolemy Euergetes II., shows them to have been employed as hydraulic machines on a grand scale, for draining lands, or conveying water over a hill from one valley to another. Their name, siphon, is evidently Oriental, and derived from the word *siph* or *sif*, to "imbibe," or "draw up with the breath," analogous to, and perhaps the origin of, our own expression "to sip." They had also invented the syringe, used for injecting liquids into the head and body of mummies during the embalming process; and an instrument is often represented in the sculptures of early times, which has the appearance of a portable pump.

Respecting the numerous inventions of the Egyptians little information is to be obtained; but I have mentioned their skill in cutting hard stones, and various branches of art; and we may conclude they tested gold by a stone. And if they applied the name *Bashan*, or *Basan* (whence *basanos*), to a basaltic stone on which gold makes no mark (nor does it on that of the "Basanite mountain"), this was probably because it included all basalts;

some of which test gold as well as our basanite—a slate to which the name has since been transferred, and confined.

I have also shown that Herodotus and others ascribe the origin of geometry to the Egyptians, but the period when it commenced is uncertain. Anticlides pretends that Mœris was the first to lay down the elements of that science, which he says was perfected by Pythagoras; but the latter observation is merely the result of the vanity of the Greeks, which claimed for their countrymen (as in the case of Thales, and other instances) the credit of enlightening a people on the very subjects which they had visited Egypt for the purpose of studying.

The discovery of the pole, the sundial, and the division of the day into twelve hours, are said by Herodotus to have been derived by the Greeks from the Babylonians. Of the two former we have no indication in the sculptures to prove the epoch when they were known in Egypt; but there is reason to believe that the day and night were divided, each into twelve hours, by the Egyptians, some centuries before that idea could have been imparted to the Greeks from Babylon.

Sufficient data cannot, of course, be expected from the sculptures of the tombs, and the accidental introduction of their occupations, to enable us to form an accurate opinion respecting the extent of their knowledge, the variety of their inventions, or the skill of their workmen in different branches of art. The objects buried with the dead were frequently mere models of those they used; and the pains taken in making them depended on the sums expended by the friends of the deceased after his death. It was left to their good intentions or their superstitious feelings to decide of what quality they should be, or what labour should be bestowed upon them; and if the kind regards of a friend frequently induced some to incur considerable expense in providing such objects, many, on the other hand, were less scrupulous in the last duties to their departed relative. The former purchased ornaments of the most costly materials, as agate, basalt, granite, alabaster, onyx, jasper, gold, and precious stones; the latter were contented with common porcelain, wax, limestone, or wood. But even the best which have been found in the tombs are evidently of inferior quality; and, like their vases and chairs, none have been discovered equal in beauty to those represented in the paintings, with the exception of a few rings and some female ornaments which had been actually worn by the deceased.

The paintings, again, indicate a very small portion of their inventions: many, with which we know they were acquainted, are omitted; and the same remark applies to some of the most common occupations, to the animals they kept, and to the ordinary productions of their country. No exact notion can even be formed of their costume and the dresses of various grades, either among men or women, though so frequently represented, partly owing to their conventional style of drawing figures, partly to their want of skill in depicting drapery; it is, therefore, only the most simple portion of their dress which can be understood.

Ordinary workmen, and indeed all the lower orders, were clad in a sort of apron, or kelt, sometimes simply bound round the loins, and lapping over in front;* and others had short drawers, extending half way to the knee.† The same kind of apron was worn by the higher orders, under an ample dress of fine linen reaching to the ankles,‡ and provided with large sleeves.§ The apron was generally fastened by a girdle, or by a sort of sash, tied in front with a bow or knot:∥ it was sometimes folded over, with a centre-piece falling down in front, beneath the part where it overlapped; and some of the poor classes, while engaged in laborious occupations, were contented with a roll of linen passed between the legs from the back to the front of the girdle.¶ This last is frequently used at the present day by the peasants, when drawing water by the *shadoóf*; some of whom are satisfied with a few leaves, in Adam-like, or in River-god, simplicity.

Herodotus mentions some Egyptian dresses, which he describes of linen, with a fringe on the border around the legs, called *calasiris*; over which they wore a cloak of white wool, similar, no doubt, to the *bornous* of the present day, so common in Egypt and the coast of Barbary. (*See above*, p. 91, and vol. i., p. 333.)

* Woodcut 459. † Woodcut 384, *fig.* 1, and *fig.* 2 *j*.
‡ Woodcut 156, *figs*. 6, 8. § Woodcuts 251 and 30, *fig.* 5.
∥ Woodcut 407. ¶ Woodcut 459, *fig.* 7.

CHAP. IX.   DRESSES.   321

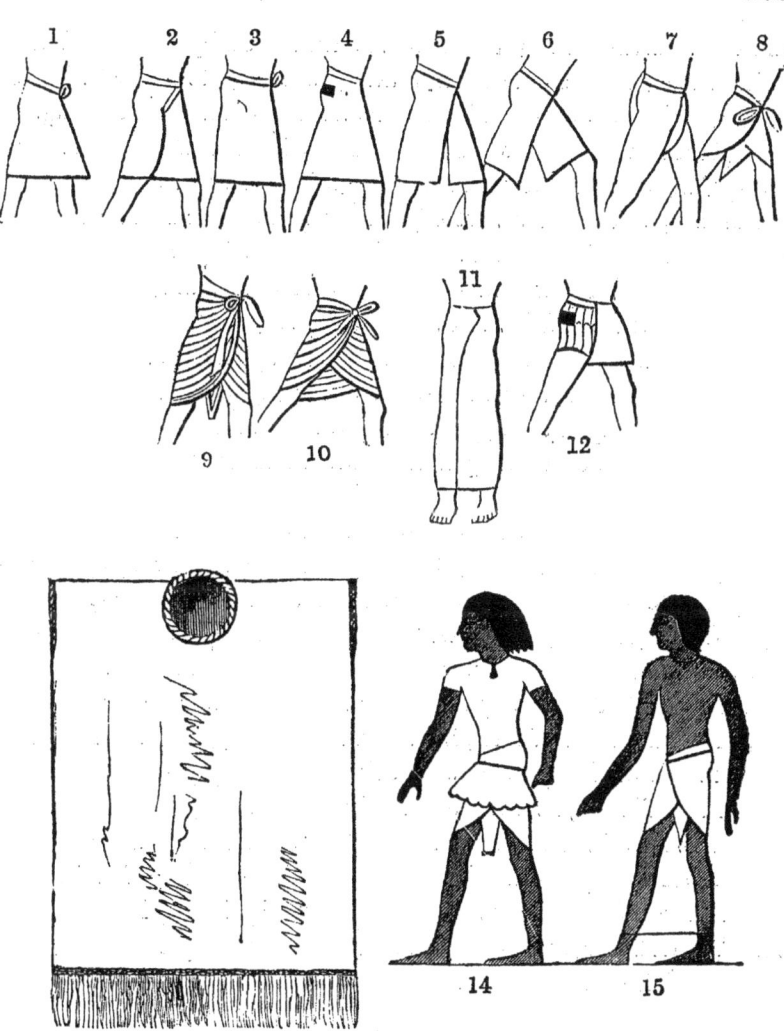

459.   Men's dresses.   13, a shirt, from the work of Prof. Rosellini.

The same custom of edging their dresses with fringes was common to the Israelites, who were ordered to make them " in the borders of their garments;" "a blue riband" being " put upon the fringe;" and, as already observed, they were only the ends of the threads composing the woof, left in order to prevent

P 2

the cloth unravelling; the blue riband added by the Israelites being intended to strengthen it, and prevent its tearing. These fringed dresses are occasionally represented in the paintings; and pieces of cloth have been found with the same kind of border, which in some instances have been sewed on.

Some people wore a sort of shirt with loose or light sleeves, open at the neck, where it was tied with strings; and except that it was linen instead of wool, it was not unlike the *bisht* of the modern inhabitants of Upper Egypt.

The dresses of the priests, which, excepting those of ceremony, were much the same as of other persons of rank, have been already mentioned, as well as the geoffreying process, by which the folds or waving lines were impressed upon the fine linen they wore.*

The princes wore a dress very like that of the sacred scribe, the apron wound round the body, and divided into three different folds, over which was a garment with long sleeves; but their distinguishing mark was a peculiar badge at the side of the head, descending to the shoulder, and frequently adorned and terminated with a gold fringe. This I suppose to have contained the lock of hair, indicative of youth, which is seen in the statues of Harpocrates, and frequently represented on the heads of children, as I have already shown.†

The robes of the sovereign varied, of course, according to his immediate occupation. When engaged as high-priest, they much resembled those worn by the principal functionaries of the sacerdotal order, with the exception of the apron and headdress, which were of peculiar form, and belonged exclusively to his rank as king.

This apron was richly ornamented in front with lions' heads, and other devices, probably of coloured leather; and the border was frequently formed of a row of asps, the emblems of royalty. Sometimes the royal name, with an asp on each side, as *supporters*, was embroidered upon it, the upper part being divided into square

---

* In vol. i. p. 334; and vol. ii. p. 92.
† *See* vol. i. p. 311, and woodcuts 279, 105, *fig.* 2.

compartments of different colours; but it is not improbable that this formed an appendage to the girdle rather than to the apron; and several straps falling down at the side of the centre-piece show that it was tied in front, and came ever the folds of the apron, and even of the upper robes.

460. Dress of the king.
2, 3, the king's apron. 3 is from a statue of Amunoph III. in the museum at Alnwick Castle. 4, wreath of the crown of Sabaco's statue at the Isle of Argo.

The head-dress of the king, on state occasions, was the crown of the Upper or of the Lower country, or the *pshent*, the union of the two. Every king, after the sovereignty of the Thebaid and Lower Egypt had become once more vested in the same person, put on this double crown at his coronation; and we find in the grand representation given of this ceremony at Medeenet Haboo, that the principal feature of the proclamation, on his ascension to the throne, was the announcement to the four sides of the world that "Remeses had put on the crown of the Upper and Lower country." (*See crowns and head-dresses in Woodcut* 461.)

He even wore his crown during the heat of battle; sometimes merely a wig; but a helmet made apparently of woollen stuff with a thick nap, not very unlike the modern Persian cap, was generally preferred; and, in religious ceremonies, he put on a striped head-dress, probably of linen, which descended in front over the breast, and terminated behind in a sort of *queue* bound with riband. This last is the one generally worn by sphinxes, which were emblems of the king.

When crowned, the king invariably put on the two crowns at the same time, though on other occasions he was permitted to wear each separately, whether in the temple, the city, or the field of battle; and he even appeared in his helmet during the ceremonies in honour of the gods. On some occasions he wore a short wig, on which a band was fastened, ornamented with an asp, the emblem of royalty.

It may appear singular that so warm a covering to the head should have been adopted in the climate of Egypt; but when we recollect that they always shaved the head, and that the reticulated texture of the groundwork, on which the hair was fastened, allowed the heat of the head to escape, while the hair effectually protected it from the sun, it is evident that no better covering could have been devised, and that it far surpassed in comfort and coolness the modern turban, which is always found, by those who are in the habit of wearing it, to be very agreeable in hot weather, provided all the particulars are attended to, which the Turks find so essential, but which those Europeans who merely put it on for effect too often neglect.

The upper portion of the wig was frequently made with curled, and not with plaited hair, this last being confined to the sides and lower part, as is the case in the wigs preserved in the British and Berlin museums; but the whole was sometimes composed of a succession of plaits, commencing from the centre of the crown, extending downwards, and increasing in length towards the bottom. Some smaller wigs, worn by persons of rank, consisted of short locks of equal length, arranged in uniform

CHAP. IX. CROWNS. WIGS. 325

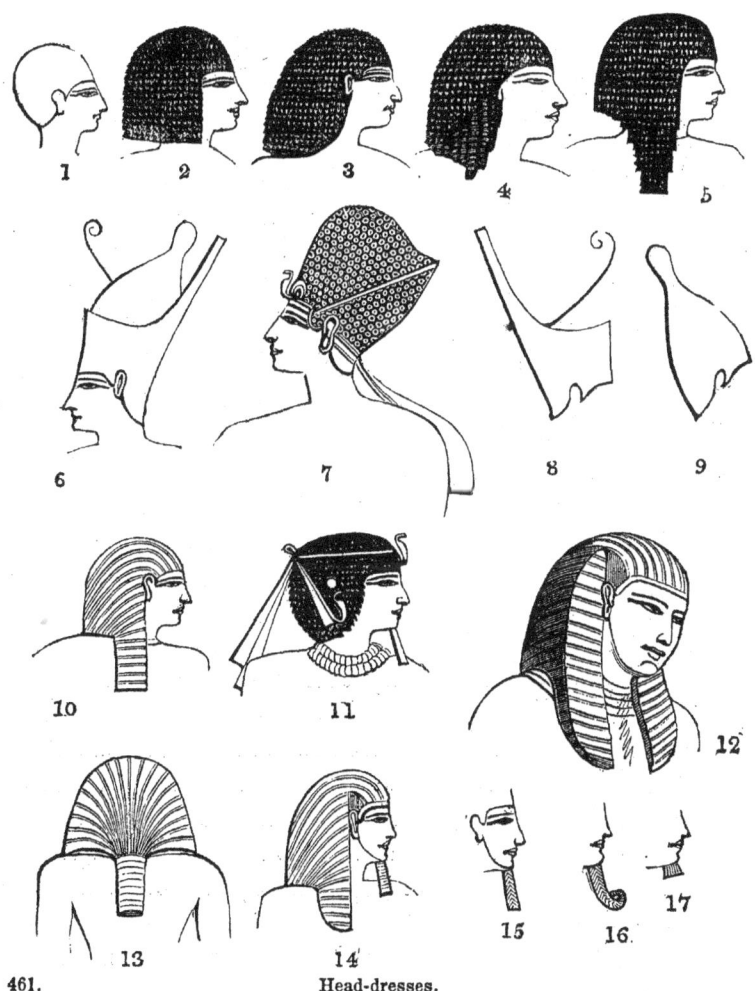

461. Head-dresses.

1, a close cap.   2, 3, 4, 5, wigs.   6, the crown *Pshent* of the upper and lower country, or 9 and 8 united.   10 to 14, royal head-dresses.   15, beard of a god.   17, of a king.   16, of a private individual of rank.

lines, imitations of which appear to have been made in woollen or other stuffs, under the denomination of false wigs, for the use of those who could not afford the more expensive quality of real hair.

Wigs were worn both within the house and out of doors, like the turban of the present day; and a priest might even officiate

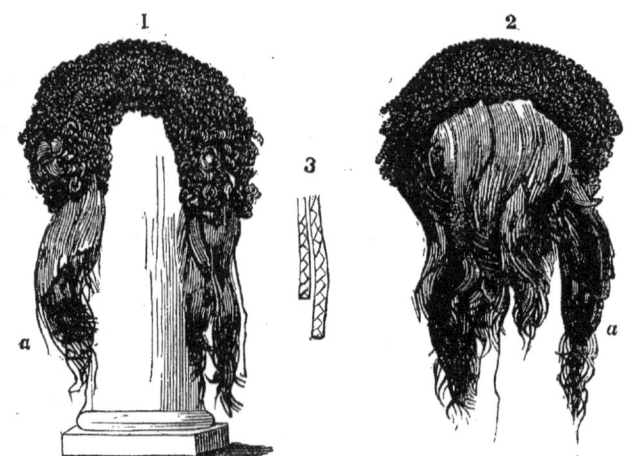

462. Front and back of an Egyptian wig, in the British Museum. 3 shows the appearance of the long plaits, *a a*.

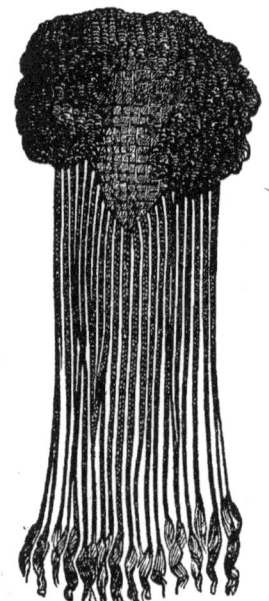

463. Wig about 2½ feet in length, seen in front. *Berlin Museum.*

on some occasions in his wig. At parties, the head-dress of every guest was bound with a chaplet of flowers, and ointment was put upon the top of the wig, as if it had really been the hair of the head; and one instance occurs of a wreath of leaves placed round the crown of a king, on a statue in the Isle of Argo, in Ethiopia, precisely similar to those worn by the Romans. (*Woodcut* 460, *fig.* 4.)

The Egyptians, says Herodotus, "only let the hair of their head and beard grow in mourning, being at all other times shaved;" which agrees perfectly with the authority of the sculptures, and of the Bible, where Joseph is said to have "shaved himself" when sent for from prison by Pharaoh. So particular, indeed, were they on this point, that to have neglected it was a subject of reproach and ridicule; and whenever they intended to convey the idea of a man of low condition, or a slovenly person, the artists represented him with a beard.· It is amusing to find that their love of caricature was not confined to the lower orders, but extended even to the king: and the negligent habits of Remeses VII. are indicated in his tomb at Thebes by the appearance of his chin, blackened by an unshorn beard of two or three days' growth. But it was likewise given as the test of hardships undergone in a severe campaign; and the warlike character of Remeses the Great is pointed out in the same manner.

The Egyptians did not confine the privilege of shaving to freeborn citizens, like the Romans, who obliged slaves to wear their beards and hair long, and only permitted them the use of a cap after they had been enfranchised; and though foreigners, who were brought to Egypt as slaves, had beards on their arrival in the country, we find that so soon as they were employed in the service of this civilized people, they were obliged to conform to the cleanly habits of their masters; their beards and heads were shaved; and they adopted a close cap.

The priests were remarkable for their love of cleanliness, which was carried so far, that they shaved the whole body every three days, and performed frequent daily ablutions, bathing twice a day, and twice during the night. It was not confined to their order; every Egyptian prided himself on the encouragement of habits, which it was considered a disgrace to neglect: we can, therefore, readily account for the disgust they felt on seeing the squalid appearance and unrefined habits of their Asiatic neighbours, whose long beards were often the subject of ridicule to the Egyptian soldier; and for their abhorrence of the bearded and long-haired Greeks, which was so great, that, according to Herodotus, "no Egyptian of either sex would on any account kiss the lips of a Greek, make use of his knife, his spit and cauldron, or taste the meat of an animal which had been slaughtered by his hand."* The same habits of cleanliness are also indicated by the "changes of raiment" given by Joseph to his brethren, when they set out to fetch their father to Egypt.

Barbers may be considered the offspring of civilization; and as a Roman youth, when arrived at the age of manhood, cut off his beard, and consecrated it to some deity, as a token of his having emerged from a state of childhood, so a people, until they have adopted the custom of shaving, may be supposed to retain a remnant of their early barbarism.

With the Egyptians it was customary to shave the heads even of young children, leaving only certain locks at the front, sides, and back ; and those of the lower classes were allowed to go out in the sun with the head exposed, without the protection of a cap ; which is the reason assigned by Herodotus for the hardness of the Egyptian skulls, compared with those of other people. " I became acquainted," says the historian, " with a remarkable fact, which was pointed out to me by the people living in the neighbourhood of the field of battle, where the Egyptians and the army of Cambyses fought; the bones of the killed being still scattered about, those of the Persians on one side, and of the Egyptians on the other. I observed that the skulls of the former were so soft that you could perforate them with a small pebble, while those of the latter were so strong that with difficulty you could break them with a large stone. The reason of which, as they told me, and I can readily believe it, is that, the Egyptians being in the habit of shaving their heads from early youth, the bones become thickened : and hence, too, they are never bald ; for, certainly, of all countries, nowhere do you see fewer bald people than in Egypt. The Persians, on the contrary, have soft skulls, in consequence of their keeping the head covered from the sun, and enveloped in soft caps. I also observed the same of those who were killed in the battle between Achæmenes and Inarus the Libyan."

It was usual for the lower orders to work in the sun without any covering for the head, as the modern peasants of Egypt, who appear (*fortunately*) to inherit from their predecessors skulls of uncommon hardness ; and we see the same class of persons represented in the paintings with and without a cap, whether in the house or in the open field.

Persons of all classes occasionally wore caps, some of which were large, others fitting tight to the head ; but these last were considered far less becoming than the wig, and suited rather to the lower orders than to persons of rank. Women always wore their own hair, and they were not shaved even in mourning, or after death.

The use of wigs was not confined to the Egyptians of all people of antiquity; the Romans, under the emperors, also adopted a sort of peruke, called *capillamentum* or *galerus*, though it seems rather to have been worn by women than men; and Juvenal describes Messalina putting on a wig of flaxen hair to conceal her own black locks, when she left the palace in disguise.

The most singular custom of the Egyptians was that of tying a false beard upon the chin, which was made of plaited hair, and of a peculiar form, according to the person by whom it was worn. Private individuals had a small beard, scarcely two inches long; that of a king was of considerable length, square at the bottom; and the figures of gods were distinguished by its turning up at the end. No man ventured to assume, or affix to his image, the beard of a deity; but after their death, it was permitted to substitute this divine emblem on the statues of kings, and all other persons who were judged worthy of admittance to the Elysium of futurity, in consequence of their having assumed the character of Osiris, to whom the souls of the pure returned on quitting their earthly abode. The form of the beard, therefore, readily distinguishes the figures of gods and kings in the sacred subjects of the temples; and the allegorical connexion between the sphinx and the monarch is pointed out by its having the kingly beard, as well as the crown, and other symbols of royalty.

This title of "Osiris" seems, in the oldest times, to have been confined to the deceased kings (as Mr. Birch has observed); and it was only on, or a little before, the accession of the 18th dynasty, that it was given to "good men" of all ranks, at their death.

The dresses of children of the lower classes were very simple; and as Diodorus informs us, the expenses incurred in feeding and clothing them amounted to a mere trifle. " They feed them," he says, " very lightly, and at an incredibly small cost; . . . . . and since most of them are brought up, on account of the mildness of the climate, without shoes, and, indeed, without any other clothing, the whole expense incurred by the parents does not exceed 20 drachmæ (13 shillings) each; and this frugality is the true reason of the populousness of Egypt." But the children of the higher orders were often dressed like grown persons, with a loose robe, reaching to the ankles, and sandals.

Infants do not appear to have been swaddled, as among the Jews, Greeks, and Romans. When too young to walk, if taken out by a mother or nurse, they were carried in a shawl, suspended at her back, or before her; a custom still retained by the

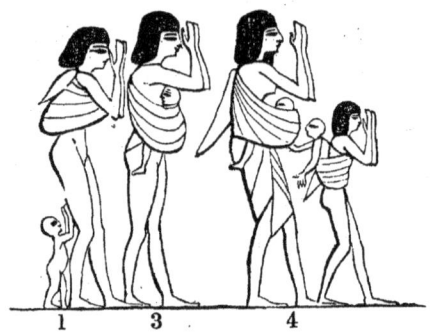

464.   Women carrying their children in a funeral procession.   *Thebes.*

women of the Moghrebin Arabs; and in Ethiopia they were carried in baskets, supported at the mother's back by a band passing over her forehead.*

Sometimes, though nearly or entirely naked, the neck of an Egyptian child was decorated with a string of beads; and occasionally a *bulla*, or charm, was suspended in the centre, representing the symbol of truth and justice, which has been supposed also to indicate the heart, and is usually found in the balance of the judgment scenes, as a representative of the good works of the deceased. A *bulla* of this kind was worn by the youthful deity Harpocrates.

It was probably of gold, or hard stone, like those of the Romans; and others worn by the poorer classes, as at Rome, and in modern Egypt, were of leather. They were supposed to prompt the wearer to virtue and wisdom, to keep off the evil eye, or to

* Woodcut 354.

CHAP. IX. CHARMS. SANDALS. 331

avert misfortune; and superstition induced many to appeal to them in danger, and derive from them omens of forthcoming events. Sometimes a charm consisted of a written piece of papyrus tightly rolled up, and sewed into a covering of linen, or other substance, several of which have been found at Thebes; and emblems of various deities were appended to necklaces for the same purpose.

Ladies and men of rank paid great attention to the beauty of their sandals; but on some occasions, those of the middle classes who were in the habit of wearing them preferred walking barefooted; and in religious ceremonies, the priests frequently took them off while performing their duties in the temple.

The sandals varied slightly in form; those worn by the upper classes, and by women, were usually pointed and turned up at the end, like our skates, and many Eastern slippers of the present day. Some had a sharp flat point, others were nearly round.

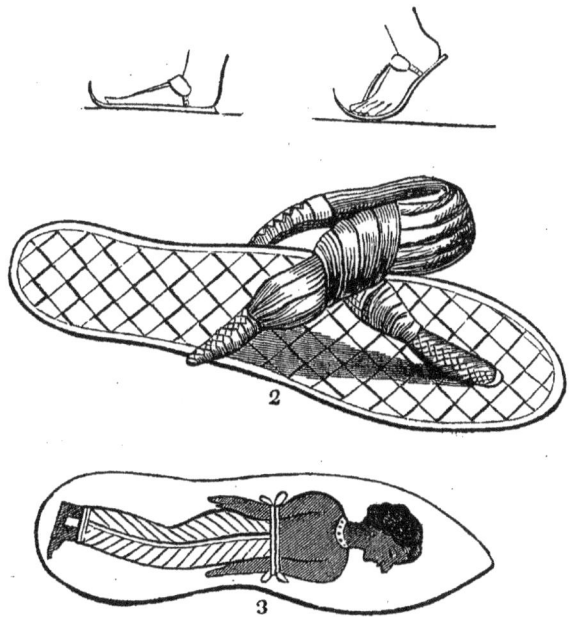

465. Sandals. *Berlin Museum.*
1. From the sculptures. 2. In the Berlin Museum; made of the papyrus.
3. Figure of a captive on the sole.

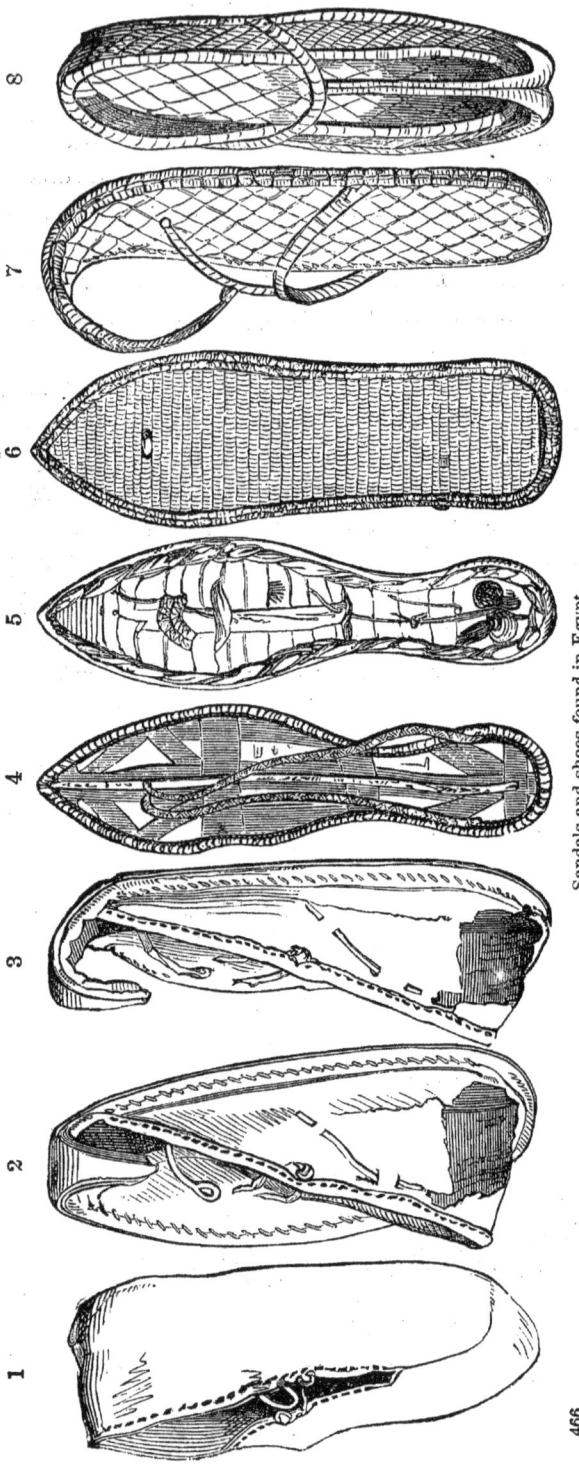

466. Sandals and shoes found in Egypt.

1, 2, 3. Shoes of green leather, probably of Greek time. Mr. Salt's Collection. 4, 5. Upper and lower side of a pair of sandals, made of palm leaves and the papyrus, 11 inches long and 3 broad. In the Museum of Alnwick Castle. 6. Sole of a sandal, 1 foot long and 3¾ inches broad. Alnwick Castle.
7. A sandal; and 8. A sandal with sides like a shoe. Both in the Berlin Collection.

They were made of a sort of woven or interlaced work, of palm leaves and papyrus stalks, or other similar materials; sometimes of leather; and were frequently lined within with cloth, on which the figure of a captive was painted;* that humiliating position being considered suited to the enemies of their country, whom they hated and despised—an idea agreeing perfectly with the expression which so often occurs in the hieroglyphic legends, accompanying a king's name, when his valour and victories are recorded on the sculptures: "You have trodden the impure Gentiles under your powerful feet."

Shoes, or low boots, were also common in Egypt, many having been found at Thebes;† but these I believe to have been of late date, and to have belonged to Greeks; for, since no persons are represented in the paintings wearing them except foreigners, we may conclude they were not adopted by the Egyptians, at least in a Pharaonic age. They were of leather, generally of a green colour; laced in front with thongs, which passed through small loops on either side; and were principally used, as in Greece and Etruria, by women.

The dresses of women consisted sometimes of a loose robe or shirt, reaching to the ankles, with tight or full sleeves, and fastened at the neck, like those of the men, with a string;‡ over which they often wore a sort of petticoat, secured at the waist by a girdle; and this last, in mourning, while bewailing the death of a relative, was frequently their only dress.§

Such was the costume of the lower classes of women; and, sometimes indeed, as at the present day, it consisted merely of the loose skirt or robe, without shoes or sandals.

The higher orders wore a petticoat, or gown, secured at the waist by a coloured sash, or by straps over the shoulders; and above this was a large loose robe, made of the finest linen, with full sleeves,‖ and tied in front below the breast; and during some religious ceremonies¶ the right arm was taken out of the sleeve, and left exposed as in the funeral processions. The petticoat or

* Woodcut 465, *fig.* 3.
† Woodcut 466, *figs.* 1, 2, 3.
‡ Woodcut 125, *fig.* 2.
§ Woodcut 280.
‖ Woodcut 282, *fig.* 5.
¶ Woodcut 282, *figs.* 1, 2, and 3.

467. Dresses of women.

The sash in figs. 1 and 2, though represented at the side, is to be understood as tied in front. In fig. 3 the side hair appears to be fixed by a comb; and before it, on the cheek, the short hair is arranged in separate plaits. 4 shows the skirt tied at the neck: it is a terra cotta statue.

gown was of richly-coloured stuff, presenting a great variety of patterns, not unlike our modern chintzes, the most elegant of which were selected for the robes of deities and the dresses of queens.

Slaves or servants were not allowed to wear the same costume as ladies, and their mode of dressing the hair was different. They generally bound it at the back part of the head, into a sort of loop, or ranged it in one or more long plaits at the back, and eight or nine similar ones were suffered to hang down at either side of the neck and face.* They wore a long tight gown, tied at the neck, with short close sleeves, reaching nearly to the elbow; and sometimes a long loose robe was thrown over it, when employed to dance, or to present themselves on festive occasions.

* Woodcuts 151 and 158.

Ladies wore their hair long, and plaited. The back part was made to consist of a number of strings of hair, reaching to the bottom of the shoulder blades, and on each side other strings of the same length descended over the breast. The hair was plaited in the triple plait, the ends being left loose; or, more usually, two or three plaits were fastened together at the extremity by a woollen string of corresponding colour. Around the head was bound an ornamental fillet, with a lotus bud, by way of *feronière*, falling over the forehead; and the strings of hair, at the sides, were separated and secured with a comb, or a band, ornamented in various ways, according to the fancy of the wearer: and occasionally a round stud, or pin, was thrust into them at the front.

468. Head-dress of a lady, from a mummy case.

The short hair at the side of the face, which the ingenuity of ancient Rome, and modern European ladies, has, by the aid of gum, compelled to lie in an immovable curve upon the cheek, was interwoven with several of its longer neighbours; and these, being bound together at the end with string, fell down before the earring, which they partially concealed, or in a simple corkscrew curl. Many of the mummies of women have been found with the hair perfectly preserved, plaited in the manner I have mentioned; the only alteration in its appearance being the change of its black hue, which became reddened by exposure to great heat during the process of embalming.

The ancient mode of plaiting the hair seems to have been very similar to that of the women in modern Ethiopia, where, too, young girls wear a girdle, or rope, of twisted hair, leather, or other materials, decorated with shells, round the hips.*

The earrings, most usually worn by Egyptian ladies, were large, round, single hoops† of gold, from one inch and a half to two inches and one third in diameter, and frequently of a still

* *See* woodcuts 98, 125, 151.   † Woodcuts 474, *fig* 5, and 159.

greater size; or made of six rings soldered together;* sometimes an asp, whose body was of gold set with precious stones, was worn by persons of rank, as a fashionable caprice; but it is probable that this emblem of majesty was usually confined to members of the royal family.

Earrings of other forms have also been found at Thebes, but their date is uncertain; and it is difficult to say if they are of an ancient Egyptian age, or of Greek introduction. Of these, the most remarkable are a dragon,† and another of fancy shape, which is not inelegant.‡ Some few were of silver, and plain hoops, like those made of gold, already noticed, but less massive, being of the thickness of an ordinary ring. At one end was a small opening, into which the curved extremity of the other caught after it had been passed through the ear;§ and others were in the form of simple studs.

Though gloves do not appear to have been worn by Egyptian women, they were known as early as the 18th dynasty, and brought as part of a tribute to Thothmes III. by the Rot-ṅ-n, an Asiatic people; and long linen gloves, ornamented with a blue stripe, have been found in Egypt.

They wore many rings, sometimes two and three on the same

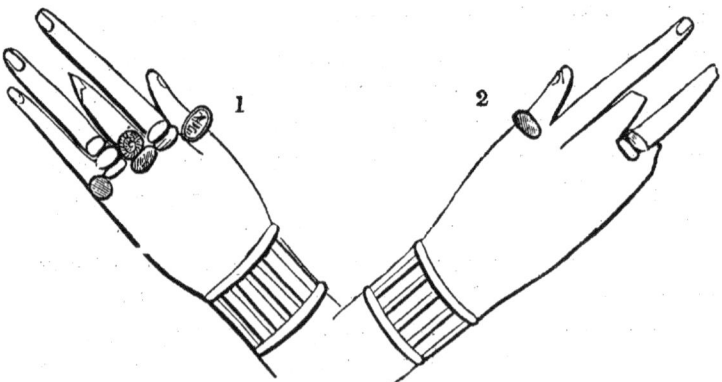

469. Hands of a wooden figure of a woman. On the lid of a mummy case in Mr. Salt's Collection, now in the British Museum. 1. The left; 2. The right hand.

* Woodcut 474, *figs.* 6 and 7.
† Woodcut 470, *fig.* 10, not unlike one of the Chinese dragons.
‡ Woodcut 470, *fig.* 21. § Woodcut 474, *fig.* 5.

finger; the left was considered the hand peculiarly privileged to bear those ornaments, and it is remarkable that its third finger was decorated with a greater number than any other, and was considered by them, as by us, *par excellence* the ring finger, though there is no evidence of its having been so honoured at the marriage ceremony. They even wore a ring on the thumb; and I have seen, upon the right hand of a wooden figure, a ring on the thumb, and two on the third finger; and upon the left, one upon the thumb and little finger, two on the fore and second finger, and three on the third. One on the third finger is in the form of a *trochus* shell, very common in the Red Sea.

Some rings were simple; others were made with a scarabæus, or an engraved stone; and they were occasionally in the form of a shell, a knot, a snake, or some fancy device. They were mostly of gold; and this metal seems to have been always preferred to silver, for rings and other articles of jewellery. Silver rings, however, are occasionally met with; and two in my possession, which were accidentally found in a temple at Thebes, are engraved with hieroglyphics, containing the name of the royal city.

Bronze was seldom used for rings, though frequently for signets. Some have been discovered of brass and iron (the latter of a Roman time); but ivory and blue porcelain were the materials of which those worn by the lower classes were usually made. The scarabæus was the favourite form both for rings and the ordinary ornaments of necklaces; in some the stone, flat on both faces, turned on pins, like many of our seals at the present day, and the ring itself was bound round at each end, where it was inserted into the stone, with gold wire. This was common not only to rings, but to signets, and was intended for ornament as well as security.

One of the largest signets I have seen contained twenty pounds worth of gold. (*Woodcut* 470, *figs*. 4, 5, 6, 7.)

It consisted of a massive ring, half an inch in its largest diameter, bearing an oblong plinth, on which the devices were engraved one inch long, six tenths in its greatest, and four tenths in its smallest breadth. On one face was the name of King Horus,

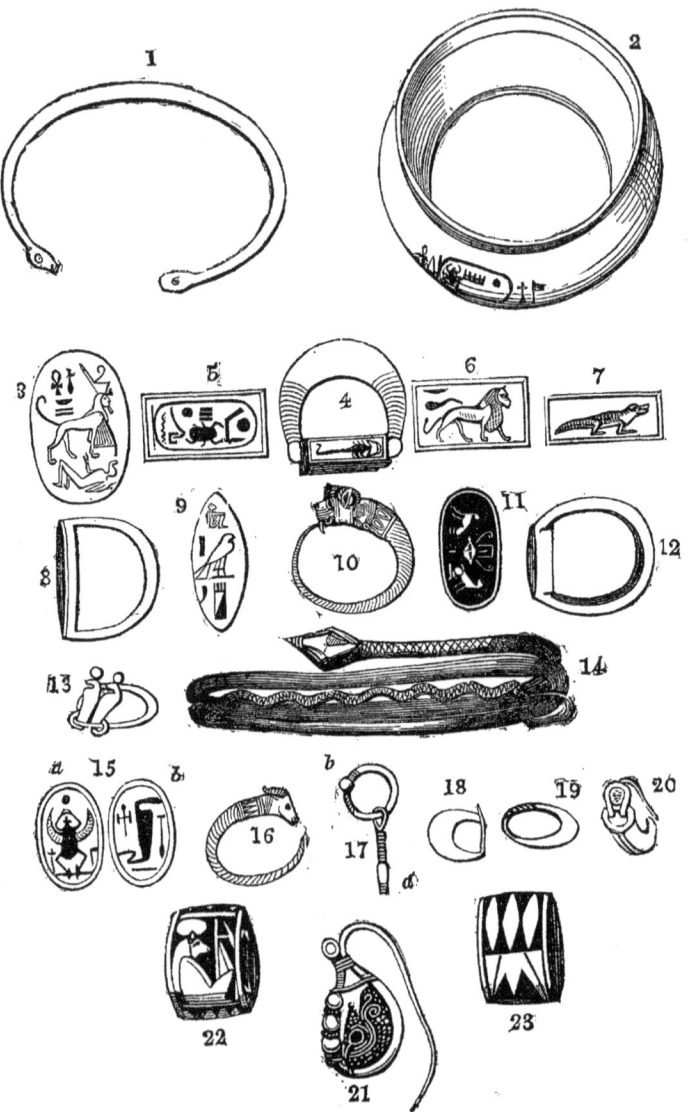

470.   Rings, signets, bracelets, and earrings.

Fig. 1. Bronze bracelet, or bangle, in the Museum of Alnwick Castle.   2. Gold bracelet in the Leyden Museum, bearing the name of Thothmes III., 1¼ inch high, and 3 inches in diameter.   3. Scarabæus of amethyst, with a sphinx, emblematic of the king trampling on a prostrate enemy; over it is the expression "Good God, Lord of the world."   4. A gold signet, mentioned in the last page.   5, 6, 7. The three other sides of the plinth.   8. A gold ring.   9. The engraved face of it.   10. A gold earring, about 1½ inch in diameter.   11. The face of it, of the real size.   12. A gold ring, in my possession, four fifths of an inch in diameter.   13. Gold ring with two asps.   14. A snake bracelet of gold.   15. A stone scarabæus.   16. Gold earring.   17. Gold earring with two pearls, *a* and *b*.   18, 19, 20. Other gold earrings.   21. Gold earring, 1 inch high and six tenths broad.   22, 23. Ring of porcelain, or blue glazed pottery, Museum of Alnwick Castle.

of the 18th dynasty; on the other a lion, with the legend " lord of strength," referring to the monarch; on one side a scorpion, and on the other a crocodile.

Two cats sitting back to back, and looking round towards each other, with an emblem of the goddess Athor between them, seem to have been a favourite device on gold rings; and I have seen three or four of this pattern. (*fig.* 11.)

They also had large gold anklets or bangles, armlets, and bracelets, frequently inlaid with precious stones or enamel, and worn by men as well as women. Some were simple bands or rings of metal; others in the shape of snakes—the last a favourite device among women in all ages, who still continue to be ignorant of the connection between their taste and Eve's temptation by the serpent, so gravely set forth by Clemens in condemnation of this graceful ornament. Kings are often represented with armlets and bracelets; and in the Leyden Museum is a gold bracelet bearing the name of the third Thothmes, which was doubtless once worn by that monarch. (*fig.* 2.)

Handsome and richly-ornamented necklaces were a principal part of the dress, both of men and women; and some idea may be formed of the number of jewels they wore, from those borrowed by the Israelites at the time of the Exodus, and by the paintings of Thebes. They consisted of gold, or of beads of various qualities and shapes, disposed according to fancy, generally with a large drop or figure in the centre. Scarabæi, gold, and cornelian bottles, or the emblems of Goodness and Stability, lotus flowers in enamel, amethysts, pearls, false stones, imitations of fish, frogs, lions, and various quadrupeds, birds, reptiles, flies, and other insects, shells and leaves, with numerous figures and devices, were strung in all the variety which their taste could suggest; and the sole museum of Leyden possesses an infinite assortment of those objects, which were once the pride of the ladies of Thebes.

Some wore simple gold chains in imitation of string, to which a stone scarabæus, set in the same precious metal, was appended; but these probably belonged to men, like the *torques* of the

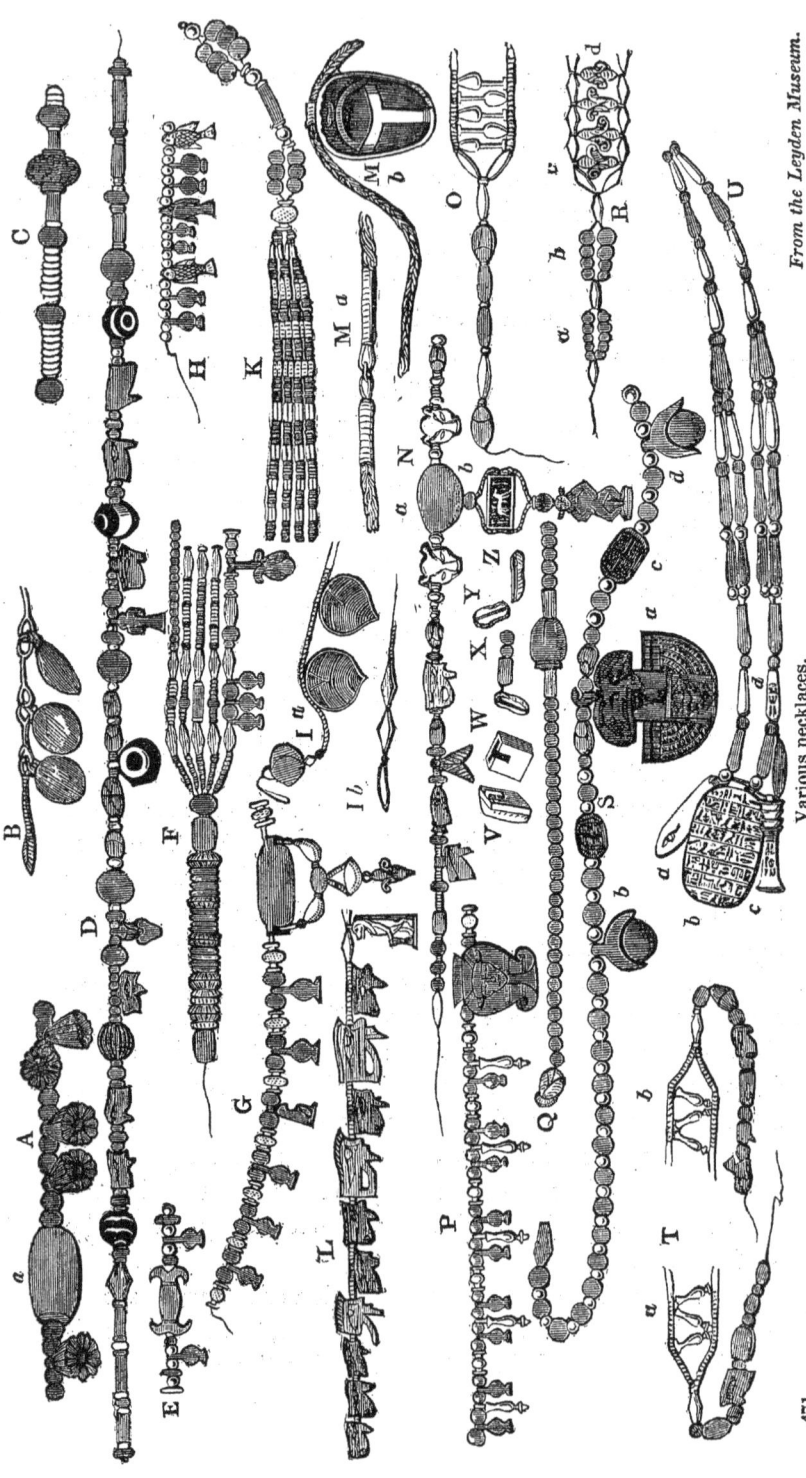

471. B is composed of small covered cups, of bronze gilt. These leaves are of gold, inlaid with lapis lazzuli and green and red stones. M a, a sort of gold *torques* or chain, of which a stone scarabæus found in gold forms the centre ornament. U, in the possession of the late Mr. Madox. V W X Y Z, gold catches of necklaces, one sliding into the other.

Various necklaces. *From the Leyden Museum.*

Romans.* A set of small cups, or covered saucers, of bronze gilt, hanging from a chain of the same materials, were sometimes worn by women, a necklace of which has been found, belonging to a Theban lady—offering a striking contrast in their simplicity to the gold leaves inlaid with lapis lazzuli,† red and green stones, of another she wore, which served, with many more in her possession, to excite the admiration of her friends.

The devices engraved on scarabæi, rings, and other objects of ornamental *luxe*, varied according to the caprice of individuals. Rings frequently bore the name of the wearer; others of the monarch in whose reign he lived; others, again, the emblems of certain deities; and many were mere fanciful combinations. The greater number consisted of scarabæi, mounted upon a gold ring passing through them: the scarabæus itself was of green stone, cornelian, hæmatite, granite, serpentine, agate, lapis lazzuli, root of emerald, amethyst, and other materials; and a cheaper kind was made of limestone, stained to imitate a harder and dearer quality; or of the ordinary blue pottery. Cylinders of stone or blue pottery, bearing devices or hieroglyphics, were also common in necklaces and as signets, one of which, bearing the name of Osirtasen I. (in the Alnwick Museum), proves them to have been of the earliest date in Egypt, and the origin of, rather than derived from, the Cylinders of Assyria. From the number of scarabæi discovered, some have hastily supposed they served as money; but they were either ornamental, funereal, or historical; and some of these last of great size, bearing the name of Amunoph III. and his queen Taia, relate to his conquests, his lion hunts, her parentage, or to public works executed during their reign.

Of the various objects of the toilet found at Thebes and other places, the principal are bottles, or vases, for holding ointment, and *kohl* or collyrium for the eyes, mirrors, combs, and the small boxes, spoons, and saucers already mentioned. The ointment was scented in various ways; some preserved in the

* Pharaoh " put a gold chain about (Joseph's) neck," Gen. xli. 42 ; and " a ring upon Joseph's hand." *See* woodcut 471, *fig*. M.

† Woodcut 471, *figs*. B, I. *a*.

museum at Alnwick Castle has retained its odour for several centuries; and the great use of ointment by the Egyptians is sufficiently indicated in the paintings representing the reception of guests.

With the exception of the little found in the tombs, we have nothing to guide us respecting the nature of Egyptian ointments. Some appear to be made with a nut oil, but it is probable that animal as well as vegetable grease was employed for this purpose, the other ingredients depending on the taste of the maker or the purchaser. Julius Pollux mentions a black kind made in Egypt, and speaks of the *sagdas* (*psagdæ*) as an ointment of that country. Theophrastus, on the contrary, states that Egyptian ointments were colourless; but we can readily account for this variance of opinion by supposing that they had in view two different qualities, which is further proved by the fact of our finding them both preserved at Thebes. (*See* p. 23, 27, 32, and vol. i. p. 259.)

Ointment was frequently kept in *alabaster* bottles, or vases (whence the Greeks applied the name of *alabastron* even to one made of other materials); sometimes in those of the onyx, or other stone, glass, ivory, bone, or shells, specimens of all of which have been discovered in the tombs.

Strabo says that the common people, both men and women, used the oil of the *kiki*, or castor-berry, for anointing themselves, the general purpose to which it was applied being for lamps; and many oils, as from the *simsim*, olive, almond, flax, *selgam* (cole-seed), *seemga*, lettuce, and other vegetable productions, were extracted in Egypt. (*See above*, p. 23 to 32.)

The Egyptian combs were usually of wood, and double, one side having large, the other small teeth; the centre part was frequently ornamented with carved work, and, perhaps, inlaid. They were about four inches long, and six deep; and those with a single row of teeth were sometimes surmounted with the figure of an ibex, or other animal.

The custom of staining the eyelids and brows with a moistened powder of a black colour was common in Egypt from the earliest times; it was also introduced among the Jews and

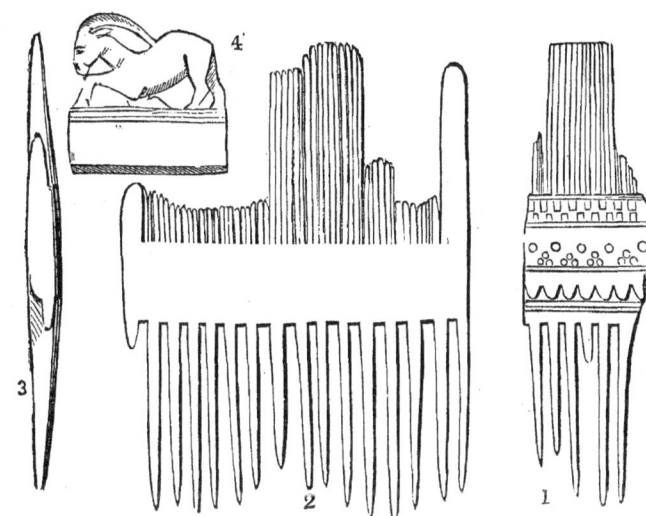

472. Combs found at Thebes.
1. Comb with the centre part ornamented. 3. Side view of fig. 2.
4. An ibex, supposed to have formed the top of a comb.

Romans; and is retained in the East to the present day. It is thought to increase the beauty of the eye, which is made to appear larger by this external addition of a black ring; and many even suppose the stimulus its application gives to be beneficial to the sight. It is made in various ways. Some use antimony, black oxide of manganese, preparations of lead, and other mineral substances; others, the black powder of burnt almonds, or frankincense; and many prefer a mixture of different ingredients for making the *Kohl*.

Mr. Lane is perfectly correct in stating that the expression "painted her face," which Jezebel is said to have done when Jehu came to Jezreel, is in the Hebrew "painted her eyes;" the same is again mentioned in Jeremiah and Ezekiel; and the lengthened form of the ancient Egyptian eye, represented in the paintings, was probably produced, as Mr. Lane supposes, by this means.

Many of the *Kohl* bottles have been found in the tombs, together with the bodkin used for applying the moistened powder. They are of various materials, usually stone, wood, or pottery, sometimes composed of two, sometimes of four and five separate cells, apparently containing each a mixture, differing slightly in its

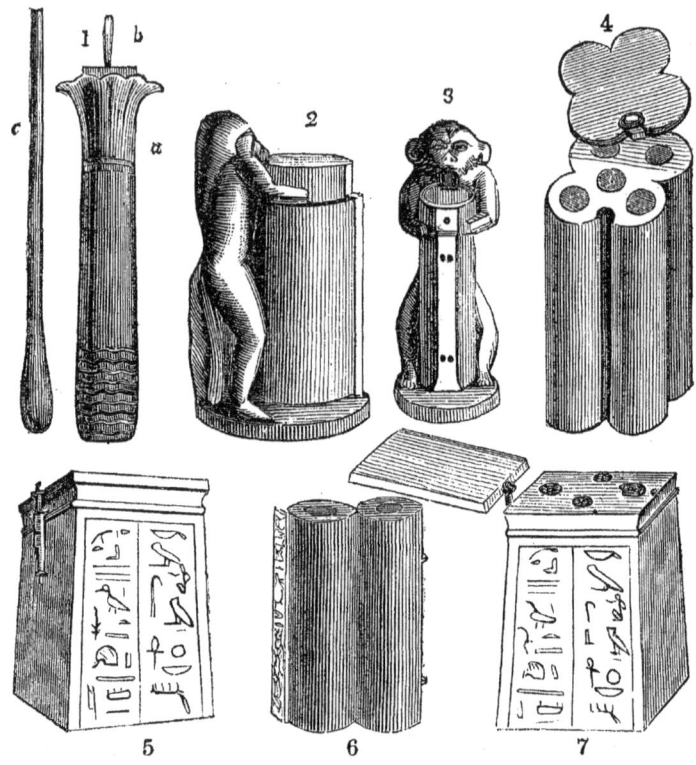

473. Boxes or bottles, holding the *Kohl* for staining the eyelids.

1. In the British Museum. *c* is the bodkin for applying the *Kohl*. The others are in the Museum of Alnwick Castle.

quality and hue from the other three. Many were simple round tubes, vases, or small boxes: some were ornamented with the figure of an ape, or monster, supposed to assist in holding the bottle between his arms, while the lady dipped into it the pin with which she painted her eyes; and others were in imitation of a column made of stone, or rich porcelain of the choicest manufacture.

Pins and needles were also among the articles of the toilet, which have been occasionally found in the tombs. The former are frequently of considerable length, with large gold heads; and some, of a different form, tapering gradually to a point, merely bound with gold at the upper end, without any projecting head (7 or 8 inches in length), appear to have been intended for arranging the plaits or curls of hair, like those used in England, in the days of Elizabeth, for nearly the same purpose.

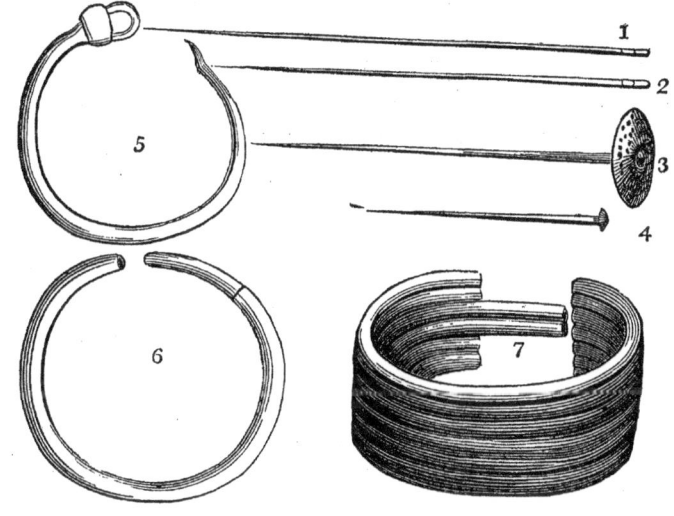

474. Needles, pins, and earrings.

1, 2. Bronze needles, in the Museum of Alnwick Castle, 3 and 3¼ inches long. 3. Large gold-headed pin in the Berlin Collection. 4. Another of smaller size. 5. Silver earring in my possession, one and four tenths of an inch in diameter. 6. Gold earring in the Berlin Museum, one and one third of an inch in diameter. 7. Another, seen from above.

Some needles were of bronze, from three to three and a half inches in length; but as few have been found, we are not able to form any opinion respecting their general size and quality, particularly of those used for fine work, which must have been of a very minute kind.

The custom of staining the fingers with red *henneh* (the pounded leaves of the Lawsonia) was probably of very ancient date in Egypt and the East; and some have attributed the Greek metaphor of "rosy-fingered Aurora" to its use in the East.

One of the principal objects of the toilet was the mirror. It was of mixed metal, chiefly copper, most carefully wrought and highly polished; and so admirably did the skill of the Egyptians succeed in the composition of metals, that this substitute for our modern looking-glass was susceptible of a lustre, which has even been partially revived at the present day in some of those discovered at Thebes, though buried in the earth for many centuries.

The mirror itself was nearly round, inserted into a handle of wood, stone, or metal, whose form varied according to the taste of the owner. Some presented the figure of a female, a flower, a column, or a rod ornamented with the head of Athor, a bird, or a fancy device; and sometimes the face of a Typhonian monster was introduced to support the mirror, serving as a contrast to the

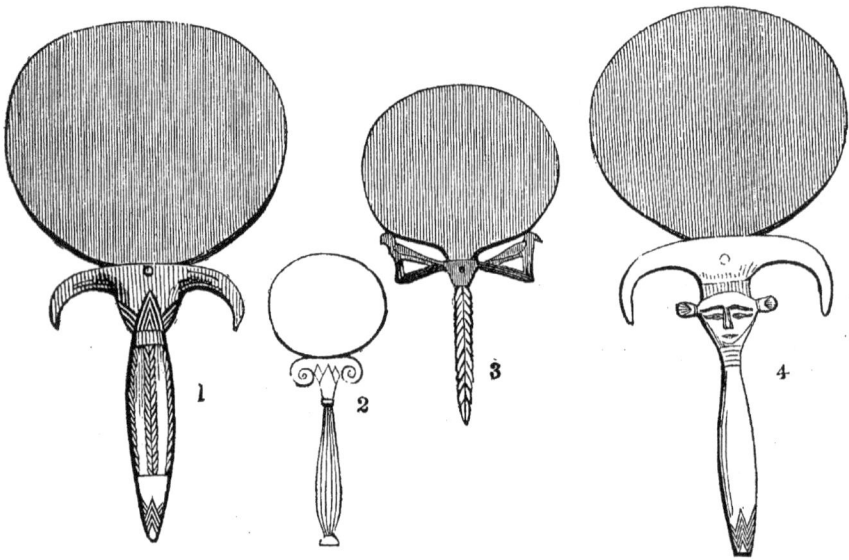

475.   Metal mirrors.   (*See* Woodcut 476, *fig.* 1.)
1, 3, 4, from Mr. Salt's Collection. 2, from a painting at Thebes. 4 is about 11 inches high.

features whose beauty was displayed within it. The same kind of metal mirror was used by the Israelites, who doubtless brought them from Egypt; and the brazen laver made by Moses for the tabernacle was composed " of the *looking-glasses* of the women, which assembled at the door of the tabernacle of the congregation." A similar one is also used to this day in China and Japan.

When walking from home, Egyptian gentlemen frequently carried sticks, varying from three or four to about six feet in length, occasionally surmounted with a knob imitating a flower, or with the more usual peg projecting from one side, some of which have

CHAP. IX.   MIRRORS. STICKS.   347

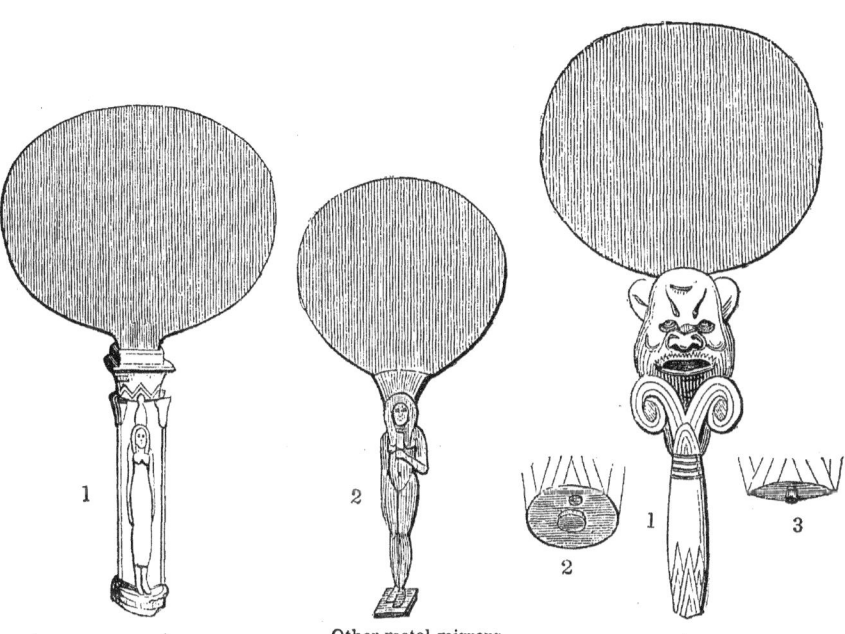

Other metal mirrors.

476. Fig. 1. From Mr. Salt's Collection; with a wooden handle. Fig. 2. In the Museum of Alnwick Castle.   475 a. Was in the possession of Dr. Hogg. 2 and 3 show the bottom of the handle, to which something has been fastened.

been found at Thebes. Many were of *cherry-wood*, only three feet three inches long; and those I have seen with the lotus head

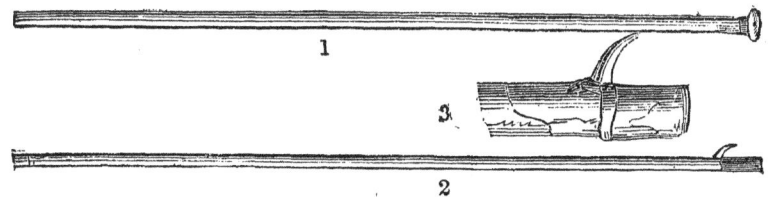

477. Walking-sticks found at Thebes.   2 is of cherry-wood, in Mr. Salt's Collection. 3 shows the peg at the side.

were generally about the same length. Others appear to have been much longer; the sculptures represent them at least six feet; and one brought to England by Mr. Madox was about five feet in length. Some were ornamented with colour and gilding.

On entering a house, they left their stick in the hall or at the door; and poor men were sometimes employed to hold the sticks

478. Priests and other persons of rank walking with sticks. *Thebes.*

of the guests who had come to a party on foot, being rewarded by the master of the house for their trouble with a trifling compensation in money, with their dinner, or a piece of meat to carry to their family. The name of each person was frequently written on his stick, in hieroglyphics, for which reason a hard wood was preferred, as the acacia, which seems to have been more generally used than any other; and on one found at Athribis, the owner had written—"O my stick! the support of my legs," &c.

We have little knowledge of the nature of their baths; but as they were forbidden in deep mourning to indulge in them, we may conclude they were considered as a luxury, as well as a necessary comfort.

The only instance I have met with in the paintings is in a tomb at Thebes, where a lady is represented with four attendants, who wait upon her, and perform various duties.

One removes the jewellery and clothes she has taken off, or suspends them to a stand in the apartment; another pours water from a vase over her head, as the third rubs her arms and body with her open hands; and a fourth seated near her holds a sweet-scented flower to her nose, and supports her as she sits. A similar subject is treated nearly in the same manner on some of the Greek vases, the water being poured over the bather, who kneels, or is seated on the ground.

Warm as well as cold baths were used by the Egyptians, though for ordinary ablutions cold water was preferred; and both were probably recommended medicinally when occasion required.

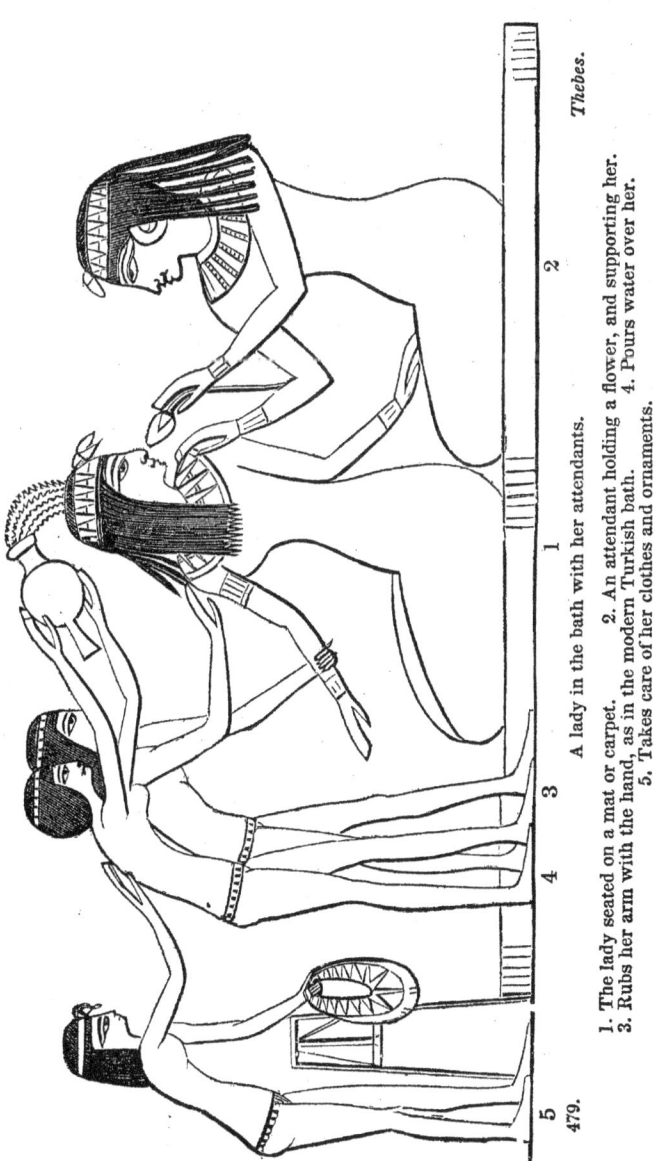

479. 1. The lady seated on a mat or carpet. 2. An attendant holding a flower, and supporting her. 3. Rubs her arm with the hand, as in the modern Turkish bath. 4. Pours water over her. 5. Takes care of her clothes and ornaments.

A lady in the bath with her attendants. *Thebes.*

The Egyptians paid great attention to health, and "so wisely," says Herodotus, "was medicine managed by them, that no doctor was permitted to practise any but his peculiar branch. Some were oculists, who only studied diseases of the eye; others attended solely to complaints of the head; others to those of the teeth; some, again, confined themselves to complaints of the intestines; and others to secret and internal maladies; accoucheurs being usually, if not always, women." And it is a singular fact that their dentists adopted a method, not very long practised in Europe, of stopping teeth with gold, proofs of which have been obtained from some mummies of Thebes.

They received certain salaries from the public treasury; and after they had studied those precepts which had been laid down from the experience of their predecessors, they were permitted to practise; and, in order to prevent dangerous experiments being made upon patients, they might be punished if their treatment was contrary to the established system; and the death of a person intrusted to their care, under such circumstances, was adjudged to them as a capital offence. If, however, every remedy had been administered according to the sanitary law, they were absolved from blame; and if the patient was not better, the physician was allowed to alter the treatment after the third day, or even before, if he took upon himself the responsibility.

Though paid by Government as a body, it was not illegal to receive fees for their advice and attendance; and demands could be made in every instance except on a foreign journey, and on military service, when patients were visited free of expense.

The principal mode adopted by the Egyptians for preventing illness was attention to regimen and diet, "being persuaded that the majority of diseases proceed from indigestion and excess of eating;" and they had frequent recourse to abstinence, emetics, slight doses of medicine, and other simple means of relieving the system, which some persons were in the habit of repeating every two or three days. "Those who live in the corn country," as Herodotus terms it, were particular for their attention to health. "During three successive days, every month, they submitted to a regular course of treatment, from the conviction that illness was wont to proceed from some irregularity in diet;" and if preventives were ineffectual, they had recourse to suitable remedies, adopting a mode of treatment very similar to that mentioned by Diodorus.

The employment of numerous drugs in Egypt has been mentioned by sacred and profane writers; and the medicinal properties of many herbs which grow in the deserts, particularly between the Nile and Red Sea, are still known to the Arabs, though their application has been but imperfectly recorded and preserved.

"O virgin, daughter of Egypt," says Jeremiah, "in vain shalt thou use many medicines, for thou shalt not be cured; and Homer, in the Odyssey, describes the many valuable medicines given by Polydamna, the wife of Thonis, to Helen while in Egypt, "a country whose fertile soil produces an infinity of drugs, some salutary and some pernicious; where each physician possesses knowledge above all other men." Pliny makes frequent mention of the productions of that country, and their use in medicine; he also notices the physicians of Egypt; and as if their number was indicative of the many maladies to which the inhabitants were subject, he observes that it was a country productive of numerous diseases. In this, however, he does not agree with Herodotus, who affirms that, "after the Libyans, there are no people so healthy as the Egyptians, which may be attributed to the invariable nature of the seasons in their country."

Pliny even says that the Egyptians examined the bodies after death, to ascertain the nature of the diseases of which they had died; and we can readily believe that a people so far advanced in civilization and the principles of medicine as to assign to each physician his peculiar branch, would have resorted to this effectual method of acquiring knowledge and experience.

It is evident that the medical science of the Egyptians was sought and appreciated even in foreign countries; and we learn from Herodotus that Cyrus and Darius both sent to Egypt for medical men. In later times, too, they continued to be celebrated for their skill: Ammianus says it was enough for a doctor to say he had studied in Egypt to recommend him; and

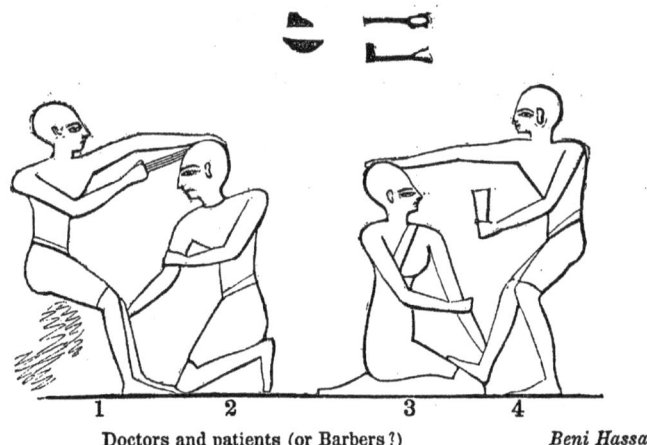

480.   Doctors and patients (or Barbers?)   *Beni Hassan.*

Pliny mentions medical men going from Egypt to Rome. But though their physicians are often noticed by ancient writers, the only indication of medical attendance appears to be in the paintings of Beni Hassan; and even there it is uncertain whether a doctor, or a barber, be represented.

Their doctors probably felt the pulse; as Plutarch shows they did at Rome, from this saying of Tiberius, " a man, after he has passed his thirtieth year, who *puts forth his hand* to a physician, is ridiculous;" whence our proverb of " a fool or a physician after forty."

Diodorus tells us that dreams were regarded in Egypt with religious reverence, and the prayers of the devout were often rewarded by the gods with an indication of the remedy their sufferings required; and magic, charms, and various supernatural agencies were often resorted to by the credulous, who " sought to the idols, and to the charmers, and to them that had familiar spirits, and to the wizards." (*Isaiah*, xix. 3.)

Origen also says, that when any part of the body was afflicted with disease, they invoked the demon to whom it was supposed to belong, in order to obtain a cure.

In cases of great moment oracles were consulted; and a Greek papyrus found in Egypt mentions divination " through a boy with a lamp, a bowl, and a pit," which resembles the pretended power of the modern magicians of Egypt. The same also notices the mode of discovering theft, and obtaining any wish ; and though it is supposed to be of the 2nd century, the practices it alludes to are doubtless from an old Egyptian source ; and other similar papyri contain recipes for obtaining good fortune and various benefits, or for causing misfortunes to an enemy. Some suppose the Egyptians had even recourse to animal magnetism, and that dreams indicating cures were the result of this influence ; and (though the subjects erroneously supposed to represent it apply to a very different act) it is not impossible that they may have discovered the mode of exercising this art, and that it may have been connected with the strange scenes recorded at the initiation into the mysteries. If really known, such a power would scarcely have been neglected ; and it would have been easy to obtain thereby an ascendency over the minds of a superstitious people.

Indeed the readiness of man at all times to astonish on the one hand, and to court the marvellous on the other, is abundantly proved by present and past experience. That the nervous system may be worked upon by it to such a degree that a state either of extreme irritability, or of sleep and coma, may be induced, in the latter case paralyzing the senses so as to become deadened to pain, is certain; and a highly sensitive temperament may exhibit phenomena beyond the reach of explanation ; but it requires very little experience to know that we are wonderfully affected by far more ordinary causes ; for the nerves may be acted upon to such an extent, by having, as we commonly term it, " our teeth set on edge," that the mere filing a saw would suffice to drive any one mad, if unable to escape from its unceasing discord. What is this but an effect upon the nerves ? and what more could be desired to prove the power of any agency ? And the world would owe a debt of gratitude to the professors of animal magnetism, if, instead of making it, as some do, a mere exhibition to display a power and astonish the beholders, they would continue the efforts already begun for discovering all the beneficial uses to which it is capable of being applied. We might then rejoice that, as astrology led to the more useful knowledge of astronomy, this influence enabled us to comprehend our nervous system, on which so many conditions of health depend, and with which we are so imperfectly acquainted.

The cure of diseases was also attributed by the Egyptians to *Ex-votos* offered in the temples. They consisted of various kinds. Some persons promised a certain sum for the maintenance of the sacred animals, or whatever might propitiate the deity; and after the cure had been effected, they frequently suspended a model of the restored part in the temple; and ears, eyes, distorted arms, and other members, were dedicated us memorials of their gratitude and superstition.

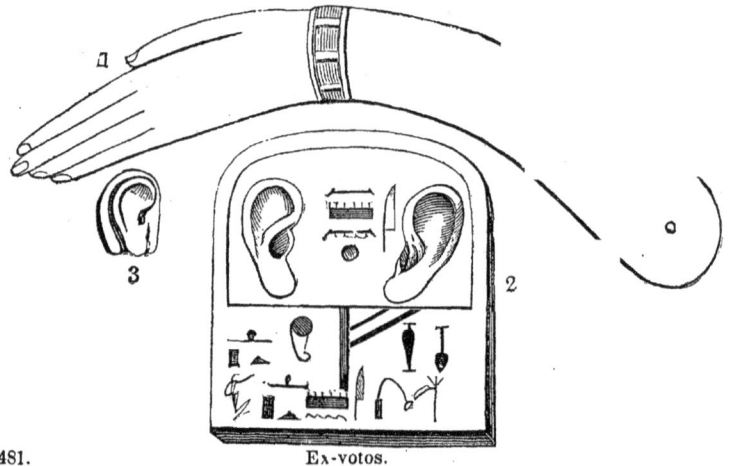

481.   Ex-votos.

1. Ivory hand, in Mr. Salt's Collection. 2 Stone tablet, dedicated to Amunre, for the recovery of a complaint in the ear; found at Thebes. 3. An ear of terra cotta in my possession, from Thebes.

Sometimes travellers, who happened to pass by a temple, inscribed a votive sentence on the walls, to indicate their respect for the deity, and solicit his protection during their journey; the complete formula of which contained the adoration (*proskunéma*) of the writer, with the assurance that he had been mindful of his wife, his family, and friends; and the reader of the inscription was sometimes included in a share of the blessings it solicited. The date of the king's reign and the day of the month were also added, with the profession and parentage of the writer. The complete formula of one *proskunéma* was as follows: "The adoration of Caius Capitolinus, son of Flavius Julius, of the fifth troop of Theban horse, to the goddess Isis, with ten thousand names. And I have been mindful of (or have made an adoration for) all those who love me, and my consort, and children, and all my household, and for him who reads this. In the year 12 of the Emperor Tiberius Cæsar, the 15th of Paüni."

The Egyptians, according to Pliny, claimed the honour of having invented the art of curing diseases. Indeed, the study of medicine and surgery appears to have commenced at a very early period in Egypt, since Athothes, the second king of the country, is stated to have written upon the subject of anatomy; and the schools of Alexandria continued till a late period to enjoy the reputation, and display the skill, they had inherited from their predecessors. Hermes was said to have written six books on medicine, the first of which related to anatomy; and the various recipes, known to have been beneficial, were recorded, with their peculiar cases, in the memoirs of physic, inscribed among the laws deposited in the principal temples.

The embalmers were probably members of the medical profession, and the Bible states that "the physicians embalmed" Jacob.

482.   Funeral Boat, or Baris.   *Thebes.*

P. Tomb at Saḳḳara, arched with stone, of the time of Psammitichus, or Psamatik, II., whose name occurs on the roof to the left, and in other places.

CHAPTER X.

FUNERAL RITES—OFFERINGS TO THE DEAD—TOMBS—FUNERAL PROCESSIONS — TRIALS OF THE DEAD — SACRED LAKE—BURIAL — EMBALMING—SARCOPHAGI—PAPYRI, &c.

THE great care of the Egyptians was directed to their condition after death, that last state towards which their present life was only the pilgrimage; and they were taught to consider their abode here merely as an "inn" upon the road. They looked forward to being received into the company of that Being who represented the Divine Goodness, if pronounced worthy at the great judgment

CHAP. X.   SERVICES, OR LITURGIES.   357

day; and the privilege of being called by his name was the fulfilment of all their wishes. Every one was then the same; all were "equally noble;" there was no distinction of rank beyond the tomb; and though their actions might be remembered on earth with gratitude and esteem, no king or conqueror was greater than the humblest man after death; nor were any honours given to them as heroes. And if ceremonies were performed to the deceased, they were not in honour of a man translated to the order of the gods, but of that particular portion of the divine essence which constituted the soul of each individual, and returned to the Deity after death. Every one, therefore, whose virtuous life entitled him to admission into the regions of the blessed, was supposed to be again united to the Deity, of whom he was an emanation; and, with the emblem of Thmei, purporting that he was judged or justified, he received the holy name of Osiris. His body was so bound up as to resemble the mysterious ruler of Amenti or *Hades*; it bore some of the emblems peculiar to him; and the beard, of a form which belonged exclusively to the gods, was given to the deceased in token of his having assumed the character of that deity. (*See above*, p. 329.)

483. Services performed to the dead by one of the family. Here it is a son. The principal part of the offering consists of onions. (*See* vol. i. p. 324.)   *Thebes.*

Offerings were also made to the god Osiris himself, after the burial, in the name of the deceased; and certain services or liturgies were performed for him by the priests, at the expense of the family; their number depending upon their means, or the respect they were inclined to pay to the memory of their parent. If the sons or relations were of the priestly order, they had the

484. The members of the family present when the services were performed. *Thebes.*

privilege of officiating on these occasions; and the members of the family had permission, and were perhaps frequently expect-

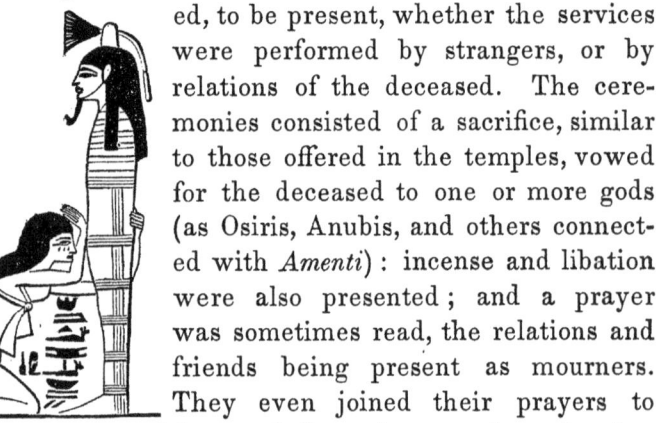

485. A woman embracing, and weeping before her husband's mummy. *Thebes.*

ed, to be present, whether the services were performed by strangers, or by relations of the deceased. The ceremonies consisted of a sacrifice, similar to those offered in the temples, vowed for the deceased to one or more gods (as Osiris, Anubis, and others connected with *Amenti*): incense and libation were also presented; and a prayer was sometimes read, the relations and friends being present as mourners. They even joined their prayers to those of the priest; and, embracing the mummied body, and bathing its feet with their tears, they uttered those expressions of

CHAP. X. SERVICES FOR THE DEAD. 359

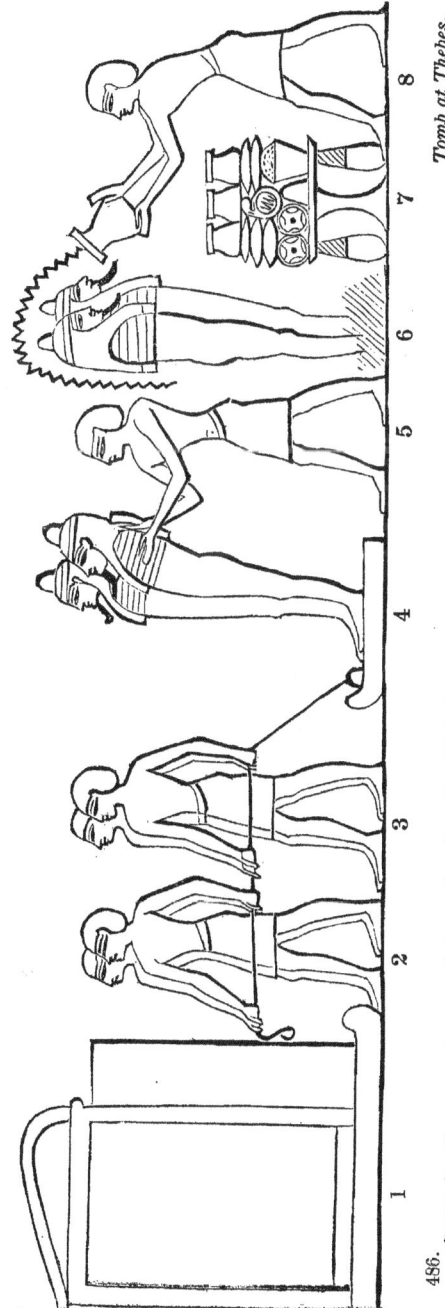

486. Conveying the mummies on a sledge to the closet in which they were kept, after the services had been performed to them. The priest (fig. 8) is pouring oil (?) over them. On the altar are three vases of oil, cakes, a basket of grapes, and some other things (which were indistinct from being much defaced). Below are two glass bottles of wine. Even in this serious subject the Egyptian artists could not refrain from their love of caricature; and one of the mummies (fig. 4) is falling down upon the priest, who supports it with his hands.

Tomb at Thebes.

grief, and praises of the deceased, which were dictated by their feelings on so melancholy an occasion.

The priest who officiated at the burial service was selected from the grade of Pontiffs who wore the leopard skin; but various other rites were performed by one of the minor priests to the mummies previous to their being lowered into the pit of the tomb, as well as after that ceremony. Indeed they continued to be administered at intervals, as long as the family paid for their performance; and it is possible that upon the cessation of this payment, or after a stipulated time, the priests had the right of transferring the tomb to another family, which the inscriptions within them show to have been done, even though belonging to members of the priestly order.

When the mummies remained in the house, or in the chamber of the sepulchre, they were kept in movable wooden closets, with folding doors, out of which they were taken by the minor functionaries to a small altar, before which the priest officiated. The closet and the mummy were placed on a sledge, in order to facilitate their movement from one place to another; and the latter was drawn with ropes to the altar, and taken back by the same means when the ceremony was over. On these occasions, as in the prayers for the dead, they made the usual offerings of incense and libation, with cakes, flowers, and fruit, and even anointed the mummy, oil or ointment being poured over its head.* Sometimes several priests attended. One carried a napkin over his shoulder, to be used after the anointing of the mummy; another brought a papyrus roll containing a prayer, or the usual

487. Pouring oil (?) over a mummy. The priest (fig. 1) has a napkin on his shoulder. Fig. 2 holds a papyrus. The mode of placing the napkin is remarkable, being the same as now adopted in the East by servants while guests are washing their hands before meals.   *Tomb at Thebes.*

* Woodcuts 486, 487.

CHAP. X.   MUMMIES KEPT IN THE HOUSE.   361

ritual deposited in the tombs with the dead; and others had different occupations, according to their respective offices.

These funeral oblations answer exactly to the *inferiæ* or *parentalia* of the Romans, consisting of victims, flowers, and libations, when the tomb was decked with garlands and wreaths of flowers, and an altar was erected before it for presenting the offerings. And that this last was done also by the Egyptians, is proved by the many small altars discovered outside the doors of the catacombs at Thebes.

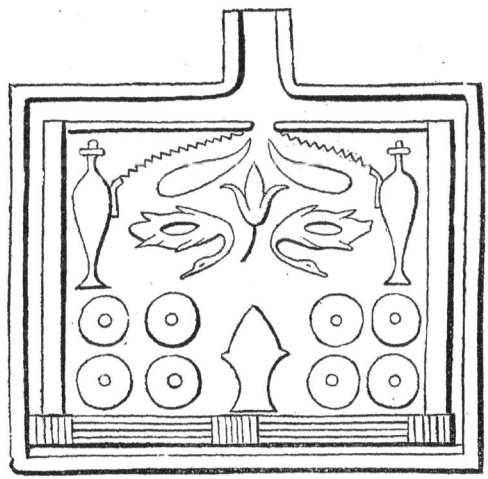

488. An altar, in the British Museum, showing that the trench is for carrying off the libation. The lower device is the ordinary hieroglyphic signifying "*chosen*," as applied to *offerings*.

It was not unusual to keep the mummies in the house, after they had been returned by the embalmers to the relations of the deceased, in order to gratify the feelings which made them desirous of having those they had loved in life as near them as possible after death, or to give time to the family to prepare a tomb for their reception. Many months often elapsed between the ceremony of embalming and the actual burial; and it was during this period that the liturgies were performed before the mummy, which were afterwards continued at the tomb. One inscription upon the coffin of a woman shows that the burial took place a whole year after her death, and some were doubtless kept, for various reasons, much longer. It was during this interval that feasts were held in honour of the dead, to which the friends and relatives were invited, as was customary among the Greeks and other people of antiquity.

Small tables made of reeds and sticks bound together, and interlaced with palm leaves, were sometimes placed in the tombs, bearing offerings of cakes, ducks, or other things, according to the wealth or inclination of the donors, one of which, found at Thebes, is now in the British Museum. On the lower compart-

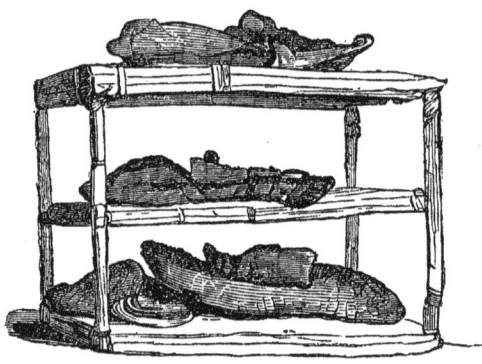

489. A table found in a tomb by Mr. Burton, on which are a duck trussed, and another cut open, with cakes. *British Museum.*

ment, or shelf, are cakes; the central shelf has a duck cut open at the breast and spread out, "but not divided asunder;" and at the top is a similar bird, trussed in the usual mode when brought to an Egyptian table. Similar offerings for "the dead" were strictly forbidden by the law of Moses; and it was doubtless the Egyptian custom that the Hebrew legislator had in view when he introduced this wise prohibition.

Though the privilege of keeping a mummy in the house was sanctioned by law and custom, care was always taken to assign some plausible reason for it, since they deemed it a great privilege to be admitted to the repositories of the dead, as their final resting-place. To be debarred from the rites of burial reflected a severe disgrace upon the whole family; and the most influential individual could not be admitted to the very tomb he had built for himself, until acquitted before that tribunal which sat to judge his conduct during life.

SUBJECTS PAINTED IN THE TOMB. 363

The tombs of the rich consisted of one or more chambers, ornamented with paintings and sculpture, the plans and size of which depended on the expense incurred by the family of the deceased, or on the wishes of the individuals who purchased them during their lifetime. They were the property of the priests; and a sufficient number being always kept ready, the purchase was made at the "shortest notice," nothing being requisite to complete even the sculptures, or inscriptions, but the insertion of the deceased's name, and a few statements respecting his family and profession. The numerous subjects representing agricultural scenes, the trades of the people—in short, the various occupations of the Egyptians, were already introduced. These were common to all tombs, varying only in their details and the mode of their execution, and were intended as a short epitome of human life, which suited equally every future occupant.

In some instances all the paintings of the tomb were finished, and even the small figures representing the future occupant were introduced; those only being left unsculptured which, being of a large size, required more accuracy in the features in order to give his real portrait; and sometimes even the large figures were completed before the tomb was sold, the only parts left unfinished being the hieroglyphic legends containing his name and that of his wife. Indeed, the fact of their selling old mummy cases, and tombs belonging to other persons, shows that they were not always over-scrupulous about the likeness of an individual, provided the hieroglyphics were altered, and contained his real name; at least, when a motive of economy reconciled the mind of a purchaser to a *second-hand* tenement for the body of his friend. Those who could afford it bought a family tomb; but this was generally confined to the owner and his wife, and their children.

Besides the upper rooms of the tomb, which were ornamented with the paintings already mentioned, were one or more pits, varying from 20 to 70 feet in depth; at the bottom or "sides" of which were recesses, like small chambers, for depositing the coffins; recalling the expression, " whose tombs are in the side of the pit," and the metaphor, " going down to the pit," applied to death. And well might the verse of the Psalmist, " our bones are scattered at the grave's mouth, as when one cutteth and cleaveth wood upon the earth," accord with the state of many an Egyptian pit a few years ago; when, to the disgrace of Christian excavators, the Moslems were obliged to interfere, and bury the bones recklessly scattered by them over the ground.

The pit was closed with masonry after the burial had been performed, and sometimes reopened to receive other members of the family. The upper apartments were richly ornamented with painted sculptures, being rather a monument in honour of the deceased than the actual sepulchre; and they served for the reception of his friends, who frequently met there, and accompanied the priests when performing the services for the dead. Each tomb, and sometimes each apartment, had a wooden door, either of a single or double valve, turning on pins, and secured by bolts or bars, with a lock, which last was protected by a seal of clay, upon which the impress of a signet was stamped when the party retired. Remains of the clay have even been found adhering to some of the stone jambs of the doorways in the tombs of Thebes; and the numerous stamps buried near them were probably used on those occasions.

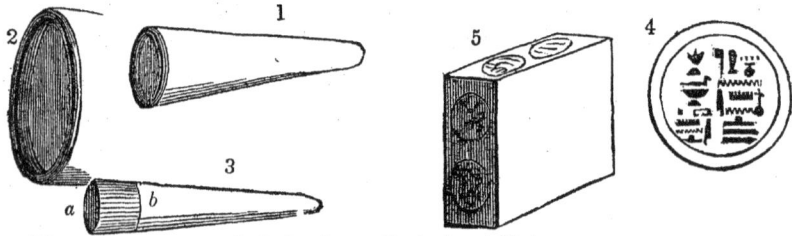

490.   Seals found near the tombs at Thebes.
1, 2. An instance of one with a raised edge round the stamped part.
3. Another, stained with red ochre from *a* to *b*.
4. Style of the inscription on some of them.
5. A brick stamped in a similar manner.

Similar seals were used for securing the doors of temples, houses, and granaries.

Tombs were built of brick and stone, or hewn in the rock, according to the position of the Necropolis. Whenever the mountains were sufficiently near, the latter was preferred; and these were generally the most elegant in their design, and in the variety of their sculptures, not only at Thebes, but in other parts of Egypt. Few, indeed, belonging to wealthy individuals were built of masonry, except those at the pyramids in the vicinity of Memphis. But Egyptian tombs were never circular, as many in Asia Minor, Etruria, and Greece.

The sepulchres of the poorer classes had no upper chamber. The coffins were deposited in pits in the plain, or in recesses excavated at the side of a rock, which were closed with masonry, like the pits within the large tombs. Mummies of the lower orders were buried together in a common repository; and the bodies of those whose relations had not the means of paying for their funeral, after being " merely cleansed by some vegetable decoctions, and kept in an alkaline solution for seventy days," were wrapped up in coarse cloth, in mats, or in a bundle of palm sticks, and deposited in the earth.

Some tombs were of great extent; and when a wealthy individual bought the ground, and had an opportunity, during a long life, of making his family sepulchre according to his wishes, it was frequently decorated in the most sumptuous manner. And so much consequence did the Egyptians attach to them, that people in humble circumstances made every effort to save sufficient to procure a handsome tomb, and defray the expenses of a suitable funeral. This species of pomp increased as refinement and luxury advanced; and in the time of Amasis and other monarchs of the 26th dynasty, the funeral expenses so far exceeded what it had been customary to incur during the reigns of the early Pharaohs, that the tombs of some individuals far surpassed in extent, if not in splendour of decoration, those of the kings themselves.

Many adorned their entrances with gardens, in which flowers were reared by the hand of an attached friend, whose daily care was to fetch water from the river, or from the wells on the edge of the cultivated land; and the remains of alluvial soil brought for this purpose may still be traced before some of the sepulchres at Thebes. Those tombs at Memphis and the Pyramids, which are of masonry, differ in their plan, and in many instances in the style of their sculptures; the subjects, however, generally relate to the manners and customs of the Egyptians; and parties, boat-scenes, fishing, fowling, and other ordinary occupations of the people, are portrayed there, as in the sepulchres of Thebes.

"When any one died, all the females of his family, covering their heads and faces with mud, and leaving the body in the house, ran through the streets, with their bosoms exposed, striking themselves, and uttering loud lamentations." Their friends and relations joined them as they went, uniting in the same demonstrations of grief; and when the deceased was a person of consideration, many strangers accompanied them, out of respect to his memory. Hired mourners were also employed to add, by their feigned demonstrations of grief, to the real lamentations of the family, and to heighten the show of respect paid to the deceased. "The men, in like manner, girding their dress below their waist, went through the town smiting their breast," and throwing dust upon their heads; but the mourners consisted chiefly of women, as is usual in Egypt at the present day; and we may suggest "dust," rather than "mud," on a dry Egyptian road.

Of the magnificent pomp of a royal funeral in the time of the Pharaohs no adequate idea can be formed from the processions represented in the tombs of ordinary individuals; and from the marked distinction always maintained between the sovereign and the highest subjects in the kingdom, we may readily believe how greatly the funeral processions of the wealthiest individuals fell short of those of the kings. From the pomp of ordinary funerals, therefore, may be inferred the grand state in which the body of a sovereign was conveyed to the tomb.

In the funeral processions of the Egyptian grandees the order was frequently as follows:

1 2

491. Closets containing figures of gods.

First came several servants carrying tables laden with fruit, cakes, flowers, vases of ointment, wine, and other liquids, with three young geese and a calf for sacrifice, chairs and wooden tablets, napkins, and other things. Then others bringing the small closets in which the mummy of the deceased and of his ancestors had been kept, while receiving the funeral liturgies previous to burial, and which sometimes contained the images of the gods. They also carried daggers, bows, sandals, and fans; each man having a kerchief or napkin on his shoulder. Next came a table of offerings, fauteuils, couches, boxes, and a chariot; and then the charioteer with a pair of horses yoked in another car, which he drove as he followed on foot, in token of respect to his late master. After these were men carrying gold vases on a table, with other offerings, boxes, and a large case upon a sledge borne on poles by four men, superintended by two functionaries of the priestly order; then others bearing small images of his ancestors, arms, fans, the sceptres, signets, collars, necklaces, and other things appertaining to the king, in whose service he had held an important office. To these succeeded the bearers of a sacred boat, and that mysterious eye of Osiris, as God of Stability, so common on funeral monuments—the same which was placed over the incision in the side of the body when embalmed, as well as on the prow and rudder of the funeral boat, was the emblem of Egypt, and was frequently used as a sort of amulet, and deposited in the tombs. Others carried the well-known small images of blue pottery, representing the deceased under the form of Osiris, and the bird emblematic of the soul. Following these were seven or more men, bearing upon staves, or wooden yokes, cases filled with flowers, and bottles for libation; and then seven or eight women, having their heads bound with fillets, beating their breasts, throwing dust upon their heads, and uttering doleful lamentations for the deceased, intermixed with praises of his virtues.

One woman is seen in the picture turning round, in the act of adoration, towards a sacred case containing a sitting Cynocephalus, the emblem of the God of Letters, placed on a sledge drawn by four men; the officiating high priest or pontiff, clad in a leopard skin, following, having in his hand the censer and vase of libation, and accompanied by his attendants bearing the various things required for the occasion.

Next came the hearse, placed in the consecrated boat upon a sledge, drawn by four oxen and by seven men, under the direction of a superintendent, who regulated the march of the procession. A high functionary of the priestly order walked close to the boat, in which the chief mourners, the nearest female relatives of the deceased, stood or sat at either end of the sarcophagus; and sometimes his widow, holding a child in her arms, united her lamentations with prayers for her tender offspring, who added its tribute of sorrow to that of its afflicted mother.

The sarcophagus was decked with flowers; and on the sides were painted alternately the emblems of Stability and Security (?) two by two (as on the sacred arks or shrines) upon separate panels, one of which was sometimes taken out to expose to view the head of the mummy within.

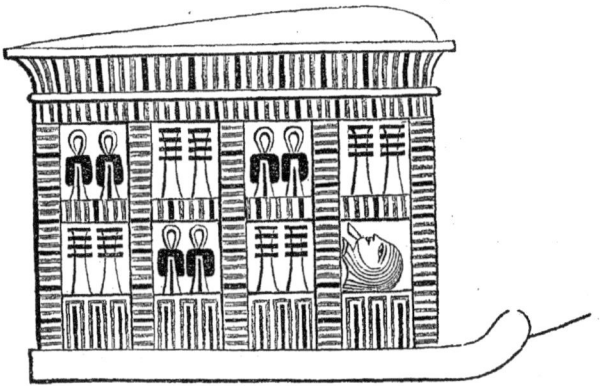

492.　　　The mummy's head, seen at an open panel of the coffin.　　　*Thebes.*

Behind the hearse followed the male relations and friends of the deceased; some beating their breasts; others, if not giving the same tokens of grief, at least showing their sorrow by their silence and solemn step, as they walked, leaning on their long sticks. These closed the procession.

Arrived at the sacred lake, the coffin was placed in the *baris*, or consecrated boat of the dead, towed by a larger one furnished with sails and oars, and having frequently a spacious cabin, which, in company with other sailing boats carrying the mourners and all those things above mentioned appertaining to the funeral, crossed to the other side. Arrived there, the procession went in the same order to the tomb, at which the priest offered a sacrifice, with incense and libation, the women still continuing their lamentations, united with prayers and praises of the deceased.

It frequently happened that the deceased, with his wife, if dead at the time of his funeral, was represented seated under a canopy in lieu of the coffin. Before him stood an altar laden with offerings; and a priest, opening a long roll of papyrus, read aloud the funeral ritual, and an account of his good deeds, "in order to show to Osiris and the Assessors the extent of his piety and justice during his life." (*Woodcut* 482.) When the boats reached the other side of the lake, the yards were lowered to the top of the cabin, and all those engaged in the ceremony left them and proceeded to the tomb, from which they appear to have returned by land, without recrossing the lake.

Such was the funeral procession of a *basilico-grammat*, or royal scribe, a member of the priestly order. He lived during the four successive reigns of Thothmes III., Amunoph II., Thothmes IV., and Amunoph III., and held the office of tutor to one of the young princesses, as the sculptures inform us, which represent him nursing her on his knee while entertaining a party of friends.

The funerals of other persons differed in the order of the procession, as well as in the pomp displayed on the occasion; and the mode of celebrating them appears to have depended on the arrangements made by the family, except in those particulars which were prescribed by law. The funeral of *Nofr-Othph*, a priest of Amun at Thebes, is thus described on the walls of his tomb; the scene of which lies partly on the lake, and partly on the way thence to the sepulchre itself:

First came a large boat, conveying the bearers of flowers, cakes, and numerous things appertaining to the offerings—tables, fauteuils, and other pieces of furniture, as well as the friends of the deceased, whose consequence is shown by their dresses and long walking-sticks—the peculiar mark of Egyptian gentlemen. This was followed by a small skiff holding baskets of cakes and fruit, with a quantity of green palm-branches, which it was customary to strew in the way as the body proceeded to the tomb, the smooth nature of their leaves and stalks being particularly well adapted to enable the sledge to glide over them.

In this part of the picture the love of caricature common to the Egyptians is shown to have been indulged in, even in the serious subject of a funeral; and the retrograde movement of the large boat, which has grounded and is pushed off the bank, striking the smaller one with its rudder, has overturned a large table loaded with cakes and other things upon the rowers seated below, in spite of all the efforts of the *prowman*, and the earnest vociferations of the alarmed steersman.

In another boat men carried bouquets, and boxes supported on the usual yoke over their shoulders; and this was followed by two others, one containing the male, the other the female mourners, standing on the roof of the cabin, beating themselves, uttering cries, and making other demonstrations of excessive grief. Last came the consecrated boat, bearing the hearse, which was surrounded by the chief mourners, and the female relations of the deceased. A high priest burnt incense over the altar, which was placed before it; and behind it stood the images of Isis and Nepthys. They were the emblems of the Beginning and the End, and were thought to be always present at the head and feet of the dead who had led a virtuous life, and who were deemed worthy of admission into the regions of the blessed.

Arrived at the opposite shore of the lake, the procession advanced to the catacombs, crossing the sandy plain which intervened between them and the lake; and on the way several women of the vicinity, carrying their children in shawls suspended at their side or at their back, joined in the lamentation. The mummy, being taken out of the sarcophagus, was placed erect in the chamber of the tomb; and the sister or nearest relation, embracing it, commenced a funeral dirge, calling on her relative with every expression of tenderness, extolling his virtues, and bewailing her own loss. In the mean time the high priest presented a sacrifice of incense and libation, with offerings of cakes and other customary gifts, for the deceased; and the men and women without continued the ululation, throwing dust upon their heads, and making other manifestations of grief.

Many funerals were conducted in a more simple manner; the procession consisting merely of the mourners and priests, with the hearse conveyed, as usual, on a sledge drawn by two or three oxen, and by several men, who aided in pulling the rope. The priest who wore the leopard-skin dress and who performed the sacrifice was in attendance, burning incense and pouring out a libation as he went; and behind him walked a functionary of an inferior grade, clad in a simple robe, extending a little below the knees, and standing out from the body. In form it was not altogether unlike a modern Abbaſeh, and was made of some stiff substance, with two holes in front, through which the arms passed, in order to enable him to hold a long taper. At the head and foot of the hearse was a female, who generally clasped one arm with her hand in token of grief, her head being bound with a fillet, her bosom exposed, and her dress supported, like that of mourning women, by a strap over the shoulder. She sometimes wore a scarf tied across her hips, much in the same manner as Egyptian women now put on their shawls both in the house and when going out of doors. She may be a type of mourning, the "chief mourner," or one who had some peculiar office on these occasions.

493. A peculiar attendant at a funeral. (See p. 373.)

A procession of this kind was all that attended the funeral of a person who held the office of "scribe, of weights and measures;" but the pomp displayed in these ceremonies depended on the sums expended by the family, and other circumstances. In another funeral, the order of the procession was as follows:

First came eight men throwing dust upon their heads, and giving other demonstrations of grief; then six females, in the usual attire of mourners, preceding the hearse, which was drawn by two oxen—in this instance unassisted by men, two only being near them, one uttering lamentations, and the other driving them with a goad or a whip. Immediately before the sledge bearing the coffin was the *sprinkler*, who, with a brush dipped in a vase, or with a small bottle, threw water upon the ground, and perhaps also on those who passed. The same is done in the funeral ceremonies of the East at the present day, being supposed to keep off the evil eye. Next came the high priest, who, turning round to the hearse, offered incense and libation in honour of the deceased, the chief mourner being seated in the boat before it; other men followed, and the procession closed with eight or more women, beating themselves, throwing dust on their heads, and singing the funeral dirge. Arrived at the tomb, which stood beneath the western mountain of Thebes, the mummy was taken from the hearse, and, being placed upright, incense was burnt, and a libation was poured out before it by the high priest as he stood at the altar, while other functionaries performed various ceremonies in honour of the deceased. The hierogrammat, or sacred scribe, then read aloud from a tablet, or a roll of papyrus, his eulogy, and a prayer to the gods in his behalf; and the same was sometimes read from the boat, immediately after the deceased had passed that ordeal which gave him the right to cross the sacred lake.

The order of the procession which accompanied the body from the sacred lake to the catacombs was the same as before they had passed it, the time occupied by the whole march depending, of course, on the position of the tomb, and the distance from which the body had been brought, some coming from remote towns or villages, and others from the city itself, or the immediate vicinity.

The tomb, in the subject above described, is represented at the base of the western mountain of Thebes, which agrees perfectly with its actual position; and from this, as from several other similar paintings, we learn that, besides the excavated chambers hewn in the rock, a small building crowned by a roof of conical or pyramidical form stood before the entrance. It is probable that many, if not all the pits in the plain below the hills, were once covered with buildings of this kind, which, from their perishable materials, crude brick, have been destroyed after a lapse of so many ages. Indeed we find the remains of some of them, and occasionally even their vaulted chambers, with the painted stucco on the walls.

Many other funerals occur on the tombs, which vary only in some details from those already mentioned. I cannot, however, omit

CHAP. X. OTHER FUNERALS. 373

to notice another instance of palm branches strewed in the way, and the introduction of two tables or altars for the deceased and his wife—one bearing a profusion of cakes, meat, fruit, vegetables, and other customary gifts, and the other numerous utensils and insignia, as flabella, censers, ostrich feathers, asps, and emblems, together with the leg of a victim, placed upon a napkin spread over the table. Another is curious, from its showing that grease was sometimes poured upon the ground or platform on which the sledge of the hearse passed, as was

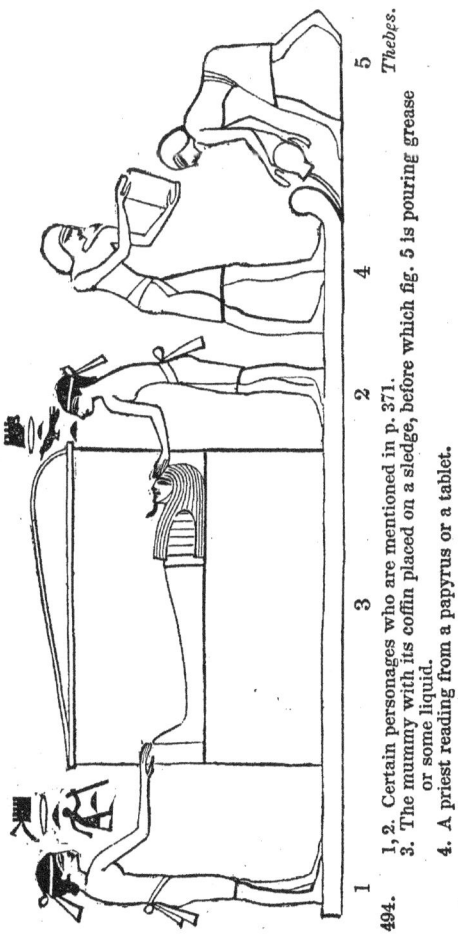

494.

1, 2. Certain personages who are mentioned in p. 371.
3. The mummy with its coffin placed on a sledge, before which fig. 5 is pouring grease or some liquid.
4. A priest reading from a papyrus or a tablet.

Thebes.

done in moving a colossus or any great weight by the same process.

The hearse containing the mummy was generally closed on all sides; but it was sometimes open, partially or entirely; and the body was seen placed upon a bier, ornamented, like some of the couches in their houses, with the head and feet of a lion. Sometimes the mummy was placed on the top of the sarcophagus, within an open hearse; and three friends of the deceased, or the functionaries destined for this office, took it thence to convey it to the tomb, where it received the accustomed services previous to interment in the pit, an affectionate hand often crowning it with a garland of "*immortelles*," bay leaves, or fresh flowers, and depositing, as the last duty of a beloved friend, some object to which, while alive, he had been attached.

Such are the principal funeral processions represented in the tombs of Thebes. It remains for me to describe the preparatory rites, and the remarkable ceremony that took place on arriving at the lake, before permission could be obtained to transport the body to the opposite shore.

The body having been conveyed to the embalmer's, the afflicted family during seventy (or seventy-two) days continued their lamentations at home, singing the funeral dirge, and fulfilling all the duties required both by custom and their own feelings on the mournful occasion.

During this period they abstained from all amusements; the indulgence in every kind of luxury, as " the bath, wine, delicacies of the table, or rich clothing;" " they suffered their beard and hair to grow;" and endeavoured to prove, by this marked neglect of their personal comfort and appearance, how entirely their thoughts were absorbed by the melancholy event that had befallen them. But they did not cut themselves in token of grief; and the command given to the Israelites, " Ye shall not cut yourselves, nor make any baldness between your eyes for the dead," does not refer to a custom of the Egyptians, but of those people among whom they were about to establish themselves in Syria, as is distinctly stated of the votaries of Baal.

The body, when embalmed, was restored to the family, and having been deposited in its case, which was generally inclosed in two or three others, all richly painted, " it was placed in a room of the house, upright against the wall," until the tomb was ready, and all the necessary preparations had been made for the funeral. The *coffin* or mummy case was then " carried forth," and deposited in the *hearse*, drawn upon a sledge, as already described, to the sacred lake of the nome ; notice having been previously given to the judges, and a public announcement made of the appointed day. Forty-two judges having been summoned, and placed in a semicircle, near the banks of the lake, a boat was brought up, provided expressly for the occasion, under the direction of a boatman called, in the Egyptian language, *Charon;* " and it is from hence," says Diodorus, " that the fable of Hades is said to be derived, which Orpheus introduced into Greece."

" When the boat was ready for the reception of the coffin, it was lawful for any person who thought proper to bring forward an accusation against the deceased. If it could be proved that he had led an evil life, the judges declared accordingly, and the body was deprived of the accustomed sepulture ; but if the accuser failed to establish what he had advanced, he was subject to the heaviest penalties. When there was no accuser, or when the accusation had been disproved, the relations ceased from their lamentations, and pronounced encomiums on the deceased. They did not enlarge upon his descent, as is usual among the Greeks, for they hold that all the Egyptians are equally noble ; but they related his early education and the course of his studies ; and then praising his piety and justice, his temperance, and the other virtues he possessed, they supplicated the gods below to receive him as a companion of the pious. This announcement was received by the assembled multitude with acclamations ; and they joined in extolling the glory of the deceased, who was about to remain for ever with the virtuous in the regions of Hades. The body was then taken by those who had family catacombs already prepared, and placed in the repository allotted to it."

"Some," continues the historian, "who were not possessed of catacombs, constructed a new apartment for the purpose in their own house, and set the coffin upright against the firmest of the walls; and the same was done with the bodies of those who had been debarred the rites of burial on account of the accusation brought against them, or in consequence of debts they or their sons had contracted. These last, however, if their children's children happened to be prosperous, were released from the impediments of their creditors, and at length received the ceremony of a magnificent burial. It was, indeed, most solemnly established in Egypt that parents and ancestors should have a more marked token of respect paid them by their family, after they had been transferred to their everlasting habitations. Hence originated the custom of depositing the bodies of their deceased parents as pledges for the payment of borrowed money; those who failed to redeem those pledges being subject to the heaviest disgrace, and deprived of burial after their own death."

The grief and shame felt by the family when the rites of burial had been refused, were excessive.

It is true that the duration of this punishment was limited according to the extent of the crimes of which the accused had been guilty; and when the devotion of friends, aided by liberal donations in the service of religion, and the influential prayers of the priests, had sufficiently softened the otherwise inexorable nature of the gods, the period of this state of purgatory was doubtless shortened; and Diodorus shows that grandchildren, who had the means and inclination, might avail themselves of the same method of satisfying their creditors and the gods.

The form of the ritual read by the priest in pronouncing the acquittal of the dead is preserved in the tombs, usually at the entrance passage, in which the deceased is made to enumerate all the sins forbidden by the Egyptian law, and to assert his innocence of each. They are supposed by Champollion to amount to forty-two, being equal in number to the assessors, who were destined to examine the deceased, at his final judgment, respecting the peculiar crime which it was his province to punish.

Every large city, as Thebes, Memphis, and some others, had

its lake, at which the same ceremonies were practised; and it is probable, from what Diodorus says of the "lake of the *nome*," that the capital of each province had one in its immediate vicinity, to which the funeral procession of all who died within the jurisdiction of the *nomarch* was obliged to repair. Even when the priests granted a dispensation for the removal of a body to another town, as was sometimes done in favour of those who desired to be buried at Abydus and other places, the previous ceremony of passing through this ordeal was doubtless required at the lake of their own province.

Those persons who, from their extreme poverty, had no place prepared for receiving their body when denied the privilege of passing the sacred lake, appear to have been interred on the shores they were forbidden to leave; and I have found the bones of many buried near the site of the lake of Thebes, which appeared to be of bodies imperfectly preserved, as of persons who could not afford the more expensive processes of embalming. This was like remaining on the wrong side of the Styx; and Diodorus has shown that the fables of the Acherusian lake, of Hecate, of Cerberus, of Charon and the Styx, owed their origin to these Egyptian ceremonies.

Of Charon it may be observed that both his name and character are taken from Horus, who had the peculiar office of steersman in the sacred boats of Egypt; and the piece of money given him for ferrying the dead across the Styx appears to have been borrowed from the gold or silver plate put into the mouth of the dead by the Egyptians. For though they did not intend it as a reward to the boatman, but rather as a passport to show the virtuous character of the deceased, it was of equal importance in obtaining for him admittance into the regions of the blessed.

The Egyptian custom of depositing cakes in the tombs probably led to the Greek notion of sending a cake for Cerberus, which was placed in the mouth of the deceased; and it was by means of a similar one, drugged with soporiferous herbs, and given to the monster at a hungry hour, that Æneas and the Sibyl obtained an entrance into the lower regions.

The judge of the dead is recognised in Osiris; the office of

Mercury, the conductor of souls, is the same as that of Anubis; the figure of Justice without a head, and the scales of Truth or Justice at the gate of Amenti, occur in the funereal subjects of the Egyptian tombs; and the hideous animal who guards the approach to the mansion of Osiris, and is called "the devourer of the wicked," is a worthy prototype of the Greek Cerberus.

It was not ordinary individuals alone who were subjected to a public ordeal at their death—the character of the king himself was doomed to undergo the same test; and if any one could establish proofs of his impiety or injustice, he was denied the usual funereal obsequies when, in the presence of the assembled multitude, his body was brought to the sacred lake, or, as Diodorus states, to the vestibule of the tomb. "The customary trial having commenced, any one was permitted to present himself as an accuser. The pontiffs first passed an encomium upon his character, enumerating all his noble actions, and pointing out the merit of each, to which the people, who were assembled to the number of several thousands, if they felt those praises to be just, responded with favourable acclamations. If, on the contrary, his life had been stained with vice or injustice, they showed their dissent by loud murmurs; and several instances are recorded of Egyptian monarchs having been deprived of the honour of the customary public funeral by the opposing voice of the people." "The effect of this," adds the historian, "was, that succeeding kings, fearing so disgraceful a censure after death, and the eternal stigma attached to it, studied by their virtuous conduct to deserve the good opinion of their subjects; and it could not fail to be a great incentive to virtue, independent of the feelings arising from a wish to deserve the gratitude of men, and the fear of forfeiting the favour of the gods."

The custom of refusing funeral rites to a king was not confined to Egypt; it was common also to the Jews,* who forbade a wicked monarch to repose in the sepulchres of his fathers. Thus Joash, though "buried in the city of David," was not interred "in the sepulchres of the kings;"† Manasseh‡ "was buried in

---

* 1 Kings, xiv. 13; 2 Kings, ix. 10. † 2 Chron. xxiv. 25.
‡ 2 Kings, xxi. 18 and 26.

the garden of his own house," and several other kings of Judah and Israel were denied that important privilege. And the speech of Samuel, on giving up his post of judge, "Whom have I defrauded?" and the answer of the people, prove that the custom was adopted by the Jews before they had the kingly form of government.* That the same continued to the time of the Asmodeans, is shown by the conduct of Alexander Janneus, who, feeling the approach of death, charged his wife, "on her return to Jerusalem, to send for the leading men among the Pharisees, and show them his body, giving them leave, with great appearance of sincerity, to use it as they might please—whether they would dishonour the dead body by refusing it burial, as having suffered severely through him, or whether in their anger they would offer any other injury to it. By this means, and by a promise that nothing should be done without them in the affairs of the kingdom, it was hoped that a more honourable funeral might be obtained than any she could give him, and that his body might be saved from abuse by this appeal to their generosity." They had also the custom of instituting a general mourning for a deceased monarch whose memory they wished to honour.

But the Egyptians allowed not the same extremes of degradation to be offered to the dead as the Jews sometimes did to those who had incurred their hatred; and the body of a malefactor, though excluded from the precincts of the necropolis, was not refused to his friends, that they might perform the last duties to their unfortunate relative.

"The Egyptians," according to Herodotus, "were the first to maintain that the soul of man is immortal; that after the death of the body it always enters into that of some other animal which is born; and when it has passed through all those of the earth, water, and air, it again enters that of a man, which circuit it accomplishes in 3000 years." The doctrine of transmigration is mentioned by Plutarch, Plato, and other ancient writers as the general belief among the Egyptians, and it was adopted by Pythagoras and his preceptor Pherecydes, as well as other philosophers of Greece.

* 1 Sam. xii. 4, 5.

Opinions varied respecting it; and some maintained that the soul passed through different bodies till it returned again to the human shape, and that all events which had happened were destined to occur again after a certain period, in the identical order and manner as before. The same men were said to be born again, and to fulfil the same career; and the same causes were thought to produce the same effects, as stated by Virgil. This was termed κυκλος αναγκης, "the circle (or orbit) of necessity."

It is even supposed that the Egyptians preserved the body, in order to keep it in a fit state to receive the soul which once inhabited it, and that their tombs were decorated so richly in order to be ready for their owners on a future occasion. But this is contradicted by the fact of the tombs being sold to later occupants; and by animals being also embalmed, the preservation of whose bodies was not ascribable to any idea connected with the soul; and the custom arose rather from a sanitary regulation for the benefit of the living, and from that feeling of respect for the dead which is common to all men.

And since it is distinctly shown that all virtuous men became "Osiris," and returned again to the Good Being whence their souls emanated, their coming to earth again at any period is improbable; and the bad alone were condemned to that degradation, going through a state of purgatory, by passing into the bodies of animals. This, which accords with the belief of the Hindoos, is more consistent with what we know of the notions of the Egyptians; and there is reason to believe from the monuments, that the souls which underwent transmigration were those of men whose sins were of a sufficiently moderate kind to admit of that purification, the unpardonable sinner being condemned to eternal fire. The Buddhists have the same notion of the soul of man passing into the bodies of animals; and even the Druids believed in the migration of the soul, though they confined it to human bodies.

The judgment scenes found in the tombs and on the papyri sometimes represent the deceased conducted by Horus alone, or accompanied by his wife, to the region of Amenti. Cerberus is present as the guardian of the gates, near which the scales of

Justice are erected; and Anubis, "the director of the weight," having placed a vase representing the good actions, or the heart, of the deceased in one scale, and the figure or emblem of Truth in the other, proceeds to ascertain his claims for admission. If on being "weighed" he is "found wanting," he is rejected; and Osiris, the judge of the dead, inclining the sceptre in token of condemnation, pronounces judgment upon him, and condemns his soul to return to earth under the form of a pig, or some other unclean animal. Placed in a boat, it is removed, under the charge of two monkeys, from the precincts of Amenti, all communication with which is figuratively cut off by a man who hews away the earth with an axe after its passage; and the commencement of a new term of life is indicated by those monkeys, the emblems of Thoth, as Time. But if, when the sum of his deeds have been recorded, his virtues so far prodominate as to entitle him to admission to the mansions of the blessed, Horus, taking in his hand the tablet of Thoth, introduces him to the presence of Osiris; who, in his palace, attended by Isis and Nepthys, sits on his throne in the midst of the waters, from which rises the lotus, bearing upon its expanded flower the four Genii of Amenti.

Other representations of this subject differ in some of the details; and in the judgment scene of the royal scribe, whose funeral procession has been described, the deceased advances alone in an attitude of prayer to receive judgment. On one side of the scales stands Thoth, holding a tablet in his hand; on the other the Goddess of Justice; and Horus, in lieu of Anubis, performs the office of director of the balance, on the top of which sits a Cynocephalus, the emblem of Thoth. Osiris, seated as usual on his throne, holding his crook and flagellum, awaits the report from the hands of his son Horus. Before the door of his palace are the four Genii of Amenti, and near them three deities, who either represent the assessors, or may be the three assistant judges, who gave rise to the Minos, Æacus, and Rhadamanthus of Greek fable. In these the *Min* and *Amenti* are very Egyptian.

Another, figured in the side adytum of the Ptolemaic temple of Dayr el Medeeneh, at Thebes, represents the deceased approaching in a similarly submissive attitude, between two figures of Truth or Justice, whose emblem, the ostrich feather, he holds in his hand. The two figures show the double capacity of that goddess, corresponding to the Thummim, or "two Truths," and according well with the statement of Diodorus respecting her position "at the gates of Truth." Horus and Anubis superintend the balance, and weigh the actions of the judged; whilst Thoth inscribes them on the tablet, which he prepares for presentation to Osiris, who, seated on the throne, pronounces the final judgment, permitting the virtuous soul to enjoy the blessings of eternal felicity. Before him four Genii of Amenti stand upon a lotus flower; and a figure of Harpocrates, seated on the crook of Osiris between the scales and the entrance of the divine abode, which is guarded by Cerberus, is intended to show that the deceased, on admission to that pure state, must be born again, and commence a new life, cleansed from all the impurities of his earthly career. It also represents the idea common to the Egyptians and other philosophers, that to die was only to assume a new form—that nothing was annihilated—and that dissolution was merely the forerunner of reproduction. Above, in two lines, sit the forty-two assessors, the complete number mentioned by Diodorus, whose office was to assist in judging the dead.

Many similar subjects occur on funeral monuments, few of which present any new features. One, however, is singular from the Goddess of Justice being herself engaged in weighing the deceased, in the presence of Thoth, who is represented under the form of a Cynocephalus, having the horns and globe of the Moon upon its head, and a tablet in its hand. Instead of the usual vase, the figure of the deceased himself is placed in one of the scales, opposed to that of the Goddess; and close to the balance sits Cerberus with open mouth, ready to perform his office of "devourer of the wicked."

Another may also be noticed, from the singular fact of the Goddess of Justice, who here introduces the deceased, being without a head, as described by Diodorus; from the deceased holding in each hand an ostrich feather, the emblem of Truth; and from Cerberus being represented standing upon the steps of the divine abode of Osiris, as if in the act of announcing the arrival of Thoth with the person of the tomb.

Sometimes the deceased wore round his neck the same vase which in the scales typified his good actions, or bore on his head the ostrich feather of Truth. They were both intended to show that he had been deemed worthy of admission to the mansions of the just; and in the same idea originated the custom of placing the name of the Goddess after that of virtuous individuals who were dead, implying that they were "judged," or "justified."

The Goddesses Athor and Netpe, in their respective trees, the Persea and Sycamore-fig, frequently presented the virtuous after death with the fruit and drink of heaven, which call to mind the ambrosia and nectar of Greek fable.

The process of embalming is thus described by ancient writers:— "In Egypt," says Herodotus, "certain persons are appointed by law to exercise this art as their peculiar business; and when a dead body is brought them, they produce patterns of mummies in wood, imitated in painting, the most elaborate of which are said to be of him (Osiris), whose name I do not think it right to mention on this occasion. The second which they show is simpler and less costly; and the third is the cheapest. Having exhibited them all, they inquire of the persons who have applied to them which mode they wish to be adopted; and this being settled, and the price agreed upon, the parties retire, leaving the body with the embalmers.

"In preparing it according to the first method, they commence by extracting the brain from the nostrils by a curved iron probe, partly cleansing the head by these means, and partly by pouring in certain drugs; then making an incision in the side with a sharp Ethiopian stone, they draw out the intestines through the aperture. Having cleansed and washed them with palm wine, they cover them with pounded aromatics; and afterwards filling the cavity with powder of pure myrrh, cassia, and other fragrant substances, frankincense excepted, they sew it up again. This being done, they salt the body, keeping it in natron during seventy days, to which period they are strictly confined. When the seventy days are over, they wash the body, and wrap it up entirely in bands of fine linen smeared on their side with gum, which the Egyptians generally use instead of glue. The relations then take away the body, and have a wooden case made in the form of a man, in which they deposit it; and when fastened up, they keep it in a room in their house, placing it upright against the wall. This is the most costly mode of embalming.

"For those who choose the middle kind, on account of the expense, they prepare the body as follows. They fill syringes with oil of cedar, and inject this into the abdomen, without making any incision or removing the bowels; and taking care that the liquid shall not escape, they keep it in salt during the specified number of days. The cedar oil is then taken out; and such is its strength that it brings with it the bowels, and all the inside, in a state of dissolution. The natron also dissolves the flesh; so that nothing remains but the skin and bones. This process being over, they restore the body without any further operation.

"The third kind of embalming is only adopted for the poor. In this they merely cleanse the body by an injection of *syrmæa*, and salt it during seventy days, after which it is returned to the friends who brought it.

"The bodies of women of quality are not embalmed directly after their death, and it is customary for the family to keep them three or four days before they are subjected to that process."

The account given by Diodorus is similar to that of the historian of Halicarnassus. "The funerals of the Egyptians are conducted upon three different scales—the most expensive, the more moderate, and the humblest. The first is said to cost a talent of silver (about 250*l.* sterling); the second 22 minæ (or 60*l.*); and the third is extremely cheap. The persons who embalm the bodies are artists who have learnt this secret from their ancestors. They present to the friends of the deceased who apply to them an estimate of the funeral expenses, and ask them in what manner they wish it to be performed; which being agreed upon, they deliver the body to the proper persons appointed to that office. First one, who is termed the scribe, marks upon the left side of the body, as it lies on the ground, the extent of the incision which is to be made; then another, who is called *paraschistes* (the *dissector*), cuts open as much of the flesh as the law permits with an Ethiopian (flint) stone, and immediately runs away, pursued by those who are present, throwing stones at him amidst bitter execrations, as if to cast upon him all the odium of this necessary act. For they look upon every one who has offered violence to, or inflicted a wound or any other injury upon a human body, to be hateful; but the embalmers, on the contrary, are held in the greatest consideration and respect, being the associates of the priests, and permitted free access to the temples as sacred persons.

" As soon as they have met together to embalm the bodies thus prepared for them, one introduces his hand through the aperture into the abdomen, and takes every thing out, except the kidneys and heart. Another cleanses each of the viscera with palm wine and aromatic substances. Lastly, after having applied oil of cedar and other things to the whole body for upwards of *thirty* days, they add myrrh, cinnamon, and those drugs which have not only the power of preserving the body for a length of time, but of imparting to it a fragrant odour. It is then restored to the friends of the deceased. And so perfectly are all the members preserved, that even the hairs of the eyelids and eyebrows remain undisturbed, and the whole appearance of the person is so unaltered that every feature may be recognized. The Egyptians, therefore, who sometimes keep the bodies of their ancestors in magnificent apartments set apart for the purpose, have an opportunity of contemplating the faces of those who died many generations before them; and the height and figure of their bodies being distinguishable, as well as the character of the countenance, they enjoy a wonderful gratification, as if they lived in the society of those they see before them."

On the foregoing statements of the two historians, I may be permitted some observations.

First. The wooden figures kept as patterns are similar (except in size) to those small ones of glazed pottery, representing the deceased in the form of Osiris, so common in our collections.

Secondly. It is evident from the mummies which have been found in such abundance at Thebes and other places, that in the three different modes of embalming several gradations existed, some of which differ so much in many essential points as almost to justify our extending the number mentioned by the historians.

Thirdly. The extraction of the brain by the nostrils is proved by the appearance of the mummies found in the tombs; and some of the crooked instruments (always of bronze) supposed to have been used for this purpose have been discovered at Thebes.

Fourthly. The incision in the side is, as Diodorus says, on the left. Over it the sacred eye of Osiris was placed, and through it the viscera were returned when not deposited in the four vases.

Fifthly. The second class of mummies without any incision in the side are often found in the tombs; but it is also shown from the bodies at Thebes that the incision was not always confined to those of the first class, and that some of an inferior kind were submitted to this simple and effectual process.

Sixthly. The sum stated by Diodorus of a talent of silver can only be a general estimate of the expense of the first kind of embalming, since the various gradations in the style of preparing them prove that some mummies must have cost far more than others; and the sumptuous manner in which many persons performed the funerals of their friends kept pace with the splendour of the tombs they made, or purchased for their reception.

Seventhly. The execrations with which the *paraschistes* was pursued could only have been a religious form, from which he was doubtless in little apprehension, an anomaly not altogether without a parallel in other civilized countries.

Eighthly. Diodorus is in error when he supposes the actual face of the body was seen after it was restored to the family; for even before it was deposited in the case, which Herodotus says the friends made for it, the features, as well as the whole body, were concealed by the bandages which enveloped them. The resemblance he mentions was only in the mummy case, or the cartonage which came next to the bandages; and, indeed, whatever number of cases covered a mummy, the face of each was intended as a representation of the person within, as the lower part was in imitation of the swathed body.

Diodorus mentions three different classes of persons who assisted in preparing the body for the funeral—the scribe, who

CHAP. X. REMARKS ON THE PROCESS DESCRIBED. 387

regulated the incision in the side; the *paraschistes*, or cutter; and the embalmers. To these may be added the undertakers, who wrapped the body in bandages, and who had workmen in their employ to make the cases in which it was deposited.* Many different trades and branches of art were constantly called upon to supply the undertakers with those things required for funereal purposes, as the painters of mummy cases; those who made images of stone, porcelain, wood, and other materials; the manufacturers of alabaster, earthenware, and bronze vases; those who worked in ivory; the leather-cutters, and many others. And it is not improbable that to the undertakers, who were a class of priests, belonged a very large proportion of the tombs kept for sale in the cemeteries of the large towns.

The number of days, seventy or seventy-two, mentioned by the two historians, is confirmed by the Scripture account of Jacob's funeral; and this arbitrary period cannot fail to call to mind the frequent occurrence of the numbers 7 and 70, which are observed in so many instances both among the Egyptians and Jews. But there is reason to believe that it comprehended the whole period of the mourning, and that the embalming process only occupied a portion of it; forty being the number of days expressly stated by the Bible to have been assigned to the latter, and "threescore and ten" to the entire mourning.

The custom of embalming bodies was not confined to the Egyptians: the Jews adopted this process to a certain extent, "the manner of the Jews" being to bury the body " wound in linen clothes with spices," as Lazarus was swathed with bandages.

The embalmers were probably members of the medical profession, as well as of the class of priests. Joseph is said to have " commanded the physicians to embalm his father;" and Pliny states that during this process certain examinations took place, which enabled them to study the disease of which the deceased had died. They appear to have been made in compliance with an order from the government, as he says the kings of Egypt had the bodies opened after death to ascertain the nature of their

* *See* above, p. 117, 118, 119.

diseases, by which means alone the remedy for phthisical complaints was discovered.

Certain regulations respecting the bodies of persons found dead were wisely established in Egypt, which, by rendering the district or town in the immediate vicinity responsible in some degree for the accident, by fining it to the full cost of the most expensive funeral, necessarily induced those in authority to exercise a proper degree of vigilance, and to exert their utmost efforts to save any one who had fallen into the river, or was otherwise exposed to the danger of his life. From these, too, we may judge of the great responsibility they were under for the body of a person found murdered within their jurisdiction.

"If a dead body," says Herodotus, "was accidentally found, whether of an Egyptian or a stranger, who had been taken by a crocodile, or drowned in the river, the town upon the territory of which it was discovered was obliged to embalm it according to the most costly process, and to bury it in a consecrated tomb. None of the friends or relations were permitted to touch it; this privilege was accorded to the priests of the Nile alone, who interred it with their own hands, as if it had been something more than the corpse of a human being."

Herodotus fails to inform us what became of the intestines after they had been removed from the body of those embalmed according to the first process; but the discoveries made in the tombs clear up this important point, and enable us to correct the improbable account given by Porphyry. The latter writer says, "When the bodies of persons of distinction were embalmed, they took out the intestines and put them into a vessel, over which (after some other rites had been performed for the dead) one of the embalmers pronounced an invocation to the Sun in behalf of the deceased. The formula, according to Euphantus, who translated it from the original into Greek, was as follows: 'O thou Sun, our sovereign lord! and all ye deities who have given life to man! receive me, and grant me an abode with the eternal gods. During the whole course of my life I have scrupulously worshipped the gods my fathers taught me to adore; I have ever honoured my parents, who begat this body; I have killed no one; I have not defrauded any, nor have I done an injury to any man; and if I have committed any other fault during my life, either in eating or drinking, it has not been done for myself, but for these things.' So saying, the embalmer pointed to the vessel containing the intestines, which was thrown into the river; the rest of the body, when properly cleansed, being embalmed."

Plutarch gives a similar account of their "throwing the intestines into the river," as the cause of all the faults committed by man, " the rest of the body, when cleansed, being embalmed;" which is evidently borrowed from the same authority as that of Porphyry, and given in the same words. But the positive evidence of the tombs, as well as our acquaintance with the religious feelings of the Egyptians, sufficiently prove this to be one of the many idle tales by which the Greeks have shown their ignorance of that people; and no one who considers the respect with which they looked upon the Nile, the care they took to remove all impurities which might affect their health, and the superstitious prejudice they felt towards every thing appertaining to the human body, could for an instant suppose that they would on any consideration be induced to pollute the stream, or insult the dead, by a similar custom.

But the inaccurate statements of the Greeks respecting Egypt and the Egyptians are numerous; and not only have we to censure them for failing to give much interesting information, which they might have acquired after their intercourse with the country became unrestrained, but to regret that what they tell us can seldom be relied on, unless confirmed by the monuments.

It might appear incredible that errors could have been made on the most common subjects, on things relating to positive customs which daily occurred before the eyes of those who sought to inquire into them, and are described by Greek writers who visited the country. But when we observe the ignorance of Europeans respecting the customs of modern Egypt—of Europeans, who are a people much less averse to inquire into the manners of other countries, much more exposed to the criticism of their compatriots in giving false information than the ancient Greeks, and to whom the modern inhabitants do not oppose the same impediments in examining their habits as did the ancient Egyptians—when we recollect the great facilities they enjoy of becoming acquainted with the language and manners, and still find many Italians, French, and others, who have resided ten, twenty, or more years in Egypt, with a perfect knowledge of Arabic, and enjoying constant opportunities for intercourse with the people, ignorant of their most ordinary customs, we can readily account for the misconceptions of the Greeks respecting the habits or opinions of the ancient Egyptians.

As far as the invocation of the Sun, and the confession pronounced by the priest (rather than the embalmer) on the part of the deceased, the account of Porphyry partakes of the character of truth; though the time when this was done should rather be referred to the ceremony on the sacred lake, or to that of depositing the body in the tomb. The confession, indeed, is an imperfect portion of that recorded in the sculptures, which has been already mentioned (p. 376).

As soon as the intestines had been removed from the body, they were properly cleansed, and embalmed in spices and various substances, and deposited in four vases. These were afterwards placed in the tomb with the coffin, and were supposed to belong to the four Genii of Amenti, whose heads and names they bore. Each contained a separate portion. The vase with a cover representing the human head of Amset held the stomach and large intestines; that with the cynocephalus head of Hapi* contained the small intestines; in that belonging to the jackal-headed Smautf were the lungs and heart; and for the vase of the hawk-headed Kebhnsnof were reserved the gall-bladder and the liver. They differed in size and the materials of which they were made. The most costly were of Oriental alabaster, from 10 to 20 inches high, and about one third of that in diameter, each having its inscription, with the name of the particular deity whose head it bore. Others were of common limestone, and even of wood; but these last were generally solid, or contained nothing, being merely emblematic, and intended only for those whose intestines were returned into the body. They were generally surmounted by the heads above mentioned, but they sometimes had human heads;

* See List of Woodcuts in vol. i., note on 278.

CHAP. X.   CLASSIFICATION OF MUMMIES.   391

and it is to these last more particularly that the name of Canopi has been applied, from their resemblance to certain vases made by the Romans to imitate the Egyptian taste. I need scarcely add that this is a misnomer, and that the application of the word Canopus to any Egyptian vase is equally inadmissible.

Such was the mode of preserving the internal parts of the mummies embalmed according to the most expensive process. And so careful were the Egyptians to show proper respect to all that belonged to the human body, that even the sawdust of the floor where they cleansed it was taken and tied up in small linen bags, which, to the number of twenty or thirty, were deposited in vases and buried near the tomb.

In those instances where the intestines, after being properly cleansed and embalmed, were returned into the body by the aperture in the side, images of the four Genii of Amenti, made of wax, were put in with them, as the guardians of the portions particularly subject to their influence; and sometimes, in lieu of them, a plate of lead, or other material, bearing upon it a representation of these four figures. Over the incision the mysterious eye of Osiris was placed, whether the intestines were returned or deposited in the vases.

For the classification of "Egyptian mummies," and the different modes of Embalming, I refer to Mr. Pettigrew's work, where they are arranged under these general heads:

I. Those with the ventral incision.
II. Those without any incision.
I. Of the mummies with the incision are,
   1. Those preserved by balsamic matter.
   2. Those preserved by natron.

1. Those dried by balsamic or astringent substances are either filled with a mixture of resin and aromatics, or with asphaltum and pure bitumen.

When filled with resinous matter they are of an olive colour; the skin dry, flexible, and as if tanned; retracted and adherent to the bones. The features are preserved, and appear as during life. The belly and chest are filled with resins, partly soluble in spirits of wine. These substances have no particular odour by which they can be recognized; but when thrown upon hot coals, a thick smoke is produced, giving out a strong aromatic smell. Mummies of this kind are dry, light, and easily broken; with the teeth, hair of the head, and eyebrows well preserved. Some of them are gilt on the surface of the body; others only on the face, or the sexual parts, or on the head and feet.

The mummies filled with bitumen are black; the skin hard and shining, and as if coloured with varnish; the features perfect; the belly, chest, and head filled with resin, black and hard, and having a little odour. Upon being examined, they are found to yield the same results as the Jew's pitch met with in commerce. These mummies are dry and heavy. They have no smell, and are difficult to develop or break. They have been prepared with great care, and are very little susceptible of decomposition from exposure to the air.

2. The mummies with ventral incisions, prepared by natron, are likewise filled with resinous substances, and also asphaltum. The skin is hard and elastic: it resembles parchment, and does not adhere to the bones. The resins and bitumen injected into these mummies are little friable, and give out no odour. The countenance of the body is little altered, but the hair is badly preserved: what remains usually falls off upon being touched. These mummies are very numerous, and if exposed to the air they become covered with an efflorescence of sulphate of soda. They readily absorb humidity from the atmosphere.

Such are the characteristic marks of the first quality of mummies, according to the mode of embalming the body. They may also be distinguished by other peculiarities; as,

1. Mummies of which the intestines were deposited in vases.
2. Those of which the intestines were returned into the body.

The former included all mummies embalmed according to the most expensive process (for though some of an inferior quality are found with the incision in the side, none of the first quality were embalmed without the removal of the intestines); and the body, having been prepared with the proper spices and drugs, was enveloped in linen bandages, sometimes measuring 1000 yards in length. It was then enclosed in a cartonage fitting closely to the mummied body, which was richly painted, and covered in front with a network of beads and bugles arranged in a tasteful form, the face being laid over with thick gold-leaf, and the eyes made of enamel. The three or four cases, which successively covered the cartonage, were ornamented in like manner with painting and gilding; and the whole was enclosed in a sarcophagus of wood or stone, profusely charged with painting or sculpture. These cases, as well as the cartonage, varied in style and richness, according to the expenses incurred by the friends of the deceased. The bodies thus embalmed were generally of priests of various grades. Sometimes the skin itself was covered with gold-leaf; sometimes the whole body, the face, or the eye-lids; sometimes the nails alone. In many instances the body or the cartonage was beautified in an expensive manner, and the outer cases were little ornamented; but some preferred the external show of rich cases or sarcophagi.

Those of which the intestines were returned into the body, with the wax figures of the four Genii, were placed in cases less richly ornamented; and some of these were, as already stated, of the second class of mummies.

II. Those without the ventral incision were also of two kinds:

1. Salted, and filled with bituminous matter less pure than the others.

2. Simply salted.

(1.) The former mummies are not recognizable; all the cavities are filled, and the surface of the body is covered with thin mineral pitch. It penetrates the body, and forms with it one undistinguishable mass. These mummies, M. Rouger conceives, were submerged in vessels containing the pitch in a liquid state. They are the most numerous of all kinds: they are black, dry, heavy, and of disagreeable odour, and very difficult to break. Neither the eyebrows nor hair are preserved, and there is no gilding upon them. The bituminous matter is fatty to the touch, less black and brittle than the asphaltum, and yields a very strong odour. It dissolves imperfectly in alcohol, and when thrown upon hot coals emits a thick smoke and disagreeable smell. When distilled, it gives an abundant oil; fat, and of a brown colour and fœtid odour. Exposed to the air, these mummies soon change, attract humidity, and become covered with an efflorescence of saline substances.

(2.) The mummies simply salted and dried are generally worse preserved than those filled with resins and bitumen. Their skin is dry, white, elastic, light, yielding no odour, and easily broken; and masses of adipocere are frequently found in them. The features are destroyed; the hair is entirely removed; the bones are detached from their connexions with the slightest effort, and they are white like those of a skeleton. The cloth enveloping them falls to pieces upon being touched. These mummies are generally found in particular caves which contain great quantities of saline matters, principally the sulphate of soda.

Of the latter, also, several subdivisions may be made, according to the manner in which the bodies were deposited in the tombs; and some are so loosely put up in bad cloths and rags, as barely to be separated from the earth or stones in which they have been buried. Some are more carefully enveloped in bandages, and arranged one over the other without cases in the same common tomb, often to the number of several hundred; a visit to one of which has been well described by Belzoni.

Some have certain peculiarities in the mode of their preservation. In many the skulls are filled with earthy matter in lieu of bitumen; and some mummies have been prepared with wax and tanning, a remarkable instance of which occurs in that opened by Dr. Granville—for a full account of which I refer the reader to his work, descriptive of the body and its mode of preservation. I cannot, however, omit to mention a wonderful proof of the skill of the embalmers in this as in so many other instances, who, by means of a corrosive liquid, had removed the internal tegument of the skull, and still contrived to preserve the thin membrane below, though the heat of the embalming matter afterwards poured into the cavity had perforated the suture and scorched the scalp.

It has been a general and a just remark that few mummies of children have been discovered—a singular fact, not easily accounted for, since the custom of embalming those even of the earliest age was practised in Egypt.

Greek mummies usually differed from those of the Egyptians in the manner of disposing the bandages of the arms and legs. The former had the arms placed at the sides, and bound separately; but the arms as well as the legs, and even the fingers of the Egyptians, were generally enclosed in one common envelope, without any separation in the bandages. In these last the arms were extended along the side, the palms inwards and resting on the thighs, or brought forwards over the groin; sometimes even across the breast; and occasionally one arm in the former, the other in the latter position. The legs were close together, and the head erect. These different modes of arranging the limbs were common to both sexes, and to all ages; though we occasionally meet with some slight deviations from this mode of placing the hands. But no Egyptian is found with the limbs bandaged separately, as those of the Greek mummies, though instances may occur of the latter having the arms enveloped with the body.

Sometimes the nails and the whole hands and feet were stained with the red dye of the *henneh;* and some mummies have been found with the face covered by a mask of cloth fitting closely to it, and overlaid with a coating of composition, so painted as to resemble the deceased, and to have the appearance of flesh. But these are of rare occurrence, and I am unable to state if they are of an Egyptian or Greek epoch. This last is most probable, especially as we find that the mummies which present the portrait of the deceased painted on wood, and placed over the face, are always of Greek time. Some remarkable instances of these are preserved in the collections of Europe; and one upon a coffin sent to England by Mr. Salt, which has been figured by Mr. Pettigrew, is now in the British Museum.

On the breast was frequently placed a scarabæus, in immediate contact with the flesh. These scarabæi, when of stone, had their

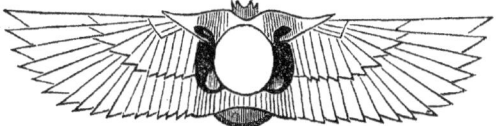

495. A stone scarabæus; covered with wings, and the sun and asps, of silver.
In my possession.

extended wings made of lead or silver; and when of blue pottery, the wings were of the same material. On the cartonage and case, in a corresponding situation above, the same emblem was also placed, to indicate the protecting influence of the Deity; and in this last position it sometimes stood in the centre of a boat, with the Goddesses Isis and Nepthys on either side in an attitude of prayer. On the outer cases the same place was occupied by a similar winged scarabæus, or the winged globe, or a hawk, or a ram-headed vulture or hawk, or both these last, or the same bird with the head of a woman, or by the Goddess Netpe; and sometimes a disk was supported by the beetle, having within it a hawk and the name of Re.

The mode of painting the mummy cases differed according to the rank of the persons, the expense incurred in their decoration, and other circumstances; and such was their variety, that few resembled each other in every particular. There was also a very great difference at different periods, which extended even to the shape of the mummy case. I shall, therefore, in describing them, confine my remarks to their general character, and to the most common representations figured upon them, from the 18th to the 26th dynasty.

In the first quality of mummies, the innermost covering of the body, after it had been swathed in the necessary quantity of bandages, was the *cartonage*. This was a pasteboard case fitting exactly to its shape; the precise measure having been carefully taken, so that it might correspond to the body it was intended to cover, and to which it was probably adjusted by proper manipulation while still damp. It was then taken off again, and made to retain tha shape till dry, when it was again applied to the bandaged body, and sewed up at the back. After this it was painted and ornamented with figures and numerous subjects: the face was made to imitate that of the deceased, and frequently gilded; the eyes were inlaid; and the hair of females was made to represent the natural plaits, as worn by Egyptian women.

The subjects painted upon the cartonage were the four Genii of Amenti, and various emblems belonging to Deities connected with the dead. On the breast was placed the figure of Netpe, with expanded wings, protecting the deceased; sacred arks, boats, and other things were arranged in different compartments; and Osiris, Isis, Nepthys, Anubis, Sokari, and other deities, were frequently introduced. In some instances, Isis was represented throwing her arms round the feet of the mummy, with this appropriate legend, " I embrace thy feet;" at once explanatory of, and explained by, the action of the goddess. A long line of hieroglyphics, extending down the front, usually contained the name and quality of the deceased, and the offerings presented for him to the gods; and transverse bands frequently repeated the former, with similar donations to other deities. But as the arrangement and character of these sacred ornaments vary in nearly all the specimens of mummies, it would be tedious to introduce more than a general notion of their character Even the cartonage and different cases of the same mummy differ, in all except the name and description of the deceased; and the figure of Netpe is sometimes replaced by a winged Sun, or a scarabæus. This goddess, however, always occurs in some part of the coffin, and often with outspread arms at the bottom of the inner case, where she appears to receive the body into her embrace, as the protectress of the dead.

The face of the cartonage was often covered with thick gold leaf, and richly adorned; the eyes inlaid with brilliant enamel; the hair imitated with great care, and adorned with gold; and the same care was extended to the three cases which successively covered it, though each differed from the next; the innermost being the most ornamented. Rich necklaces were placed or represented on the neck of each, for all were made in the form of the deceased; and a net-work of coloured beads was frequently spread over the breast, and even the whole body, worked in rich and elegant devices.

The outer case was either of wood or stone. When of wood, it had a flat or a circular summit, sometimes with a short square pillar rising at each angle. The whole was richly painted, and some of an older age frequently had a door represented near one of the corners. At one end was the figure of Isis, at the other Nephthys; and the top was painted with bands or fancy devices. In others the lid represented the curving top of the ordinary Egyptian canopy (*figs*. 9, 1, 2).

The stone coffins, usually called sarcophagi, were of oblong shape, having flat straight sides, like a box, with a curved or pointed lid. Sometimes the figure of the deceased was represented upon the latter in relief, like that of the queen of Amasis in the British Museum; and some were in the form of a king's name, or royal oval. Others were made in the shape of the

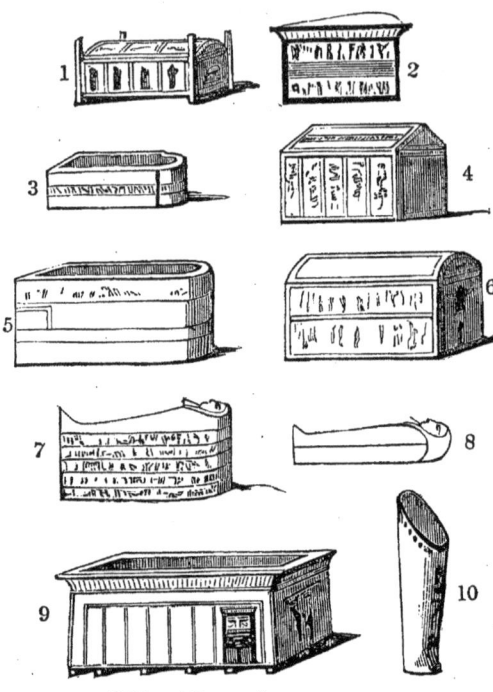

496.   Different forms of mummy cases.
1, 2, 4. Of wood.   3, 5, 6, 7, 8. Of stone.
9. Of wood, and of early time—before the 18th dynasty.
10. Of burnt earthenware.

mummied body, whether of basalt, granite, slate, or limestone, specimens of which are met with in the British Museum and other collections. I have even seen one of this form, found during my stay at Thebes, of a red earthenware, very similar to our tiles, made in two pieces sewed together, small holes having been made in the clay before it was burnt for this purpose. The upper part was broken off, but it was evidently a continuation of the human figure in the form of the mummy it contained.

With regard to the question when the custom of embalming the body ceased in Egypt, it may be observed that some are of opinion that it ceased at an early time, when Egypt became a Roman province. But this has been fully disproved by modern discoveries; and it not only appears that the early Christians embalmed their dead, but according to "St. Augustine, mummies were made in his time, at the beginning of the 5th century." The custom may not have been universal at that period; and it is more probable that it gradually fell into disuse, than that it was suddenly abandoned from any accidental cause connected with change of custom, or from religious scruple.

The disposition of various objects placed with the dead varied in different tombs according to the rank of the person, the choice of the friends of the deceased, or other circumstances, as their number and quality depended on the expense incurred in the funeral. For, besides the richly decorated coffins, many vases, images of the dead, papyri, jewels, and other ornaments were deposited in the tomb; and tablets of stone or wood were placed near the sarcophagus, engraved or painted with funeral subjects and legends relating to the deceased. These last resembled in form the ordinary Egyptian shield, being squared at the base, and rounded at the summit; and it is probable, as already observed, that their form originated in the military custom of making the shield a monument in honour of a deceased soldier.

Many of the objects buried in the tomb depended on the profession or occupation of the individual. A priest had the insignia of his office, as the scribe his inkstand or palette, the high priest the censer, the hieraphoros a small model of a sacred shrine, or a figure bearing an image or emblem of a deity, and others according to their grade. In the soldier's tomb were deposited his arms; in the mariner's, a boat; and the peculiar occupation of each artisan was pointed out by some implement employed in his trade.

Besides the four vases with the heads of the Genii of Amenti were many of smaller size, of alabaster, hard stone, glass, porcelain, bronze, and other materials, many of which were of exquisite workmanship; but these were confined to the sepulchres of the rich, as were jewellery and other expensive ornaments.

Papyri were likewise confined to persons of a certain degree of wealth; but small figures of the deceased, of wood or vitrified earthenware, were common to all classes, except the poorest of the community. These figures are too well known to need a detailed description. They usually present a hieroglyphic inscription, either in a vertical line down the centre, or in horizontal bands round the body, containing the name and quality of the deceased, with the customary presentation of offerings for his soul to Osiris, a chapter from the ritual, or some funereal formula. In the hands of these figures are a hoe and a bag of seed. Their arms are crossed in imitation of certain representations of Osiris, whose name and form the dead assumed; and their beard indicates the return of the human soul which once animated that body to the Deity from whom it emanated.

I do not enter into a minute description of all the modes of arranging the objects in the tombs, the endless variety of Egyptian mummies, or the subjects of their painted cases. I have confined myself to a general view of this, as of other subjects connected with the manners and customs of this ancient and remarkable people; and now, having accompanied the Egyptians to the tomb, I take my leave of them with this wish,

"Sedibus ut saltem placidis in morte quiescant."

Q.   Mummy-pit. A woman searching for ornaments.   *Thebes.*

INDEX.

AARON, embroidered fine linen coat of, ii. 81.
Abbott, collection of Dr., i. 194, 195, 368, 383.
Abrek, Berek, "bow the knee," ii. 203.
Abstract ideas, i. 327, 328, 330.
Abydus, Temple of Osiris at, i. 301, 307.
—— false arch at, ii. 301.
——, some preferred to be buried at, ii. 377.
Abyssinia. *See* Monkeys.
Abyssinian branch of the Nile, ii. 19.
—— called "*blue*" properly "*black* river" ii. 20.
Abyssinians do not eat geese and ducks, i. 166.
Acacia, or Mimosa, several kinds of, i. 57; ii. 28, 37, 38. See *Sont*.
——, a sensitive —, in Ethiopia, ii. 28.
—— *seál*, of the Eastern desert, ii. 38, 106.
Acanthus, or *Sont*, groves of, ii. 28, 37, 110.
Adaptability. *See* Taste, i. 21; ii. 288.
Admired the knick-knacks and furniture of the rooms, i. 146.
Ægyptus the old name of the Nile, i. 303.
—— not the land of Egypt, in Homer, i. 303.
African enemies of Egypt, i. 403, 404.
Agathodæmon, the Asp, i. 46.
Age, respect for old, ii. 226.
Agesilaus took back chaplets of papyrus to Sparta, i. 57, 81.
—— entertained by Tachos, i. 81.
Agility. *See* Feats of —.
Agriculture, ii. 3–54.
Agriculture. *See* Land, Plants, Plough.
—— led to scientific discoveries, ii. 247–250.
—— led to the adjustment of the year, ii. 251, 252.
—— and manufactures of Egypt, ii. 255.

Agweh, preserve of dates, i. 55.
Alabaster used for vases and bottles, i. 156, 157; ii. 70, 342.
——, walls lined with, ii. 288, 292.
Alabastron, vase called, ii. 342.
Alcaline plant called *Boréeth*, ii. 106.
Alexander's conquest of Egypt, i. 309.
Alexandria, population of, i. 305.
——, number of persons who sold vegetables in, i. 168.
—— much wine to be obtained at, i. 54.
Alitta or Mylitta, i. 333.
Alloys in bronze, i. 148.
Almond tree in Egypt, i. 57; ii. 27.
—— oil, ii. 24, 27.
Alluvial deposit in the Valley of the Nile, i. 306; ii. 8, 9.
—— rise of, and proportion of the, ii. 8, 9. *See* Nile.
—— quality, and analysis of the, ii. 19.
Alphabet, twenty-five letters said to compose the Egyptian, i. 291.
Altars, ii. 361.
Amasis, wisdom of, ii. 228.
—— population of Egypt under, i. 304.
—— foreigners saw little of Egypt till after reign of, ii. 231.
Amenti, or Hades, i. 285; ii. 357, 358.
——, four genii of, ii. 381, 382, 390, 391, 396, 399.
America and England, ii. 240.
Americans, North, like Europeans, i. 303.
Ames, or Amosis, i. 111, 307.
"Ames," a harper called, i. (woodcut, 122) 112.
Amphoræ, or wine-jars, i. 47, 48.
——, how fixed upright, i. 48, 49.
——, stopped and sealed, i. 48.
——, pitch, or resinous sediment in, i. 48.
Amun (God of Thebes), i. 327, 328, 331, 332.

Amun expelled from the Pantheon, i. 308.
——, women of, i. 133.
Amunophs, i. 306, 308.
Amunoph III. *See* Lions.
Amusements of Egyptians, lively, i. 210.
Analysis of alluvial deposit, ii. 19.
Animal magnetism, use of, ii. 353.
Animals of Egypt, list of the, i. 245-255.
—— chiefly hunted, i. 224.
—— of Egypt, most noted, i. 227.
——, fabulous, or fanciful, i. 226; ii. 263.
—— not represented, i. 244.
—— sometimes placed entire on the altars, i. 173, 263.
—— skill in rearing, ii. 169.
Anointing the King, i. 275.
—— the statues of gods, i. 275.
——; a customary ceremony, i. 77, 275.
—— guests at a party, i. 77, 78.
Antelopes, various, i. 227, 247.
Anthylla, wine of, i. 50.
Anubis, ii. 358, 378, 381, 382, 396.
——, rites of, i. 129.
Aphôphis, Apôp, the "giant," the "great serpent," the emblem of sin, i. 330.
Apis, the soul of Osiris, i. 288.
——, fête of, i. 288, 291.
——, fête of, lasted seven days, i. 291.
—— called Epaphus, i. 288, 290.
—— and Mnevis, i. 288, 289.
——, colour and marks of, i. 289.
——, clean oxen belonged to, i. 290.
—— called Hapi, i. 290. *See* ii. 390, *note.*
—— kept at Memphis, i. 290.
——, stables of, i. 290, 295.
—— shown to strangers, i. 290.
—— said to have been drowned after living twenty-five years, i. 291.
—— embalmed and buried with great pomp, i. 291.
—— died and another chosen, i. 291.
——, children prophetic who smelt the breath of, and attended the processions in honour of, i. 291, 295.
——, expense of the funeral of, i. 292.
——, discovery of burial place of, i. 292.
—— generally lived 17 to 20 years, i. 292.
——, rejoicings on finding the new, i. 293, 294.
—— consulted as an oracle, and omens drawn from him, i. 294.

Apis the living image of Osiris, i. 288, 294, 300.
——, mode of consulting, i. 295.
——'s influence on crocodiles, i. 295.
——, care respecting food and water given to, i. 293, 295, 322.
Apollinopolis. *See* Crocodile.
Apries took Gaza and Sidon, i. 309.
Arab invaders of Egypt, i. 2.
Arabs had very fine parchment, ii. 100.
—— used at first the shoulder-blades of sheep to write upon, ii. 100.
Arch, bricks led to the invention of the, i. 18; ii. 304.
——, bricks and stones at first placed lengthways in forming the, ii. 304.
—— in Egypt very ancient, i. 18, 31; ii. 300.
—— in Greece, ii. 302.
——, true and false, ii. 302, 303.
—— of brick, ii. 300-303.
—— of stone, ii. 300, 301, 303.
——, principle of the, not depending on the material, nor on the keystone, ii. 300.
——, the pent roof the predecessor of the, ii. 303.
——, pointed, very early, ii. 304.
——, pointed, very early, at Tusculum, in Italy (woodcut), ii. 261.
——, substitutes for, and origin of the, ii. 302-304.
Archers of Egypt, i. 337.
—— of the infantry, i. 354.
——, attack of, i. 405.
Architecture of Egypt, derived much from natural productions, ii. 280, 288.
——, some parts from wood, ii. 280.
——, at first simple, ii. 297.
—— a creation of the mind, ii. 271.
——, constructed—borrowed pillar from the quarry, but rock-temples and tombs took other members from constructed—ii. 281.
——, Byzantine, and Romanesque, Lombard, Saxon, Norman, Saracenic, pointed, ii. 305.
——, progress and modification of styles of, ii. 305. *See* Saracenic.
Ark, or boat, of Sokari, i. 284, 285.
Arks. *See* Shrines.
Armed troops, light and heavy, i. 338, 340, 368.
Arms of Egyptian soldiers, i. 344-369.
—— of their allies, i. 338.
—— of heavy and light armed troops, i. 368.
Army, amount of the, i. 337.

INDEX. 403

Army, discipline of the, i. 337, 338, 340.
———, regiments of the, i. 338, 340. *See* Soldiers.
———, standards of the, i. 342, 343.
———, return of the. *See* War.
Aroura, or *Arura*, land measure, ii. 256.
Arouras, twelve given to each soldier, i. 336; ii. 228.
Arrivals of guests at a party, i. 73–76, 141.
Arrows, length of, i. 353.
——— of reed, i. 352, 353; ii. 30.
——— tipped with metal, or with flint, i. 222, 353.
——— with flint heads used by the Greeks also, and others, i. 353, 354.
———, spare, i. 351, 352.
Arsinoe, on the Red Sea, ii. 235, 236.
———, or Crocodilopolis, i. 307.
Arsinoite nome, i. 242; ii. 28.
Artificial flowers, i. 57.
Arts, ii. 277–280. *See* Taste.
——— of production and arts of design, ii. 295.
——— and inventions older than we suppose, ii. 57.
Aryandes coined money in Egypt, ii. 150.
Ascalon and Asmaor (Samaria?), i. 403.
Ashúr of ten strings, a Jewish instrument, i. 126, 130.
Asiatic enemies of Egypt. *See* Enemies.
A'Souán, or Syene, Cuphic inscriptions at, ii. 142.
———, quarries at, ii. 309, 311.
Asp, or Agathodæmon, guarding a store-room, i. 46.
——— sacred to Neph (Nû, or Nûm), i. 253.
Assemblies, the great, i. 280.
Asses numerous in Egypt, i. 231.
———, wild, not represented, i. 244.
Assessors, ii. 369, 376, 381.
———, forty-two, ii. 376, 382.
Assyria, i. 308.
Assyrian art borrowed, and archaïc style of, not yet found, ii. 263. *See* Nimroud Sculptures and Cylinders.
Assyrians, cruelty of the, i. 3, 410.
Astarte, i. 333.
Atesh, or Kadesh, fort of, i. 403.
Athenian coins of commerce had the old type, ii. 151.
Athor, cow or heifer the emblem of, i. 260, 261, 299.
———, Venus of Egypt, i. 333.

Athor, the Persea the sacred tree of, ii. 383.
Athribis (or Crocodilopolis), i. 307.
Attendants collecting the game, i. 236.
Axe, or hatchet, used in war, i. 361, 362, 419.
———, with a metal blade, used by peasants also, ii. 18.
A'zrek means "black" as well as "blue," ii. 20.

BAALBEK, large stones of, ii. 299.
———, mode of removing large stones from the quarry at, ii. 316.
Babel (Babylon), tribute from, i. 397.
Babylon, arched tunnel under the Euphrates at, ii. 302.
———, mode of carrying Gods of, i. 269.
———, golden statues at, ii. 243.
Babylonian embroidered cloths, and cloths of different colours, ii. 81.
Babylonians, pole, sun-dial, and division of day, from the, ii. 319.
Bacchus, fête of, i. 287.
———, resemblance of, to Osiris, i. 285.
Bags containing gold dust, i. 148.
Bagpipes of the Abruzzi, i. 129.
Bais, palm branches, i. 71.
Baker and cook formerly the same office, i. 177.
Balance, ii. 148, 152. *See* Scales.
Balanites. *See* Egleeg.
Ball, or bullet, the pointed, i. 358.
———, games of, i. 198–200.
———, they mounted on each other's backs while playing at, i. 198, 200.
Balsam, ii. 27.
Bargains, length of time in concluding, ii. 104.
Barley, ii. 21. *See* Wheat, and Beer.
Barrels not wanted in Egypt, ii. 166.
Basin of Amasis, golden, i. 186.
Baskets for fruit when gathered, i. 43.
Bastinado, punishment of the, i. 418; ii. 4, 210, 211, 215.
——— of women, ii. 211.
——— of workmen, ii. 212.
——— of *shereéfs* and great men, ii. 212.
——— of a Copt at Cairo, ii. 213.
Baths, ii. 349.
Bats represented, i. 234.
Battle-axe, i. 362, 363.
——— with bronze blade and silver casing to the handle, i. 363.
Battles formerly decided by hand-to-hand fighting, i. 364.
Beads, ii. 64, 65, 339, 340.

Beans and other vegetables eaten, but not by the priests, i. 323.
Bear, i. 228, 245.
Beards, false, ii. 329.
——— of gods, kings, and private individuals, ii. 329.
Bedroom furniture, i. 70, 71.
Bedsteads, i. 72.
Beef and goose favourite meats of the Egyptians, i. 66.
——— not wholesome, i. 66.
Beer, men drunk with, i. 54.
——— offered, i. 266.
——— called barley-wine, and *zythos* (*zythus*), i. 53–55.
Bees and hives, i. 36.
——— taken on the Nile in boats, i. 36.
Bellows worked by the feet, i. 174.
Benha-el-Assal or "Benha of honey," town of, i. 37.
Beni Hassan, strange shields at, i. 348.
———, wrestlers at, i. 204, 205.
———, dwarfs and deformed persons at, i. 204.
Benno sacred bird of Osiris (apparently the Phœnix), i. 251, 252.
Berek. See *Abrek.*
Berenice, on the Red Sea, ii. 235–237.
Berkel, pyramids of Gebel, ii. 301, 304.
Bersheh. *See* Colossus.
Bident spear, i. 237–239.
Biot, reign of Thothmes fixed by, ii. 255.
Birds of Egypt, i. 232–234, 249–252.
———, fanciful and allegorical, i. 252; ii. 396.
———, salted and dried, i. 173; ii. 184, 185.
——— sometimes placed whole on the altar, i. 173, 263.
——— served up with the feet and pinion-joints taken off, i. 173.
——— caught in nets and traps, ii. 180–185.
Birthday of the King celebrated, and of Typho, i. 281.
Bitumen called *sift*, or *zift* "pitch," i. 397; ii. 259. *See* Rot-n̄-n.
Black slave holding a plate, i. 141.
——— and white slaves. *See* Slaves.
——— puddings made in Egypt, i. 170.
Blades of tools, and weapons, mode of fastening, ii. 113, 164.
Blocks. *See* Stones.
Blood used for cooking, i. 170.
Boar, wild, in Egypt, i. 244.
———, wild, eaten by some people about Damietta, i. 244.

Boards, mode of joining two, ii. 111, 112.
Boat towed on a lake in the grounds of a villa, i. 25.
——— with sail made of papyrus, i. 413, 414.
——— of the dead, or Baris, ii. 355.
Boat-builders of two kinds, ii. 119.
Boatmen of the fleet, or navy. *See* Sailors.
——— of the Nile, of the 3d class, ii. 55.
——— of guard ships, ii. 55.
———, steersman a high office among, ii. 55.
Boats of Egypt, i. 414; ii. 119–131. *See* Ships.
——— with double mast in early times, i. 413, 414.
———, punts, or canoes of papyrus, osiers, &c., pitched, ii. 119, 120, 123.
———, various kinds of, in Egypt, ii. 123, 130.
——— going up and down the Nile, ii. 122–124.
———, sails of, like those of China, but generally of sailcloth, ii. 123.
——— of burthen, ii. 121, 122.
——— of large size only used during high Nile, ii. 125.
——— made of the papyrus, ii. 119–123.
———, mentioned by Pliny and Strabo, at the Cataracts, ii. 119, 121.
——— of the papyrus safe against crocodiles, ii. 120.
——— of papyrus not sent to India, as Pliny pretends, ii. 122.
——— of the Armenians covered with hide, ii. 121.
——— of Egypt had no beaks, ii. 128.
———, construction of, ii. 130.
———, lotus painted on, ii. 127.
———, eye on prow of, confined to the funeral boats, ii. 127, 367.
———, eye on Maltese and Indian, ii. 127.
———, ornaments on head and stern of, ii. 128.
———, streamers of, ii. 127.
———, raised places at the head and stern of, i. 413; ii. 128.
———, painted, ii. 127.
———, clean and well washed, ii. 129.
——— made of *sont*, or Acacia wood, ii. 129.
———, pulleys, doubtful if used in, ii. 130, 131.
———, rigging of, ii. 130.

INDEX. 405

Boats, built with ribs, and little or no keel, ii. 126.
—— with and without a cabin, ii. 123–125, 127, 129.
——, of burthen, cabins of, ii. 129.
——, square sails of, ii. 126, 128.
—— with coloured and embroidered sails, ii. 131, *cut* 167.
——, sails of, how reefed and furled, i. 412; ii. 126, 130.
—— sails of, had yard at the top and bottom, ii. 126, 128.
—— sails, had one yard in old times, ii. 126.
Bocchoris the Wise, a great legislator, ii. 217.
Body, reason for preserving the, ii. 380.
Boiled meats seldom eaten by Homer's heroes, i. 173.
Bottle held on the thumb, i. 165.
Bottles, i. 155, 157, 158, 164, 165.
—— and vases stopped with leaves, i. 165.
Bouquet of the Mareotic wine, i. 49.
Bouquets at parties, i. 57.
—— among the offerings to the Gods, i. 257, 258.
Bow of the Koofa, i. 349.
—— of Egypt, i. 349, 350.
——, mode of stringing the, i. 350.
——, mode of drawing the, i. 222, 351.
——, guard on the wrist, in using the, i. 351.
—— and arrows for the chase, i. 221.
—— cover used by infantry, i. 354.
—— case, i. 354.
—— suspended at the side of a chariot, i. 375.
—— string of catgut, i. 351.
—— string used for entangling an enemy, i. 351.
Bow the knee, *abrek*, *bérek*, ii. 203.
Box, curious mode of fastening the lid of a, i. 163, 164.
Boxes of wood of various forms for ornament, and for the toilet table, i. 159–164.
—— and furniture, ii. 110, 111, 115–117.
—— veneered with rare woods, i. 163; ii. 115.
—— of ivory, i. 158.
—— in the form of geese, i. 161.
—— with handle in form of a fox, or a fox-dog, i. 161.
——, lids of, ii. 115–117.
—— of ebony and ivory, ii. 117.

Boxes with pointed top, i. 164; ii. 115, 116.
——, mode of opening, ii. 116, 117.
Boy. *See* Child.
Boys watched the grapes, i. 43.
Brass cups, i. 82, 180.
—— money, ii. 150.
Bread with seeds, i. 177, 179.
——, cakes of, in form of leaves, crocodile's head, &c., i. 177, 266.
——, shape of rolls of, i. 176, 177, 179, 266.
—— made of wheat, or barley, or *doora*, i. 179. See *Doora*.
——, error of Herodotus respecting wheaten, i. 180.
Brickmakers. *See* Bricks.
—— with taskmasters, as described in the Bible, ii. 195.
Bricks led to the invention of the arch, i. 18; ii. 304.
——, houses of crude, i. 6, 18; ii. 8.
——, houses of crude, stuccoed, i. 6.
—— derived from mass of mud first used for building, ii. 281.
——, captives and Egyptians made, ii. 195.
—— made with, and without, straw, ii. 194.
—— preserved to this day, ii. 194.
——, horizontal courses of, in curved lines, ii. 194.
——, burnt, of Roman time, ii. 194.
—— a government monopoly, ii. 194, 195.
——, stamped, ii. 195.
——, great use of, ii. 194, 195.
——, Jews made, but not represented on the monuments, ii. 195, 197.
—— called *Tobi*, as in Arabic, ii. 197.
British bronze weapons, perhaps Phœnician, ii. 136.
Bronze, or brass, cups, i. 82, 180.
——, alloys in, i. 148.
—— blades elastic, i. 148; ii. 159.
—— of excellent quality, i. 148.
——, the earliest cast, ii. 160, 161.
——, use of, ii. 152–155.
——, gilt, ii. 146, 147, 159.
—— tools for cutting stone, ii. 156, 158.
—— used at least 2000 years B.C., ii. 134.
—— weapons in Britain. *See* British.
—— tools, how tempered, ii. 156.
—— chisel found at Thebes, ii. 158.
——, patina upon, ii. 159. *See* Metals, and Metallurgy.
Bruce's harpers, i. 108–110.

Bubastis, Tel Basta. *See* Fête.
—— raised more than any town, as a protection against the inundation, ii. 9, 209.
Buffoonery, the Egyptians fond of, i. 73, 100, 210.
Buffoons, i. 100–103.
Buildings. *See* Architecture.
——, oldest, were of limestone, ii. 305.
Bull-fights, i. 209, 300, 301.
Bulls, sacred, i. 248, 288, 289. *See* Apis.
Bureaucratie in Egypt, ii. 176.
Burial refused, i. 325; ii. 376.
—— refused even to a king if bad, i. 314, 379.
Bushes dragged over the mud, ii. 11.
Butchers sharpening knives on a steel, i. 169, 170.
Buto, fête of Latona at, i. 296, 298.
Byblus. *See* Papyrus.
Byrsa, the citadel of Carthage, ii. 93.
——, a name found in the East, ii. 93.
Byssus is linen, not cotton, ii. 73.
Byzantine and other styles of architecture, ii. 305.

CABBAGES eaten to excite them to drink, i. 53.
Cabinet-makers. *See* Carpenters.
Cabins. *See* Boats.
Calasiries (*Klashr*) soldiers, i. 337, 338.
Calasiris, fringed dress called, ii. 91, 321.
Cambyses invaded Egypt, i. 309.
Caffass of palm branches, i. 71.
Cairo, *Mulkufs* on the houses of, vignette A, i. 1.
Cakes of various shapes in offerings, i. 266.
—— with seeds, i. 177, 266; ii. 31.
Calf, golden, i. 140.
Camel not represented, i. 234.
Camp, i. 406, 407.
Camp-stools, i. 63.
Canals carrying the water through the lands, ii. 5, 7, 10.
——, mouths of the, dammed up to keep in the water, ii. 11.
Canopus vase, ii. 391.
Captives. *See* Prisoners. *See* Enemies.
—— represented supporting tables and chairs, and on sandals, i. 68, 69; ii. 287, 333.
—— represented slain by the king on the façades of the temples, allegorical, and found on the monuments of the Ptolemies and Cæsars, i. 411.
Car. *See* Chariot.
Carchemish, defeat of Necho at, i. 309.
——, fortified town of, i. 308, 309.
Caricatures of women, i. 52; ii. 276.
Carpenters and Cabinet-makers, ii. 109, 111–119.
——, tools of the, ii. 111–114.
——, work of the, ii. 111–119.
Carpets, i. 68; ii. 92, 93.
Carriage with four wheels, i. 384.
—— for travelling (or *plaustrum*), i. 384, 385.
Carthamus, ii. 22, 34.
Cartonage of mummies, ii. 396, 397.
Carts of the Tokkari, i. 392.
Cassiterides, ii. 134–136.
Castes. *See* Classes.
Castor oil, and castor-berry tree, ii. 23, 24, 29.
—— mode of extracting, ii. 23, 24.
Cat used as a retriever, i. 236, 238.
——, sacred, i. 246.
——, wild, or *chaus*, i. 230, 246.
Catgut strings of lyre and other instruments, i. 118, 122, 123, 125.
Cattle of different kinds, i. 231.
——, stall fed, i. 27; ii. 49.
——, marked with a hot iron, i. 217, 218.
——, account of, given to a steward, ii. 178. *See* Shepherds. *See* Superintendents.
Cavalry of Egypt, i. 338, 340.
Cedar and fir wood, from Syria, ii. 38.
Celtes not found in Egypt, ii. 164.
Cerberus, ii. 377, 378.
Ceremonies of Egypt, i. 267–288, 296–301.
——, other, i. 280, 285, 287.
——, the Egyptians delighted in, i. 267.
Ceres and Isis, i. 297.
——, wolves led a priest to the temple of, i. 299.
Chair, a monkey tied to the leg of a, i. 145.
Chairs, i. 58–65.
——, double and single, i. 62.
——, the Egyptians sat on, i. 58.
——, kangaroo, i. 64, 65.
Changes made in the Egyptian religion, i. 328–330.
Chaplets, numerous, i. 57.
—— of nightshade in Egypt, ii. 33.
Character of the Egyptians, i. 2, 3, 210; ii. 210, 227. *See* Conquest.
——, modes of telling the, i. 210, 211.

INDEX. 407

Chariot with complete furniture, i. 376.
—— held two persons, i. 368, 370.
—— sometimes held three, i. 368, 370.
——, the king alone in his, i. 371.
——, the king had a " second," i. 371.
—— had no seat, i. 373.
—— was of wood, i. 373.
——, bent pole of the, i. 374.
——, driver was on the off side of the, i. 371.
——, parts of the, i. 375.
——, process of making a, i. 377, 378.
——, partly made by carpenters, partly by curriers, i. 377.
—— makers, ii. 117.
——, bow and arrow, and spear cases suspended on the, i. 377.
——, wheels of the, i. 379.
——, drawing of, in perspective, i. 380, 382.
——, mode of fastening, and parts of the harness of a war, 1 379, 381.
—— had only two horses, i. 381.
—— for travelling (or *plaustrum*), i. 384, 385.
—— or car in the Florence Museum, i. 385, 386.
—— with mules, i. 384, 385.
—— of the Rot-ñ-n, i. 376.
Chariot-corps, i. 368, 371, 386.
Charioteer, i. 368, 370, 371.
—— often a person of consequence, i. 372.
Chariots of silver and gold, others painted, i. 375.
——, guests arrived in, i. 73, 74, 76.
—— of gentlemen in towns, i. 371.
—— of princes, i. 370.
Charms, ii. 352.
——, or bullas, worn by children, ii. 330.
Charon, origin of, ii. 375, 377.
Chase, i. 212, 214, 218, 221, 224.
—— a favourite pastime, i. 212.
—— in the grounds of grandees, and nets enclosing a space for the, i. 213.
Chemistry and metallic oxides, knowledge of, ii. 67.
—— and dyeing cloths, ii. 67.
Cherubim like the winged figures of Truth in the arks, i. 271.
Chevron ornament in Egypt, ii. 290.
Chickens, or fowls, treatment of, ii. 184.
Child, lock of hair indicative of a, i. 311, 372.
—— accompanied its parents when fishing and fowling, i. 235, 237.

Children of priests, education of, i. 321.
——'s hair, ii. 328.
——, education of, ii. 226.
—— of common people, i. 322.
—— of slaves, ii. 225.
——, severity of duties of, ii. 225.
——, respect of, to parents, ii. 225.
——, not swaddled, and mode of carrying, ii. 330.
Chinese bottles, ii. 68, 69, 70.
——, probable date of, ii. 70.
Chisels, ii. 113, 114. *See* Bronze.
Choristers, i. 92.
—— often blind, i. 94, 95.
Chorus of many persons, i. 92.
Christian story offers fine subjects for art, ii. 294.
Clappers, or *Crotala*, i. 99, 100, 129, 130, 135, 296.
—— used in dances, i. 135.
Clapping the hands, i. 92. *See* Hands.
Class the 1st and the 2d, priests and soldiers, i. 316; ii. 2.
Class 3d, huntsmen, gardeners, boatmen, peasants, &c., ii. 2, 54, 55.
Class 4th, members of the, ii. 2, 56.
Class 5th, members of the, ii. 2.
Classes, five, of the Egyptians, not castes, i. 316; ii. 2.
—— according to Herodotus, Diodorus, Strabo, and Plato, ii. 1, 2.
Clay used for pottery, ii. 107.
—— kneaded by the foot, ii. 107.
Cloth, manufacture of, ii. 85, 86, 89.
——, calendering, ii. 91, 92.
Clover, dried, called in Arabic *Drees*, ii. 21, 48, 49.
Club of rude shape, i. 364.
—— (*lissán*) or curved stick, i. 365.
—— used by foreigners (woodcut), i. 338, 365.
Cock's head. *See Rhyton*.
Cocks and hens, not represented, i. 234.
—— originally from Asia, i. 234.
Coffin makers, ii. 117–119.
Coffins, ii. 119, 368, 375, 397.
—— of foreign woods, ii. 19.
Coin of Athens, of old type, being known in commerce, ii. 151.
Coinage, oldest, ii. 147, 150.
Coins of Electrum, Lydian, ii. 150.
—— of real gold were of Darius, ii. 150.
—— oldest silver, ii. 147, 150. *See* Gold.
Colossi. *See* Statues.
Colossus on a sledge, at El Bersheh, ii. 307, 308. *See* Frontispiece to vol. ii.

Colour of temples, ii. 281, 290, 291.
—— of statues, ii. 279.
Colours, nature of their, ii. 292.
—— taste in the arrangement of, ii. 293.
—— applied to wood on a coating of stucco, ii. 111.
Coloured and glazed tiles, ii, 288, 292.
Column thrown down by one of the guests at a party, i. 146.
—— supporting a statue, not good taste, i. 21.
Columns, eight orders of Egyptian, ii. 285, 286.
——, palm tree and other, ii. 283.
——, Caryatide from the Osiride, ii. 286.
——, slender, reaching to the top of the house, i. 20, 21 ; ii. 286.
—— of our modern houses, i. 20.
——, variety of, in the same hall, ii. 296, 297.
——, square, or pillars, the oldest, ii. 281.
——, polygonal, ii. 282–284.
——, half drums of, ii. 284.
Combs, ii. 342, 343.
Committees never responsible, ii. 295.
Commutation. *See* Punishments.
Confectioners, i. 174, 177.
Confession of the dead, ii. 201.
Conquest of a country does not entirely change the character of a people, i. 2 ; ii. 227.
Conquests of the Egyptians, i. 308, 390–416.
Convent, or college, of women, i. 319.
Conversation considered the charm of society, i. 146.
Cook. *See* Baker.
Cooking meat, i. 174, 175, 178.
Cooks, i. 170, 174–178.
Coopers, ii. 117.
——, occupation of, ii. 166.
Copper, use of, or bronze, when alloyed with tin, ii. 152, 158.
—— mines in Egypt, ii. 155. *See* Bronze.
Copt, refusing to pay taxes, story of, ii. 213.
Coptos, pottery of, ii. 107.
Corbag whips, i. 240.
Corn, six ears of, offered by the king, i. 273.
—— and other produce sown, ii. 39. *See* Wheat.
Corn country, i. 173.
Coronation. *See* King.

Corslet, or coat of scale armour, i. 366, 367.
—— worked in colours, i. 367, 368.
—— bronze, scales of, with the name of Sheshonk (Shishak), i. 368.
—— of Amasis, with gold thread, ii. 81, 82.
Cotton cloth, ii. 74.
—— used by the priests, ii. 74.
—— not Byssus, ii. 73.
Couches, i. 68, 69.
Cow. *See* Athor.
Cow's head on a pilaster, ii. 286.
Credulity, reaction of, i. 211.
——, injury arising from, i. 325, 328.
Criminals. *See* Punishments. *See* Bastinado.
—— when not transported, ii. 215.
Crocodile, mode of catching the, i. 241, 242, 244.
—— venerated in some, hated in other places, i. 242, 332.
—— attacked by the Tentyrites, i. 242.
—— a timid animal, i. 242.
——, mode of attack of the, i. 243.
——, size of the, i. 243.
—— eaten at Apollinopolis, i. 241.
—— held in abhorrence at Apollinopolis, Tentyris, and Heracleopolis, i. 242.
—— and the trochilus, i. 243.
—— moves the lower jaw, i. 197.
——, toy of the, i. 197.
——, eggs of the, i. 243.
Crocodile's eggs destroyed by the ichneumon, i. 229.
Crocodilopolis. *See* Arsinoë. *See* Athribis.
Crops, several, ii. 20, 21, 25, 39, 49, 50. *See* Plants.
Cross, sign of life put for the, i. 277.
Cross-legged, poor people sat, i. 58.
——, they did not generally sit, i. 58.
Crotala, or clappers. *See* Clappers.
Crown of Upper and Lower Egypt (called *Pshent*), i. 257, 269 ; ii. 323, 325.
—— put on by the king, i. 273.
—— put on the king's head by the gods, i. 276.
Cruelty of Asiatics, i. 3.
—— not commonly practised by the Egyptians, i. 3, 406, 410.
——, occasional acts of, i. 410.
Cubit, ii. 256–259.
—— of same length at different times, ii. 257.
—— of the Nilometer, ii. 257–259.

INDEX. 409

Cullenders. *See* Strainers.
Cups, i. 180. *See* Vases.
Cups of brass, or bronze, i. 82.
Curriers and shoemakers, ii. 10–105.
Cush, or Ethiopia, i. 402, 404.
Cutch, club of the people of, i. 364.
Cylinders very ancient in Egypt, long before, and not borrowed from, the Assyrians, ii. 341.
Cymbals, i. 99, 100.
Cyperus, various kinds of, ii. 96.

DAGGERS, i. 358.
——, mode of wearing and using, i. 359.
—— with sheaths, and ornamented handles, i. 360.
—— of bronze, i. 360, 361.
Damascening, art of, ii. 159, 161, 162.
Damietta, wild boar eaten by some people about, i. 244.
Dance, i. 133–140.
——, steps in the, i. 139.
——, figure, i. 137, 140.
——, gestures in the, i. 133–135, 138.
—— of the lower orders, i. 139.
Dancers, i. 96.
Dancing not taught to the upper classes, i. 135.
—— of the Greeks and Romans, i. 135, 138.
—— of Hippoclides, i. 135.
——, posture in, i. 138.
——, pirouette in, i. 138.
—— women, dresses of the, i. 138.
——, sacred, i. 140.
—— taught to slaves, i. 138.
——, clapped their hands while, i. 135.
—— in the temple, i. 140.
Darabooka drum, i. 93, 98.
Darics gold coins, ii. 150, 151.
Darius introduced good laws into Egypt, ii. 229.
Date-wine, i. 56.
Dates, i. 55.
——, preserve of, i. 181.
—— of *Korayn*, called *Amaree*, ii. 37.
David danced, i. 140.
——, gold and silver collected by, ii. 243.
Days of the Epact, the 5 days added to the 360, i. 281; ii. 252, 254.
—— and night divided into 12 hours, ii. 319.
Dead, did not cut themselves for the, ii. 374.
——, no degradation offered to the, ii. 379.

Dead, numerous ceremonies of the, ii. 119, 357–363, 365–375, 383–390.
—— body, if found, was embalmed at the expense of the district, ii. 388.
——, trial of the, ii. 375, 377, 378.
——, intestines of the, ii. 388, 390, 391.
——, lake of the, ii. 377.
——, objects buried with the, ii. 319.
Death of individuals, songs on the, i. 97.
Death, soul after, ii. 329, 357.
Debt, laws respecting, ii. 217, 218.
——, no arrest for, ii. 217.
——, gave tomb of a parent as a pledge for, ii. 218, 376.
—— increased by luxury and fondness for imitation, ii. 218, 219.
Decimal and duodecimal calculation, ii. 178.
Decorative design, the province of, ii. 288.
—— works by celebrated artists, ii. 280.
Decoy bird, i. 236.
Dedication of a temple, i. 271, 272.
Deeds, mode of executing, ii. 219.
——, number of witnesses for, ii. 219, 222.
——, form of, for sale of small property, ii. 220–222.
Deity, division of the, into his attributes, i. 327, 329.
——, unity of the, i. 327.
Delta, villages of the, like islands during the inundation, ii. 7.
——, the water and the land rise less in the, ii. 7, 9.
Dentists, ii. 350.
Desert, edge of the, cultivated, ii. 20.
Diana. *See* Pasht.
Dice, i. 195, 196.
Dido and the bull's hide, ii. 93. *See* Byrsa.
Dining, mode of, i. 167.
Dinner, they sat round a small table at, i. 167, 181, 182.
——, number of dishes at, i. 167, 180.
——, preparation of, i. 165.
—— at noon, i. 73, 174, 179.
——, occupation of guests before, i. 76.
Discoveries and inventions often effects of chance, ii. 84.
Dishes of various kinds, i. 167, 180.
Divans, i. 58.
Doctors, ii. 350–352.
——, feeling the pulse, ii. 352.
Dog, mummies of the fox-, i. 231.
Dogs in fashion at different times, i. 231.

VOL. II.   T

Dogs often appear to be chosen for their ugliness, i. 231.
——, breeds of, i. 230, 231.
——, hunting with, i. 218.
—— coupled, i. 218, 219.
Dóm tree, or Theban palm, i. 56, 57.
——, nut of the fruit of the, i. 56; ii. 28, 113.
——, fruit of the, like our gingerbread, i. 56.
Doora, or *holcus* sorghum, bread of the, i. 179; ii. 3, 22, 25.
——, plucked up by the roots, and the head stripped off by a spiked instrument, ii. 50, 51.
Doors, i. 13, 15-17, 28.
——, hinges, and keys, i. 15, 16.
——, single and double valves, opened inwards, i. 17.
——, sentences written over, i. 6.
—— of store-rooms for grain, i. 14, 32.
Doorways, i. 9, 15-17, 26.
Doqáq, of ground lupins, for washing, instead of soap, i. 186.
Double pipe, i. 128, 129.
—— used in sacred music, i. 129.
Dovetailing, ii. 111.
Doura. See *Doora*.
Dramatic entertainments, Greek, i. 100.
Draughts, game of, i. 189, 190, 191, 192, 193.
Drawing much studied in France, ii. 275.
—— and sculpture preceded writing, ii. 270.
Dress, leopard skin, of the priests, i. 319. See Leopard-skin Dress.
—— of a king and a queen, i. 317.
Dresses of dancing women, i. 138.
—— of huntsmen, i. 215.
—— of priests, i. 319, 320, 333-335.
—— of soldiers, i. 365, 366.
—— of mercenary troops, i. 337.
—— and arms of foreign people the enemies of Egypt, i. 390-404.
—— of the kings, i. 317; ii. 322-325.
—— of the queens, i. 317.
—— of men, ii. 320-322.
—— of women, i. 318-335.
—— of children, ii. 329, 330.
—— at a party, i. 81.
—— simple, like that of a river god, ii. 320.
—— embroidered and coloured, ii. 81, 83.
—— with fringes, i. 333; ii. 91, 320, 321.
——, head, of men, ii. 325.

Dresses, head, of women, ii. 335.
—— of poor people, ii. 320.
—— not fully described on the monuments, ii. 320.
Drill (or centrebit), i. 56; ii. 94, 111-113.
Drinking to each other, i. 82.
——, excesses in, i. 52, 53.
Drum, i. 98, 104, 105, 106, 107.
Drum. See *Darabooka* Drum.
Drumstick, i. 107.
Drums of columns, ii. 284.
Dwarfs and deformed persons in the service of grandees, i. 203, 204.
Dykes, ii. 5, 7, 10.
—— watched by guards and kept up at great expense, ii. 7.
——, punishment for injuring the, ii. 7.
Dynasty, Thinite, Memphite, Theban, i. 307. See Saite.
——, 18th, i. 308.

EARRINGS, women talking about, i. 145.
——, patterns of, ii. 335, 338, 345.
Education of the priests and other classes, i. 321, 322.
—— of youth, strict, ii. 226.
Egleeg, or Balanites, tree, ii. 28, 37, 38, 110.
Eglon, King of Moab, parlour of, i. 11.
Egypt, influence of, on Greece, i. 1.
——, influence of, on early civilization, i. 3.
——, antiquity of, i. 3, 4.
——, treatment of women in, i. 4; ii. 223.
——, plants and trees of, i. 57.
—— famous for medicinal plants and drugs, i. 50; ii. 351.
——, history of, i. 307-309.
——, Menes, the first king of, i. 307.
——, dynasties of the kings of, i. 307.
—— once divided into several independent kingdoms, i. 307.
—— Ames (or Amosis) became sole king of, i. 111, 307.
——, Shepherds invaded, and were driven out of, i. 307, 308.
——, lost all its conquests in Asia, i. 309.
—— conquered by Cambyses, i. 309.
—— recovered by native kings, i. 309.
——, Alexander conquers, i. 309.
——, rule of the Ptolemies in, i. 309.
—— rule of the Romans in, i. 310.
—— of limited extent, i. 304.
——, number of square miles in, i. 304.

INDEX. 411

Egypt, towns and villages of ancient, i. 304.
——, population of, i. 305.
—— had Ethiopians, Libyans, and others under its sway, i. 305.
——, produce of, greater in old times, but capable of producing more now, i. 305.
——, no great encroachments of sand in, i. 306.
——, some towns of, placed on the edge of the desert, i. 306, 307.
—— glass. *See* Glass. *See* Etruscans.
—— has more cultivable land now than formerly, i. 306.
—— emblems, and crowns, of Upper and Lower, i. 257, 269; ii. 323, 325.
—— productiveness of, ii. 2, 3.
—— called "the world," ii. 227.
—— nomes or provinces, and limits of, ii. 229.
——, divisions of, at different times, ii. 229, 230, 231.
——, foreigners confined to certain parts of, ii. 231.
—— became commercial after the fall of Tyre and building of Alexandria, ii. 133.
——, long the dominant nation, and set the fashion in art, &c., ii. 263.
——, foreign woods imported into, ii. 111.
—— produced little wood for ornamental purposes, ii. 109.
——, boats of. *See* Boats.
——, wealth of, ii. 238, 239, 242. *See* Tribute.
——, wines of, ii. 238, 239, 240.
——, known to foreigners for its manufactures, ii. 247. *See* Agriculture.
——, exports of, ii. 233, 234, 256.
——, offices in, at different times, ii. 231.
——, Greek information respecting, imperfect, ii. 231, 389.
—— under the Romans, ii. 233.
"Egyptian," artificial flowers called, i. 57.
Egyptian. *See* Embroidery. *See* Chemistry.
—— yarn, ii. 84.
—— architecture, ii. 280–304.
—— architecture, all painted, ii. 290. *See* Architecture.
—— painters and scribes, ii. 275, 276, 277.
—— inkstands and sketches, ii. 276.
—— art, ii. 262.

Egyptian paintings on panel, ii. 277.
—— laws, sanctity of old, ii. 227.
—— lawgivers, ii. 226.
—— temples, subjects of the sculpture in, ii. 295, 296.
—— colours, ii. 292, 293.
—— scribes with a pen behind the ear, ii. 275.
—— figures drawn in squares, ii. 266, 267.
—— figures often spirited, but wanting in life and reality, ii. 268.
—— statues, ii. 272.
—— sculptures in low relief and intaglio, ii. 272.
—— sculptures of a new style of Remeses III., ii. 273.
—— sculpture, revival of, ii. 274.
Egyptians, origin of the, i. 302, 303.
——, a Caucasian race, i. 302.
—— went to Egypt as conquerors, i. 303.
—— placed some towns on the edge of the desert, i. 306, 307.
——, early government of the, hierarchical, i. 307.
—— restless under all foreign rulers, i. 310.
——, social habits of the, i. 3, 4, 5, 144.
—— not guilty of great cruelty. *See* Cruelty. *See* Humanity.
—— thought to be a gloomy people, i. 2.
——, character of the, i. 2, 3, 210.
——, character of the modern, i. 2; ii. 210, 227.
—— very fond of their country, ii. 227.
—— fond of flowers, i. 19, 57.
—— fond of wine, i. 53.
—— fond of variety, i. 58; ii. 297.
—— fond of ceremonies and religious pomp, i. 267.
—— sat on chairs, i. 58.
—— did not recline at meals, i. 58.
—— victories and power of. *See* Conquests.
—— had only one wife, i. 5; ii. 224.
—— kept to their old customs, ii. 226.
——, "wisdom of the," i. 325; ii. 202.
——, gratitude of the, ii. 227.
—— had some elegant vases, but generally deficient in taste, and very inferior to the Greeks, ii. 109.
—— had the *guilloche, chevron*, and other patterns at a very early time, ii. 290.
—— coated walls with stucco, ii. 291.
—— used gilding, ii. 293.
—— avoided uniformity and studied

THE ANCIENT EGYPTIANS.

variety in their architecture, ii. 296, 297, 298.
Egyptians had columns of different styles in the same hall, ii. 296, 297.
—— skill of the, in drawing lines, ii. 274.
—— pencils and brushes of the, ii. 275.
—— did not bear innovation in sacred subjects, ii. 264.
—— did not alter their style of drawing, and were bound by fixed rules, ii. 264, 266.
—— deficient in taste, ii. 265–269, 272.
—— drew animals better than men, ii. 269.
——, "all equally noble," ii. 357.
—— first who taught that soul of man was immortal, ii. 379.
Elasticity of bronze, i. 154, 360; ii. 159.
Electric fish, called in Arabic Raad, "thunder," ii. 192.
Electrum, coins of, ii. 150.
Elizabethan rooms, i. 58.
Embalmers, ii. 119, 374, 387.
Embalming process, ii. 383–387.
——, supposed reason for, ii. 380.
——, when given up, ii. 398, 399.
Emblems offered, i. 260.
——, sacred and other, i. 257.
Embroidery of the Egyptians, Hebrews, Babylonians, and Romans, ii. 81.
—— with gold, ii. 81.
Emeralds, false, in glass, ii. 63, 64.
——, large statues of, ii. 63.
Enamelling on gold, ii. 70.
Encaustum, the colours burnt in, ii. 70.
Enemies of Egypt, Asiatic, i. 390, 391–403.
——, African, i. 402, 403, 404.
——, wounded, i. 373.
——, heads of, represented on window-sills, i. 68; ii. 287.
Epact, the five days of the. *See* Days.
——, third day of the, Typho's birthday, i. 281.
Epaphus, clean oxen belonged to, i. 290. *See* Apis.
Ethiopia, Jupiter going into, i. 269.
——, gods taking refuge in, i. 269.
——, a princess of, coming to an Egyptian king, i. 384, 385.
Ethiopian kings of Egypt, i. 308.
Ethiopians, tribute of the, i. 404.
Etruscans, Greeks, and Assyrians had some bottles and vases from Egypt, ii. 70, 71.
Evil, ii. 372.

Europe had an indigenous population, i. 303.
Europeans differ from Asiatics, i. 303.
Excesses of men and women in drinking, i. 52, 53.
—— in eating and drinking, i. 173.
Expenses of the Egyptians trifling, the necessary, ii. 219. *See* Food.
Extremities of the world possess the greatest treasures, ii. 240.
Ex-votos, ii. 354.
Eye of Osiris, i. 257.
—— signifying "Egypt," i. 244, 257.
—— on boats, ii. 127. *See* Boats.
Eyes painted, or blackened with *Kohl*, ii. 343.

FALCHION, *Shopsh*, or *Khopsh*, i. 361.
Fanbearer of the king a high office, i. 283, 284.
——, investiture to the office of, i. 283.
Father, abstract idea of, i. 327, 332.
——, murder of a, ii. 209.
——'s trade followed by a son. *See* Son.
Fauteuil of the master of the house, i. 145.
—— some pet animal tied to the leg of a, i. 145.
Fauteuils, i. 60, 61, 62.
——, highly ornamented, i. 60, 61.
Feast, ruler of the, i. 82.
Feats of strength and dexterity, i. 201, 205, 207.
—— of agility, i. 188, 189.
Feet, clay kneaded with the, ii. 107.
——, paste kneaded with the, i. 177.
Fescennine verses of Italy, i. 101.
Festivals, i. 280–287. *See* Fêtes. *See* Sacred.
—— connected with agriculture, ii. 52, 53, 54.
—— of harvest-home, i. 282.
Fête of Diana at Bubastis, i. 296, 297.
—— of Isis at Busiris, i. 296, 297.
—— of Minerva, or Neith, at Saïs, i. 296, 298.
—— of burning lamps, ii. 71.
—— of the Sun at Heliopolis, i. 296, 298, 301.
—— of Latona at Buto, and of Mars at Papremis, i. 296, 298.
—— of Thoth, i. 299.
—— in honour of the daughter of Mycerinus, i. 299.
Fêtes, many, in the year, i. 296.
—— at the new and full moon, i. 299.
—— other, i. 301. *See* Sacred.

INDEX.   413

Fêtes of the peasants during the high Nile, ii. 52. *See* Festivals.
Fig trees and vines, i. 41, 57.
——, wild, ii. 30.
Figs, i. 54.
——, sycamore, 44, 57, 181, 259. *See* Sycamore.
—— and grapes, fond of, i. 181.
—— and grapes on altars, i. 262.
—— in a basket, the hieroglyphic signifying "wife," i. 323.
Figl (or *Raphanus*), i. 167, 259, 323.
Figure, proportions and Egyptian mode of drawing the human, ii. 266.
Figure. *See* Foot, the standard for the.
Firmán, or royal order; custom of kissing, ii. 203.
First fruits, offerings of the, i. 274, 299.
Fish not eaten by the priests, i. 322.
——, sacred, i. 254; ii. 191, 192.
—— and meat at dinner, i. 167.
——, how brought to table, i. 173.
—— of Egypt most prized, ii. 191.
—— of the Nile of muddy flavour, ii. 193.
——, great consumption of, ii. 189, 193.
——, dried, ii. 181, 189, 190.
—— of Egypt regretted by the Israelites, ii. 191.
——, electric. *See* Electric.
—— of the sea not appreciated, ii. 193.
Fishponds, i. 37, 215.
Fisheries, revenue from the, ii. 193.
—— of the Lake Mœris, ii. 193.
Fishermen, ii. 181, 186.
Fishing, ii. 181, 186-193.
Fishing, an amusement of gentlemen, i. 238.
——, they sat on a mat, or in a chair, while, i. 238.
—— with a fly unknown, i. 239.
—— nets and leads of, ii. 187-189.
Fishing-rod and hook, i. 239; ii. 186.
Flax, process of cultivating, or steeping, and preparing for cloth, ii. 88, 89.
——, comb for preparing, ii. 90, 91.
—— used for ropes, ii. 93.
——, nets of string, made of, ii. 95.
——, much in Egypt, ii. 50.
Flaxman, the great taste of, ii. 289.
Flower offered from each other's bouquet, i. 146.
—— garden, i. 37, 57.
—— of the lotus, i. 39. *See* Lotus.
Flowers, as emblems, i. 257.

Flowers presented as offerings, i. 257-259.
—— produced in Egypt. i. 57.
—— much used, i. 19, 57.
——, artificial, called "Egyptian," i. 57.
—— presented to guests, i. 78-81, 141.
——, wreaths of, i. 57, 79.
——, stands for, i. 79.
——, fondness of the Egyptians for, i. 19, 57.
——, bowl crowned with, i. 80.
—— brought as part of a foreign tribute, i. 57, 395.
—— of the lotus much used for chaplets and wreaths, i. 57.
——, tables decked with, i. 57.
—— and plants of Egypt, from Pliny, ii. 27-32. *See* Plants.
—— in the paintings, ii. 36.
——, "*immortelles*," placed in the tomb, ii. 374.
Flute, length of the Egyptian, i. 127.
——, antiquity of the, i. 126, 127.
—— of reed, bone, wood, or ivory, i. 127.
—— not allowed in the rites of Osiris and Anubis, i. 129.
——, Minerva's aversion for the, i. 127.
Fly-fishing. *See* Fishing.
Food, i. 166-168.
—— of the peasants, i. 167; ii. 3.
—— of the poor people and shepherds, ii. 175.
—— of poor people simple and cheap, i. 179; ii. 219, 330.
"Fool or a physician at forty," origin of, ii. 352.
Foot, watering with the, i. 34.
——, standard, or unit for the human figure, ii. 266.
Foot-machine, i. 34.
Footmen, running, i. 76.
Footstools, i. 68.
Foreleg and shoulder, called "the chosen part," i. 264.
Forks not used at dinner, i. 181.
—— known to the Jews and Etruscans, but not used at table, i. 182.
—— used in an Egyptian kitchen, i. 174, 175.
—— of wood used by the peasants, ii. 42, 45.
Fortification, regular system of, i. 407.
Fowling, a great amusement, i. 234.
Fox, i. 227, 245.
—— dog, i. 231.
Fringes on dresses (sometimes sewed

on), ii. 91, 322. *See* Dresses with fringes.
Fruit in wicker baskets, i. 43.
—— gathering, i. 40, 41, 43, 44.
Fruit trees, i. 36, 55, 57.
Fruits on the altar, i. 259.
Fullers, ii. 106.
Funerals, mourners at, ii. 366.
Funerals of kings, ii. 366.
——, some grand, ii. 366-373.
Furniture of Egyptian rooms, i. 58-72.
Fyoom, or Arsinoite nome, i. 49, 229, 244, 304.
——, extremity of the, artificially irrigated, i. 307.
—— remains of vineyards on the western borders of, i. 49; ii. 20.
——, wild boars found in the, i. 244.

GAME, preserves for, i. 37.
——, parks and covers for, i. 215.
Game-cart, substitute for the, i. 218.
Games in honour of the gods, i. 282.
—— most usual, i. 188, 189.
—— of ball, i. 198-200.
——, various, i. 192-207.
—— of single-stick, i. 206, 207.
——, board of, found by Dr. Abbott, i. 194, 195. See *Mora* and Draughts.
Gardens, i. 25, 32, 35-37.
Garlands or chaplets, i. 57, 79-81.
Gazelle, i. 214-216, 219, 220, 223-225, 227, 247.
Geese, boxes in the form of, i. 161.
—— fed, i. 215. *See* Goose.
—— potted, ii. 185.
Geoffreying machine, ii. 92.
Geography, in the books of Hermes, i. 274.
Geometry, i. 321.
——, arithmetic, and astronomy, ii. 319.
—— invented in Egypt, ii. 248, 251.
Gilding, ii. 145-147.
Giraffe, i. 231, 247.
Gladiators not employed in Egypt, i. 210.
Glass, early use of—blowers, bottles and blowpipe, and glazed pottery, ii. 58.
—— bottles, ii. 58, 67.
—— bottles of various colours, ii. 60.
—— beads with name of Amun-m̀-het, ii. 59.
—— beads, ii. 64, 65. *See* Beads.
—— beads rarely found with a name, ii. 60.
——, discovery or invention of, ii. 60.
——, Egyptians famed for particular kinds of, ii. 60.

Glass counterfeits of precious stones, ii. 60, 63. *See* Precious Stones.
—— shows advance of luxury, ii. 65.
—— of many colours attempted at Venice, ii. 61.
—— mosaics of pictures in Venice, ii. 61, 63.
——, false emeralds of, ii. 63, 64.
——, coloured, 60, 63-65, 67, 71.
——, coloured imitations of murrhine vases, ii. 71.
—— applied to various uses, ii. 65.
—— coloured porcelain, ii. 66, 71. *See* Vitrified.
——, cut, ground, and cast, ii. 67.
—— cut by the diamond, emery powder, and wheel, ii. 67.
—— bottles inclosed in wicker casing, ii. 67, 68.
—— lamps, ii. 71, 72.
Glazed tiles in Egypt, ii. 287, 292.
Gloves, i. 283, ii. 336.
—— brought by the Rot-ǹ-n, i. 397.
Glue, ii. 114, 115.
Goats browsing on vines after the vintage, i. 45.
God, division of, into various attributes, i. 327.
——, spirit of, was Nef, Nû, Nûm, or Nûb, i. 327.
——, or Goddess, with several names, i. 329.
Gods of Egypt, i. 327, 328, 330, 331.
——, figures of the, i. 328.
——, nature, i. 332, 333.
—— worshipped throughout Egypt, i. 331.
—— of different cities, i. 331, 332.
Goddesses with various names, in different countries, really the same, i. 333.
Gold-dust in bags, i. 148, 260, 261; ii. 149.
Gold in Egypt and in Britain, and quartz veins broken up, ii. 141.
—— thread, ii. 81.
—— wire, ii. 82.
—— workers, ii. 137, 138.
——, great use of, for ornaments, ii. 138, 140, 141.
——, hieroglyphic signifying, ii. 149. (*Woodcut, figs. a, b.*)
——, fusing, ii. 139.
——, washing ore of, ii. 139.
——, vases of, ii. 140, 141.
—— mines of Egypt and Ethiopia in the Bisharee desert, and Mr. Bonomi's account of them, ii. 141.
—— of Australia and California, ii. 143.

INDEX. 415

Gold mines described by Diodorus, ii. 143, 144.
——, cruelty to people condemned to the mines, ii. 144, 145.
—— at first used very pure, ii. 145.
—— leaf, at first thick, ii. 145.
—— on vases, mummies, &c., ii. 146.
—— beating, improvements in, ii. 146.
—— used before silver, shown by the latter being called "White gold," ii. 147, 241. (*Woodcut* 408, *fig. c.*)
—— used for overlaying humbler materials, ii. 147.
——, greater use of, for ornamental purposes, ii. 147.
——, rings of, as money, ii. 149.
——, a quantity in bags already counted, ii. 149.
—— darics of Persia, ii. 150.
—— staters, the oldest coins, originally mere dumps, ii. 150.
——, fetters of, in Ethiopia, ii. 155.
—— of Colchis, ii. 240.
—— of Spain, ii. 240, 242.
—— and silver, ii. 238–247.
—— and silver, relative value of, at different times, ii. 242.
——. *See* Precious Metals, Wealth, and Jewellery, ii. 243, 244.
——, quantity of in ancient countries, ii. 243.
——, teeth stopped with, ii. 350.
——, statues of, ii. 243.
—— of David and Solomon, ii. 243.
—— loss by wear and other causes, ii. 245.
—— in Rome, ii. 244, 245.
—— before and after the discovery of America, ii. 246.
Golden calf ground and reduced to powder, ii. 136.
——, mode of worshipping with dances, i. 140.
—— mosaics. *See* Mosaics.
—— ewer and basin, i. 76, 77.
Good, Goodness, i. 327; ii. 358. *See* Osiris.
Goose and beef much eaten, i. 66.
——. *See* Abyssinians.
——, emblem of the God Seb, i. 251.
—— and globe, "son of the Sun," of Egypt, found on Greek vases. *See* Vases.
Grace before meals, i. 186.
Grain, pigs and other animals trod in the, ii. 11, 12, 13.
Grain, abundance of, ii. 3.

Grain of "seven plenteous years" laid up, shows the abundance of, ii. 3.
—— exported and belonging to government stores, ii. 3.
Granaries, i. 13, 31, 32; ii. 43, 46.
—— with vaulted roofs, i. 31, 32.
Granite, difficulty of cutting, ii. 157.
—— not cut and worked when less hard, ii. 157.
——, stunning the crystals of, ii. 157.
——, early use of squared, ii. 287.
——, painted, ii. 291.
——, imitation of, ii. 292.
——, walls cased with, ii. 292.
Grapes, gathering of, i. 40–43.
—— watched by boys, i. 43.
Gratitude of the Egyptians, ii. 227.
Grease used in moving large stones, ii. 309.
Greece, pictures of, ii. 278, 279.
—— in its infancy, when Egypt had long been the leading nation, ii. 263.
—— borrowed from Egypt, ii. 264, 283.
——, influence of Egypt on, i. 1, 4; ii. 263.
Greek temples traced from wooden buildings, i. 5.
—— lyres. *See* Lyres.
—— instruments, name of, i. 126.
—— flute, name of, i. 126.
—— mercenaries in Egypt, i. 309.
—— statues coloured, ii. 279, 280.
—— artists painted on panel, not on walls, the best, ii. 278, 280.
—— pictures in temples and galleries, ii. 279.
—— pictures carried off to Rome, ii. 279.
——, oldest paintings monochrome, ii. 279.
—— statues and bas-reliefs coloured, ii. 279, 291.
—— colours, ii. 291.
—— taste, colour, form, and proportion, ii. 293.
—— architecture at first simple, ii. 297.
—— towns wanted lofty buildings, i. 21.
——, Ionic, and Corinthian capitals, ii. 297.
—— and Egyptian temples of a different character, ii. 298.
—— architecture and bas-reliefs coloured, ii. 291.
Greeks claimed discoveries of others, ii. 109.

Greeks, vases of the, far superior to those of Egyptians in taste, ii. 109.
—— did not copy natural objects for ornament, ii. 288.
—— copied from the "Barbarian" what was beautiful, and made it their own, ii. 289.
—— knew but did not use the arch in buildings, ii. 302.
—— considered music a necessary accomplishment, i. 94.
—— indebted to Asia for stringed instruments, i. 111.
——, long haired, ii. 327.
Grove or *Temenos. See* explanation of Frontispiece, List of woodcuts, vol. i.
—— or *Temenos*, i. 409.
Guard at the gate of a camp, i. 407.
—— had no shield, i. 406.
Guards, royal, i. 337.
Guests, reception of, and arrival of, i. 73.
—— had flowers and wine brought them on arriving, i. 81, 141.
—— anointed on arriving, i. 78.
—— received bouquets of flowers and necklaces, i. 78, 79.
—— crowned with flowers, i. 78, 80.
—— admired the furniture and knick-knacks, i. 76, 146.
—— at dinner sat on the ground, or on chairs, i. 181, 182.
—— amused with music and dancing, i. 141.
Guilloche ornament, i. 19; ii. 290.
Guitar of 3 strings, i. 84, 86, 123, 124.
—— knowledge required for the invention of the, i. 84.
—— *Kithára, Chitarra*, i. 124, 129.
—— an instrument found at Thebes not unlike the, i. 125.
Gúsla of Montenegro, with one string, i. 125.

HAIR of women, ii. 335.
—— of children, i. 312; ii. 328. *See* Child.
—— of men shaved, i. 312; ii. 327.
—— of servants, ii. 334.
Halfeh or *Poa* grass, i. 57.
Handwriting to tell a character, i. 211.
Hands cut off, as a return of the enemy's killed, i. 373.
——, clapping the, i. 89, 90, 92, 95, 101, 128, 135, 139, 296.
Handles of vases, i. 153, 154.
Hare, i. 227, 228, 246.

Harness. *See* Chariot.
Harp of the Paris Collection, i. 113, 114.
—— unknown to the Greeks, i. 111.
——, head of a, from Thebes, i. 110.
Harps, the oldest, i. 85, 111.
—— of various sizes, i. 110, 111.
——, catgut strings of. *See* Catgut.
—— with a support, i. 87, 111, 112.
—— of wood covered with bull's hide, i. 87, 113.
—— of tortoise shell, i. 87, 113.
—— of coloured leather, i. 88, 89, 90, 113.
——, shortening the strings of the, i. 113.
—— had no pedals and no pole, i. 113.
—— used for religious services, i. 113, 129, 130.
—— in the hands of Deities, i. 113.
Harpers, i. 108–112.
—— of the tomb of Remeses III., called Bruce's, i. 108–110.
—— standing to play, i. 86, 87, 88, 89, 90, 108, 109, 111, 112.
Harpocrates, with his finger to his mouth, not silence, ii. 182.
——, ii. 53. *See* Horus.
——, or reproduction on dissolution, ii. 382.
Harvest home, i. 282.
Hatchet, or axe, i. 361, 362, 419; ii. 114.
Hatching eggs artificially, ii. 170.
——, the modern oven for, ii. 170–172.
Hawking, no instance of, i. 221.
Head of an animal given to a poor man, i. 171.
—— cut off first, i. 170, 263.
—— placed on altars and taken to the kitchen, i. 172.
—— said by Herodotus not to have been eaten, i. 172.
——, imprecations on the, as on the scapegoat, probably not extended to every one, i. 172. *See* Enemies.
Heads, men and women carried loads on their, i. 177.
Heads of Egyptians, hard, ii. 328.
Head-stools, or wooden pillows, i. 63, 71, 335, 336.
Hearse of the dead, ii. 368, 373, 375.
Heavy-armed troops, arms of, i. 368.
Hedgehog, i. 227, 229, 245.
Heliopolis, wine not taken into the temple at, i. 51.
—— Re, the Sun, was the God of, i. 296, 298, 300, 331; ii. 312.
——, Mnevis, the sacred bull of, i. 288.

Heliopolis said to have been founded by Arabs (or a Semitic race), i. 302.
Helmet, quilted, i. 365, 366.
—— with crest, from Asia, i. 366.
Henneh, ii. 345.
Heracleopolis, i. 243.
Hermæ of Greece not the origin of statues, ii. 271.
Hermes, books of, i. 274; ii. 251. *See* Medicine.
——, or Mercury, ii. 228. *See* Thoth.
Hermotybies, soldiers, i. 337.
Heroes, no divine honours paid to, i. 328.
Hieraphori, bearers of standards, images, &c., i. 273, 284, 285.
Hierogrammat (sacred scribe), *Hieroscopus*, and *Stolistes*, i. 276.
Hieroglyphics cut to great depth in granite, ii. 156.
Hippopotamus hide, use of the, i. 240. *See* Corbag and Shields.
——, blade for spearing the, i. 241.
——, chase of the, i. 239–241.
—— emblem of Typho, i. 288.
——, cakes with, stamped on them, i. 288.
—— sacred to Mars, i. 246.
History of Egypt, i. 307–309.
Hoe, ii. 11, 14, 16, 17, 18.
—— used with and without the plough, ii. 12, 18.
—— called *Toré*, and put for the letter M, ii. 17.
—— had not a metal blade in early times, ii. 17.
Holydays, i. 281.
—— of peasants, ii. 52.
Hoop, game with a, i. 194, 195.
Horizontal courses of masonry, great antiquity of, ii. 287.
Horizontal line in architecture, i. 20.
Horns for instruments, i. 105.
Hors d'œuvres to excite the appetite, i. 174.
Horses exported from Egypt, i. 386.
—— originally from Asia, i. 234, 386.
—— called *Sus* as in Hebrew, i. 386.
—— abundant, i. 231.
—— of Egypt esteemed, i. 234.
——, trappings of, i. 381.
Horus, or Orus, i. 242, 275, 288, 300, 312, 330.
——, the child, or Harpocrates, i. 256, 312, 333; ii. 182, 382.
House in the British Museum, model of a, i. 13, 14.
Houses, plans of, i. 11, 12.

Houses, they slept in summer on the roofs of, i. 7.
——, small, i. 13.
——, large, i. 20, 24, 27, 29.
—— at Karnak, i. 14.
——, remains of, i. 11.
—— of crude brick, i. 6.
—— of priests, luxurious, i. 7, 322.
——, plans and number of stories of, i. 8.
—— irregular in plan, i. 11, 28.
——, they sought coolness in their, i. 5, 6.
——, tombs, and temples painted, ii. 290–292.
—— painted, in Greece, ii. 278.
Human sacrifices in Egypt, no, ii. 411.
Human figure. *See* Figure.
Humanity of the Egyptians recorded by their sculptors, i. 406. *See* Cruelty.
Hunting, mode of, i. 218, 221, 224.
Huntsmen, i. 213, 215, 218.
—— of the 3rd class. *See* Class 3rd.
Hyæna, i. 213, 224, 227, 246.
—— caught, i. 213, 224.
—— apparently not eaten, i. 224.
——, spotted, i. 227, 246.
Hyrax, or *Wabber*, i. 228, 247.

Jackal, i. 227, 246.
Javelin lighter than the spear, i. 355.
—— of reed, an inferior kind of, i. 357.
Ibex, i. 227, 247.
Ibis, two kinds of, sacred, i. 251.
——, shoulder of an, broken and set, ii. 172.
Ichneumon, i. 227, 229, 246.
—— destroys serpents and the eggs of crocodiles, i. 229, 243.
Jerboa, i. 227, 230, 246.
Jerusalem, temple of, pillaged, i. 308, 340.
Jewels of silver and gold, &c., i. 146; ii. 147, 336–341.
Jewish music, i. 94, 95.
—— musicians, numerous, i. 96.
—— instruments and music, i. 94, 96, 98, 105, 120, 129, 130, 140.
—— trumpets, i. 96, 104, 105.
Jews, features of the, ii. 197.
—— included among Syrians by the Egyptians, ii. 197.
—— anointed the king, i. 275.
—— brought in the ark, i. 268.
—— mourning and songs at funerals, i. 98.

THE ANCIENT EGYPTIANS.

Jews embalmed the dead, ii. 387.
—— had forks; not at table, i. 182.
——, investiture to office among the, i. 275.
—— sold as slaves by the Phœnicians, i. 417.
——, brickmakers at Thebes not. ii. 195, 197.
——, features of Eastern not like those of Western, ii. 197–199.
——, features of Western, not given to the Saviour, ii. 198.
Jingling instrument, i. 89, 92, 93.
Immigration does not always destroy the aborigines, and conquest never, i. 2; ii. 227.
Inapplicableness and adaptability, i. 21; ii. 288.
Incense, i. 265.
—— offered, i. 324.
—— offered to the dead, ii. 358.
—— brought from Asia, ii. 397.
India, resemblance of the religions of Egypt and, i. 329.
——, arrival of the Hindoos in, i. 329.
——, aborigines of Scythian origin in, i. 329.
—— trade with, ii. 134, 234, 235, 237.
——, Solomon's trade with, ii. 235.
——, trade of Tyrians with, ii. 235.
Indian productions went to Egypt, ii. 134, 235, 237.
Indigo used by the Egyptians, ii. 78, 79.
Infantry, heavy and light, i. 386, 387.
Inn, this life only an, i. 187; ii. 356.
Insects of Egypt, i. 255.
—— fabulous, i. 255.
Instruments. *See* Musical.
—— with a neck for shortening the strings, i. 84.
—— with three strings, i. 84.
——, unknown, i. 133.
—— to which they danced, i. 133.
—— resembling lyres, i. 118–122.
—— of sacred music, i. 129.
——, triangular, i. 118, 119, 126.
——, names of Greek, i. 126.
—— of jingling sound, i. 89, 92, 93, 119.
—— held on the shoulder, i. 121.
—— found at Thebes not unlike a guitar, i. 125.
—— of one string, i. 125.
Interest not allowed to increase beyond double the original sum lent, ii. 217.
Intestines of the dead, how buried, ii. 388, 390, 391.

Inventions, few represented, ii. 320.
—— of the Egyptians, ii. 315–319.
Inventions, many older than we suppose, ii. 57.
Investiture to office, i. 275, 282, 283.
Inundation, water of the, retained by dykes, ii. 11.
—— kept out from certain crops, ii. 11.
——, subsiding of the, ii. 11.
——, the land dries quickly after the, ii. 11.
—— beginning of the, ii. 5.
—— caused by rains of Abyssinia, ii. 5.
—— Nile red and green, and red again in the, ii. 5.
—— as described by Virgil (Georg. IV. 289), ii. 5.
—— makes the villages of the Delta like islands, as of old, ii. 7.
——, height of the, ii. 8, 9.
—— artificially improved when low, ii. 7.
——, plough and hoe used after the ii. 11.
—— now rises high above the base of old monuments, ii. 9. *See* Bubastis.
——, cattle rescued from the, ii. 6, 7.
See Vignette at head of Chap. VIII.
——, fêtes of peasants during the, ii. 52.
——, observations on the, ii. 248–250, 255.
—— led to the invention of sluices, Nilometers, levelling, geometry, &c., ii. 249.
Joints of meat, i. 170, 171.
—— of peculiar form, i. 171.
—— on the altar, i. 264.
—— boiled and roasted, i. 173.
Ionic movements, i. 138.
Joseph sold, i. 417.
Joseph's brethren sat according to age, i. 58, 179.
—— silver cup, i. 82.
Iron, use of, very ancient, ii. 153–155.
——, use of, in Egypt, ii. 155.
—— bedsteads. *See* Og.
—— mentioned in Homer as tempered by plunging, ii. 153.
—— blades sharpened on a steel, ii. 155.
—— easily decomposed and not likely to be found, ii. 155.
—— known to the Egyptians, ii. 154.
——, "*Ferrum*" Latin for sword, ii. 155.
Irrigation, i. 32–34; ii. 4, 5, 11.
—— prolonged, ii. 7, 11.

INDEX. 419

Isaac, savoury meats brought to, i. 173.
Isis "with ten thousand names," i. 329.
—— the mother of the child, i. 333.
—— and Athor (Venus), i. 300.
—— and Ceres of the Greeks, i. 297.
——, festival of, i. 296, 297
Isis and Nepthys, the beginning and the end, ii. 381.
Isle. *See* Wight, Isle of.
Israelites regretted the fish of Egypt; the onions, and other vegetables, i. 167, 169.
Israelites. *See* Jews. *See* Jewish.
Italian Pantomime and Fescennine verses, i. 101.
Judgment, the future, i. 331. *See* Osiris.
——, mode of passing, ii. 207.
—— scenes, ii. 380, 381.
Judge, the king was, ii. 202.
—— of the dead. *See* Osiris.
Judges received salary from government, ii. 204.
——, ii. 229, 232.
——, figures of, without hands, ii. 206.
——, bench of, ii. 30, 203.
——, the Arch Judge chief of, ii. 203, 206.
Judging a case, mode of, ii. 206, 207.
Justice given gratuitously, ii. 204.
Justice, goddess of, without a head, ii. 382.
——, figure of, i. 272. *See* Truth.
Jupiter going into Ethiopia, i. 269.
Jupiters, several, i. 329.
Juvenile offenders, ii. 215.
Ivy, i. 256, 285; ii. 33.

KANAAN (Canaan), i. 403.
Karnak, temple of, i. 397.
—— and our churches, ii. 302.
Kasr-Kharóon (in the Fyoom), i. 307.
Kebsh, wild sheep, i. 227, 247.
Khem, the God, the abstract idea of father, i. 273, 327, 332.
——, or Amun-Khem, or Amun-Re *generator*, i. 273.
——, or Pan, i. 286.
Khita, or Sheta, i. 399, 401.
——, supposed to be the Hittites, i. 403.
——, fort of the, called Atesh or Kadesh, i. 400.
——, bridges over a river and ditch of the, i. 399, 400.
Khonfud, or clod-crushing machine, ii. 1, 14.
Killed, hands of the, i. 373.
King called Phrah, "the Sun" (Pharaoh), i. 280, 310. (First observed by the D. of Northumberland and Colonel Felix.)
King, feelings towards the, i. 310.
——, hereditary title of, i. 310.
——, either of the priestly or of the military class, i. 311.
——, duties of the, i. 312.
——, companions of the, i. 312.
——, rules for the conduct of the, i. 312–314.
—— could do no wrong, and never died, i. 313.
——, prayer for the, and praise of the, by the priest, i. 313.
——, mourning for the death of the, and funeral of the, i. 315; ii. 366, 378.
——, people could prevent the, being buried in his tomb, i. 326; ii. 378.
——, coronation of the, i. 272, 273.
——, anointed, i. 275.
——, Gods laid their hands on the, i. 276.
—— passing through towns on his return from victory, i. 278.
—— sacrificed daily in the temple, i. 281, 313.
—— confidential advisers, or ministers of the, i. 316; ii. 202.
——, respect for, ii. 226.
——, was judge, ii. 202.
—— could commute punishments, ii. 209.
—— wore his helmet or a wig in battle, ii. 324.
King's birth-day celebrated, i. 281.
Kisirka, or Nubian lyre, i. 117.
Kissing a royal order, ii. 203.
Kitchen (woodcuts), i. 175, 176.
——, cooks and others in the, i. 177, 178.
Knee, bow the. *See* Bow. *See Abrek*.
Kneph, with a ram's head. *See* Nû.
Knife, semicircular, for cutting leather, ii. 103.
Knives, stone. *See* Stone and Metal.
Koofa (Kufa), i. 395, 399.
Korayn, A'maree, dates of, ii. 37.

LABOUR, division of, ii. 185.
Ladles of bronze gilt, i. 185.
Lake of the dead at every large city, ii. 377.
Lamps, festival of burning, i. 298; ii. 71.
Land rented from the kings and others, ii. 4.
—— cultivated with little labour, ii. 14.
See Sowing and Grain.

Land, overseer of the. *See* Steward.
——, alluvial doposit on the, ii. 11.
——, dries soon after the inundation subsides, ii. 11.
Land, levels of the, different, ii. 10, 11.
——, rise of the, ii. 8, 9.
——, varies in different parts, ii. 8, 9.
——, lower near the edge of the desert than on the banks of the Nile, ii. 7, 10.
Large blocks of stone. *See* Stone.
Lasso, use of the, i. 213, 220.
Laws of Egypt, ii. 202–218.
——, respect for the, ii. 207.
——, primitive character of some, ii. 214.
——, sanctity of old, ii. 227.
Lawgivers, ii. 207, 218, 228.
Lazarus, swathed in bandages, ii. 387.
Leather, twisting, ii. 93.
—— cutters of Thebes, ii. 93.
——, circular cut of, ii. 93, 94.
—— used for writing paper, ii. 99.
——, tanning of, ii. 102.
—— cutters, ii. 102.
—— stamped of time of Shishak, ii. 102.
——, objects made of, ii. 102.
——, curing skins for, ii. 102.
——, stretching and binding, ii. 103.
——, semicircular knife for cutting, ii. 103.
—— cutter, holding strap with his toes, ii. 104.
——, great use of, ii. 105.
Lemanon, i. 403.
Lentils, much eaten, i. 167, 177, 181.
—— supposed by Strabo to be imbedded in the rock at the Pyramids, i. 167.
—— of Pelusium, famous, i. 167.
——, porridge or soup of, i. 177.
Leopard skin dress, i. 291, 319. *See* Prophet. *See Nebris.*
Leopard's spotted skin suspended on a staff near Osiris, i. 285.
Lepidotus, fish, ii. 192.
Levels of the land. *See* Land.
Libation, they first began with a, i. 264.
—— of wine, i. 265.
—— vases used in, i. 266.
Life given to the king, i. 277.
—— sign of, taken by the Christians as a cross, i. 277.
——, or *Crux ansata*, i. 257.
——, mode of, account given before magistrates of, ii. 199–201.

Light armed troops, arms of, i. 368, 386.
Limestone used in the oldest Egyptian buildings, ii. 305.
Linen corslet of Amasis, ii. 80.
——, fine, of Egypt, exported, ii. 72, 73, 80.
—— bandages of mummies, ii. 73, 74, 77.
—— experiments respecting, ii. 73.
——, peculiarity in the manufacture of, in the number of threads of the warp and woof, ii. 76, 77, 80.
—— threads double, ii. 76.
—— threads coloured before worked in, ii. 79.
—— cloths fringed, ii. 77, 91, 320, 321. *See* Calasiris.
——, beauty of texture of, ii. 75, 76.
——, singularly fine piece of, ii. 75, 80.
——, selvages of, dyed with indigo, as of modern Nubians, ii. 77–79.
——, dresses worn by votaries of Isis in Italy, ii. 74.
——, the word ειλικρινης, "sincere," taken from fine, ii. 80.
——, different qualities of, ii. 80. *See* Byssus.
Linus, song of, i. 97.
Lion, i. 224, 229, 246.
—— formerly in Syria and Greece, i. 229.
—— hunting, i. 224; ii. 341.
Lions trained for the chase, i. 221.
—— killed by Amunoph III., i. 224.
Liturgies. *See* Services.
Lively character of the Egyptians, i. 2, 210.
Locust in the sculptures, i. 234.
Looms, horizontal and upright, ii. 85, 86, 87.
——, rude, but the work fine, ii. 75.
Lots, casting of, i. 196.
Lotus, i. 34, 36, 57; ii. 29. *See* Nufar.
—— eaten, i. 168; ii. 3.
—— a symbol, i. 257.
—— presented to guests, i. 79.
—— a favourite flower, i. 57.
——, or nelumbium, not represented except by the Romans, i. 57.
——, or Lotos, of Cyrene (a thorny tree, an acacia), ii. 121.
Lowbgeh, or palm wine, i. 55.
Lupins, ii. 21. *See Doqáq.*
Luxury increasing, led to debt, ii. 219.
Lyre, fabulous invention of the, i. 114, 115.
—— ornamented with heads of animals, i. 114.

INDEX. 421

Lyre, number of strings of the, i. 115.
—— used in sacred music, i. 129.
—— of the Greeks, i. 115–117.
—— of Greece, with three strings, i. 124.
——, construction of the, i. 115–117.
—— of the Berlin and Leyden Museums, i. 116, 117.
——, or *Kisirka*, of Nubia, i. 117.
——, mode of tuning the, i. 117.
——, other instruments resembling the, i. 118, 119.
——, standing, i. 119, 120.
—— of three strings really a guitar, i. 86, 123.
—— of 18 strings, i. 115.
—— with many strings might be invented at an early time, i. 84.

MAABDEH, crocodile mummies at, i. 242.
Maces, weapons with metal head, i. 364.
Machine for crushing clods. *See Khonfud.*
Magic, by a boy, &c., ii. 352, 353.
Magnetism, animal, effect on nerves, ii. 353.
Mándara, or reception-room, i. 10.
Maneros, song of, i. 97.
Manufactures of Egypt, ii. 247, 255.
Marathon and other places, flint arrowheads found at, i. 354.
March of the army, i. 342, 404.
—— of the army home after war, i. 415.
Mareotic wine, i. 49.
Mareotis belonged to Egypt, ii. 229.
Marriage ceremony and contracts not found, ii. 223.
—— with sisters, ii. 224.
Marriages of the Egyptian royal family with foreigners, i. 308.
Mars. *See* Papremis.
Masara, quarries of El, ii. 306.
Mashoash, an Asiatic people, i. 398.
Mast of the old ships of Egypt was double, i. 413.
Master and mistress of the house sat on one chair, i. 145.
Mat-making, ii. 86.
Mats, i. 68.
Maut, the abstract idea of mother, i. 333. *See* Mother.
—— "proceeded from herself," or her own mother, i. 327.
Measure of land, of length (stadium), ii. 256. *See* Cubit, Weights.
Measures of capacity, ii. 260.
—— of liquids, ii. 261.

Measures for grain, made of wood, ii. 167.
Meat eaten without being kept, i. 165, 174.
——, great quantity of, served up, i. 166.
Mecca. *See* Mekkeh.
Medeenet Haboo, i. 73, 272, 284, 285, 394, 401.
Medicinal plants in Egypt, i. 50; ii. 351.
Medicine, six books of, ii. 355.
Medicines, ii. 351, 352.
Medusa's head like that of the Typhonian monster in Egypt, i. 153; ii. 263.
Mekaukes, Coptic governor of Egypt, i. 37.
Mekkeh pilgrims, the number of, made up by angels, i. 297.
Memlooks, club (or *dabôs*) of the, i. 364.
Memnonium, palace-temple of Remeses II., usually called the, i. 401, 407.
Memphis, i. 209, 290, 295, 307, 331.
—— Pthah, the god of, i. 331.
——, capital of Lower Egypt, ii. 229, 230.
—— "Menofr," ii. 96.
Memphite dynasties and kings, i. 307.
Men and women sat together at a party, i. 144.
Menes first king of Egypt, i. 307.
—— introduced luxury, i. 173.
—— changed the course of the Nile, ii. 249, 251, 287.
——, science before the time of, ii. 251, 287.
——, Amun of Ptolemaic time would have been recognized by, ii. 264.
Menophres, the Egyptian name of, uncertain, ii. 255.
Mercenaries. *See* Soldiers.
Mercury, the inventor of the lyre and of music, i. 84, 118, 123.
Mesopotamia, i. 308, 397, 403.
——, Egyptian conquests in, i. 308.
——, tribute from, i. 397.
Mesoré, offering in the month of, i. 299.
Metal implements of Egypt and Europe of a different character, ii. 164.
——, stones used for arms and tools before, ii. 163.
Metals, skill in the compounding of, i. 148; ii. 159.
——, inlaying of. *See* Damascening.
——, oldest casting of, ii. 160. *See* Bronze and Metallurgy.

Metals, Samians famous for casting, ii. 160.
——, soldering, ii. 162.
Metallurgy, skill in, ii. 133, 136, 156, 158, 159.
—— carried to perfection in Egypt and at Sidon, ii. 133.
Military class, i. 336.
—— punishments, i. 418.
—— music, i. 104-106.
—— bands of music, i. 104.
Milk offered to the gods, i. 266.
Mimosa. *See* Acacia.
Mina, *men*, or *mna*, weight, ii. 259, 260.
Minerva, fête of, at Sais, i. 296, 298.
—— reputed inventress of the trumpet, i. 104.
——. *See* Neith.
Minervas, several, i. 329.
Ministers and confidential advisers of the king, i. 316; ii. 202.
Minos, Æacus, and Rhadamanthos, Egyptian names, ii. 381.
Mirrors of metal, ii. 346, 347.
Mnevis, the black bull, i. 289.
——, the sacred bull of Heliopolis, i. 288.
Mœris, king, i. 307.
——, revenues from the fish of the lake, ii. 193.
Money, sheep and oxen valued as, ii. 117.
—— formerly taken by weight, ii. 148.
—— in rings, ii. 149.
——, Persian, the first coined, in Egypt, ii. 150.
——, oldest coined, ii. 150. *See* Gold. *See* Silver.
Monkey, or other pet, tied to the leg of a chair, i. 145.
Monkeys assisting to gather fruit, i. 44.
—— in Abyssinia held torches, i. 44.
Monochordium of one string, i. 125.
Monolith of Sais, and of Buto, ii. 310. *See* Saïs.
Months originally lunar, i. 299; ii. 252.
—— and seasons of the year, ii. 252, 253.
Moon, fêtes at the new and full, i. 287, 299.
——, erroneously supposed to be related to Osiris, i. 289.
—— was the god Thoth, i. 328. *See* Thoth.
Mora, game of, i. 188, 189, 190.
Mordants, the use of, ii. 83, 84.
Mosaics, golden, ii. 305.
—— in vaults and ceilings, ii. 305.

Moses broke down the superstitions of Egypt, i. 325.
—— did not mention the future judgment, reason why, i. 331.
Mother, goddess, i. 332, 333.
——. *See* Maut.
—— of the child found in Asia, Egypt, India, Italy, Mexico, the nature goddess, i. 333.
Mourners, hired, ii. 366.
——, chief, or type of mourning, ii. 371, 373.
Mud, after the inundation, bushes dragged over the, ii. 11.
—— of the Nile. *See* Nile and Alluvial deposit.
Mulkuf on houses, i. 6.
Mummies, making coffins and bandaging, ii. 117-119.
——, embalming of, ii. 383, 387.
——, classification of, ii. 391, 394.
——, offering and services to, ii. 358-360, 362.
—— of poor people, ii. 365.
—— strewed over the ground by Christian excavators, ii. 364.
——, different qualities of, ii. 391-396.
Mummy cases, old, resold, ii. 363.
—— cloths, of linen, some coarse, ii. 75-78. *See* Linen.
Mummy pit. *See* Vignette, ii. 400.
—— pits, ii. 363, 364.
Mummy's head seen in the coffin at an open panel, ii. 368.
Murder of a child by a parent, ii. 209.
—— of a parent by a son, ii. 209.
—— of a slave, punished by death, ii. 208, 209.
Murrhine vases, doubtful of what stone, ii. 71.
——, false, probably a glass-porcelain, ii. 71.
Music, i. 82-133.
—— before dinner, i. 82.
—— after dinner, i. 188.
——, style of, i. 83.
—— studied by the priests, i. 83.
——, Egyptians fond of, i. 83, 84.
—— at Greek entertainments, i. 83.
—— part of education, i. 83, 94.
——, skill of the Egyptians in, i. 83, 84, 86.
——, at first metrical, i. 83.
——, a Greek accomplishment, i. 94.
—— of the Jews, i. 94, 95, 96.
——, military, i. 104, 105.
—— allowed in religious ceremonies, i. 301.

INDEX. 423

Music not in the temple of Osiris, i. 301.
—— of mournful kind, i. 301.
Musical notation, i. 96.
—— instruments, the oldest were those of percussion, i. 83.
—— instruments at first rude, i. 84.
—— instruments, combination of many, i. 86, 89, 91, 92.
—— instruments of jingling kind, i. 89, 92, 93, 119.
—— instruments had strings of catgut, i. 118, 122, 123, 125.
Musicians, six hundred, together, i. 91.
——, hired, i. 96.
——, great number of Jewish, i. 96.
Mutton not eaten at Thebes, i. 166.
—— not eaten by the priests, i. 324.
Mycerinus, fête in honour of the daughter of king, i. 299.
Mylitta, or Alitta, i. 333.
Myos Hormos, port on the Red Sea, ii. 235–237.
Mysteries, greater and less, i. 321.
—— of Osiris, i. 298, 331.

Nabl, or viol, of the Jews, i. 121, 126.
Nahrayn, i. 397. See Mesopotamia.
Napkin brought for wiping the mouth after drinking, i. 144.
Nations gifted with certain qualities, i. 3.
Natron lakes, nome of Nitriotis, i. 166; ii. 229.
Natural productions for decorative purposes, a mistake to copy, ii. 288.
—— objects, the Greeks preferred taking the sentiment of, ii. 288.
—— objects not always imitated by the Egyptians, ii. 290.
Nature gods, i. 332, 333.
—— Goddess, i. 333.
——, the vivifying and producing principles of, i. 332, 333.
Navigation, origin of, ii. 132.
—— indebted to the Phœnicians, ii. 132.
Navy included in the army, i. 311.
Neboot, or long pole, game with the, i. 207–209.
Nebris, or fawn of Bacchus, taken from the spotted leopard-skin suspended near Osiris, i. 285.
Nebris and the leopard-skin dress of priests in Egypt, i. 291.
Nebuchadnezzar deprived Egypt of its influence in Syria, i. 309.
Nechesia and the Leucos Portus, ii. 235, 237.

Necho lost all the conquests of Egypt in Asia, i. 309.
Necklaces, ii. 339, 340, 341.
—— and jewellery offered in the temple, i. 260.
Nectanebo, i. 309.
Needles, ii. 344, 345.
Nef, or Nûm. See Nû.
Neith, i. 296, 298, 328. See Minerva.
Nelumbium not represented growing in Egypt, i. 57.
—— only represented by the Romans, i. 57.
Nepenthes probably the *Hashéesh* (or opium?), ii. 35.
Netpe, i. 181, 256; ii. 396, 397. See Sycamore.
Netting needles, ii. 91, 95.
Nets of different kinds, i. 214.
—— enclosing part of the desert, i. 214.
—— of flax string, ii. 95.
—— of very fine quality, ii. 80.
—— for birds, ii. 180–185.
—— for fishing. See Fishing-nets.
"Newest" things recommended instead of the "best," ii. 289.
Nightshade used in Egypt for chaplets, ii. 33.
Nile, valley of the, has more arable land than formerly, i. 306.
—— deposit the same throughout its course from Abyssinia, ii. 19. See Alluvial.
—— water, fattening properties of the, i. 293, 295, 322.
—— water red and green at the beginning of the inundation, ii. 5.
—— water laid up in jars before it is green, and error of Aristides, ii. 5.
——, Osiris the beneficent property of the, i. 298.
——, white and *Blue*, properly " *Black*," ii. 19, 20.
——, fertilizing properties of the, ii. 20.
Niloa, festival of the Nile, i. 282.
Nilometer of Elephantine, ii. 257.
Nilometers made, ii. 249.
——, daily rise according to the, ii. 52, 249.
Nilus, the god, of a blue and red colour, ii. 5.
—— called "*Hapi.*" See *List of Woodcuts*, 278.
Nimroud or Nineveh sculptures, i. 152; ii. 263. See Nineveh.
——, weights brought by Mr. Layard from, ii. 260.
Nineveh (*Niniee*), tribute from, i. 397.

Nineveh sculptures, cruelty of the Assyrians shown by the, i. 3, 410.
—— marbles not so old as some have supposed, ii. 263.
—— ornaments, i. 152, 153.
—— ornaments late compared to those of Egypt, ii. 290.
Nisroch, the head of a bird on a vase like that of the god, i. 152.
Nitriotis. *See* Natron Lakes.
Nitrous top-dressing, on the land, ii. 19.
Nofre (or Nofr), Atmoo, i. 256, 284, 285. *See* Nufar.
Nomarchs, ii. 230, 231.
Nomes of Egypt, furnishing soldiers, i. 337.
——, thirty-six, afterwards fifty-three, ii. 229.
Nóreg, probably used of old, answering to the Hebrew *moreg*, ii. 47.
——, like the Roman *tribulum*, ii. 48.
Notaries, public, ii. 165.
—— or public scribes punished for fraud, ii. 214, 217.
Nû, Nûm, Noub, Nef, Neph, or Kneph (Chnuphis), the god, i. 271, 327, 332.
——, the spirit, i. 327. *See* Asp or Agathodæmon.
Nufar, name of the lotus, perhaps related to Nofr, " Good," i. 256.
Numbers placed over cattle, sheep, &c., ii. 178, 179.
Nummulite rock at the Pyramids, i. 167.

OAR, of boats, ii. 126.
Oasis, i. 55, 277; ii. 191, 229.
Obelisk, object of, to contrast with the horizontal line, ii. 311.
——, barbarous additions to the point of, ii. 311.
—— in a quarry, ii. 311.
Obelisks, transported from quarries of Syene, ii. 309.
——, the largest, ii. 309, 312.
——, effect of, i. 21.
—— removed to Europe, ii. 311.
Offerings of various kinds, i. 323.
—— to different Gods at various periods of the year, i. 263.
—— most common, i. 263.
—— of flowers, fruits, ointment, i. 259–261.
—— of emblems, jewels, i. 260.
—— for the dead, ii. 362.
Og, King of Bashan, iron bedstead of, i. 72.
Oils, ii. 23, 24, 27, 29, 30, 32.

Ointment. *See* Anointing.
——, offering of, i. 259, 260.
—— on heads of guests, i. 77, 78.
—— to anoint the statue of a God, i. 259.
—— of various kinds, i. 259; ii. 23, 24, 27, 32.
—— found in jars in the tombs, i. 78.
——, pots of different materials for holding, i. 155, 157.
——, *sagdas*, or *psagdæ*, i. 259; ii. 342.
Olive, i. 57; ii. 24, 28.
——, soldiers carried a twig of, at the sacrifice of thanks for victory, i. 279.
Ombos (Ombite nome), i. 242.
Onions, i. 168, 169.
—— offered and eaten, i. 323, 324.
——, a particular mode of presenting, i. 324; ii. 357.
——, error respecting, i. 168.
—— of Egypt of excellent flavour, i. 169.
——, stories respecting, i. 169.
Orchard, i. 37–39.
Ornaments worn by women, ii. 336–346.
Ornan, threshing instruments of, ii. 46, 47.
O'Sioót, or O'sioút (formerly Lycopolis), wolf mummies at, i. 228.
Osirei, King. *See* Sethi.
Osiris, loss of, Osiris found, i. 287, 300.
——, fêtes in honour of, i. 286–288, 300.
——, offerings to, ii. 358.
——. *See* Benno, sacred bird of.
—— wosrhipped under the form of Apis, i. 288–291.
——, Judge of the dead, i. 331; ii. 377.
——, allegorical history of, i. 298.
——, character and mysteries of, i. 298, 331.
——, history of, the great mystery, i. 298.
——, the abstract idea of good, or goodness, i. 330; ii. 356.
——, before 18th dynasty only kings called after death, ii. 329.
——, after that time all good men called, ii. 357, 367, 380.
——, souls of good men returned to, ii. 329, 357.
——, remarkable and peculiar character of, i. 331.
——, eye of, i. 244, 257; ii. 127, 367, 386, 391.
——, sceptres of, i. 257, 266; ii. 381.
——, chamber of, at Philæ, i. 257.
——, they beat themselves in honour of, i. 264.

INDEX. 425

Osiris, or Bacchus, i. 286. *See* Bacchus.
—— and Anubis, rites of, i. 129. *See* Flute.
——, rites of, i. 129, 299, 301.
—— and the Nile, i. 298. *See* Nile.
—— invented the pipe, i. 127.
—— the Great, Deity of the future state, i. 331.
—— mummies in form of, ii. 383, 385.
——, small figures of the dead, in the form of, ii. 367, 400.
——, wooden figure of, brought to table, i. 186, 187.
——, allegories connected with the land of Egypt, and, i. 300; ii. 53.
Osirtasen I., i. 204, 307.
—— the original Sesostris, i. 307.
Osirtasens, fashionable dogs in the reigns of the, i. 231.
Ostrich feathers and eggs, i. 224.
—— caught for its eggs and plumes, ii. 54.
Ottomans, i. 58, 67.
Oxen for sacrifice not necessarily free from black spots, i. 290.
——, clean, belonged to Epaphus, or Apis, i. 290.
Oxyrhinchus, city of, i. 307.
—— fish, i. 254; ii. 191.

PAAMYLIA, i. 286.
Painted walls and panels, i. 19–21.
—— houses and temples, ii. 290, 291, 292.
Painters and carvers in stone, distinct from sculptors, ii. 56.
Painting before sculpture, ii. 281.
—— and sculpture, origin of, ii. 270, 271.
——. *See* Greek.
——, oldest in Egypt and Greece, ii. 277, 278.
—— on panel in Egypt, ii. 277.
—— in fresco, not in Egypt, ii. 278.
Palace. *See* Pavilion.
Palimpsests, ii. 99.
Palanquins, i. 73, 75; ii. 119.
Pallaces, Pallacides, Pellices Jovis, i. 96, 133, 317.
Palm, or date tree, split, and used for roofing, i. 18.
Palm tree, i. 39, 55–57.
——, used for various purposes, parts of the, i. 56.
—— miscalled "of the desert," i. 55, 168.
—— requires water to enable it to grow, i. 168.

Palm-tree a great gift to the people, i. 168
—— branch type of a year, i. 256.
——, the *Dôm*, or Theban, i. 56, 57. *See Dôm* tree.
—— formerly said to be sterile in Lower Egypt, ii. 36.
Palm-wine, i. 55.
—— of the Oasis called *Lowbgeh*, i. 55.
—— used in the embalming process, ii. 383, 385.
Panegyries, or assemblies, i. 280.
Panels, houses with painted, i. 19–21.
——, walls with, i. 28, 29.
Pantheism, i. 328.
Pantomime, Italian, i. 101.
Paper, earliest substitutes for, ii. 100.
——, when first made from linen rags, ii. 101.
—— of cotton and silk, ii. 101.
—— in Arabic called "leaf," ii. 100.
——, leaves used for, ii. 100.
—— very old in China, ii. 101.
—— when first used in England, ii. 101.
Papremis, or Mars, fête of, i. 209, 298.
Papyrus or byblus plant, ii. 26, 29, 95, 96.
—— used for making punts, baskets, &c., a more common kind, ii. 95, 96.
—— of different kinds, ii. 96.
——, early use of the, ii. 98.
—— or book, i. 274.
—— eaten, i. 168; ii. 3.
—— garlands, i. 57, 81.
—— punts, i. 236; ii. 5.
—— punt a security against crocodiles, i. 236.
—— and another water plant, emblems of Upper and Lower Egypt, i. 257.
—— not now in Egypt, ii. 97, 100.
—— grows only in Sicily and Syria, ii. 97, 100.
——, prophecy fulfilled respecting the, ii. 100.
——, its name perpetuated in "paper," ii. 100.
——, modern paper made from the, ii. 97.
——, or paper, when found very brittle, ii. 96.
——, mode of making, ii. 96–98.
——, different qualities of, ii. 98.
—— of fine quality, ii. 96.
——, Pliny wrong in supposing, not used before the time of Alexander, ii. 98.
——, breadth of sheets of, ii. 98.
—— continued in use till the time of Charlemagne, ii. 98.

Papyrus, monopoly of, resold, the original writing erased, ii. 99.
——, substitutes for, of pottery, board, &c., ii. 98–100.
Parchment, invention of, ii. 98, 99.
——, excellent Arab, ii. 100.
Parks and covers, i. 37, 215.
Parlour, i. 11.
Party. *See* Guests.
Pasht, Bubastis, Diana, i. 296.
Passport system in Egypt, ii. 200, 201.
Paste kneaded by the hands, and the feet, i. 174, 177.
Pastry, i. 174, 177.
Pavilion and palace of the King, i. 22.
Pavilions, i. 22.
Payment, evasion of, ii. 200, 211, 213.
Peasants, frugal mode of living of the, i. 168; ii. 3.
—— allowed to grow the crops they chose, ii. 3.
—— rented the land from the King and others, ii. 4.
——, agricultural skill of the, ii. 3.
——, fêtes of the, during the high Nile, ii. 52. *See* Festivals.
Pelusium beer famous, i. 54.
—— lentils, i. 167.
Pelusium, i. 404.
People, task to be performed by different, i. 3.
Periploca secamone, or *ghulga* plant, i. 256; ii. 36, 38.
—— used for curing skins, ii. 103.
Perpendicular style abandoned the variety of the original pointed architecture, ii. 297.
Persea tree, ii. 28. *See* Egleeg.
—— sacred to Athor, i. 256.
Phalanx of infantry, Egyptian, i. 340–342.
——, Egyptian, in the army of Crœsus, i. 342.
Pharaoh. *See* Phrah.
Pharos never was a day's sail from the shore, i. 303.
Philæ, view of (vignette F), i. 212.
Philoteras Portus, on the Red Sea, ii. 235, 236.
Phœnicians traded in slaves, i. 417.
—— the great navigators of old, ii. 132.
—— doubled the Cape of Good Hope, ii. 133.
—— traded in tin, ii. 133. *See* Tin.
—— exchanged manufactures for tin, ii. 136.
—— went to Britain for tin, ii. 134, 135.
——, commercial jealousy of the, ii. 134.

Phœnicians, trade of the, ii. 133–136. *See* Spain, and Gold.
Phœnix bird, apparently the *Benno*, i. 252.
Phrah, "the sun," changed into Pharaoh, i. 310. *See* King.
Physician, origin of saying "a fool or a, after forty," ii. 352.
Pig sacrificed to the moon, i. 286.
—— to Typho, i. 323.
——, paste figure of a, offered by poor people, i. 387.
——'s flesh abhorred by the priests, i. 322, 324.
——, treatment of, not kept in a sty, i. 231.
—— eaten sometimes by the Egyptians, i. 323.
—— turned into the fields, ii. 18, 19.
—— rarely found in the sculptures, and never before the 18th dynasty (woodcut), ii. 18.
Pillows, or head stools, of wood and other materials, i. 63, 71, 335, 336.
Pins, ii. 344, 345.
Pipe, the Egyptian, very old, i. 127.
—— of reed and of straw, i. 127–129.
—— invented by Osiris, i. 127.
——, double, i. 128, 129.
——, double, was among the sacred instruments, i. 129.
——, double, of modern Egypt, or *Zummara*, i. 128.
Pipes and flutes at first rude, i. 84.
Pirouette danced 4000 years ago, i. 138.
Pitch called "*zift*" or "*sift*," i. 397; ii. 120, 259.
Plants of Egypt, i. 57, 167–169; ii. 20–22, 25, 26.
—— from Pliny, ii. 23, 24, 27–35.
—— sacred, i. 256.
—— brought as part of a foreign tribute, i. 57, 395.
—— number of, in Egypt about 1300, ii. 26.
—— producing oil. *See* Oils.
—— raised in ancient Egypt, ii. 26.
—— now grown before and after the inundation, ii. 21, 22, 25.
——, wild and indigenous, of the desert; few introduced into Egypt, ii. 26.
Plate, or silver, few pieces of Greek or Roman, ii. 147.
Plaustrum, or travelling carriage, drawn by two oxen, i. 384, 385.
Plough, ii. 13–16.
——, light furrows made by the, ii. 14.
——, oxen and cows yoked to the, ii. 15.

INDEX. 427

Plough perhaps shod with metal, ii. 15, 17.
Ploughing the land, ii. 13, 14.
—— with an ox and an ass, not in Egypt, ii. 16.
Pointed ball, the principle of the, known to the Greeks, i. 358.
Pole and bucket, or *Shadóof*, i. 33, 35, 72. *See* Shadóof.
Pole-axe, i. 363.
Pomegranate, i. 36, 54, 57, 256.
—— tree represented, i. 36.
——, the *Rhodon* (rose) that gave its name to Rhodes, ii. 29.
Pompeii, red panels, and "reeds for columns" painted at, i. 19–21.
Population of Egypt in old times, i. 304, 305.
—— of the world the same now as of old, i. 305.
—— of Alexandria, i. 305.
Porcelain, or glass-porcelain, ii. 66, 70, 71.
—— of many colours, yellow put on afterwards, and parts added to, ii. 66.
Porches, i. 9.
Porcupine, i. 216, 225, 228, 246.
Porte, the Sublime, or "High Gate," ii. 202.
Potters, ii. 107, 108.
Potter's wheel, ii. 107.
Pottery, &c., used for writing upon, ii. 99.
——, Coptic names for different kinds of, ii. 107.
—— of modern Egypt has succeeded to that of old time, ii. 107.
—— Egyptian, far inferior in taste to that of Greece, ii. 109.
Poulterers, ii. 184, 185.
Poultry. *See* Cocks and hens.
Pounders, ii. 165, 166.
—— used stone mortars, ii. 165, 166.
Pount, Asiatic people of, i. 396.
Power of Egypt, i. 308, 418; ii. 263.
Precious stones imitated in glass, ii. 60, 63.
—— cut with the diamond, ii. 67.
—— metals formerly used, ii. 245.
——, amount of, in old times, ii. 247. *See* Gold, Wealth.
Preserves, or covers, i. 37, 215.
Prevention of crime in youth a modern suggestion, ii. 215.
Priest, each, had one wife, i. 5; ii. 224.
Priestesses, i. 316, 317. *See* Women, holy.

Priesthood kept up their influence partly by pomp and ceremonies, i. 267.
Priests, worldly possessions of the, i. 7.
——, the law was in the hands of the, i. 311.
—— and military class had the highest rank, i. 316.
—— of various grades, i. 316, 319.
—— of the King, i. 316.
——, dress of the, i. 333, 334.
—— dressed in fawn (or leopard) skins, i. 291.
—— who wore the leopard-skin dress. *See* Prophet.
——, chief, and the prophets called "*Sem*," i. 270, 319. *See* Prophet.
—— enjoyed great privileges, i. 319, 321, 325.
—— paid no taxes, but had public allowance of food, &c., i. 319.
—— initiated into the mysteries, i. 321.
——, education of the children of the, i. 321.
—— had great ascendency over the people, i. 321, 325, 326.
——, abstinence of the, i. 322, 324, 325.
—— abstained from pork, fish, beans, &c., i. 322, 324, 325.
—— abstained from salt on certain occasions, i. 324.
——, ablutions of the, i. 324.
—— fond of cleanliness, ii. 327.
—— left the people in ignorance, i. 325.
—— raised their own class, and degraded the people, i. 325.
—— were moral, and set a good example, i. 322, 325.
—— did not disregard social ties, performed the duties of fathers and husbands, i. 326.
—— governed the country well, i. 326.
—— did not assume power over the King as the Ethiopian pontiffs did, i. 326.
——, system of the, not suited to all times, and too unbending, i. 326.
—— slept on a wooden pillow, i. 335, 336.
—— brought in the shrine, i. 269.
—— carrying the table, or stand, i. 268.
—— wore the leopard-skin dress when with the shrines, one of the, i. 269.
Primitive habits traced long after a people have been settled, i. 5.
—— mountains in the desert, i. 228.
Princes, dress of the, i. 311.
——, lock of hair, the badge of, i. 312; ii. 322.

Princes in chariots, i. 370.
——, office of, i. 311, 342, 344.
—— carried flabella, i. 342, 344.
—— commanded parts of the army, i. 342.
Principles of nature, the vivifying and producing, i. 332, 333.
Prisoners of war, i. 373, 416.
——, treatment of, i. 406, 410.
——, employment of, i. 416.
Private life gives an insight into character, i. 5, 210.
Prizes for gymnastic exercises, cattle, dresses, and skins, i. 210; ii. 52.
Procession of the ark of Sokari, i. 284, 285.
—— at the King's coronation, i. 272, 273.
Processions, order of, from Clemens, i. 274.
Professions, only two, i. 311; ii. 1.
Prophet clad in the leopard-skin dress, he was called "*Sem*," i. 270, 275, 284, 319, 320, 324.
——, duty of the, i. 319.
Proportion understood by the Egyptians, but particularly by the Greeks, and now by the Italians, ii. 293.
Prostration before great people, i. 58; ii. 203.
Psagdæ, ointment, i. 259; ii. 342.
Psalms of David, some written after the captivity, ii. 251.
Psammitichus, Psammaticus, or Psamatik, court for Apis of, i. 290.
"*Pshent*," double crown called, i. 269; ii. 323. *See* Crown.
Pthah, the creative power, i. 327.
——, Memphis, the city of, i. 331.
—— accompanied by the figure of Truth, i. 327.
Pthah-Sokari-Osiris, i. 204.
——, boat of, i. 284, 285.
Ptolemies, titles of some of the, in a deed, ii. 220.
——, tyranny of the, ii. 229.
——, corruptions under the later, ii. 232.
Pulleys known in Egypt, but may not have been used in boats, ii. 130, 131.
Pump, ii. 318.
Punishment of the offending member, ii. 214, 217.
——. *See* Prevention of crime.
—— for adultery, ii. 210. *See* Murder.
Punishments. *See* Bastinado.
——, military, i. 418; ii. 210.
—— with the corbag whip and the bastinado, i. 240, 418.

Punishments, commutation of, ii. 209.
—— of great men now in Egypt, ii. 212.
—— of public weighers, notaries, shopkeepers, forgers, and others, for fraud, ii. 214, 217.
Pyramid, granite casing of the Third, ii. 292.
——, pent roof construction over entrance-passage of the Great, ii. 303.
Pyramidal, or sloping, line, and in rock temples, ii. 298.
Pyramids, i. 307.
—— during the inundation (vignette G), i. 302.
——, tombs near the. *See* Tombs.
——, dimensions of the, ii. 256.
——, claim of superiority of brick over stone, ii. 304.
——, arches of crude brick, ii. 301–303.
—— of Gebel Berkel in Ethiopia, ii. 301, 304.
—— the oldest monuments, ii. 287.

QUAILS, numerous, i. 234.
Quarry, mode of beginning a, ii. 303, 306.
Quarries of Syene, ii. 309, 311.
Quartz veins broken up for gold, ii. 141.
Queens, sceptre of, i. 276.
—— held priestly offices, i. 317.
Quiver, mode of carrying the, i. 314.

RAHAB, an instrument of one string, i. 125.
Rain, very little, in Egypt, i. 7; ii. 250.
—— falls occasionally, and signs of heavy rain at the tombs of the Kings, at Thebes, ii. 250.
Raphanus, or *figl*, i. 167; ii. 23, 30.
—— among the offerings, i. 259.
—— gives an oil, ii. 23, 30.
Rebo, an Asiatic people, i. 393–395.
—— chosen as the type of Asia, i. 394.
Reclining, not an Egyptian custom, i. 58.
Red paint on walls, censured by Vitruvius, i. 19.
—— Sea, ports on the, ii. 235–237.
Religion of Egypt, system of the, i. 326, 327.
——, changes in the, i. 329, 330, 332.
——, doctrines of the, i. 327.
——, abuses crept into the, i. 326.
—— a Pantheism rather than a Polytheism, i. 328.
—— had no mixture of Sabæism, i. 328.
——, subjects connected with, i. 257–301, 313–334. *See* Sacred.

INDEX. 429

Remeses II., or the Great, i. 308, 392, 396, 401, 403, 418.
——, name of Sesostris transferred from an older king to, i. 307.
Remeses III., pavilion of, i. 73 (Vignette C, 401).
——, treasury of, i. 155.
——, probably the same as the Rhampsinitus of Herodotus, i. 155.
——, change in the sculptures, in the reign of, ii. 273.
——, conquests of, i. 308, 394, 398, 401, 418.
——, naval fight in reign of, i. 406, 410.
—— playing at draughts, i. 191-193.
Reptiles of Egypt, i. 252, 253.
——, fabulous, i. 253.
Rhampsinitus probably the same as Remeses III., i. 155.
——, story of the daughter of, i. 299.
——, treasury of, i. 15, 155.
——, strength of the trap set in the, ii. 182.
Rhyton, or drinking-cup, i. 153, 154.
—— in form of a cock's head, i. 153.
Ring-finger, third of the left hand, ii. 337.
Rings, ii. 336, 339, 341.
Robbers, chief of the, a man of integrity, like their modern Shekh, ii. 216.
Romans, state of Egypt under the, ii. 233.
Roof of houses of palm branches and mud, i. 7; ii. 280, 281.
——, they slept in summer on the, i. 7.
—— and floors of palm tree beams, i. 18.
Roofs vaulted, i. 18; ii. 301, 302, 303.
Ropes of flax and date fibres, and of twisted leather, ii. 93.
Rose, or *rhodon*. See Pomegranate.
Rot-ñ-n, a people of Asia, i. 153, 395-397.
——, women of the, i. 397, 398, 416.
——, tribute of the, i. 397.
—— mentioned with Nahrayn, or Mesopotamia, i. 397. See Gloves.
——, vases of the, i. 153.
—— brought bitumen to Egypt, called *zift*, i. 397.
Rudders of boats, ii. 125, 129.

SABACO, i. 308.
—— raised the towns, especially Bubastis, to protect them from the inundation, ii. 9.
Sabæism not part of the Egyptian religion, i. 328.

Sacred music, instruments of, i. 129-133, 108, 109.
—— rites. See Religion.
—— scribe, dress of the, i. 334.
—— trees and vegetables, i. 256.
—— animals, i. 245-256.
—— emblems, i. 257.
—— fêtes, or festivals, i. 272, 286, 288, 296-301.
—— dancing, i. 140.
——, subjects in painting had prescribed rules, ii. 264, 266.
Sacrifice, i. 264. See Offerings.
——, daily, in the temple, attended by the king, i. 281.
—— after victory, i. 279, 416.
Sacrifices, human, not in Egypt, i. 411.
Sagdas. See *Psagdæ*.
Sails of some boats, of the papyrus, resembling those of the Chinese, i. 413, 414.
—— furled in ships of war, i. 412.
Sailors of Egypt, i. 411.
——. See Boatmen.
—— of the fleet, or "king's ships," ranked with the soldiers, i. 411; ii. 55.
Sails of modern lighters and Ethiopian boats, ii. 126. See Boats.
Sais, city of, i. 296, 298, 299.
——, lake of, i. 298.
——, nome of, i. 337.
—— monolith, ii. 55, 309, 310.
Saïte Dynasty, Kings, i. 309.
Salt sometimes excluded from the tables of the priests, i. 324.
Sandals of the priests, i. 335.
—— of women and others, ii. 331-333.
Sands, error respecting the great encroachment of the, i. 306.
Sandstone generally used after the 12th dynasty, ii. 306.
Sapt, "the chosen part," i. 264.
Saracenic architecture, progress of, ii. 305.
—— gave us the pointed arch, ii. 305.
Sarapeum of Memphis discovered, i. 292.
Sarapis, temple of, i. 292.
Sarcophagi, ii. 397, 398.
Sarcophagus, ii. 368, 374.
Satan, the Manichæan, i. 330.
Saviour, portrait of the, ii. 198.
Saw, ii. 113, 114, 118.
Sawing, mode of, ii. 114, 118.
Saxon, Norman, and Lombard styles, ii. 305.
Scales for weighing, ii. 136.
—— gold, ii. 151, 152.

Scarabæi, ii. 341, 395, 397.
Scarabæus, or beetle, i. 255.
Sceptre hereditary, i. 310.
—— of Queens, i. 276.
Sceptres of Osiris, i. 257, 266; ii. 381.
Science in Egypt advanced by the effects of the Nile, ii. 248-250.
—— already advanced in time of Menes, ii. 251, 287.
Scorpion, i. 254.
Scourers or fullers, ii. 106.
Scouring plants, used by fullers, ii. 106.
Sea-fight, i. 406, 410, 411.
Seáleh, or acacia Seál, i. 228; ii. 38, 106.
Seals on doors, i. 15, 16.
—— of tombs, ii. 364, 365.
Seats of chairs and stools, i. 64.
Seb, goose, emblem of, i. 251.
Semneh, fortresses of, i. 408.
Sennacherib, i. 309.
Serapis. *See* Sarapis.
Services or liturgies performed for the dead, ii. 357-362, 373.
Sesostris, ships of, i. 311, 411. *See* Ships.
——, a name transferred to Remeses II., i. 307.
—— gave lands to the soldiers, i. 336.
——, division of the country by, ii. 230.
Seth, i. 275, 330, 331.
——, the brother of Osiris, banished from the Pantheon, i. 330.
——, the abstract idea of Evil, i. 330, 331.
—— and Horus pouring emblems over the king, i. 275, 330.
——, with Hor-Hat, i. 275.
—— the same as Typho, or Typhon, i. 330.
Sethi, or Sethos, or Osirei I., i. 308, 396, 403, 418.
Seventy days, time of embalming, ii. 374, 383, 384, 387.
Shadóof, or pole and bucket, i. 33-35; ii. 4, 5, 22, 26.
——, Vignette, i. 72.
Shafts of a cart or carriage, found, i. 383.
Sharetana, an Asiatic people, i. 390-392.
—— had a helmet with horns, i. 390.
Shart, a people of northern Arabia, i. 396.
——, name of the Red Sea, i. 396.
Shaved their beards, priests, ii. 327.
—— their whole body, ii. 327.
—— heads of children, ii. 328.
Sheaves bound up, ii. 47.
Shekel, meaning weight, ii. 148.

Sheep, fear of diminishing the stock of, i. 166.
——, large flocks of, i. 166; ii. 172.
—— valuable for their wool, i. 166.
Shepherds, invasion of the, i. 111, 307.
—— invasion and their expulsion, i. 307, 308.
——, music dated before the, i. 111.
—— hated in Egypt, ii. 168, 169.
—— caricatured in the paintings, ii. 169, 175.
——, care of breeds of sheep by the, ii. 172.
——, various grades of, ii. 175.
—— chosen by the steward, ii. 176, 177.
—— gave account of the stock to the scribes, ii. 176.
Sheshonk (Shishak) took Jerusalem, i. 308, 340.
——, i. 308, 330, 340.
Shield of the Egyptians, i. 345.
——, battlements in the form of the, i. 23, 408.
—— used as an umbrella, i. 73, 75.
——, boss of the, i. 349.
——, form and handle of the, i. 345, 347.
—— slung at the back, i. 346, 347.
——, concave form of the, i. 347.
—— covered with hide, i. 345.
——, a light kind of, perhaps foreign, i. 348.
——, a large kind of, i. 349.
Shields of the Egyptians used by the Greeks for firewood, i. 345.
—— made of hide of hippopotamus and crocodile, i. 240.
Shinar (Shingar, Sinjar), tribute from, i. 397.
Ships of war, i. 411-413; ii. 130.
——, rigging of, i. 412, 414; ii. 130.
—— of Sesostris in the Arabian gulf, i. 411; ii. 133.
—— of great size, ii. 131, 132.
—— originally mere rafts, ii. 132.
Shishak pillaged temple of Jerusalem, i. 308, 340. *See* Sheshonk.
Shoemakers and curriers, ii. 103.
Shops, ii. 103, 184.
——, name and occupation of the owner put up over, ii. 105.
" Shrine of King Ptolemy," i. 268.
Shrines, or arks, or sacred boats, i. 267-272, 284, 285.
—— procession of, i. 267-270.
——, golden, i. 268.
Sieges of fortified towns, i. 387-390.
Sieves of string, the oldest of rushes, ii. 95.

INDEX. 431

Sift. See Zift.
Silence, Egyptian mode of indicating, ii. 182.
——, God of. See Harpocrates.
Silsilis, large quarries at, ii. 306.
Silver, use of, for money in Abraham's time, ii. 148, 240.
—— called "white gold," ii. 147, 241. See Gold.
Silver, hieroglyphic signifying, ii. 149. (Woodcut, fig. c.)
—— much used for money, ii. 147.
—— soon followed gold, ii. 148.
—— thread and wire, ii. 82.
Simple dress of the Egyptians, like a River God's, ii. 320.
Simpula, or ladles, i. 184, 185.
—— with a hinge, i. 184, 185.
Simsim, or sesame, gives an oil, ii. 23, 26, 31.
"Sincere," ειλικρινης, ii. 80.
Singing and music after dinner, i. 188. See Music and songs.
—— at work, ii. 308.
——, a solo, i. 92.
Single-stick, i. 206, 207.
Siphons, i. 174, 175; ii. 317, 318.
Sistrum, i. 131-133.
—— held by women, i. 133.
—— has been found, i. 132, 133.
Sitting on their heels, i. 58.
Sketches made on pieces of stone, board, &c., ii. 99, 276.
Skins imported into Egypt, and part of tribute, ii. 105, 106.
——, tanning and curing, ii. 102, 106.
Skins. See Leopard skins. See Water skins. See Prizes.
Slave, a black woman holding a plate in the way the African women now do, i. 141.
——, murder of a, capital offence, ii. 208.
Slaves, black and white, i. 416, 417; ii. 225.
——, traffic in, customary in those days, i. 417.
——, the Jews also had, i. 417.
——, Caucasian, like the modern Circassian, i. 418.
——, treatment of, i. 417.
——, children by, ii. 225.
Slaughtering for the table, i. 169.
Sling, i. 357, 419.
—— looked upon with contempt by some of the Greeks, i. 357.
—— used by some of the Greeks, i. 358.

Sling, the people of the Balearic Islands famed for their skill with the, i. 358.
——, the Greeks used a leaden-pointed ball for their, i. 358.
—— bullets of Egypt were round pebbles, i. 358.
Snakes of Egypt, i. 253.
——, sacred, i. 40, 253. See Asp.
——, horned, i. 253.
Soap, i. 186.
—— plant, ii. 106.
——, earths, steatite, ground lupins, &c., used for, i. 186.
Sokari. See Pthah-Sokari-Osiris.
——, necklace of, i. 260, 261.
——, ark of, i. 284, 285.
Soldering metals. See Metals.
Soldiers. See Army. See Class 2nd.
——, pay and rations of the, i. 336, 337.
—— from certain nomes or provinces of Egypt, i. 337.
——, mercenary, auxiliaries and allies, i. 337, 338.
—— of different corps, i. 369. See Olive.
See Frontispiece of vol. ii.
Solomon's trade, ii. 235.
—— wealth, ii. 243.
Soltána Valideh, influence of the, i. 4.
Sons followed the profession of their fathers, but not always, i. 316; ii. 57.
Song, a solo, i. 92.
—— of Maneros or Linus, i. 97.
—— of the threshers, ii. 43.
Songs, or dirges, on the death of individuals, i. 97; ii. 370, 372.
Sont, Mimosa, or Acacia, Nilotica, ii. 28, 37, 38, 106, 110, 129.
——, pods of the, used for tanning, ii. 106.
——, groves of, ii. 28, 37, 110.
Sooez (Suez), ii. 236, 237.
Sothic period, ii. 255.
—— and solar year, ii. 253-255.
Sothis, rising of, in reign of Thothmes III., ii. 254, 255.
Soul, transmigration of the, ii. 379.
—— immortal, first taught by the Egyptians, ii. 379.
Sowing the land, ii. 11, 12.
—— broadcast, ii. 139.
Spear, or pike, with metal head, i. 355.
—— had nothing at the lower end to fix it in the ground, i. 355.
—— and javelin heads, i. 355, 356.
Sphinx, i. 226, 248.
Sphinxes, ii. 290, 315, 324.
Spiked stand for offering birds, i. 263.
—— instrument. See Doora.

Spindles, ii. 84–88.
Spinning, employment of women, ii. 84, 85.
Spoil of the enemy, i. 406.
Spoonbill, i. 251.
Spoons, i. 183, 184.
Stables, i. 30.
Stag, i. 227, 247.
Stamps. *See* Seals.
Standards of the Egyptians, i. 342, 343.
Stands for flowers, i. 79.
Staters, the oldest coins, ii. 150.
Statue on a column, not good taste, an instance of inadaptability, i. 21.
—— on a sledge at El Bersheh, ii. 307, 308.
Statues of the Greeks, some as large as those of Egypt, ii. 300.
—— painted, ii. 279, 280.
——, large, ii. 309, 310, 314, 315.
—— at Thebes, ii. 309, 310.
—— of great size, not good taste, i. 21.
——, early, ii. 270, 271.
——. *See* Greek Statues. *See* Hermæ.
——, polishing and painting granite, ii. 314, 315. *See* Granite.
Steel. *See* Iron.
Steelyard of Roman time, ii. 152.
Steersman a high office, ii. 55.
Steward, or overseer of lands, i. 32; ii. 4.
Stick. *See* Throw-stick. *See* Walking-stick.
Sticks, fights with, i. 206–209, 298.
Stimulants for drinking, i. 53.
Stone, large blocks of, used in other countries as well as in Egypt, ii. 299.
—— knives of early time, and long retained, ii. 163, 164.
—— on a sledge, taken from a quarry, ii. 306.
——, mode of squaring, ii. 313, 315.
Stones of very great size taken by land, ii. 307, 309.
Stones on sledges, ii. 306.
——, transport of large, ii. 307–312.
——, mode of squaring, ii. 313, 315.
—— dragged for Temple of Isis, ii. 307.
——, men condemned to hew, ii. 307.
Stools, i. 58, 61–65, 67.
—— for the head. *See* Pillows.
Story of the man and his wife and the jars of gold, i. 23, 24.
Strainers or cullenders of bronze, i. 185.
Stranger Kings, i. 308, 330, 403.
Straw for provender, ii. 48.
—— in making bricks, ii. 194.
String, instruments of one, i. 125.
Strings of catgut, i. 111, 118, 122, 125.

Strings not of wire, i. 125.
——, mode of shortening, by a neck, i. 84.
—— limited to three, shows an improvement in music, i. 84.
Styx, the dead who remained on the wrong side of the, ii. 377.
Suez. *See* Sooez.
Sun, worship of the, i. 328, 329, 339.
——, distinct from Sabæism, i. 328.
——, festivals in honour of the, i. 296, 298, 300, 301.
—— worship introduced by the Stranger kings, i. 308.
—— worshipped at Heliopolis, i. 331. *See* Heliopolis. *See* Phrah.
——, the bull Mnevis said to be sacred to the, i. 289.
Superintendents of cattle, a high post, ii. 176, 178.
Surveying, land, or mensuration, ii. 248.
Swineherds in Egypt and India despised, ii. 2.
——, most ignoble, ii. 169.
Swine. *See* Pig.
Swords and daggers, i. 358, 419.
Sycamore, i. 44, 57, 259; ii. 27, 37, 110.
—— figs heavenly fruit, i. 181.
—— figs if eaten supposed to ensure a return to Egypt, ii. 110.
—— tree sacred to Netpe, i. 256; ii. 383.
Symmetry avoided, ii. 296. *See* Variety.
Symphony, the triple, i. 86.
Syringe, ii. 318.

TABLE for dinner, i. 167, 179, 182.
—— not covered with linen, i. 179.
——, mode of sitting at, i. 179.
Tables, i. 69, 70, 167, 179, 182, 190.
—— brought in and removed with the dishes, i. 180, 181.
——, offerings in the tombs on small, ii. 362.
Tabret, or timbrel (the *Taph* of the Jews), i. 129, 130, 140.
Talent, ii. 259, 260.
Tamarisk, ii. 37.
—— wood, use of, ii. 110.
—— tree, sacred to Osiris, i. 256.
Tambourine, i. 98, 129.
—— of various kinds, i. 129.
—— used in sacred music, i. 129.
—— played by goddesses, i. 129.
Tanning skins, pods of the acacia (*sont*), bark of *sealeh* and rhus, for, ii. 106.
Tapestry (*tapeta*) carpets, ii. 92.
Taste, ii. 288, 289. *See* Inapplicableness.
——, encouragement of, ii. 293–295.

INDEX. 433

Taxes, very great in Egypt, ii. 234.
Temenos. *See* Grove.
Temperance, exhortations to, i. 53, 187.
Temple, dedication of a, i. 271, 272.
——, a complete. *See* Frontispiece, vol. i.
Temples, subjects represented in the, i. 264.
——, coloured, ii. 290.
——, sculptures of, ii. 295.
—— not derived from excavated monuments, ii. 298.
——, or sanctuaries, at first small, ii. 299.
Tentyris (now Dendera), i. 242, 307.
Tentyrites overcame the crocodile, i. 242.
Testudo and battering-ram, i. 387–389.
Thales, improbable story of, teaching his instructors, ii. 109, 319.
Thanksgivings, i. 260. *See* Grace.
—— after victory, i. 278, 416.
Theban dynasty, i. 307.
Thebes, pavilion of Remeses III.; two colossi of the plain before the temple of Amunoph III.; vignettes C, E, i. 73, 141, 306.
——, i. 306, 331, 407.
——, capital of Upper Egypt, ii. 229, 230.
—— and Memphis had no walls round them, i. 409.
——, tombs of the kings at, i. 394.
——, plain of, formerly of less breadth, i. 306.
Theft, ii. 216.
——, mode of discovering, by divination, ii. 353.
Thieves had a chief, to whom they reported what they stole, and to whom the person robbed applied, ii. 216.
Thimble-rig, i. 203.
This, the Thinite dynasty, i. 307.
Thomson, Mr., on linen or mummy cloths, ii. 73–77, 79, 80.
Thoth, the Mercury or Hermes of Egypt, i. 274, 275.
——, books of Hermes, or, i. 274.
——, fête of, i. 299.
——, the intellect, i. 123.
—— month of, i. 299.
——, the Moon and God of letters, with an Ibis head, i. 328.
——, answered to Time, ii. 381.
Thothmes, the kings, i. 308.
—— III., i. 153, 308, 395, 397, 399, 418.
——, rising of Sothis in reign of, and date of, ii. 255.
Threshers, song of the, ii. 43.

Threshing. *See* Wheat. *See* Ornan.
Throwstick, i. 235, 237.
—— not on the principle of the *boomerang* of Australia, i. 235.
Thummim. *See* Truth.
Thyrsus carried by the priests, i. 291.
—— suggested by the staff or ivy-bound flower, i. 285.
Tiles, glazed, ii. 288, 292.
Tin, early use of, ii. 133, 134.
—— taken to the Isle of Wight as a depôt, ii. 135.
—— called *Kassiteros* in Greek, and *Kastira* in Sanscrit, ii. 133.
—— sought in Britain by the Phœnicians, ii. 134, 135.
——, some found in Spain even now, ii. 134.
Tirhaka, i. 308.
——, captives of, i. 393, 395–398.
Tnephachthus' curse of Menes, i. 173.
Toersha, a people of Asia, i. 398.
Toes, a strap held between the, ii. 104.
Tokkari, an Asiatic people, i. 392.
——, carts of the, i. 392.
Tomb of Remeses III., i. 77, 108.
——, some not allowed to be buried in their own, i. 314, 325; ii. 376, 379.
Tombs and funeral rites, ii. 356–400.
——, visit of women to the (as at present), i. 93; ii. 364.
—— of the kings, i. 394.
—— of poor people, ii. 365.
—— all finished except the name of the owner, and ready for sale, ii. 363.
——, seals of the, ii. 364.
—— of great size, ii. 365.
——, gardens at the, ii. 365.
—— at base of mountain of Thebes, ii. 372.
—— never circular in Egypt, ii. 365.
—— at the Pyramids, i. 111; ii. 287, 365.
Tomtom drum, i. 103–106.
Towers, movable, used in sieges, i. 390.
Towns raised above the inundation, ii. 9.
Toys for children, i. 196, 197.
Trade of Egypt, ii. 134, 234, 235, 237.
—— of a father generally followed by his son, ii. 57.
Tradesmen not allowed to meddle with politics, nor to follow more than one pursuit, ii. 57.
Transmigration of the soul, ii. 379.
—— in India, ii. 380.
Traps for birds, ii. 180, 182.
——, spring, very strong, ii. 182.
Treasure, story of, found, i. 23, 24.

Treasury. *See* Remeses III.
Trees of Egypt, i. 35–37, 57.
——, sacred, i. 256.
—— represented on monuments, ii. 36–38.
Triad of gods, i. 329–332.
Trial of the dead, i. 325; ii. 376, 379.
Tribute paid to Egypt, i. 396, 397, 399, 404, 417; ii. 233, 241.
—— of Ethiopia, i. 404.
——, jar of, i. 397.
—— from Asia and Africa, ii. 233.
——, vases brought as part of a, i. 152, 153, 397, 399.
Triclinium not used by the Egyptians, i. 58.
Trimalchio's exhortation at his feast, i. 187.
Triumph of the king after victory, i. 277. *See* Thanksgiving.
Trochilus, story of the, i. 243.
Trumpet, i. 104, 105.
——, troops summoned by the, i. 344.
—— of the Israelites, Greeks, and Romans, i. 105. *See* Jewish instruments.
Truth, the figure of, i. 260, 271, 272, 327.
Truth, i. 271, called *Thmei* (θεμις). *See* Pthah.
—— and Justice, i. 272; ii. 205.
——, the two figures of Thmei or, answer to *Thummim*, ii. 205, 382.
——, or Justice, the great cardinal virtue, ii. 207.
——, goddess of, with her eyes closed, ii. 205.
Turkish tent traced in the house, i. 5.
Typho or Typhon, or Seth, i. 105, 241, 242, 244, 249, 288, 323, 330.
——, the 3rd day of the Epact the birthday of, i. 281.
——, sow sacrificed to, i. 323.
——, chase of a boar by, i. 244.
——, hippopotamus and crocodile, emblems of, i. 241, 288.
Typhonian monster, i. 152, 153.
——, head of, resembled that of Medusa, i. 153; ii. 263.

Variety, the Egyptians fond of, i. 58; ii. 296.
Vase like a caldron, i. 154.
—— of bronze, with an elastic cover, i. 154, 158.
Vases, i. 147–158.
—— of glass and porcelain, i. 78, 82.
—— with the head of a bird and of a Typhonian monster, i. 152, 153.
—— with a human head for a cover, i. 155.

Vases of porcelain, or of enamel on gold, i. 152.
—— from Asia, i. 152, 153.
—— often of as bad shape as our flower-pots, i. 153.
—— and bottles in a case, i. 80.
—— and bottles, closed with leaves, i. 142, 165, 262.
—— of gold and silver, and other materials, i. 82, 148.
—— of gold, with so-called Greek patterns, i. 147.
—— of same form as some Greek, but most ancient, i. 147.
—— used in the temple and the kitchen, i. 154, 156.
—— of bronze, glass, and other materials, i. 148.
—— studded with precious stones, i. 148.
—— variously ornamented with animals, &c., i. 152, 153.
—— of the Greeks, with the "Goose and Sun" of Egypt (first noticed by Mr. Stuart Poole), ii. 263.
—— of elegant form in Egypt, sometimes imbricated, with plates of metal, ii. 162.
—— from Egypt. *See* Etruscans.
Vaults, vaulting. *See* Arches.
Vectis. *See* Wight, Isle of.
Vegetables, great quantity of, at dinner, i. 166.
—— forbidden to the priests, some. *See* Beans.
—— food of the lower orders, i. 167. *See* Food.
——, great number of people in Egypt who sold, i. 168.
——, sacred, i. 256.
Veneering with rare woods, i. 19; ii. 114, 115.
Vertical line in architecture, i. 21; ii. 302.
Veterinary art in Egypt, ii. 173, 174.
Victim, mode of slaying and cutting up a, i. 263, 264.
Victory, return of a king after, i. 277–279, 415.
——, thanksgiving after, i. 279, 416.
Villa, arrangement of a large, i. 27, 28.
——, boat towed on a lake in the grounds of a, i. 28.
Villas, i. 24–28.
—— of irregular plan, i. 28.
——, entrances to, i. 25.
Vine, i. 39–45; ii. 29, 36.
Vines trained, i. 38, 41.

INDEX. 435

Vines browsed on by kids after the vintage, i. 45.
—— grown on the edge of the desert, i. 49; ii. 20.
Vineyard, i. 38, 41–43.
Vitrified coating over figures and sarcophagi of stone, ii. 64, 65, 70.
Vitruvius censures quantities of red paint on walls, and "reeds for columns," i. 19, 21.
Umbrella over a chariot, i. 73, 75, 76, 384, 385.
——, shield used for an, i. 73, 75.
Undertakers, ii. 119, 387.
Volutes from Egypt, ii. 297.
Vows, public and private, i. 261.
Usury condemned, ii. 217.

Wabber, or *hyrax* (a sort of marmotte), i. 228, 247.
Walking-sticks, ii. 347, 348.
War, preparation for, i. 404.
——, mode of attack in, i. 405.
——, return of the army from, i. 278, 415, 416.
Wars of the Egyptians, i. 390–416.
Washerwomen, ii. 92.
Washing before dinner, i. 76, 77.
—— after dinner, i. 185.
Water of the Nile. *See* Nile.
—— pitcher or *hydria*, i. 287.
—— skins, i. 35, 213.
—— wheel, hydraulic screw, and foot machine, i. 34.
Wealth of ancient people, ii. 243, 244, 245.
—— of individuals at Rome, ii. 244, 245.
Weighers, public, ii. 165.
——, public confidence in, and punishment of, ii. 214, 217.
Weighing rings of gold and silver, ii. 148.
Weight, *shekel*, meaning, ii. 148.
——, money taken by, ii. 148.
——, things sold by, ii. 165. *See* Scales.
Weights, game of raising, i. 207.
—— and measures, ii. 259–261.
——, talent, mina, and other, ii. 259, 260.
Wheat, ii. 21.
—— and barley, when cut, the best, ii. 39.
——, all bearded, the seven-eared quality of, ii. 39.
—— found in tombs, said to have been grown in England, ii. 39.
—— cropped a little below the ear, ii. 39, 48.

Wheat cropped now close to the ground, ii. 47.
—— carried to the threshing floor, ii. 39.
——, sowing, reaping, carrying, threshing, winnowing, and housing, ii. 40, 41, 44–46.
——, treading out, or *tritura*, with oxen, ii. 41–46.
——, oxen unmuzzled when treading out the, ii. 46.
Wheaten bread, i. 180. *See* Bread.
Wheel and shafts of a cart found by Dr. Abbott, i. 383.
Wheels of chariots, i. 374, 376–380, 384.
—— had four or six spokes, i. 374, 379, 384.
Wheelwrights, ii. 117.
Wheeled carriage, four, i. 384.
Whip, i. 372.
—— suspended from the wrist, i. 373.
Wife, hieroglyphic signifying, i. 323.
——, the priests and other Egyptians had only one, i. 5; ii. 224.
"Wife" and weaving, ii. 84.
—— said to rule at home, ii. 223.
—— of Potiphar, ii. 224.
Wight, Isle of, made the depôt for tin, and the port of traders from the continent, ii. 135.
Wigs, ii. 325, 326, 329.
Wild animals kept for the table, i. 215.
—— animals, i. 226–231, 239–248.
—— ass and wild boar not represented, i. 244.
Wild boar, i. 244, 247. *See* Damietta.
—— ox or cow, a species of antelope (the *Antilope Defassa*), i. 227, 247.
Windows of houses, i. 14, 20, 22.
—— not covered with hangings, i. 22.
—— hanging up between columns, i. 20.
Wine of various kinds, i. 49–51, 266.
—— in the cellar, i. 49.
—— presented to guests, i. 81, 141.
—— presented before dinner, i. 82.
—— brought by an upper servant, i. 141.
——, it was not rude to refuse, i. 144.
——, not forbidden to women, i. 51, 52.
—— presented with a complimentary speech, i. 144.
—— offered in two cups to the gods, i. 266.
—— offered to the gods, i. 51. *See* Heliopolis.
—— called *Erp*, i. 48, 266.
—— of the Upper and Lower country, i. 266.
—— of the palm. *See* Palm wine.

Wine also imported from Phœnicia and Greece, i. 53.
—— used medicinally, i. 50.
Wines of a choice kind confined to the rich, i. 54.
——, fictitious or medicated, i. 50.
Wine-cellars, i. 47, 48.
Wine-jars, or amphoræ, i. 48.
——, resinous substance put into the, i. 48.
—— press, i. 45–47.
Wire, when first drawn, ii. 82.
"Wisdom of the Egyptians," i. 325; ii. 202.
Witnessing a murder or any violence, without giving information, was participation in guilt, ii. 208.
Witnesses, number of, required for deeds, ii. 176.
Wolf, i. 227, 228, 245.
Wolf mummies at O'Sioót. *See* O'Sioót.
Women, treatment and influence of, in Egypt, ascended the throne, i. 4; ii. 223.
—— sat with the men, i. 144.
—— in Greece secluded, i. 144; ii. 224.
—— not secluded in Rome, i. 144.
—— attended festivals, ii. 224.
—— sacred, or holy, i. 316–319.
—— held offices connected with religion, i. 317, 318.
—— of Amun, i. 133. *See* Pallaces.
——, a sort of college or convent of, i. 319.
——, rights and duties of, i. 4.
—— talked about their earrings, i. 145.
—— carried loads on their heads, sometimes on their shoulders, i. 177.
—— occupied in weaving, and other occupations in doors, ii. 223.
—— of the *hareem*, ii. 225.
—— guilty of capital crimes, punishment of, ii. 209–211.
——, dresses of, ii. 334.

Wood brought from Syria and other countries, i. 18; ii. 38, 111.
——, little, in Egypt, ii. 109.
—— painted on a coating of stucco, ii. 111.
Woods, veneering. *See* Veneering.
—— most used in Egypt, ii. 38.
Wooden figure of Osiris at table, i. 186, 187.
Woof pushed upward and downwards, ii. 85.
Wool. *See* Sheep.
Woollen cloths, none buried in, i. 353; ii. 72.
—— cloths worn by common people, i. 333.
—— upper garment worn by priests, ii. 72.
World not more peopled now than formerly, i. 305.
Wounded enemies, i. 373.
Wreaths of flowers, i. 57, 79, 80.
Wrestling, i. 204–206.
Writing, everything done in, ii. 176.
Writing-paper, leather used instead of, ii. 99. *See* Paper. *See* Papyrus.

Year, division of the, ii. 251–254.
—— of 365 and 365¼ days, ii. 252–254.
—— intercalated, ii. 254, 255.
Yoke for carrying waterpots and other things, i. 33.
—— of a plough, ii. 15.
—— of a chariot, i. 379, 381.
Yoking oxen and cows to the plough, ii. 15.
Young animals for stocking preserves, i. 215, 216.

Zift, or bitumen, brought in tribute from Asia, i. 397; ii. 120. *See* Rot-ñ-n.
Zummára, a double pipe of modern Egypt, i. 128.
Zythus, or Zythos, beer, i. 53–55.

THE END.

www.ingramcontent.com/pod-product-compliance
Lightning Source LLC
Chambersburg PA
CBHW041436300426
44114CB00025B/2900